MW00784347

WHISKEY
OPUS

WHISKEY OPUS

THE DEFINITIVE GUIDE TO THE WORLD'S GREATEST DISTILLERIES

REVISED AND UPDATED BY

JONNY McCORMICK & GAVIN D. SMITH

CONTENTS

WHISKEY GOES GLOBAL

Whiskey is in a very good place at the moment. Global demand is at a record high and traditional territories, such as Scotland, are working flat out to meet it. And all the indicators suggest the boom days won't end any time soon. Nor is it just whiskey from traditional territories, either. The whiskey industry is benefiting from a demographic shift toward new emerging middle classes across the planet, combined with a trend in the West of drinking less but better, and seeking heritage and provenance in what is consumed.

Whiskey is both extremely easy to make—it's simply a combination of grain, yeast, and water, brewed into beer and then distilled into grain spirit—and yet it is extremely difficult to make well. Scotland, in particular, makes whisky very well indeed, dominating the category, and drawing on centuries of experience to produce its world-famous single malts and blended whiskies.

Nevertheless, variations of whiskey have been created successfully in Ireland, the US, Canada, and Japan, all of which are also benefiting from the current boom. But it doesn't stop there. The rise in global demand has been accompanied by an equally dramatic growth in new distilleries appearing in new territories such as Taiwan, India, Australia, New Zealand, England, and the Nordic countries—many of them producing excellent, world-class tipples. Hundreds of new and small distillers have sprung up, many of them experimenting with wood types, cask finishes, drying techniques, and using peat and local grains to develop the category into new areas.

An affordable luxury

We live in a rapidly changing world. China, India, and countries in South America, Southeast Asia, and emerging states across Africa are growing on a massive scale. Their burgeoning middle classes are seeking to enjoy the rewards of their wealth. When it comes to alcohol, few drinks can match whiskey as an attainable symbol of wealth and luxury. Traditionally, Scotch single malt whisky has been the greatest beneficiary of this trend for affordable luxury, but in many of the emerging economies, single malt Scotch whisky isn't having it all its own way. Quality blended whiskies and whiskey from many other countries are also benefiting from this demand, and before long, many an entrepreneurial person turns to distilling their own.

A book for the times

Whiskey is a dynamic and organic industry that is constantly evolving. Traditional distilleries are increasing capacity to meet demand and seeking to supply new trading partners. New distilleries are popping up in the most unlikely of places to help evolve the category and create new and exciting grain spirits. *Whiskey Opus* provides a detailed and comprehensive account of these changes. Drawing on their extensive experience and contacts in the whiskey world, the authors have identified the distilleries and whiskies that are fueling the current boom.

WHISKEY EXPRESSIONS

The Tasting Notes

The whiskey expressions featured in the book, with their accompanying tasting notes, should be readily available, whether on their home market or on the export market. However, not all distilleries, especially small craft producers and world whiskey distilleries, export widely. And sooner or later, the featured whiskies will be discontinued or become obsolete, but fortunately, whiskey auctions enable anyone eager to try something that's out of stock with the opportunity to track a bottle down if they hunt for it!

The Grande Whisky Museum, Asia's first rare whisky collection. Home to a comprehensive collection of fine and rare Scotch and Japanese whiskies in Suntec City, Singapore.

WHAT MAKES WHISKEY SUCH A UNIQUE DRINK?

No other spirit attracts the same degree of dedication and loyalty, creates the same frisson of excitement, or prompts so much study and investigation as whiskey. How does whiskey weave such magic on its followers? Perhaps it's the heady mix of craftsmanship, history, and mystery wrapped up with the drink. Or because a spirit of such nobility and elegance, that is notoriously difficult to make well, is yet distilled from the roughest, ready-on-hand ingredients. Quite how only three basic ingredients—grain, yeast, and water—can be combined to create such a plethora of different flavors has been called "The Great Wonder of Whiskey." Who can resist?

THE BASICS OF WHISKEY MAKING

Barley is the most common grain used in whiskey. It is the sole grain in Scotch malt, and a percentage of malted barley is used in almost all whiskey.

Malting Barley goes through a malting process to activate enzymes and maximize its starch content, which is later converted to sugar and then alcohol. If peat is burned to flavor the grains, the whiskey will have a smoky flavor.

Mashing Malt is milled to produce a coarse flour called "grist." The grist is then mixed with hot water in a mash tun to extract soluble sugars. The sugar-laden water, known as "wort," is piped off for use.

Fermentation The wort is mixed with yeast and heated in a washback. The yeast feeds off the sugars in the wort, so producing alcohol and carbon dioxide. This fermentation results in what is effectively a strong and rather tart beer, called "wash."

Distillation The next stage is for the wash to be distilled in order to extract the alcohol spirit from it. The essential process is simple: alcohol boils at a lower temperature than water, so as the wash is boiled, the alcohol is driven off as vapor, which is then condensed back into liquid and collected. Most whiskey is distilled twice.

The Cut The first and last parts of the "run" during the second distillation are not pure enough for use. Known as the "foreshots" and the "feints," respectively, they will go back for redistillation along with "low wines" from the first distillation. The desired part of the distillation is the middle section, and this is known as the "middle cut," "the hearts," or just "the cut." This usable spirit, which is called "new make," is drinkable and exhibits some of the characteristics that will be found in the final whiskey. The distiller must assess the spirit and identify the cut.

Floor malting at Stauning, Denmark. Malting unlocks sugars in the grains by steeping in water to stimulate germination, then kilning the malt to halt germination.

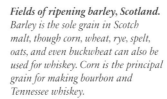

Fields of ripening barley, Scotland. Barley is the sole grain in Scotch malt, though corn, wheat, rye, spelt, oats, and even buckwheat can also be used for whiskey. Corn is the principal grain for making bourbon and Tennessee whiskey.

Maturation The new make will have its strength slightly reduced to about 63 or 64 percent ABV—the optimum strength to begin maturation. The spirit is then piped from a holding tank into wooden casks. The process that turns raw, clear new make into the richly hued, complex-tasting drink we know as whiskey is maturation. The length of time varies, depending on climatic conditions, the size and type of casks used, the storage method, and legal requirements.

The mash tun at Blair Athol distillery, where hot water extracts soluble sugars from the milled malt to create the worts.

HOW WHISKEY EVOLVED

As for its origins, there have been many claims and counterclaims regarding where grain distillation began, with the Middle East and East Asia as favorites. Truth be told, no one really knows and the chances are that the separating of alcohol from water to make it stronger came about in different parts of the world at roughly the same time. What seems likely is the clergy had something to do with it, and that its origins are tied up with medicine. Alcohol comes from an Arabic word, and the theory that traveling priests brought the secrets of distillation back to Ireland and from there to the west coast of Scotland is not without merit.

WHISKEY—MOMENTS IN TIME

The history of whiskey is studded with significant moments, both in terms of the drink's discovery and evolution and the economic and political context in which it has developed. The most important moment? The invention of the column or Coffey still continues to be a strong contender, as is the introduction of oak casks and the charring of oak. Maybe the greatest defining moment, however, for anyone who loves whiskey is the moment when you take a sip and the taste makes total sense. Is there any moment greater than that?

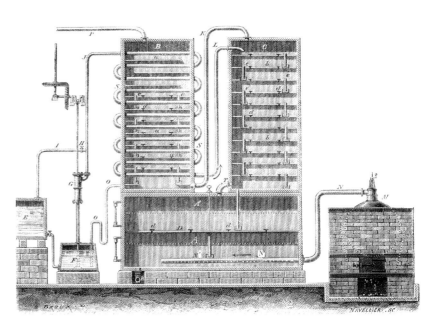

Continuous innovation. Scotch's world story began with the invention of the Coffey still in 1826, Known as the Coffey (after its inventor), patent, column, or continuous still, it allowed for continuous rather than batch distillation and led to the production of grain whiskey, a lighter style that could blend with malts for mass appeal.

TIME DISTILLED—KEY EVENTS IN THE HISTORY OF WHISKEY

The origins of whiskey are lost in time, but they stretch back hundreds of years, possibly thousands. Moreover, there is great debate as to how the spirit evolved and who was responsible. Here, then, are a few key signposts.

The first whiskey
Nobody knows who first distilled whiskey, but there are suggestions that distillation was first carried out in China or Mesopotamia, for medicine and perfume. Certainly, there are big links between health and alcohol: just consider a drinks toast in virtually any language.

Blame it on the clergy
The church has a lot to answer for when it comes to alcohol. Pilgrims traveled widely in the Middle Ages and probably brought distilled spirits back to Europe. Monasteries were the guardians of brewing and distilling, and the Dissolution of the Monasteries in England probably helped spread these skills.

Into the daylight
In Scotland, it took the Excise Act of 1823 to legalize an already thriving trade in whisky. In Ireland, whiskey went legal in 1608 with the world's first whiskey license. In the US, it took a rebellion and a resettlement into new frontiers in the South to establish whiskey making on the banks of the Ohio River. Japan started making whisky in 1923.

Roll out the barrel
Nobody can pinpoint exactly when oak casks became part off the whiskey story, but it was almost certainly a happy accident. As the need to export grew, containers were required. In Scotland, it's likely whisky was stored in casks that had previously carried all manner of things, including casks of wine and sherry coming into the country by sea.

The Old Bushmills distillery, founded in 1784, is based in Northern Ireland, and today holds the title of oldest licensed whiskey distillery in the world.

Dr. Jim Swan was a scientist and whiskey consultant who advised new distilleries all over the world and is credited with the popularity of the STR cask.

Japan's whisky master Masataka Taketsuru learned the secrets of single malt production in Scotland and used this knowledge to help create the Japanese whisky industry, known today for producing some of the best single malts in the world.

Jasper "Jack" Daniel learned to make whiskey from Nearest Green, but his success at selling it led to the establishment of the Jack Daniel's distillery in Lynchburg, Tennessee. His whiskey is now sold in more than 165 countries around the world.

George Urquhart of Gordon & MacPhail in Elgin is remembered as a pioneer of single malt Scotch whisky and laid down the casks that would become some of the oldest whiskies ever bottled. He died in 2001 at the age of 82.

Bill Lark is credited with driving forward Australia's whisky industry after starting a distillery in Tasmania. Lark and his contemporaries supported each other in establishing a craft whisky scene on the island, and he helped introduce Australian whisky to the rest of the world.

Blazing a trail
There are many legends surrounding the "invention" of bourbon whiskey in the US. In fact, the technique of charring casks crossed over from the Old World to the New, and the corn in the mashbill was simply the most abundant local grain. The pattern stills plays out today with American single malt flourishing in the Pacific Northwest.

The rise of Japan
Masataka Taketsuru learned to make whisky in Scotland and was the first distiller at Yamazaki with the company that became Suntory. He left to set up his own company, which became Nikka Whisky, opening Yoichi distillery in 1934. Global recognition of Japanese whisky and the flavors of Mizunara oak have truly blossomed in the 21st century.

Single malt Scotch
Interest in single malt Scotch whisky began to grow during the 1980s, with more distilleries gradually offering bottled malts at a variety of ages. Such is the modern thirst for single malts that by 2023 exports around the world exceeded the $2.5 billion (£2 billion) mark for the first time, with global sales headed by The Glenlivet and Glenfiddich.

The first visitor center
The first whiskey distillery visitor center opened at Glenfiddich in 1969, and "whiskey tourism" has subsequently come to provide welcome income in many countries. Many distilleries now offer a "menu" of visitor experiences, with behind-the-scenes tours and cask sampling for more knowledgeable members of the public.

The first finished whiskeys
David Stewart, former malt master of The Balvenie, decided to put mature single malt aged in an American oak cask into a sherry cask to see if it would add extra flavor, and it worked. This became Balvenie Classic, now called Balvenie Doublewood. Finishing is now practiced globally, using virgin oak, wine, beer, spirit, and fortified wine casks.

STYLES OF WHISKEY

Whiskey is now made in many different countries around the world, from its traditional origins in Scotland, Ireland, Canada, and the US to new locations stretching from China and Lebanon to Mexico and South Korea. Whiskey is spelled with or without an "e'"'by different countries, though it doesn't bear any greater significance than giving a clue to its country of origin; Scotland, Japan, and Canada call it whisky, while Ireland and the US prefer to use whiskey, with an "e."

BLEND
A combination of single malt and single grain whiskies. Irish blends can be any combination of two or more Irish whiskey styles. American blends are the exception, containing a minimum of 20 per cent straight whiskey or a blend of straight whiskey, while the remainder can include cheaper neutral spirits or other younger whiskeys.

BLENDED MALT
A combination of single malt whiskeys from more than one distillery. Previously, these were known as vatted malts. Monkey Shoulder is a blend of single malts made by one company loved by bartenders for mixing, while independent bottlers and blenders such as Douglas Laing, Elixir Distillers, and Compass Box blend parcels of different single malts to create specific flavor profiles.

SINGLE MALT
Made from 100 percent malted barley at a single distillery. It is a style of whiskey most famously made in Scotland, but it is now also a leading style in Japan, Taiwan, Ireland, England, Wales, mainland Europe, and Australia, and it is growing in importance in the US, Canada, and New Zealand.

SINGLE GRAIN
Made from corn, wheat, malted barley, and other cereals distilled in a column still at a single distillery. Most grain whiskey is produced for blending or bottled as cheaper options for mixing. The most interesting single grains hail from distilleries such as Loch Lomond and Nikka's Coffey still at Miyagikyo, independent bottlers, and blenders like Compass Box for Hedonism Wines.

SINGLE POT STILL
A classic style of Irish whiskey made in pot stills using both malted and unmalted barley, and small amounts of other adjunct grains such as oats or rye. This style of whiskey came close to dying out in the 20th century but was popularized again by Irish Distillers. It is now flourishing once more with numerous Irish producers focusing on single pot still whiskey production.

Where the distiller makes the spirit cuts influences the style of whiskey produced. This is at Mackmyra, Sweden.

Regulations around whiskey-making vary between countries, from the rigor of the Scotch Whisky Regulations 2009 to nations with no set regulations where distillers are free to follow their own path, working toward the day when a set of national standards can be agreed.

Fortunately, the definitions of different styles of whiskey are largely observed and respected internationally, so the explanations below cover the basic whiskey styles you might find printed on a bottle label.

WORLD WHISKEY

The term "*world whiskey*" can indicate a blend or whiskeys from more than one country, but the term is also used to refer to whiskeys made outside of the traditional whiskey-producing countries.

CANADIAN

This can be made from any cereal grain, and it must be mashed, aged, and distilled in Canada and aged for three years in cask. It is often blended to make the final whisky. A rye made in Canada does not need to follow the US definition of being made from a mashbill of at least 51 percent rye. Single malt is also made in Canada, though this is made clear on the label.

TENNESSEE WHISKEY

Made from 51 percent corn in Tennessee. It is distinguished by the Lincoln County process, where filtering through vats of sugar maple charcoal helps mellow the spirit before it is filled into the barrel. Globally, the category is dominated by Jack Daniel's, but it's worth exploring all the state's distilleries as they have earned a solid reputation for innovation.

BOURBON

Made from at least 51 percent corn and can contain smaller amounts of wheat, rye, malted barley, and other small grains; and must be matured in new charred oak casks. Although it is synonymous with Kentucky, bourbon is made across the US. While there is no minimum aging requirement, a straight whiskey must be aged for two years.

RYE

In the US, this is made from a mashbill of at least 51 percent rye and can contain smaller amounts of corn, wheat, malted barley, and other small grains. Many Canadian whiskies are called rye, though confusingly, they don't need to contain anywhere close to 51 percent rye. Outside of the US, rye is now being made in Scotland, England, India, across Europe, and Australia.

CORN

Made from at least 80 percent corn, this can be aged in uncharred new oak barrels or used barrels, or sold as an unaged product. While they remain a niche product, the US corn whiskeys make interesting counterpoints for comparative tastings with the heritage corn whiskeys being produced at new distilleries in Mexico and Peru.

THE TASK OF THE CASK

It's true that whiskey is made of just three ingredients, but there are two other major contributors to flavor: the peat that is sometimes used in drying the green malt, and the wood used in maturation. Malt spirit comes off the still as a clear liquid and is placed in wooden casks to start its journey to whiskey. How long it stays there depends on a myriad of different factors, including what country you are making it in, what style of whisk(e)y it is, and how light or robust the spirit is to stand up to the strong flavors from the oak. Up to three-quarters of the flavor of a single malt whiskey will come from the cask, and considerably higher than that for bourbon. It's from the wood that the magic and mystery of whiskey stems.

Nobody knows just when it was discovered that if fiery new spirit was left in wooden casks for a period of time, the quality could improve significantly, with the development of a more mellow and "rounded" character. The discovery was almost certainly a happy accident, with wooden vessels primarily being used for storage purposes.

Many legally defined styles of whiskey stipulate the use of oak for maturation purposes, principally because oak is a hard wood, relatively easy for coopers to work, and with just enough porous qualities to allow the spirit to "breathe," without leaking.

The two principal types of oak used for aging whiskey are American white oak (*Quercus alba*) and European oak (*Quercus robur*). Scotch whisky maturation was traditionally carried out in European oak casks, which had previously contained Spanish sherry, due to its popularity in Britain during the 18th and 19th centuries.

The use of American oak casks that had previously been used to mature bourbon was a 20th-century innovation, with large numbers of surplus barrels being available to Scottish distillers due to the legal requirement for all newly charred bourbon casks to be used only once.

This requirement coincided with a dramatic decline in the British love affair with Spanish sherry. There are approximately 18 million casks of whisky maturing in Scottish warehouses today, but only around 5 percent formerly held sherry. A good-quality sherry cask can cost 10 times as much as a bourbon cask. Both European and American oak casks are seasoned with sherry prior to their new lives in Scotland, and a number of Scottish distilleries such as The Macallan, The Dalmore, and Glenfarclas remain notable for their extensive use of former sherry casks. While oak is by far the most favored wood for

whiskey maturation, other types are employed from time to time, in locations where oak is not a legal requirement. Ireland is one such location, giving rise to the use of French and Japanese chestnut, cherrywood, and mulberry wood for finishing single pot still spirit by Irish Distillers at Midleton in County Cork, while acacia has been employed by Bushmills in County Antrim, Northern Ireland. Japanese mizunara oak casks are in high demand by distillers around the world for finishing, given the desirable sandalwood and incense characteristics they impart to Japanese whiskies. Amburana casks are becoming increasingly chosen by distillers for the spicy, cinnamon flavors they can deliver to maturing whiskey.

Whatever the wood, casks are constructed by highly skilled coopers who spend long apprenticeships learning how to build and repair the precious vessels. The art of coopering involves very precise jointing and fitting, with no glue or nails, and while labor-saving devices have made the coopers' life easier in recent

*The American white oak (**Quercus alba**) is the most common type of oak used to make barrels for the global whiskey industry.*

decades, creating and maintaining casks that will last for perhaps 50 years without leaking, ultimately comes down to sheer craftsmanship.

Casking explained

Much of the final taste of a whiskey can come from both the type of wood used to make the cask and what that cask contained before whiskey spirit was put into it, though the finest whiskeys have their flavors enhanced by the cask and not dominated by it. Advanced age is not necessarily a good thing: long maturation in an overactive cask can lead to the spirit being dominated by wood-derived flavors.

INTERACTION OF SPIRIT AND WOOD New-make spirit enters the cask as a clear liquid, but once in wood, four reactions take place. First, the spirit gently expands and contracts as it moves in the cask with the passing of the seasons, pushing deeper into the staves, taking flavor and color from it. But a second effect takes place: the wood removes impurities and negative compounds in the spirit. Third, the wood and spirit react with each other to produce a myriad of flavors; this is the unexplained magic of whiskey. The final part of the maturation is created by oxidization, because oak allows air to pass into the cask as some of the liquid evaporates.

CASK SIZE Although whiskey is nearly always matured in oak, the size of the cask affects the speed of maturation. The smaller the cask, the more the spirit comes into contact with the wood that has a greater the effect on maturation. Sherry butts and puncheons hold 110 gallons (500 liters), hogsheads hold 55 gallons (250 liters), while standard American barrels hold 44 gallons (200 liters).

AGE OF CASK Whether the cask is new or used will also affect maturation. Bourbon must be matured in new charred white oak barrels (toasting the inside is an option). While some Scotch single malt is now matured in virgin oak casks, most is aged in a cask that has already been used for producing something else, normally bourbon or sherry. Different types of casks are increasingly being used, however, particularly for giving whiskey a secondary period of aging, or "finishing," often in former wine casks, in order to impart different aroma and flavor characteristics to the spirit.

ATMOSPHERIC FACTORS Maturation will also be affected by average temperature, extremes of temperature, humidity, atmospheric pressure, and the size and type of warehouse. The traditional warehouse is cool, damp, earth-floored, and with casks racked two- or three-high, which causes spirit to reduce its strength but retain high volume. In the US, by contrast, racked warehouses stack casks up to eight-high and the atmosphere can be warm—even hot—close to the roof, and dry. In these conditions, the volume reduces, but the strength remains high, so they often fill the barrels at a lower proof. In subtropical climates in India and Taiwan, whiskies reach peak maturation in much less time than it takes in Scotland, so the distilleries need fewer warehouses, and age statements are rare.

The length of maturation is the most influential factor in the flavor of the mature whiskey. There is no optimum time—this depends on the history of the cask. Whiskeys of the same vintage and distillery are discernibly distinct from one cask to the next. This is at the A. Smith Bowman distillery in Virginia, owned by Sazerac.

Burning the inside of the cask, here at Kavalan in Taiwan, causes chemical changes to the wood, without which the spirit will not mature. European casks tend to be lightly "toasted" while American barrels are "charred."

PEOPLE MAKE WHISKEY

Whiskey is an important industry to the economy and supports hundreds of thousands of jobs across the agriculture, food and drink, manufacturing, hospitality, retail, and tourism sectors. And so there is a myriad of opportunities for people with different skills to be a part of the ongoing story.

Whiskey may be made from cereals, yeast, and water, but there's a whole team of people working hard in different jobs behind every bottle you buy. Here are some of the people putting their heart and soul into every drop in your glass.

The maltster manages the steeping of the barley, germination, and the kiln, drying the malt to the required moisture content. Single malt whiskey distilleries mostly rely on commercial maltings for their needs, but some retain traditional floor maltings.

The brewer manages mashing and fermentation, critical steps to maximizing the production of alcohol and flavor. Hot water extracts the sugars from the grist in the mash tun to make wash, which is then pumped into the fermenters where yeast is added to convert sugar into alcohol, and a wonderful array of fruity flavors are created along the way. Bourbon distillers may use a hammer mill and cook the corn and small grains before adding yeast.

The distiller safely controls the process of distillation using the stills, manages the spirit safe, takes samples and analyzes the spirit run, documents the outcome of each batch, and ensures the stills are cleaned and fully maintained, calling in the coppersmith for repairs to the stills when needed.

The cooper performs a highly skilled task involved in the manufacture and repair of oak casks. A mastery of different tools and machines is required to shape the staves, raise the barrels, hammer the hoops, toast and char the cask interior to the required level, and fit the heads to produce the end product: a spirit-tight vessel. Larger companies, such as William Grant & Sons, Loch Lomond Group, and Brown-Forman, have their own on-site cooperages, whereas smaller ones may purchase casks from an independent cooperage, which their own coopers will maintain and repair throughout their useful working life. Coopers serve a four-year apprenticeship, then become a journeyman cooper.

Ashok Chokalingam's career with Amrut in India saw him rise from brand ambassador to become Amrut's head of distilling, global sales, and marketing.

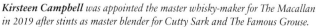
Kirsteen Campbell was appointed the master whisky-maker for The Macallan in 2019 after stints as master blender for Cutty Sark and The Famous Grouse.

The experience of buying whiskey in the 21st century has evolved from a physical retail store, such as here at The Whisky Exchange at Covent Garden in London, to purchasing from online retailers such as The Whisky Exchange, Amazon, and ReserveBar. The whiskey enthusiast can also shop directly from distillery websites and buy whiskey through cask offers, barrel pick schemes, whiskey auctions, as NFTs, and from delivery platforms such as Uber Eats. Go buy something new today!

The warehouse worker manages the storage and removal of casks from a bonded warehouse or rickhouse and is responsible for identifying any leaking casks; the drawing of samples; and the safety and security of the warehouse, its contents, and its staff. In days gone by, Scotch whisky distilleries would also have an excise officer on site to ensure every drop of maturing whisky was accounted for inside the distillery's bonded warehouses.

The brand director is in charge of the marketing, communication, strategy, and long-term vision of the brand, including the key responsibility for its commercial success. Concepts for new expressions, ranges, and packaging designs can be conveyed to the blending team to work on the liquid for the new expressions.

The master blender is responsible for the quality, consistency, and supply of current whiskey ranges, working with analytical scientists to monitor the new-make quality, driving innovation for special bottlings, and embracing media work and greeting consumers at whiskey festivals.

The bottling hall operative works on bottling lines to maintain quality control as the final whiskey is filled, sealed, and labeled, then packed into cartons before being boxed into cases ready for shipping all over the

world. It's a role that's crucial to ensuring the whiskey's authenticity, helping to deter counterfeiters through the use of security measures built into the packaging.

The brand ambassador embodies the whiskey brand, bringing the stories of the distillery and its whiskey to life for consumers at shows and festivals, while building and maintaining relationships with important trade customers, journalists, bloggers, and social media influencers.

The visitor center guide leads distillery tours, describing how whiskey is made and hosting multisensory tastings, managing the retail and bar environment, and delivering memorable experiences to visitors from all over the world.

The bartender/mixologist thrills you with dazzling cocktails and introduces you to new flavors with whiskey flights tailored to your every need, showcasing their creativity and skills with jigger, shaker, ice, and garnish, while demonstrating a deep knowledge of contemporary drinks culture.

The retailer brings together the greatest selection of whiskeys for your convenience, from everyday easy sippers, hot new releases, cask-strength independent bottlings for your home bar, luxury pours, collectibles, and rare vintage bottlings for your whiskey shelf.

WHERE TO NOW?

Whiskey is perpetually moving forward. As traditional producers take advantage of growing global demand, they remain grounded by the understanding that whiskey's attraction is centered around heritage, provenance, and integrity. When making fine spirits, you cannot cut corners. A new generation of producers has arrived, and they're eager to push forward new innovations. Much of it cannot be called whiskey, but all bets are off as to whether new, closely related drinks categories will be invented in the future.

New start-ups and pushing the boundaries

New distilleries are flourishing across Ireland, England, Japan, Australia, and New Zealand, with pioneering distilleries opening in new whisky-producing countries such as China, Peru, Lebanon, and South Korea. New distillers often think outside the box and are prepared to push the boundaries, taking advantage of the lack of regulations and agreed standards in new whisky-producing countries.

Super premium categories

Aided and abetted by the staggering growth of the secondary market for whiskey, producers have been eager to supply collectors with an ever-expanding choice of rarities, tactical limited editions, and one-off opportunities. The first Macallan to be sold for more than $1 million dollars was auctioned in 2018. By 2023, the first Macallan to break $2 million dollars had been sold.

Innovation and sustainability

Whiskey producers the world over recognize the urgent need to address issues of sustainability, and many are already global leaders in carbon reduction, energy and water efficiency, and the production of more environmentally friendly packaging solutions.

Organic barley sounds attractive, but this involves greater land use to match the yield of other varieties. Malted barley continues to be exported internationally to distilleries built in parts of the world unsuitable for growing barley.

The interest in finishing in exotic woods like amburana, cedar, chestnut, hickory, and sakura can lead to extra freight costs to transport these vessels around the world. Australian distillers recognize this well, and make a point of difference through using the wine, tawny, and apera casks available locally.

As well as taking their environmental responsibilities seriously, distilleries such as Domaine des Hautes Glaces, Nc'Nean, Westland, and Ardnamurchan are finding ways to convey this message authentically and build loyalty and respect from fans of their whiskies.

Small stand-alone distilleries may make headlines on sustainability, but the much greater change comes at scale from the positive actions of the bigger players in the industry such as Diageo, Brown-Forman, Suntory Global Spirits, Pernod Ricard, and International Beverages.

What's old is new again

Alongside such technology-driven innovations, there has also been a move among many small-scale distillers to effectively turn the clock back when looking to the future. With optimum flavor creation in mind, they have embraced the use of "heritage" barley and corn varieties, superseded by higher yielding varieties, and differing yeasts—again, with maximization of flavor as their goal. In Ireland, several distillers have sought to redefine "single pot still" whiskey by using higher proportions of adjunct grains, such as oats and rye, much as their predecessors did a century and more ago.

LOOKING AHEAD

The Future of Energy
Whiskey production is an energy-intensive process. In Scotland alone, it has been estimated that the whisky industry accounts for 10 percent of Scotland's total energy consumption. The drive to carbon negativity requires a shift away from fossil fuels, and the greater use of renewable sources through wind and solar, on-site generation of biogas through anaerobic digestion, smarter energy use in the stillhouse such as thermal vapor recompression systems and mechanical vapor recompression systems, and the potential for distilleries to benefit from advances in the hydrogen industry, following hydrogen trials at Bruichladdich and Yamazaki distilleries.

The future is female. More women are embarking on successful careers in the industry, particularly in underrepresented areas such as production. Dr Abbie Jaume is co-founder at Cooper King Distillery, England.

An arctic whisky experience at the top of the world, whisky visitors flock to the Aurora Spirit Distillery in northern Norway to sip a dram of Bivrost single malt under the spectacle of the Aurora borealis.

At the Komoro Distillery in Nagano Prefecture, Japan, former Kavalan master distiller Ian Chang is now making high-quality Japanese whisky in a state-of-the-art distillery, and they offer educational classes to whisky aficionados of all levels.

While rye is popularly associated with Canadian whisky and America's rye whiskeys, it is now firmly rooted in European distilling culture with strongholds in Germany, Austria, England, and The Netherlands.

Ad Gefrin is England's most northerly distillery and is exploring heritage barley varieties with their cooperative of local farmers.

SCOTLAND

SCOTLAND

SCOTCH WHISKY EVENTS

Scotch whisky has long been at the heart of many of the country's principal celebrations. A dram to welcome in the New Year at midnight on Hogmanay is practically mandatory, while Burns' Suppers, held to commemorate the birth of Scotland's national bard on January 25, 1759, always feature the national drink. In 2012 Aberdeen University student Blair Bowman, now a whisky consultant, came up with the concept of celebrating World Whisky Day (www.worldwhiskyday. com), staged annually on or around the third Saturday in May.

Whisky may now be a truly global drink, enjoyed in many countries around the world and produced in a number of them, but to most people, its roots lie in the Scottish Highlands (though the Irish would certainly dispute that Scotland was the birthplace of whisky). The popular image of whitewashed distilleries silhouetted against the grandeur of a heather-clad moor with a burn of pure water flowing by is derived partly from the work of generations of advertising and marketing folk, who wish to equate their product with the beautiful, the natural, and the archetypally "Scottish." Most consumers don't want to imagine high-speed bottling lines in 1980s concrete structures located on industrial estates when they pour a dram and raise it to their lips.

Scotland boasts an extraordinarily diverse range of distilleries scattered across some of the most scenic parts of the country, especially the Highlands and the Islands, and the survival of almost 100 malt distilleries well into the 21st century is in itself remarkable in an unsentimental, commercial world where policies of consolidation and rationalization have long been preeminent. Many of those distilleries still surviving were founded during the remarkable Victorian period of popularity when blended Scotch ruled the waves around the world.

Record export sales have led to the expansion of existing distilleries and the creation of entirely new ones in recent years. Indeed, some 40 dedicated whisky distilleries have been established during the past two decades, ranging from locations in the Borders to the far north mainland coast. Most of these distilleries are independently owned and operated, but in terms of scale, ownership remains concentrated in relatively few hands. The two major players, Diageo and Pernod Ricard's subsidiary Chivas Brothers, own 41 of the 135 malt-producing facilities, accounting for nearly half of overall capacity.

After a lengthy period of increasing growth in global Scotch whisky sales, there are signs that some key markets are experiencing a slowdown or even a downturn, while output of malt whisky has continued to grow. For the first time, production of malt and grain spirit are approximately equal. There is surely a danger that supply is outstripping demand and that the days of what the press dubbed the "whisky loch," or "lake," back in the early 1980s may return. The US and France remain the two most valuable overseas markets for Scotch whisky.

The Strathisla distillery cuts a handsome figure, outfitted with a high gabled roof and a pair of pagoda-capped kilns.

SCOTCH WHISKY REGIONS

The regions of Scotch malt whisky production have evolved for both practical and administrative reasons and also as a result of perceived stylistic similarities between whiskies distilled within proximity of each other. The division between "Highland" and "Lowland" came about as a result of the 1784 Wash Act, which imposed varying levels of duty in the two areas, while the whiskies produced on Islay, for example, were noted for their heavily peated profile.

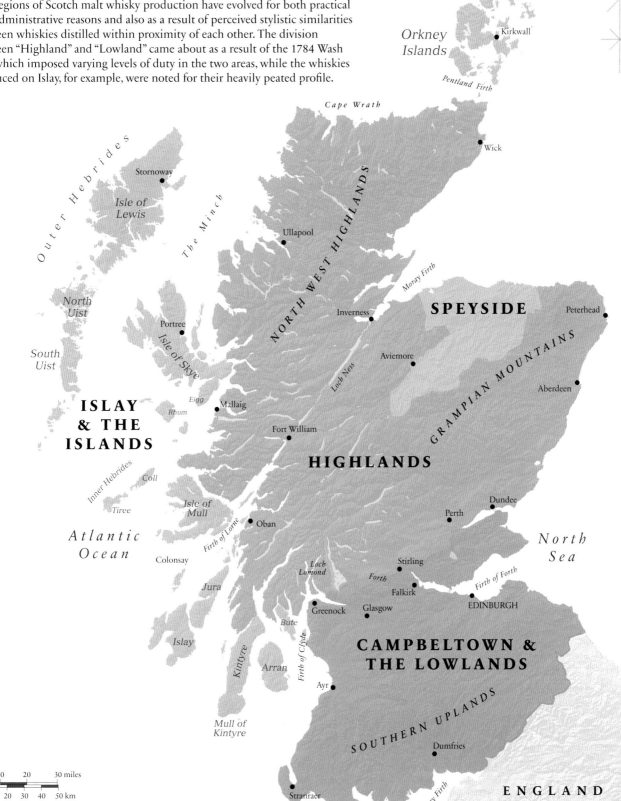

SPEYSIDE

REGIONAL STYLES
Traditionally, Speysides have been known as elegant, complex whiskies, but there are dramatic differences between the light, grassy, floral profile of a single malt such as Glen Grant and the full, rich, sherried character of The Macallan nearby.

AUTHOR'S CHOICE
BALVENIE A classic Victorian distillery in family ownership and one of only a handful still operating floor maltings. Its single malt is widely available yet never commonplace, and its owners are not afraid to innovate. TORMORE Not a "big hitter" but still a must-see for its visionary architecture.

REGIONAL EVENTS
Eight distilleries, including Historic Scotland's silent Dallas Dhu site, plus the fascinating Speyside Cooperage, are part of the official Malt Whisky Trail (www.maltwhiskytrail.com), while many other distilleries also provide facilities for visitors. For details, visit www.scotlandwhisky.com. Two annual whisky festivals are staged, with the Spirit of Speyside Whisky Festival (www.spiritofspeyside.com) taking place over five days in May and the Spirit of Speyside: Distilled festival, which occupies two days in September.

Known as "The Golden Triangle," Speyside is the very heartland of malt whisky production. The adjective "golden" is apt in two ways: not only does it imply something precious, but Speyside is also a notable center for the cultivation of malting barley and the summer months see acre after golden acre of the raw material of Scotch whisky swaying in the breeze.

Located in northeast Scotland, the Speyside single malt region is also a place of remote highland glens where winter lingers long and where, in days gone by, illicit distillers were able to ply their trade in relative safety away from prying eyes.

At the center of the region is the great Spey River, Scotland's fastest-flowing and second-longest river, which has a fine reputation among anglers for its world-class salmon fishing. The river rises in the highlands of Badenoch and flows past Grantown, Aberlour, and Rothes until it reaches the sea between Elgin and Buckie. From a whisky-making perspective, however, Speyside embraces an area extending from the Findhorn River in the west to the Deveron in the east and as far south as the city of Aberdeen.

Speyside's historical popularity as a location for distilleries is due to the fact that the area provided the key ingredients needed for making whisky of plentiful pure water, high-quality barley, and peat, all within relatively close proximity. It is now home to about half of all Scotland's malt whisky distilleries.

The arrival of the railroads in the second half of the 19th century meant that the Speyside distilleries could transport their spirit to the great blending centers further south, and when the increasing popularity of blended whisky caused a distilling bonanza, it was on Speyside that development was at its most dramatic. Today, the Scotch whisky industry is experiencing another such bonanza, and Speyside remains firmly at the center of activities, with major distillers such as Diageo and Chivas Brothers investing heavily in its future. For the whisky lover, visiting Speyside offers wonderful opportunities for exploration and discovery.

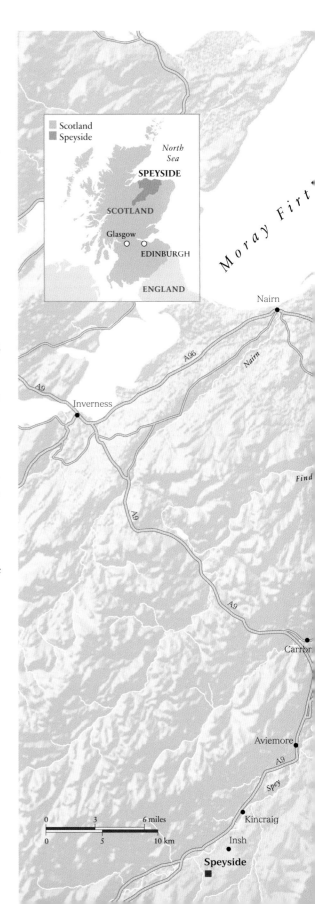

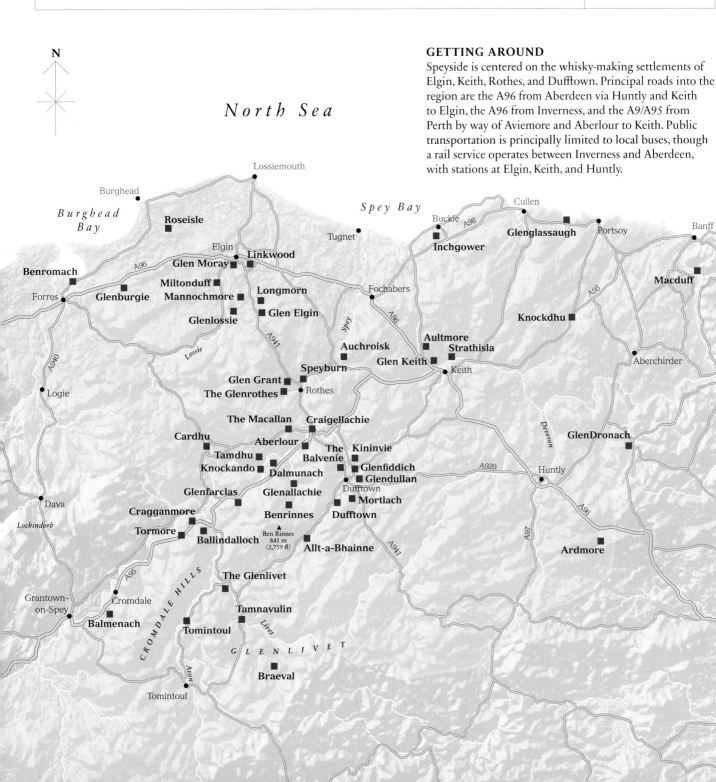

N

North Sea

GETTING AROUND
Speyside is centered on the whisky-making settlements of Elgin, Keith, Rothes, and Dufftown. Principal roads into the region are the A96 from Aberdeen via Huntly and Keith to Elgin, the A96 from Inverness, and the A9/A95 from Perth by way of Aviemore and Aberlour to Keith. Public transportation is principally limited to local buses, though a rail service operates between Inverness and Aberdeen, with stations at Elgin, Keith, and Huntly.

Lossiemouth

Burghead

*Burghead
Bay*

Spey Bay

Cullen

Roseisle

Buckie   Glenglassaugh   Portsoy   Banff
A98

Tugnet
Inchgower

Elgin
Benromach   Linkwood
Glen Moray
A96   Fochabers   Macduff
Forres   Glenburgie   Miltonduff   Longmorn   Knockdhu
Mannochmore
Aultmore
Glenlossie   Glen Elgin   Auchroisk   Strathisla
Glen Keith   Aberchirder
Lossie   Speyburn   Keith
A941   Spey
A940   Glen Grant
Logie   The Glenrothes   Rothes

The Macallan   Craigellachie   Devon   GlenDronach

Cardhu   Aberlour   The   Kininvie
Tamdhu   Balvenie
Knockando   Dalmunach   Glenfiddich
Dava   Glendullan   A920   Huntly
Glenfarclas   Glenallachie   Dufftown
Cragganmore   Benrinnes   Mortlach   A96
Lochindorb   Tormore   Dufftown
Ballindalloch   Ben Rinnes   A97
841 m   Ardmore
(2,759 ft)   Allt-a-Bhainne   A941
Grantown-
on-Spey   Cromdale   A95   The Glenlivet
Balmenach   *CROMDALE HILLS*   Tamnavulin   Livet
Tomintoul
GLENLIVET
Avon
Braeval
Tomintoul

THE CAIRNGORMS

Cairn Gorm
1,245 m
(4,085 ft)
Gairn

ABERLOUR

Aberlour 18-Year-Old

OWNER Chivas Brothers Ltd (Pernod Ricard)

FOUNDED 1826

WEBSITE www.aberlour.com

Close to the busy A95 road on the southwestern skirts of Aberlour, the distillery stands at the opposite end of the village from a factory that produces one of Scotland's other great iconic products, namely shortbread. Walkers Shortbread Ltd is an independent family firm, which makes one of the best-known brands, and while Aberlour single malt is not such a household name in the UK, mention single malt Scotch whisky in France, and Aberlour is likely to be the name on almost everyone's lips. It is now the eighth bestselling single malt in the world.

Aberlour was one of the first single malt distilleries to be purchased by a non-British company when France's Pernod started its acquisition campaign in 1974. One consequence was that Pernod focused on building the reputation of Aberlour in France and played a key role in developing the single malt category there. To this day, Aberlour is brand leader in that key market, the world's biggest for Scotch whisky. More than half of Aberlour's sales are generated in France.

To meet demand for Aberlour, both as a single malt and as a component of Chivas Brothers' blends, a major program of expansion is being undertaken, including the construction of a new stillhouse, tun room, and mash house, accommodating 16 washbacks and four stills. This will double capacity to almost 2.11 million gallons (8 million liters) per annum.

At present, the distillery is equipped with a 13-ton semi-lauter mash tun, six stainless steel washbacks, and two pairs of large stills. To achieve the desired fruity style of new-make spirit, the stills are run very slowly, with the "middle cut" lasting for two hours.

Sherried heritage

Aberlour Distillery was founded by Peter Weir and James Gordon in 1826, though the present plant actually dates from 1879 when the banker James Fleming built it close to the site of the original one, which had been seriously damaged by fire. Aberlour remained in a variety of independent hands until 1974–1975, when Pernod purchased its then owner,

Aberlour 10-Year-Old

Campbell Distilleries. In 2001, Pernod Ricard, as the company had become, acquired Chivas Brothers, and Aberlour joined the Chivas group of distilleries.

Aberlour is one of a number of single malts that have clung to the tradition of using significant amounts of ex-sherry wood for maturation purposes, highlighted by the cask strength, oloroso sherry cask-aged Aberlour a'bunadh (Gaelic for "of the

The late-Victorian distillery was designed by Charles Doig after a fire destroyed the original building in 1898.

Aberlour A'bunadh

origin") expression, launched in 2000. Aberlour is regarded as one of the best sherry-matured whiskies in the world, with Aberlour A'bunadh attaining cult status among whisky connoisseurs.

Throughout the rest of the range, a definite sherry influence is prevalent, although it is usually apparent as part of the "double-cask" maturation style, which mixes whisky matured in sherry casks with whisky matured in bourbon casks, giving depth and versatility to the range. From its medium-size pot stills, Aberlour produces a balanced spirit that takes well to maturation in ex-sherry casks but also has the elegance to shine through following ex-bourbon cask maturation.

The principal bottlings of Aberlour include 12-, 14,- 16-, and 18-year-olds, plus the bourbon- and oloroso-matured Casg Annamh and A'bunadh.

WHISKY TALES

The Aberlour Experience
While Aberlour was a late starter when it came to offering public access to the distillery, since getting in on the visitor center act in 2002 it has become synonymous with in-depth connoisseur tours, opting for quality over quantity. At present, a range of tasting options are available, including Single Casks Explored and The A'bunadh Collection, while there are plans to upgrade and augment facilities and offerings in due course as part of the distillery expansion project.

TASTING NOTES

Aberlour A'bunadh
Single malt, cask strength, matured in ex-oloroso sherry casks, non-chill-filtered, 61% ABV
Rich on the nose, with sherry, furniture polish, nutty malt, apples, and smoke. The full palate is intensely sherried and fruity, with more apples, nuts, and smoke, plus ginger. The finish is long, with honey, spices, and plain chocolate.

Aberlour 10-Year-Old
Single malt, matured in a mix of ex-bourbon and ex-sherry casks, 40% ABV
A sweet sherry and honey nose, balanced by spiciness and a touch of Jaffa oranges. Caramel and quite dry sherry on the palate, with barley sugar in the medium-long sweet finish.

Aberlour 18-Year-Old
Single malt, 43% ABV
The nose offers sweet sherry, honey, and orange creams. Spices and figs emerge. The palate is rich, with spicy sherry, apricots, and peaches. The finish is long, with cream, more spices and figs, and gentle oak.

THE BALVENIE

OWNER William Grant & Sons Ltd

FOUNDED 1892

WEBSITE www.thebalvenie.com

One of the great pleasures of Scotch whisky is the almost infinite number of variables that shape the essential style of each single malt and make it different from all others. The Balvenie is distilled on a site adjacent to its big brother Glenfiddich yet produces a spirit with an entirely different profile.

As David Stewart MBE, The Balvenie Malt Master, explains, "There is a honeyed sweetness right through The Balvenie from the new make spirit. It's sweet, biscuity, and malty. It's more fruity, floral, and aromatic than Glenfiddich, with deeper malt notes."

William Grant & Sons Ltd is known as a company in which members of staff serve for long periods of time, with several generations of the same family often being employed. David Stewart began his career with Grant's back in 1962. He became Master Blender a dozen years later, remarkably being only the fifth person to occupy that role in the history of the firm. In 2009, Stewart handed over the blending reins to his long-standing "apprentice" Brian Kinsman, while Stewart continued in his parallel role as The Balvenie Malt Master.

The Balvenie is also an important component of William Grant's major blended brand Family Reserve, and David Stewart explains, "When it comes to blending, Glenfiddich adds fruity, floral, estery, aromatic character, while The Balvenie gives malty, nutty depth, and sweetness to a blend."

A sister to Glenfiddich

The Balvenie dates from 1892–1893, when it was constructed as a sister distillery to Glenfiddich. While Glenfiddich had been built on a shoestring, by the time The Balvenie was established, the Grant family's financial fortunes had improved to the extent that it was possible to spend some $10,000 (£2,000) on the new distillery, more than two and a half times the outlay for Glenfiddich.

Nonetheless, second-hand stills from Lagavulin on Islay and Glen Albyn in Inverness were acquired, the reason being not so much a desire to save money but rather a wish to have "seasoned" stills,

The Balvenie 12-Year-Old Doublewood

The Balvenie Caribbean Cask 14-Year-Old

which had already proved themselves capable of producing good whisky.

The single malt produced by the distillery was first officially bottled in its own right during 1973, and today Balvenie boasts five wash stills and six spirit stills. The brand is now in the top-ten single malts in the US and enjoys strong sales in the UK, Taiwan, France, Canada, and travel retail outlets.

Approximately 80 percent of new make spirit is filled into ex-bourbon casks and another 20 percent goes into former sherry casks, with maturation taking place in some of the 40-plus warehouses, which also hold the make of Glenfiddich and Kininvie distilleries.

In addition to its own maltings, The Balvenie boasts a cooperage and coppersmith facilities. The cooperage and maltings are popular elements of the distillery tour, which is aimed at the more knowledgeable whisky aficionado, lasting for about three hours and limited to a maximum of eight people.

An esoteric whisky

David Stewart says, "With The Balvenie we have created an esoteric image—it's easier to do smaller bottlings here than it is at Glenfiddich, due to the scale of the operations. The Balvenie brand tends to be where we experiment a little and offer limited editions. We used to bottle The Balvenie Classic and it was finished in a sherry cask. In fact, it was probably the first-ever cask finish, although that wasn't mentioned on the label. That led directly to DoubleWood and PortWood."

The Balvenie 12-year-old DoubleWood and 21-year-old PortWood expressions are both part of the current core range, along with Caribbean Cask 14 and French Oak 16, while 25-, 30-, and 40-year-old variants are available in the Rare Marriage series.

DoubleWood is initially filled into ex-bourbon casks then transferred to sherry casks for the final two years of maturation. PortWood is first matured in ex-bourbon casks before spending a secondary period of maturation in 20-year-old port pipes.

Rare expressions

As well as being smaller in scale than Glenfiddich, The Balvenie is able to trade on its traditional, "craft" image, giving scope for the sort of bottlings already noted, and other more obscure expressions. These have embraced releases such as The Balvenie 14-year-old Roasted Malt and 17-year-old Peated Cask. The former was the first single malt Scotch whisky to be

made using a batch of dark, roasted malted barley, more commonly used to make stout, while the latter comprises a mixture of 17-year-old matured in new wood and 17-year-old finished in casks that previously contained a heavily peated batch, distilled in 2001.

Other Balvenie rarities include The Balvenie Sixty, released to celebrate David Stewart's six decades in the Scotch whisky business. Just 71 bottles from a 1962 European Oak hogshead were produced, and this is the oldest Balvenie expression ever released. Other fascinating recent releases are A Rare Discovery from Distant Shores—a 27-year-old with a rum finish—and a Revelation of Cask and Character—a 19-year-old matured in oloroso sherry casks, which highlights the vital role played by the craftsmen working in the Balvenie cooperage.

Turning the barley as it germinates is a skilled job. *At The Balvenie distillery, it is turned up to four times a day.*

WHISKY TALES

New Use for the New House

Most distilleries, whatever their vintage, were created from scratch for the role of distilling whisky. The Balvenie is unusual in that while the majority of its structures were newly built, the derelict mansion of Balvenie New House was incorporated into the design, serving as extremely unconventional maltings and warehousing. This situation continued until 1929, when the upper floors of Balvenie New House were demolished and the stone was used to build more conventional malt barns. Today, The Balvenie is one of only a handful of Scotch whisky distilleries to continue malting some of the barley it uses on its own floor maltings.

TASTING NOTES

The Balvenie 12-Year-Old DoubleWood
Single malt, matured in ex-bourbon casks, finished in sherry casks, 40% ABV
Nuts and spicy malt on the nose, with banana, vanilla, and sherry. Full-bodied, with soft fruit, vanilla, sherry, cinnamon, and a hint of peat on the palate. Dry and spicy in a luxurious finish.

The Balvenie Caribbean Cask 14-Year-Old
Single malt, finished in Caribbean rum casks, 43% ABV
The nose offers honey, vanilla, and tropical fruits, while the palate yields white rum, caramel, more tropical fruit, and spicy oak.

The Balvenie PortWood 21-Year-Old
Single malt, finished in first-fill port pipes, 40% ABV
Notably fruity, with marzipans and almonds on the nose, and a palate of red wine, brittle toffee, and a hint of aniseed, which slowly dries.

BENROMACH

Benromach 10-Year-Old

OWNER Gordon & MacPhail

FOUNDED 1898

WEBSITE www.benromach.com

The distillery was founded in 1898 by the Benromach Distillery Company, opening two years later, but closing almost immediately, with a crisis of overproduction decimating the distilling landscape. The plant was revived between 1907 and 1910, and again after World War I, but was silent for much of the economically troubled 1930s.

Benromach changed hands several times during its first half century of existence, before finding itself part of the Distillers Company Ltd portfolio in 1953. Thirty years later, however, Benromach was to cease production once again, when the same problem of overproduction that eventually ended the Victorian whisky boom caused major rationalization during the 1980s, with the Distillers Company alone closing 23 of its distilleries.

Happily, Benromach was one of those silenced distilleries that were subsequently revived, thanks in this instance to the foresight of renowned Elgin-based bottlers and retailers Gordon & MacPhail, who took over Benromach in 1993, a decade after its closure. Production resumed five years later, coinciding with the distillery's centenary.

A new and smoky style

Gordon & MacPhail's Managing Director and Whisky Supply Manager, Ewen Mackintosh, explains, "When we purchased Benromach distillery, we undertook a great deal of work and research to identify the type of whisky we wished to create. When sampling Speyside whiskies from the 1960s and before this time, we identified that each retained a smoky characteristic. We attributed this smokiness to the use of traditional floor maltings at the time. At Benromach, we wished to create a whisky that embraced the smoky style that is prevalent in whiskies pre-1960s."

Accordingly, malt for general production is peated to a level of 10–12 parts per million, or ppm, and given that many Speyside malts are only very lightly peated, this is a significant element in the ultimate character of the whisky. "Benromach is

Benromach
Contrasts: Organic

The revived Benromach distillery, then the smallest in Speyside, was officially opened in 1999 by the Prince of Wales.

WHISKY TALES

An Early Maturing Spirit
Benromach is the smallest distillery on Speyside, operated by just two members of staff, one of whom is the manager! Benromach's current production facilities differ quite significantly from those originally in place, being redeveloped during the 1990s on a much more modest scale. The new stills installed there were considerably smaller than those they replaced and were designed with relatively broad necks to capture the heavier flavors created during the first distillation. The aim is to produce a spirit that matures early but also has enough substance to last in cask for two or three decades prior to bottling.

a medium-to-heavy style of spirit, helped by the use of malt peated to this level," says Distillery Manager Keith Cruickshank. In May 2004, the new style of Benromach was showcased with the release of Traditional, an expression with no age statement and the first release of spirit to have been distilled under Gordon & MacPhail's ownership of the distillery.

An innovative range

Innovation has continued ever since, with variants such as the heavily peated Peat Smoke and Organic, the first single malt whisky certified by the UK's Soil Association, which guarantees that the whole process, from raw materials to bottling, meets with organic standards. Maturation is in virgin oak casks, made with wood from sustainable forests in Missouri.

As Gordon & MacPhail has built up stocks of Benromach, it has been able to offer a core range based around age statement releases. These now include 10-, 15-, and 21-year-olds, along with a Cask Strength Vintage. The Contrasts range embraces an ongoing program of special releases, with Organic 2014, Peat Smoke 2014, Air-Dried Oak, and Kiln Dried Oak, with the latter pair intended to showcases the differences between the two methods used to remove moisture from oak designed for cask construction.

As Keith Cruickshank notes, "At Benromach, we believe that making single malt whisky is a little like creating a jigsaw. Like each part of a jigsaw, each element of the whisky-making process plays a tiny but important role in the overall picture."

Consistency of distillation

While an increasing amount of the spirit bottled as Benromach has now been distilled under the Gordon & MacPhail regime, older expressions such as the annually released 40-Year-Old were produced when the distillery was owned by the Distillers Company. Consumers could be forgiven for expecting little similarity between the "old" and "new" Benromachs, but Ewen Mackintosh says, "We feel there is a common thread that connects vintages distilled by the previous owners and spirit distilled by Gordon & MacPhail. When Gordon & MacPhail purchased Benromach, we were fortunate to obtain a sample of the new-make spirit from the previous owners. When we analyzed this sample against our distillations, we noticed this common thread. This is despite the fact that we reequipped Benromach with all-new equipment. The only constant that remains the same is the water source!"

TASTING NOTES

Benromach 10-Year-Old
Single malt, 43% ABV
Slightly smoky on the nose, with new leather, Jaffa orange, licorice, and marzipan, while the palate offers rich orchard fruits, more leather, and a hint of cardamom, closing with hot chocolate and sherry.

Benromach 21-Year-Old
Single malt, 43% ABV
The nose offers subtle smoke and leather, with baked apples and pears. while malt and chocolate feature on the rich palate, with stewed apricots, developing black pepper and wood smoke.

Benromach Contrasts: Organic
Single malt, virgin American oak casks, non-chill-filtered, 46% ABV
Sweet on the nose, with bananas, toasted malt loaf, and fresh oak aromas. Sweet in the mouth, with vanilla, brittle toffee, and a hint of resin. The finish features fruity, lively oak.

Benromach 21-Year-Old

CARDHU

OWNER Diageo plc

FOUNDED 1824

WEBSITE www.malts.com

The first licensee of what was originally known as Cardow Distillery was John Cumming who possessed three convictions for illicit distilling. He took over the lease of Upper Cardow farm in 1813, settling there with his wife, Helen.

Elizabeth's regime

Cumming was persuaded to operate on the right side of the law as a result of the groundbreaking Excise Act of 1823 and was granted a license to make whisky the following year. After his death in 1846, his son, Lewis, and daughter-in-law, Elizabeth, ran the distillery, and upon Lewis's death in 1872, Elizabeth adopted the role of principal distiller. She was one of the first women in Scotland to hold such a position. Under Elizabeth Cumming's regime, the distillery was extended in 1887, with the old equipment, including a somewhat worn pair of stills, being sold to a Johnny-come-lately former shoemaker by the name of William Grant who was establishing his own Glenfiddich distillery just across the valley.

Six years later, Cardow was acquired by John Walker & Sons of Kilmarnock for $102,500 (£20,500), and the Cumming family continued to run the operation for a time under the new name of Cardhu. This was the era when blended Scotch whisky was taking the world by storm, and as a leading proponent of blending, the Walker company required a sizable distillery to supply it with malt.

Walker heart malt

Today, an expanded and upgraded Cardhu is part of the Diageo portfolio. Cardhu was one of four distilleries—along with Clynelish, Caol Ila, and Glenkinchie—chosen by Diageo to represent the "Four Corners of Scotland," with each being designated as providing a key component of Johnnie Walker. As the blend's "brand home," the visitor center was significantly upgraded, reopening in 2021.

Today, the blend sells in excess of 270 million bottles a year, and the old familiar Red Label and Black Label variants have been augmented by the

Cardhu 12-Year-Old

Cardhu 15-Year-Old

The old maltings at Cardhu, with their distinctive traditional pagoda-style roofs.

Cardhu 18-Year-Old

likes of Gold Label Reserve, Double Black Label, and Blue Label. Cardhu itself has the status of Diageo's leading single malt in terms of sales, with Spain as its principal market, and growth of the brand outstripped supply of the liquid itself for a time, leading to few available expressions.

Now, however, there is a wide range of Cardhu single malts available, including 12-, 15-, and 18-year-old expressions, along with the NAS Amber Rock and Gold Reserve. The year 2021 saw the release of a much-praised 16-year-old Four Corners of Scotland bottling, exclusive to the distillery and www.malts. com while Diageo's 2022 Special Releases collection included a 16-year-old Cardhu finished in Jamaican rum casks.

TASTING NOTES

Cardhu 12-Year-Old
Single malt, 40% ABV
The nose is relatively light and floral, quite sweet, with pears, nuts, and a whiff of distant smoke. Medium-bodied, malty, and sweet in the mouth. Medium-length in the finish, with sweet smoke, malt, and a hint of peat.

Cardhu 15-Year-Old
Single malt, 40% ABV
Ripe apples, caramel, and almonds on the nose, with flavors of candied orange peel, overripe bananas, and cereal, becoming malty, with cinnamon and light oak.

Cardhu 18-Year-Old
Single malt, 40% ABV
Nutty toffee, honey, and orange aromas lead into a rounded palate of figs, dates, and soft oak spice.

GLENFARCLAS

OWNER J. & G. Grant

FOUNDED 1836

WEBSITE www.glenfarclas.com

When it comes to the Scotch whisky equivalent of the French grand cru designation for top-quality wines, Speyside is home to a comparatively high number of the leading contenders. Among these are two single malts whose expressions are principally defined by their heavily sherried style, namely The Macallan and Glenfarclas.

While The Macallan is probably the most collectible whisky in the world, with the rarest expressions commanding record-breaking prices of up to $156,400 (£125,000), connoisseurs of Glenfarclas tend to buy it simply in order to consume the product rather than look at the bottle or hope that it will appreciate in value. This is partly due to the prevailing philosophy of Glenfarclas supremo John Grant, who represents the fifth generation of his family to own the distillery.

Whisky for drinking

John Grant believes that whisky is for drinking and prices Glenfarclas accordingly. He eschews the contemporary trend for overelaborate packaging, noting of the Glenfarclas 40-year-old expression, launched in 2010, "It's affordable because it's not overpackaged—it just comes in a plain carton—and we have lots of it. We make a reasonable margin, and I'd rather people drank it than collected it.

"I think we should ban all secondary packaging—cartons, tubes, and so on—from a carbon footprint point of view. If you buy a bottle of Château Latour or something similar, no matter how expensive and prestigious the wine, all you get usually is a bottle with a label. So why has the Scotch whisky industry gone down the route of using so much extravagant packaging?"

Although Glenfarclas distillery was first established in 1836 by Robert Hay, in the shadow of Ben Rinnes in the parish of Ballindalloch, it was not acquired by the Grant family until 1865. It was then a further five years before it actually came to be operated by J. & G. Grant Ltd, as father John and son George initially leased the plant to John Smith, until

Glenfarclas 40-Year-Old

Glenfarclas 10-Year-Old

he left to establish Cragganmore distillery nearby. Since then various members of the Grant family have presided over the distillery up to the present day, managing it through both good times and bad.

An independent spirit

"The great advantage of being independent is that we can take a long-term view and plan long-term strategies," says John Grant of the current generation. "We aren't answerable to those terrible men in the City who are only interested in higher share prices and bigger dividends and don't care how it is achieved. We don't have that burden."

Having the ability to take a long-term view of the business is one of the reasons why the distillery's inventory boasts the sort of quantities of old whisky stocks most distillers would kill for. Long-term strategic thinking also explains the well-established use of oloroso sherry casks, rather than ex-bourbon barrels. If the need to restrain costs in order to maintain or increase shareholder dividend were the overriding consideration, it would be ex-bourbon barrels all the way, as a good European oak ex-sherry butt can cost as much as 10 times that of its American oak cousin.

Much of the distillery that we see today, standing in the bulky, broad shadow of the Ben Rinnes mountain and within sight of the A95 road connecting Aberlour to Grantown on Spey, was constructed in the postwar era, with the original pair of stills being augmented by two more in 1960, while a major rebuilding program during the mid-1970s added yet another pair.

Given the distillery's well-deserved reputation for producing a consistently high-quality sherried Speyside whisky, it is not surprising that larger rivals have often cast covetous eyes over the fiercely independent Glenfarclas operation. "I regularly get offers for the distillery," says John Grant. "But I just say no thank you. We are in charge of our destiny, because we do everything, including our own bottling, at Broxburn, near Edinburgh. The distillery will only be sold over my dead body, and I hope it will carry on after me."

The Glenfarclas lineup

Glenfarclas can now offer a wide range of aged single malt expressions, from 10 to 50 years old. This is thanks to a concerted effort to market Glenfarclas as a single malt, first begun in the mid-1970s when John Grant joined the firm, at the time headed by his father, George.

The Glenfarclas distillery sits at the foot of Ben Rinnes mountain, with barley fields in the foreground.

"By 1979–1980, we had enough stock to offer a 15-year-old," says Grant, "and by the mid-eighties we could offer a 21-year-old. In the late eighties we added 25- and 30-year-olds. Now we are able to have a 40-year-old as part of the current permanent range."

In 2007 came the release of the innovative and highly collectible Family Casks range, which comprises single-cask bottlings of Glenfarclas from every year between 1952 and 1994. As John Grant notes, "We do it because we have the stock, whereas many of our competitors don't, it's as simple as that." In 2021, a limited edition 185th anniversary bottling appeared, while other notably old offerings include Pagoda Ruby Reserve 62- and 63-year-old. In 2022, a 50-year-old expression was released to celebrate John Grant's 50 years in the Scotch whisky industry.

WHISKY TALES

Direct-fired Stills
Glenfarclas boasts six of the largest stills on Speyside, and unusually, they are direct-fired by gas, rather than heated by steam. According to company Chairman John Grant, "We once put a steam coil borrowed from Miltonduff into one of our spirit stills for a few weeks, and what came out nosed bland. All the character and body and guts had gone. You definitely do get a different spirit. You get really individual character from direct-fired stills. A lot of character has gone from many whiskies and the change from direct-firing to indirect was enormous. It's much more efficient, but different alcohols come off at different rates."

TASTING NOTES

Glenfarclas 10-Year-Old
Single malt, ex-sherry casks, 40% ABV
Aromas of sherry, raisins, nuts, and spices on the nose, with just a lingering hint of smoke. The palate offers quite dry sherry, with a developing and gradually sweetening full body. The finish is long, nutty, and comparatively dry.

Glenfarclas 25-Year-Old
Single malt, 43% ABV
Oloroso sherry on the nose, with raisins and dark chocolate. malt, ginger, hazelnuts, and cocoa on the fruity palate, plus a long, oaky finish.

Glenfarclas 40-Year-Old
Single malt, ex-sherry casks, 43% ABV
Full and lush on the nose, with aromas of sweet sherry, orange marmalade, new leather, and spicy fruit. Big-bodied and rich on the fruity palate, with developing flavors of black coffee and some licorice notes. The spicy finish is very long.

GLENFIDDICH

Glenfiddich 21-Year-Old Gran Reserva

OWNER William Grant & Sons Ltd

FOUNDED 1886

WEBSITE www.glenfiddich.com

There is a tendency among those who consider themselves whisky aficionados to dismiss Glenfiddich because of its popularity, much as they might dismiss Ford cars because so many people drive them. But just as Fords are well-made and reliable vehicles, so Glenfiddich is actually a very good whisky. Selling nearly a million bottles per annum, the brand has been the world's top single malt for longer than anyone cares to remember.

As Glenfiddich's Master Blender, Brian Kinsman declares, "You get some people coming into whisky who say Glenfiddich is old hat. But the more they learn, the more they appreciate what we've done. We've paved the way for lots of other single malts. The more they learn, the more polite they become!" Kinsman does concede, however, that the whisky itself has evolved. "We've been very protective of the distillery character, but it's now 12 years old, where previously it didn't carry an age statement, and it's deeper, richer, and more complex than it was back in the 1970s."

A giant among distilleries

Glenfiddich currently operates no fewer than 43 stills, giving it the joint highest capacity of any Scottish malt distillery, along with Glenlivet. The scale of production has risen enormously since its establishment by William Grant, at which point it was only the second distillery in Dufftown after Mortlach. What has not changed, however, is the ownership. The current chairman of the firm is Glenn Gordon, a direct descendant of William Grant, a member of the fifth generation of the family to run the organization.

As the largest family-owned distilling company in Scotland, William Grant & Sons Ltd embraces Glenfiddich and the neighboring Balvenie distillery, along with Kininvie, established in 1990 and adjacent to Balvenie. Kininvie was built to provide additional malt whisky for the firm's "Grant's Family Reserve" blend, the world's fourth-biggest blended Scotch whisky. Since 1963, Grant's has also operated Girvan grain distillery, and its blending and warehousing

Glenfiddich 12-Year-Old
Special Reserve

facilities on the Ayrshire coast, while a new and flexible malt distillery was developed within the Girvan complex during 2007–2008. Named Ailsa Bay, it has an annual capacity of 1.65 million gallons (6.25 million liters).

Glenfiddich was the first Scottish distillery to open its doors to the public on a regular basis, back in 1969, and since then more than 3 million visitors have sampled its delights.

The extent of the range

The core Glenfiddich lineup embraces 12-, 15-, and 18-year-olds, while 30-, 40-, and 50-year-old bottlings are available in the Time series. The Grand series offers a number of luxury "finished" whiskies, including 21-year-old Gran Reserva, 22-year-old Gran Cortes, 23-year-old Grand Cru, 26-year-old Grand Couronne and 29-year-old Grand Yozakura, which is finished in

One of three stillhouses at Glenfiddich. Together, they are home to no fewer than 46 stills.

Japanese Awamori casks that previously held rice spirit. There is also a 38-year-old Glenfiddich Ultimate and a number of vintages in the Rare Collection.

The Experimental Series

Since 2016, several unusual releases have appeared in the Experimental Series. The first two were Project XX (component casks selected by 20 individuals) and IPA Cask Finish (finished in IPA ale casks), followed by 21-year-old Winter Storm (finished in Canadian icewine casks). Fire & Cane (including peated malt finished in rum casks) and Orchard Experiment (finished in casks that previously held Somerset Pomona spirit).

WHISKY TALES
Direct-Fired Stills
Glenfarclas boasts six of the largest stills on Speyside, and unusually, they are direct-fired by gas rather than heated by steam. According to company Chairman John Grant, "We once put a steam coil borrowed from Miltonduff into one of our spirit stills for a few weeks, and what came out nosed bland. All the character and body and guts had gone. You definitely do get a different spirit. You get really individual character from direct-fired stills. A lot of character has gone from many whiskies and the change from direct-firing to indirect was enormous. It's much more efficient, but different alcohols come off at different rates."

Glenfiddich 30-Year-Old

TASTING NOTES

Glenfiddich 12-Year-Old Special Reserve
Single malt, 40% ABV
A delicate, floral, slightly fruity nose; well mannered in the mouth, malty, elegant, and soft. Rich fruit flavors dominate the palate, with a developing nuttiness and an elusive whiff of peat smoke in the fragrant finish.

Glenfiddich 30-Year-Old
Single malt, vatting of ex-oloroso sherry and ex-bourbon casks, 43% ABV
Coconut, fruit salad, oak, and sherry on the nose. Complex palate, with cinnamon, ginger, oak, and dark chocolate. Long and honeyed with sweet oak in the finish.

Glenfiddich 21-Year-Old Gran Reserva
Single malt, 40% ABV
Malt, honey, red apples, and light rum aromas, leading to a palate of caramel, cream, oak, and pecan pie, with nougat and oak in the finish.

GLEN GRANT

Glen Grant 10-Year-Old

OWNER Gruppo Campari

FOUNDED 1840

WEBSITE www.glengrant.com

Glen Grant has the distinction of being the only Scottish distillery directly named after a person or persons, in this case the brothers John and James Grant, who established the first distillery in the town of Rothes during 1840. In 1872, the distillery was inherited by James Grant's son, also James, frequently referred to simply as "the Major"—an astute businessman who carried on the good work of his father and uncle in developing Glen Grant into one of the largest distilleries of its day.

While the Major was a traditional figure in many ways, the woodland garden he made at Glen Grant was planted with new and exotic species not usually found in the north of Scotland. One feature of it always remembered by visitors was the "dram safe" set in the rocky bank of the burn that flows through the picturesque glen in the distillery grounds. Installed by the Major, this provided the *pièce de résistance* of a walk through the gardens in his company; visitors were suitably astonished when the Major unlocked the safe, pulled out a bottle of Glen Grant, and poured drams for them, accompanied, if required, by crystal-clear water from the burn itself.

Glen Grant expands

At the height of the Victorian whisky boom, in 1897, the Major constructed an entirely new Glen Grant No. 2 distillery on the opposite side of the main road through Rothes in order to increase capacity. Later rechristened Caperdonich, this facility was demolished during 2010.

In 1953, J. & J. Grant, Glen Grant Ltd merged with George & J. G. Smith of Glenlivet to form Glenlivet & Glen Grant Distillers Ltd, and in 1972, the company became part of The Glenlivet Distillers Ltd, acquired five years later by The Seagram Company Ltd. The complement of stills was increased from four to six in 1973, and from six to ten in 1977. During 2001, Glen Grant was one of the Seagram distilleries acquired by Chivas Brothers, and in 2006 the distillery and brand name were sold to the Italian drinks company Campari.

Glen Grant 18-Year-Old

Italian style

One of the first and most astute decisions taken by Campari was to headhunt Dennis Malcolm to manage their new acquisition. Nobody knows Glen Grant better than Malcolm, who was born in a

Glen Grant The Major's Reserve

distillery house on the site where his father was a stillman and his grandfather had also served as a mashman and stillman. Malcolm started working at Glen Grant in 1961 as an apprentice cooper, and has had a connection with the distillery in one capacity or another for most of his working life.

"Campari bought Glen Grant because they wanted a really good spirits brand. Glen Grant has a huge following in Italy. In terms of volume, it's the leading single malt Scotch in the country," explains Malcolm. Of the spirit, he says, "The wash still had what you might term a 'German helmet' to it, which helps to prevent a buildup of solids from the fermented wash. The stills are fitted with purifiers, which work all the time, and they create a huge amount of reflux, which gives the spirit a comparatively light and delicate character. Using wooden washbacks also adds to the whisky's character."

The drams

The core Glen Grant range includes the NAS The Major's Reserve, the NAS Arboralis—aged in a combination of bourbon and sherry casks—and 10-, 12-, 15-, 18-, and 21-year-olds. The 15-year-old is offered at batch strength. The year 2023 saw the release of the oldest Glen Grant distillery bottling to date, namely a 70-year-old, launched to celebrate 70 years of the late Queen Elizabeth II's reign. Just seven decanters—at 55 percent ABV—were produced.

Although Glen Grant has the image of a pale and youthful whisky, Dennis Malcolm says, "Just because our whisky is usually light and young doesn't mean it can't grow old very gracefully. It matures beautifully. It's very dense and complex when it's matured in a sherry cask."

WHISKY TALES

Bye-way of Rothes
Major James Grant was in many ways an archetypal Victorian Highland laird and, in later life, a passionate sportsman, devoted to shooting, fishing, and big game hunting. During a safari in Matabeleland in 1898, the Major and his party came across an abandoned child and took him home to Rothes. The boy was christened Biawa Makalaga, having been discovered in Makalaga state, and was known locally as "Bye-way." He was educated in Rothes and subsequently became butler to the Major. After the Major's death, Biawa lived on in Glen Grant House until he died in 1972.

TASTING NOTES

Glen Grant The Major's Reserve
Single malt, 40% ABV
Delicate on the nose, with gentle vanilla, malt, lemon, and the aroma of damp leaves. Malt and vanilla take center stage on the palate, too, along with citrus fruit and hazelnuts. The finish is brisk.

Glen Grant 10-Year-Old
Single malt, 43% ABV
Aromas of ripe pear, honey, malt, and vanilla, with flavors of red apple, pear, and Brazil nuts, finishing on a note of cinnamon and oak.

Glen Grant 18-Year-Old
Single malt, 43% ABV
Floral on the nose, with soft orchard fruits, while the palate offers subtle spice, malt, milk chocolate, and nougat, leading into a finish of green apples and a little white pepper.

THE GLENLIVET

OWNER Chivas Bros Ltd (Pernod Ricard)

FOUNDED 1824

WEBSITE www.theglenlivet.com

During the past few years, The Glenlivet and Glenfiddich have fought it out on the global stage to determine the world's bestselling single malt. The pendulum has swung both ways, but in 2022, The Glenlivet had the upper hand, selling over 20 million bottles. The Glenlivet's owner Chivas Brothers also has high-volume blends such as Ballantine's and Chivas Regal in its stable, so it is hardly surprising that the output of Glenlivet has increased dramatically. The first phase of expansion came in 2008–2009 when a new $12.5 million (£10 million) production building was constructed next to the existing distillery.

The Glenlivet is another of those historic distilleries where the impetus to expand swiftly at various periods in its history has led to the construction of some less-than-attractive structures, but its most recent growth spurt has gone a long way to righting past aesthetic wrongs.

The additional production building was clad in local stone, with stills visible to visitors upon arrival. Since its construction, however, another phase of expansion has seen the creation of an entirely new distilling operation behind a set of warehouses. This takes total capacity to 84.8 million gallons (321 million liters) per annum courtesy of no fewer than 14 pairs of stills.

Smith's Glenlivet

The Glenlivet was the first distillery to be granted a license in the wake of the highly influential 1823 Excise Act, and its owner and licensee was George Smith, whose family had been distilling whisky on his farm at Upper Drumin, about 1 mil (1.6km) from the present Glenlivet distillery, since 1774.

In 1840, George Smith leased the Cairngorm distillery at Delnabo, near Tomintoul, and his son, William, took charge of the distillery at Upper Drumin. However, demand for Smith's whisky outstripped supply, and in 1858, a new, significantly larger distillery named Glenlivet was established on the present Minmore site, with Upper Drumin and Cairngorm closing the following year.

The Glenlivet 12-Year-Old Double Oak

The Glenlivet
Founder's Reserve

The magnificent scenery that surrounds The Glenlivet distillery is an added attraction for tour visitors.

Family ownership continued for almost a century, with George & J. G. Smith Ltd merging with J. & J. Grant Glen Grant Ltd to form Glenlivet & Glen Grant Distillers Ltd in 1953. In 1972, the company joined Hill Thompson & Company Ltd and Longmorn-Glenlivet Distilleries Ltd to create The Glenlivet Distillers Ltd; Seagram of Canada then acquired that company in 1977, and in 2001, The Glenlivet was one of the former Seagram assets purchased by Pernod Ricard subsidiary Chivas Brothers, for whom it is now the jewel in their Scotch whisky portfolio.

The definite article

The powers that be at Chivas Brothers stress that the distillery should always be referred to as The Glenlivet. The definite article usage stems from an 1880 legal action, fought by John Gordon Smith, who felt that the name was being devalued by its widespread employment by distilleries often many miles from the glen itself.

Indeed, so many distilleries attempted to capitalize on the fame and reputation of The Glenlivet that during the second half of the 19th century the place was jokingly referred to as "the longest glen in Scotland." The court decided that only Smith's Glenlivet distillery could use the definite article in front of its name, while all other distillers had to use "Glenlivet" as a hyphenated prefix or suffix.

Visiting The Glenlivet

The Glenlivet boasts an array of award-winning visitor experiences, including The Archives warehouse tour, where participants explore the maturing whisky stocks and sample a dram straight from the cask. Single cask tasting sessions are also available, and whiskies and cocktails may be enjoyed in the Drawing Room bar.

The Glenlivet today

The core Glenlivet range includes the NAS Founder's Reserve, Captain's Reserve (finished in cognac casks), Caribbean Reserve (finished in rum casks), 12-year-old Double Oak, 15-year-old French Oak Reserve, and an 18-year-old. The Sample Room Collection comprises a 21-year-old, finished in oloroso, vintage port, and cognac casks, and a 25-year-old, finished in PX sherry and cognac casks. Cask Finished Editions include a 20-year-old Rum Barrel Finish and a 9-year-old Beer Cask Finished Edition.

TASTING NOTES

The Glenlivet 12-Year-Old Double Oak
Single malt, 40% ABV
A honeyed, floral, fragrant nose. Medium-bodied, smooth, and malty on the palate, with vanilla sweetness; not as sweet, however, as the nose might suggest. The finish is pleasantly lengthy and sophisticated.

The Glenlivet Founder's Reserve
Single malt, 40% ABV
Light toffee, vanilla, and ripe apples on the floral nose. Ripe pear, fudge, and soft spices on the palate, finishing with raisins, hot chocolate, and light oak.

The Glenlivet 15-Year-Old French Oak Reserve
Single malt, 40% ABV
Orchard fruits, almonds, and honey on the nose, with a palate of cinnamon, pineapple, and vanilla fudge, leading into a spicy, nutty finish with drying oak.

WHISKY TALES

Hair-Trigger Pistols
Glenlivet is a remote area of Speyside, once renowned for both the quantity and quality of illicit whisky distilled there. When he decided to operate on the right side of the law, George Smith of The Glenlivet distillery found himself with more enemies than friends among his fellow whisky makers, so the Laird of Aberlour presented him with a pair of hair-trigger pistols with which to protect himself and his distillery. As Smith later recalled, "I got together two or three stout fellows for servants, armed them with pistols, and let it be known everywhere that I would fight for my place to the last shot." The distillery survived!

The Glenlivet 15-Year-Old French Oak Reserve

GLEN MORAY

OWNER La Martiniquaise

FOUNDED 1897

WEBSITE www.glenmoray.com

Glen Moray represents a good example of a single malt that does not have too many competing high-profile brands and is flourishing under the ownership of a large company that is prepared to focus on its merits.

Back to capacity

While in the Glenmorangie plc portfolio this whisky from the Speyside capital of Elgin was always going to play second fiddle to Glenmorangie itself and could sometimes be found in supermarkets at a price per liter that was more or less comparable with some of the higher-quality blends.

Indeed, sales of Glen Moray have grown significantly in recent years, topping 2.2 million bottles in 2021. To cope with increasing single malt sales and those of Glen Turner, Label 5, and the historic Cutty Sark blend, acquired by La Martiniquaise in 2019, the distillery in Elgin has been progressively expanded. It now boasts a capacity of 2.25 million gallons (8.5 million liters) per annum, compared to 580,000 gallons (2.2 million liters) 15 years ago. Increasing capacity has taken place in three stages, with the most radical being completed in 2023–2024. The distillery now includes a 11-ton full lauter mash tun, a 6.6-ton semi-lauter mash tun, and 21 external stainless steel fermenting vessels. Four wash and six spirit stills complete the extensive production apparatus.

Peaty possibilities

In common with several other Scottish distilleries whose make has long been at the opposite end of the stylistic spectrum to peaty malts, Glen Moray distills from heavily peated malt for a short period each year. The first peated spirit was in 2009, and up to 66,000 gallons (250,000 liters)—peated to 48ppm—is now produced each year. It is used in the owner's blends and in peated finish Glen Moray single malt expressions.

Brewery background

There is a close relationship between brewing beer and distilling whisky, with both breweries and

Elgin Classic Peated

Elgin Classic

distilleries requiring a guaranteed supply of grain for malting and pure process water, and whisky is, in essence, simply distilled beer. Several breweries have been converted into distilleries over the years, including Glenmorangie, the late lamented Lochside in Montrose, and Glen Moray itself.

The distillery was established in 1897, when the Speyside region was at the heart of a vast expansion in whisky production, and was developed within the former West Brewery of Henry Arnot & Company, trading as the Glen Moray Glenlivet Distillery Company Ltd.

After the whisky bubble burst amid a crisis of overproduction around the turn of the century, expansion was swiftly followed by contraction, and Glen Moray fell silent in 1910. With the exception of a brief revival two years later, the Elgin distillery was silent until 1923, when it reopened in the hands of new owners Macdonald & Muir Ltd. The Leith-based company already owned Glenmorangie, and it was left up to the manager of that distillery to choose between Aberlour and Glen Moray to add to the portfolio. He chose the latter.

During 1958, a degree of reconstruction took place at Glen Moray, with the existing floor maltings being replaced by Saladin boxes, though on-site malting ended entirely in 1978. A year after malting ceased, the complement of stills was doubled to four.

French connections
Macdonald & Muir changed its name to Glenmorangie plc in 1996, and in 2004 the company was acquired by French luxury goods group Louis Vuitton Möet Hennessy (LVMH). It would be unfair to suggest that LVMH had little interest in Glen Moray, since they invested in a new visitor center at the distillery and proceeded to release various limited editions and vintage expressions.

"The Fifth Chapter," a 1992 cask strength bottling, appeared during 2005, while two well-regarded, cask strength, limited editions of Glen Moray "Mountain Oak" were released in 2003 and 2007. The whisky for "Mountain Oak" had been matured since filling during 1991 in what Glen Moray described as "a unique selection of toasted and charred mountain oak casks from North America."

Despite such innovations at Glen Moray, however, in 2008 LVMH divested itself of its blending operations, blended Scotch whisky brands, and the Glen Moray operation in order to concentrate on its Ardbeg and Glenmorangie single malts. Ownership

of the Glen Moray distillery and single malt brand remained in French hands, however, with a buyer found in the form of the French drinks firm La Martiniquaise.

La Martiniquaise opts for a much lower profile than the owner of the Louis Vuitton designer fashion house, and the Moët Champagne and Hennessy Cognac brands. Indeed, if you read most whisky books, you won't find mention of the fact that the company now operates a large grain distillery near Bathgate in West Lothian. The Starlaw Distillery has a capacity of 6.6 million gallons (25 million liters) per annum and provides spirit for Cutty Sark, La Martiniquaise's Glen Turner malt whiskies, the bestselling malt brand in France, and the Label 7 blend, both of which also enjoy strong sales in overseas markets.

Glen Moray today
Glen Moray offers an extensive range of single malts across several key ranges. The entry-level NAS Classic lineup includes Classic, Port Cask Finish, Sherry Cask Finish, Chardonnay Cask Finish, Cabernet Sauvignon Cask Finish, and Classic Peated. The Heritage range takes in 12-, 15-, and 18-year-old expressions, plus 10-year-old Fired Oak and 21-year-old Port Wood Finish. Curiosity offers a number of intriguing bottlings, including Madeira Cask, Rhum Agricole Cask Finish, Curiosity Chenin Blanc Matured, and Rye Cask Finish. The Warehouse 1 collection continues the theme of finished single malts with Barolo, Tokaji, and manzanilla finishes.

TASTING NOTES

Elgin Classic
Single malt, 40% ABV
Notably fresh on the nose, with aromas of barley, wet grass, and gentle fruit notes. The palate is balanced and mild with a taste of nuts, citrus fruit, and oak. Citrus notes continue in the finish with a little extra spice.

Elgin Classic Peated
Single cask, 40% ABV
Earthy peat, pineapple, honey, and vanilla aromas, with flavor of wood smoke, leather and ripe pears, leading into a finish of peppery peat.

Glen Moray 18-Year-Old
Single malt, 47.2% ABV
Orchard fruits, milk chocolate, vanilla, pepper, and subtle smoke on the nose, while the palate features stewed fruits, malt, butterscotch, and cinnamon, closing with orange, toffee apples, and a hint of chili.

Glen Moray 18-Year-Old

THE MACALLAN

OWNER The Edrington Group

FOUNDED 1824

WEBSITE www.themacallan.com

In single malt global sales, The Macallan occupies third place behind Glenfiddich and The Glenlivet, but when it comes to sheer whisky cachet, it surely ranks highest of them all. The brand boasts an unparalleled reputation both for the quality of its liquid and the high prices that rare and collectible bottlings fetch at auction. In December 2023, a bottle of 60-year-old Macallan, featuring a label designed by Italian artist Valerio Adami, sold at Sotheby's auction house in London for a world record price of $2.76 million (£2.2 million). It was one of only 40 bottled by Macallan in 1986, and one of 12 featuring the Adami label.

Collaborations

Part of The Macallan's attraction for collectors is the fact that they are guaranteed a regular supply of limited edition releases, which are very likely to appreciate in value over the years. These have included projects such as "Masters of Photography," which featured collaborations with the likes of Rankin and Albert Watson, and The Red Collection of old and very rare expressions. Others include Fine & Rare, offering single cask bottlings from 1926 to 1993; and the Harmony Collection, featuring a 30-year-old Double Cask bottling; and the 81-year-old The Reach—the oldest single malt Scotch whisky bottled to date. The year 2023 saw the release of the Color Collection, a series that celebrates two of the pillars upon which The Macallan legacy is built: natural color and sherry seasoning.

The Macallan heritage

Today's iconic Macallan single malt first saw the light of day in 1824 when the distillery was licensed to Alexander Reid, though for much of its subsequent existence it was in the hands of the Kemp family, with the Japanese distilling giant Suntory acquiring 25 percent of the stocks in what had become Macallan-Glenlivet plc in 1986. A decade later, Highland Distilleries Ltd bought the rest of the stocks, and in 1999, a partnership of The Edrington Group and William Grant & Sons Ltd purchased

The Macallan Double Cask 12-Year-Old

The Macallan 30-Year-Old
Sherry Oak

The Macallan Double Cask
18-Year-Old

Highland Distilleries, going on to form the 1887 Company.

The Macallan distillery was progressively enlarged over the years, until an entirely new distillery with a notably radical design was unveiled in 2018. It cost $175 million (£140 million) and contains no fewer than 36 of Macallan's distinctive small stills, arranged in three circular "pods," along with 21 stainless steel fermenters and a 19-ton mash tun, said to be the largest in Scotland. Externally, the distillery and visitor center was inspired by traditional Scottish brochs, or roundhouses, and features a stunning undulating grass and wildflower-topped roof. The visitor facilities in the "new" Macallan are among the finest anywhere in the world.

The Macallan distillery is far from conventional in design and houses no fewer than 36 small stills.

WHISKY TALES

From Barley to Casks
A number of factors influence the character of The Macallan single malt, starting with the barley. The use of a proportion of the Minstrel variety helps produce a rich, oily new make spirit character. The spirit stills are notably small and are run slowly, with a narrow cut of around 16 percent being filled into casks, again helping to ensure an oily, rich new make spirit that is ideally suited to lengthy maturation in ex-sherry casks. The Macallan also has its own Spanish oak casks made on a custom basis and seasoned with sherry in Spain, while American oak cask staves are also imported to Spain for sherry seasoning.

The Macallan Sherry Oak 18-Year-Old

The whiskies

While there are many limited editions and collections to consider, The Macallan core range includes 8-, 12-, 26-, and 30-year-old expressions in its "traditional" Sherry Oak lineup, along with 12-, 15-, 18-, and 30-year-old expressions of Double Oak—matured in a mix of sherry-seasoned European and American oak casks.

TASTING NOTES

The Macallan 12-Year-Old Sherry Oak
Single malt, matured in ex-sherry casks, 40% ABV
Buttery sherry and Christmas cake on the nose, rich and full on the palate, with ripe oranges and sweet oak. Long and malty in the finish, with gently smoked, spicy oak.

The Macallan 30-Year-Old Sherry Oak
Single malt, matured in ex-oloroso sherry casks, 43% ABV
Big sherry notes on the full, mature nose, with spice and tangerines. Luxurious rounded palate with sherry, honey, raisins, and allspice. Long, fruity finish with coffee and plain chocolate.

The Macallan Double Cask 12-Year-Old
Single malt, 40% ABV
Warm leather, toffee, relatively dry sherry, and cherry blossom on the nose, while the palate offers richer sherry, honey, orange, vanilla, hot chocolate, and spicy oak.

The Macallan Double Cask 18-Year-Old
Single malt, 43% ABV
The nose is floral, with wood polish, vanilla, toffee, and cloves. Jaffa orange, dark chocolate, Christmas spices, caramel, and ginger on the palate, which closes with citrus fruit, black coffee, and black pepper.

The Macallan Sherry Oak 18-Year-Old
Single malt, 43% ABV
Cinnamon, dried fruits, cloves, leather, and ginger aromas lead into flavors of orange, ginger, smoky sherry, and soft oak.

CRAGGANMORE

Cragganmore 12-Year-Old

OWNER Diageo plc

FOUNDED 1869

WEBSITE www.malts.com

By 1869, when John Smith set out to establish Cragganmore, close to the Spey River, he could already boast a strong track record as a distiller. In 1988, the current owner, United Distillers, selected Cragganmore 12-year-old as the regional representative in its Classic Malts portfolio. Cragganmore had long enjoyed the reputation of being a first-class blending malt, as well as a fine dram in its own right.

Making the malt

The essential character of Cragganmore single malt is partly due to comparatively lengthy fermentations of around 60 hours, with fermentation times being long enough to produce some of the floral, light fruit notes that characterize Cragganmore.

However, it is the distillation regime that has the greatest influence on the style of the whisky. The wash still lyne arms slope downward toward the worm tubs, thereby limiting the opportunity for the vapor to interact with copper, while the T-shaped tops of the spirit stills encourage a degree of reflux. The wash stills produce a comparatively sulfury character, while the spirit stills give a lighter spirit. "Sulfury" and "meaty" are desirable components of Cragganmore, so in order to combat the lighter style of spirit produced in the spirit stills, they are not given time to "rest," which would allow the copper to rejuvenate. The stills are recharged as soon as they are empty, making the copper less active than would otherwise be the case.

Cragganmore Distiller's Edition (Bottled 2022)

TASTING NOTES

Cragganmore 12-Year-Old
Single malt, 40% ABV
A complex nose of sherry, brittle toffee, nuts, heather, mild wood smoke, and mixed peel. Malty on the palate, with almonds, herbal, and fruit notes. Medium in length, with a slightly peppery, smoky finish.

Cragganmore Distiller's Edition (Bottled 2022)
Single malt, single cask, cask strength, matured in refill American oak casks, 40% ABV
Orange fondant cream on the nose, with marzipan and malt, deepening to molasses. Fresh citrus fruits on the palate; lively and spicy, becoming drier and more oaky, with ginger and licorice in the lengthy finish.

GLENALLACHIE

OWNER The GlenAllachie Distillery Company

FOUNDED 1967

WEBSITE www.theglenallachie.com

Whisky made at GlenAllachie, nestling at the foot of Ben Rinnes, near Aberlour, has gone from being well-nigh invisible in consumer terms to having significant visibility and a proactive releases policy. GlenAllachie was established in 1967–1968 principally to supply malt whisky for the popular Mackinlay blend. Led by industry veteran Billy Walker, the current owners, The GlenAllachie Distillery Company (which capitalized the middle A in the name, just as they had capitalized letters in their BenRiach and GlenDronach distilleries and brands), have moved the focus to building a single malt brand. Around 211,000 gallons (800,000 liters) of spirit are produced each year. The distillery has a capacity of 1.1 million gallons (4 million liters), far beyond current requirements, and production has been slowed down to allow for fermentations lasting 160 hours.

Along with the distillery, the owners acquired a large inventory of stock from Chivas Brothers, some dating back to the 1970s. Over 500,000 casks are maturing in 16 on-site warehouses, and a range of single malts carrying age statements are available. The core portfolio comprises 8-, 10- (cask strength), 12-, 15-, 18-, 21- (cask strength), 25-, and 30-year-old (cask strength) expressions; and there is also a Virgin Oak Series, offering French, Hungarian, Scottish, Spanish, and Chinquapin Oak–matured bottlings. Additionally, there is a Wood Finish Range and a Wine Cask Series, along with half a dozen single cask variants. Tours and tastings are available.

TASTING NOTES

GlenAllachie 10-Year-Old Cask Strength, Batch 11
Single malt, 58.6% ABV
A spicy nose with red wine, honey and furniture polish leads into a palate focusing on milk chocolate, stewed fruits, red berries, and more lingering, lively spice.

GlenAllachie 18-Year-Old
Single malt, 46% ABV
Nutty and spicy on the nose, with barley sugar and malt. Almonds, apricots, nutmeg, and wood spice on the palate.

GlenAllachie 10-Year-Old Cask Strength, Batch 11

GlenAllachie 18-Year-Old

GLEN ELGIN

OWNER Diageo plc

FOUNDED 1898

WEBSITE www.malts.com

Given that it operates 28 malt distilleries in Scotland, Diageo does not give single malt prominence to the whisky produced in all of them but focuses on a core range representing a variety of regions and styles. Yet away from the Taliskers and Cardhus, Lagavulins and Dalwhinnies, there are some seriously fine single malts waiting to be discovered. One such is Glen Elgin, long favored by blenders and an important component of the historic White Horse blend, but since 2005 also embraced by Diageo's Classic Malts portfolio.

Low-profile classic

Glen Elgin is one of Speyside's more elusive distilleries, in keeping with its profile. With three pairs of relatively small stills and traditional wooden worm tubs to condense the spirit, it offers a good example of how a distillery can be set up to produce a style of spirit that is essentially at odds with the expectations of its equipment. In theory, that spirit should be relatively full-bodied and rich, but lengthy fermentation and slow distillation actually result in a comparatively fruity and light character.

Established in 1898, production commenced in May 1900, just as the industry suffered a dramatic downturn from which it took more than 50 years to recover. Glen Elgin made whisky for just five months before closing. In 1930, the distillery was acquired from Glasgow blender J. J. Blanche & Company by the Distillers Company Ltd subsidiary Scottish Malt Distillers (SMD), becoming part of Diageo.

TASTING NOTES

Glen Elgin 12-Year-Old
Single malt, 43% ABV
A nose of rich, fruity sherry, figs, and fragrant spice, plus honey and cut flowers. Full-bodied, soft, malty, and honeyed in the mouth, with ginger and orange. Lengthy and slightly perfumed, with spicy oak in the finish.

Glen Elgin 18-Year-Old (Diageo Special Releases 2017)
Single malt, 54.8% ABV
Aromas of fresh leather, orchard fruits, brittle toffee, and vanilla lead into a voluptuous palate of fudge, apricots, cinnamon, ginger, and lingering oak.

Glen Elgin 12-Year-Old

GLENGLASSAUGH

OWNER Glenglassaugh Distillery Company Ltd
(Brown-Forman)

FOUNDED 1873

WEBSITE www.glenglassaugh.com

The original distillery, standing close to the southern shores of the Moray Firth, was built in 1873–1875, but in 1986 it was mothballed—there are few sadder sights for the whisky lover than a silent distillery, its copper pots cold and tarnished, with no smell of mash on the air or bustle of human activity. Fortunately, the distillery found its savior in Scaent Group, which has global energy interests and was eager to expand into Scotch whisky. Scaent bought the distillery in early 2008, forming the Glenglassaugh Distillery Company Ltd, and spent around $2 million

(£1 million) on refurbishment. In 2013, The BenRiach Distillery Co Ltd acquired Glenglassaugh, and since 2018, it has been owned by the US company Brown-Forman. A new core range was introduced during the summer of 2023, comprising a 12-year-old and two NAS expressions, Sandend and Portsoy.

TASTING NOTES

Glenglassaugh 12-Year-Old
Single malt, 45% ABV
Red berries, walnuts, and caramel on the nose, with developing coconut. Caramel, vanilla, and red wine on the palate, with milk chocolate and salted peanuts in the finish.

Glenglassaugh Portsoy
Single malt, aged in sherry, bourbon, and port casks, 49.1% ABV
A nose of soft peat, dried fruits, chocolate, and a sprinkling of salt. The palate offers charcuterie, blackberries, and gingerbread.

Glenglassaugh 12-Year-Old

THE GLENROTHES

OWNER The Edrington Group

FOUNDED 1878

WEBSITE www.theglenrothes.com

As a malt whisky, The Glenrothes has long enjoyed a high reputation among blenders, one of only a few Speyside whiskies accorded the blender's grading of "Top Class." Its profile began to grow significantly after 1993 when the owners opted to release a series of vintages of its single malt, rather than age-specific bottlings. That practice lasted until 2017–2018, with Edrington introducing a select portfolio of aged expressions during the latter year, placing the brand firmly in the "ultra-premium" market. The range culminates in a 42-year-old, described by master whisky maker Laura Rampling as "Part science, part alchemy, and a little bit of magic." A long-standing relationship existed with fabled London wine and spirits merchants Berry Bros & Rudd, who owned the brand—but not the distillery—from 2010 to 2017, when Edrington took it back "in house."

An unusual arrangement

Located in the small town of Rothes, the distillery has historically had a complicated ownership. In 1887, the then-owner William Grant and Company merged with the Islay Distillery Company, and the new group became Highland Distilleries, later Highland Distillers, and now part of The Edrington Group.

The Glenrothes distillery lies in a pretty wooded location on the edge of the town of Rothes.

TASTING NOTES

The Glenrothes 18-Year-Old
Single malt, 43% ABV
Tropical fruits, marzipan, and allspice on the nose, while the palate offers caramel, vanilla, raisins, cinnamon, and ultimately dark chocolate, black pepper, and oak.

The Glenrothes 25-Year-Old
Single malt, 43% ABV
Aromas of sherry, apple pie, cinnamon, and tobacco lead into a palate of dates, plums, worn leather, and faint smoke.

The Glenrothes 42-Year-Old
Single malt, 43% ABV
Tropical fruits, hazelnuts, and sherry on the nose, with a palate featuring treacle, brown sugar, almonds, aniseed, and spicy oak.

The Glenrothes 42-Year-Old

KNOCKANDO

Knockando 12-Year-Old

OWNER Diageo

FOUNDED 1898

WEBSITE www.malts.com

Knockando has long been the heart malt in the J&B blended Scotch whisky brand, globally the third-best seller behind Johnnie Walker and Ballantine's, and particularly popular in France, Spain, Portugal, South Africa, and the United States.

The J&B "Rare" blend was established by the fashionable London wine and spirits merchants Justerini & Brooks especially for the US market during the era of Prohibition (1920–1933); its pale color and light style suited the mood of the era, making it keen competition for Cutty Sark.

Born in the whisky boom

However, the history of Knockando began in 1898–1899, when it was established just before the end of the great Victorian whisky boom. Knockando was active for only about 10 months before being forced to close, with Gilbey's purchasing it for the knocked-down price of just $17,500 (£3,500) in 1904.

The connection between Knockando and J&B dates back to a 1962 merger between W&A Gilbey Ltd and United Wine Traders (then owners of J&B), which led to the creation of International Distillers & Vintners and the capacity of Knockando doubling in 1969 by the installation of a second pair of stills. Subsequent mergers and acquisitions eventually led Knockando and the J&B brand into the Diageo whisky portfolio.

From the 1970s onward, Knockando whisky was bottled for most markets according to its vintage instead of carrying specific age statements, but this practice ended with the release of 12-, 15,- 18-, and 21-year-old bottlings. Only the 12-year-old remains.

The Knockando stillhouse is home to two pairs of distinctive copper stills.

TASTING NOTES

Knockando 12-Year-Old
Single malt, 43% ABV
Delicate and fragrant on the nose, with hints of malt, worn leather, and hay. Quite full in the mouth, smooth, and honeyed, with gingery malt. Medium length in the finish, with cereal and more ginger.

LONGMORN

OWNER Chivas Brothers Ltd (Pernod Ricard)

FOUNDED 1894

WEBSITE www.secret-speyside.com

While The Glenlivet is Chivas Brothers' pin-up single malt and Strathisla is notable for its popularity with visitors and its role as the brand home of "Chivas Regal," Longmorn principally provides malt whisky for blending. It has an enviable reputation among blenders as one of the top-flight Speysides. It also fulfills its role as the provider of malt for the Chivas Regal, Queen Anne, and Something Special blends with aplomb.

The distillery was constructed by John Duff and his associates, but Duff took sole control in 1897. This was clearly not a judicious move, since he filed for bankruptcy the following year, with Longmorn being bought by one James Grant. Private ownership continued until 1970, when The Glenlivet Distillers Ltd was formed, and in 1978 Seagram of Canada acquired it. Longmorn was one of the former Seagram assets subsequently acquired by Pernod Ricard's subsidiary Chivas Brothers Ltd in 2001.

Longmorn operates eight large, onion-shaped stills that produce a rich, full-bodied, fruity, new-make spirit. Until 1994, the wash stills were direct-fired, using coal, while the spirit stills, located in a separate stillhouse, were heated by steam. Some 18 mashes per week currently produce approximately 793,000 gallons (3 million liters) per annum, though the distillery's annual capacity is 1.2 million gallons (4.5 million liters).

TASTING NOTES

Longmorn 18-Year-Old
Single malt, 48% ABV
Apricots, marzipan, crushed almonds, malt and milk chocolate on the nose, with a soft palate offering ripe pears, fudge brownies, vanilla and gentle spice. Long in the finish, with nutty oak and citrus fruit.

Longmorn 22-Year-Old
Single malt, 54.5% ABV
The nose yields baked apple, poached pears, coconut and ginger, while the palate features dried apricot, Jaffa orange, vanilla and milk chocolate, with ginger, nutmeg and cocoa in the finish.

Longmorn 18-Year-Old

Longmorn 22-Year-Old

MORTLACH

OWNER Diageo plc

FOUNDED 1823

WEBSITE www.malts.com

Of all Scottish distilleries, Mortlach deserves a prize for having the most complex whisky-making regime, with the spirit distilled 2.8 times. Key to the process is the role of No.1 spirit still, nicknamed the "Wee Witchie." In total, there are six stills, all of different shapes and sizes, and the "Wee Witchie" is charged three times during each run. Condensation of spirit takes place in six worm tubs, five made of timber and one of stainless steel. The spirit that results from this unique distillation process is notably rich and robust, suited to lengthy maturation in ex-sherry casks.

The development of Mortlach

Mortlach was the first distillery to be built in Dufftown, and William Grant worked there for 20 years, latterly as manager, before leaving to establish his own Glenfiddich operation in 1886.

    Mortlach is an important component of the Johnnie Walker Black Label, and when demand grew in recent years Mortlach became even more elusive as a "house" bottling. However, an increase in production at the distillery has allowed this fascinating single malt to achieve much higher visibility, and since 2018, there has been a trio of core bottlings, 12-year-old Wee Witchie, 16-year-old Distiller's Dram, and 20-year-old Cowie's Blue Seal, more readily available.

Mortlach 16-Year-Old
Distiller's Dram

TASTING NOTES

Mortlach 12-Year-Old Wee Witchie
Single malt, 43.4% ABV
Milk chocolate, baked apricot, ginger, and black pepper on the nose, with a slightly savory palate of vanilla, orchard fruits, and cinnamon, closing with chocolate, ginger, plums, and subtle oak.

Mortlach 16-Year-Old Distiller's Dram
Single malt, 43.4% ABV
The nose is quite earthy, with tobacco, ginger, and subtle sherry, while the palate yields peaches in syrup, figs, and cinnamon, ending on orange, leather, and oak.

Mortlach 20-Year-Old Cowie's Blue Seal
Single malt, 43.4% ABV
Meaty on the nose, with instant coffee, nuts, and milk chocolate. The palate is waxy, with apricots, almonds, and spicy orange.

Mortlach 12-Year-Old Wee Witchie

SPEYBURN

OWNER International Beverage Holdings

FOUNDED 1897

WEBSITE www.speyburn.com

On the outskirts of the distilling town of Rothes, Speyburn is one of five Scottish distilleries operated by Inver House Distillers Ltd, part of the mighty International Beverage Holdings since 2001. As a single malt, Speyburn is best known in the US, but the majority of the distillery's "make" finds its way into Inver House blends such as Catto's, Hankey Bannister, and Pinwhinnie.

Established in 1897, when Speyside was at the center of a distillery boom, Speyburn was designed by Elgin architect Charles Doig, and the structures remain little changed. Doig is the doyen of distillery architects, and his most enduring creation, the Chinese-style kiln pagoda head, is regarded as a symbol of Scotch whisky distilling.

Diamonds and gold

Speyburn was commissioned by John Hopkin & Company, already owners of Tobermory distillery, and operated under the auspices of the Speyburn-Glenlivet Distillery Company Ltd. The founders were anxious to distill some spirit during Queen Victoria's

Diamond Jubilee year (1897) for a commemorative release, but this could be accomplished only by working the stills in a snowstorm in December, before the doors or windows had been fitted to the newly constructed stillhouse.

The Distillers Company Ltd purchased Speyburn in 1916, and it served as a production facility for the supply of blending malt until 1991, when Inver House Distillers Ltd took control. The following year, they released a 10-year-old expression of the single malt, and that is now accompanied by 15- and 18-year-olds and the NAS Bourbon Cask.

Speyburn Bourbon Cask

Speyburn 10-Year-Old

TASTING NOTES

Speyburn 10-Year-Old
Single malt, 40% ABV
The nose is spicy and nutty, with pencil shavings and sweet malt. In the mouth, sweet and easy-drinking, with herbal notes and a hint of smoke. Medium length in the finish, with barley and oak.

Speyburn Bourbon Cask
Single malt, 40% ABV
The nose is fruity and floral, with oranges, honey, and malt; the palate is nicely balanced, with fresh fruit, vanilla, spice, and subtle oak. Spicy oak features in the relatively lengthy finish.

Speyburn 18-Year-Old
Single malt, 46% ABV
Fudge, figs, cinnamon, and cooked pineapple on the nose. The rich palate offers honey, orange, lively spices, and a final hint of wood smoke.

SPEYSIDE

OWNER Speyside Distillers Company Ltd

FOUNDED 1990

WEBSITE www.speysidedistillery.co.uk

Although the first spirit flowed from Speyside's stills in 1990, the founding year could easily be stated as 1956 or 1962. The former date was when Glasgow whisky broker George Christie bought the site on the banks of the Tromie River, not far from Kingussie, and the latter was the year in which dry-stone waller Alex Fairlie began construction of the distillery. Building proceeded on a leisurely basis, taking almost three decades. Once completed, the project was called Speyside, which may seem slightly generic but was actually the revival of an old, local distillery name.

The "new" Speyside may have taken a long time to build, but it did not take long for its spirit to find its way into bottles, with the Drumguish single malt first released in 1993, when it could only just have been legal as Scotch whisky. Since 2012, Speyside has been in the hands of Harvey's of Edinburgh, a firm with origins stretching back to 1770. Harvey's has significantly increased the number of expressions available, establishing a core range that comprises Tenne (with a port cask finish), Trutina (bourbon cask matured), Fumare (made from peated malt), and the duo Chairman's Choice and Royal Choice— both multivintage vattings from European and American oak casks.

Speyside also produces Beinn Dubh, a near black single malt designed to replicate the late and largely unlamented Loch Dhu brand, created by United Distillers in the 1990s using Mannochmore single malt matured in double-charred casks.

TASTING NOTES

Spey Tenne
Single malt, 46% ABV
Berry fruits, chocolate, orange peel, and ginger on the nose, with a palate of vanilla, peach, red wine, blackberries, and oak.

Spey Chairman's Choice
Single malt, 40% ABV
Poached pears, marzipan, and spice on the nose, while the palate reveals baked apple, vanilla, malt, fresh wood, and cloves, ending on black pepper and oak.

Spey Chairman's Choice

Spey Tenne

STRATHISLA

OWNER Chivas Brothers Ltd (Pernod Ricard)

FOUNDED 1786

WEBSITE www.chivas.com

Standing on the outskirts of the town of Keith, Strathisla is arguably the oldest working distillery in the Scottish Highlands. It is marvelously photogenic, featuring an exaggerated pair of pagoda-capped kilns and even a waterwheel.

Miltonic beginnings

The history of Strathisla begins in 1786, when it was established under the name of Milltown. The name Strathisla was adopted for the first time during the 1870s, though in 1890, the name reverted to Milton. Isla is the river that cuts through the town of Keith, and "strath" means a river valley.

Seagram on the scene

In the late 1940s, the Seagram Company of Canada bought Milton at auction for just $295,000 (£71,000) for the Canadian distilling giant's recently acquired Chivas Brothers subsidiary. A program of refurbishment and upgrading was instigated, and the name became Strathisla again in 1951. With sales of Chivas Regal, one of the world's bestselling luxury blends, growing in North America during the postwar period, Chivas Brothers built an entirely new distillery named Glen Keith (currently silent), adjacent to Strathisla, in order to augment malt whisky production. In 1965, the number of stills at Strathisla was doubled to four. The company developed a significant power base in Keith, constructing vast tracts of warehousing outside the town where about 100 million casks of malt whisky are now maturing, and bonds where Chivas Regal is blended, prior to bottling near Glasgow.

Seagram expands

In 1978, The Glenlivet Distillers Ltd was acquired by Seagram, adding a number of prestigious distilleries such as The Glenlivet itself to the company's portfolio, along with a pair of Speyside distilleries created purely to supply malt whisky for blending. Braes of Glenlivet (later rechristened Braeval) had been built in 1973 and Allt-a-Bhainne two years later. Both now provide a significant amount of spirit for use in the Chivas Regal family of blends.

Strathisla Distillery, along with Seagram's other spirits assets, was purchased by Pernod Ricard in 2001 and subsequently became the "Home of Chivas Regal," reflected in the emphasis on the popular visitor center. Strathisla has been sold as a single malt for more than two centuries, and the principal expression available today is a highly regarded 12-year-old.

Strathisla 17-Year-Old Single Cask Edition

Strathisla 12-Year-Old

TASTING NOTES

Strathisla 12-Year-Old
Single malt, 43% ABV
Sherry, stewed fruits, spices, and malt on the nose. Almost syrupy on the palate, with toffee, honey, nuts, a whiff of peat, and oak. The finish is slightly smoky, with more oak and a final flash of ginger.

Strathisla 17-Year-Old Single Cask Edition
Single malt, 52.4% ABV
Pineapple, popcorn, new timber, and barley on the nose, with a full palate of vanilla, malt, citrus fruit, and lively oak.

TAMDHU

OWNER Ian Macleod Distillers

FOUNDED 1897

WEBSITE www.tamdhu.com

Tamdhu is located close to Knockando distillery, near the banks of the Spey River, and dates from the late Victorian heyday of Scottish distilling expansion. Ownership passed to Ian Macleod Distillers in 2011. That firm already had Glengoyne in its portfolio and has subsequently acquired and revived Rosebank.

Tamdhu has three pairs of stills and an annual capacity of 1.1 million gallons (4 million liters). No fewer than 28 warehouses are located on site, housing not only casks of Tamdhu but also Glengoyne and Rosebank. Emphasis is very much on offering Tamdhu as a sherry cask-matured single malt, and core expressions include 10,- 12-, 15-, and 18-year-olds, along with annual releases of the NAS Batch Strength variant. A Cigar Malt is also offered on a limited release basis.

TASTING NOTE

Tamdhu 12-Year-Old
Single malt, 43% ABV
Dry sherry, hazelnuts, and citrus fruit predominate on the nose, while the palate offers richer sherry, cinnamon, baked bananas, and orange, closing with dark chocolate, cloves, and drying oak.

Tamdhu 12-Year-Old

TOMINTOUL

OWNER Angus Dundee Distillers plc

FOUNDED 1964

WEBSITE www.tomintouldistillery.co.uk

Tomintoul's workaday appearance is emphasized all the more by contrast with the grandeur of the surrounding Highland scenery. The distillery, located in the parish of Glenlivet, is equipped with six stills and takes its name from the nearby settlement of Tomintoul, the highest village in the Highlands. It took more than a year to find the pure water source of the Ballantruan Spring in the Cromdale hills. Once discovered, the distillery was subsequently built close to the spring. Tomintoul was created for the Tomintoul-Glenlivet Distillery Ltd, a company set up by a group of whisky blenders and brokers, and now belongs to Angus Dundee Distillers plc who bought the distillery from Whyte & Mackay in 2000.

The Tomintoul range
Tomintoul was first marketed as a single malt during the 1970s, and examples dating from that time and presented in distinctive "perfume bottles" are now sought after by collectors. However, the brand became best known after the current owners bought the distillery, going on to add a blend center on the site.

Today there is maturation capacity for 116,000 casks, and stocks of whisky up to 40 years old are held there.

The single malt range comprises the no age statement Tlath and Seiridh bottlings, plus 10-, 14-, 16-, 18-, 21-, and 25-year-old expressions and Cigar Malt, along with a number of limited-edition finished releases. For more than two decades, Tomintoul has produced annual batches of heavily peated spirit in addition to its standard make. Principally, this is intended to give Angus Dundee peated malt for blending purposes, but there is an NAS Tomintoul Peated bottling and a 15-year-old Peaty Tang. A more heavily peated stand-alone lineup is marketed as Old Ballantruan.

TASTING NOTES

Tomintoul 10-Year-Old
Single malt, 40% ABV
A light, floral, and pleasantly malty nose. Light-bodied and delicate, with vanilla fudge, apples, and lemon on the palate. The finish is medium in length, with honey and lingering malt.

Tomintoul 21-Year-Old
Single malt, 40% ABV
Melons, pears, warm spices, and barley sugar on the nose. A rich, spicy palate presence, plus toffee and malt notes. Quite lengthy in the finish; mildly mouth-drying, with cocoa powder and spicy to the end.

Tomintoul 21-Year-Old

ALLT-A-BHAINNE

OWNER Chivas Brothers Ltd (Pernod Ricard)

FOUNDED 1975

WEBSITE www.alltabhainne.com

Located between Dufftown and Tomintoul, Allt-a-Bhainne Distillery stands in beautiful countryside and dates from 1975. It was built at a cost of $6 million (£2.7 million) by the Canadian distilling giant Seagram's subsidiary Chivas Brothers for the express purpose of providing bulk malt whisky for blending,

notably for the 100 Pipers brand, which was a major seller at the time. There are a number of independent bottlings available and a 15-year-old in Chivas Brothers' Distillery Reserve Collection.

TASTING NOTE

Allt-a-bhainne 15-Year-Old Distillery Reserve Collection
Single malt, 58.8% ABV
Vanilla, toffee and honey on the sweet nose, with pear drops, melons and developing red berry fruit on the smooth, balanced palate.

Allt-a-Bhainne 15-Year-Old Distillery Reserve Collection

ARDMORE

The Ardmore Legacy

OWNER Suntory Global Spirits

FOUNDED 1898

WEBSITE www.ardmorewhisky.com

In 1898–1899, Ardmore Distillery was constructed by the Glasgow-based firm of Teacher & Sons to provide malt whisky for their increasingly popular Highland Cream blend, created by William Teacher in 1863. Today, the distillery, on the eastern fringes of Speyside, continues to fulfill that role. The distillery and the Teacher's brand are now in the ownership of Suntory

Global Spirits, and Ardmore produces both an unpeated spirit and spirit distilled from malt peated to 12–14ppm. The smoky style of Ardmore gives the Teacher's blend its distinctive full and rich character. The distillery's capacity was gradually increased to the present four pairs of stills.

TASTING NOTE

The Ardmore Legacy
Single malt, 40% ABV
Ashy peat, orchard fruits, and vanilla on the nose, while the palate offers honey, vanilla, charcoal, citrus, and spicy oak.

AUCHROISK

OWNER Diageo plc

FOUNDED 1974

WEBSITE www.malts.com

Auchroisk is located near the distilling and bonding hub of Keith, and from 1986 to 2001, Auchroisk single malt was bottled under the Singleton name. In the hands of Diageo, the distillery provides malt whisky for a range of blends, and the site is also used to mature malt spirit made in other Diageo distilleries in the area. Additionally, malts are vatted together at

Auchroisk and transported to bottling plants, where the grain element of blended Scotch whiskies is introduced. Auchroisk is equipped with eight stills and has an annual capacity of 1.6 million gallons (5.9 million liters). Its stillhouse was used as the model when Diageo came to construct Roseisle near Elgin in 2009.

TASTING NOTE

Auchroisk 10-Year-Old
Single malt, 43% ABV
Spice and citrus fruits, nuts, and malt on the nose. Fresh fruit and malt on the palate, with more malt, plus milk chocolate in the finish.

Auchroisk 10-Year-Old

AULTMORE

OWNER John Dewar & Sons (Bacardi)

FOUNDED 1896

WEBSITE www.aultmore.com

Aultmore was established in 1896 by local landowner and distilling entrepreneur Alexander Edward. In 1998, it became part of Bacardi, who proceeded to launch a range of expressions. The distillery that stands today, close to the town of Keith, largely dates from a rebuilding project carried out at the beginning of the 1970s. Production takes place seven days per week and up to 850,000 gallons (3.2 million liters) of spirit are produced each year. Expressions include 12-, 18-, and 21-year-olds, along with a 25-year-old, exclusive to Asia.

Aultmore 12-Year-Old

TASTING NOTE

Aultmore 12-Year-Old
Single malt, 40% ABV
A floral and fudge note on the nose with elements of spice. Fresh citrus fruits on the palate, with vanilla, more spice, and lemon zest. The finish is nutty and quite drying.

BALLINDALLOCH

OWNER The Macpherson-Grant family

FOUNDED 2014

WEBSITE www.ballindallochdistillery.com

One of Speyside's newer distilleries, Balllindalloch was created by the Macpherson-Grant family, who have lived in nearby Ballindalloch Castle since 1546. The distillery is very traditional in design and operation and boasts wooden worm tubs for condensing the spirit made in its single pair of stills. The barley is grown on the estate, and the owners were happy to wait for almost a decade before releasing their first whisky. Ballindalloch will surely take its place among the great whisky names of the region. There is a distillery store and several tour options.

Ballindalloch Edition No. 1 Seven Springs Collection

TASTING NOTE

Ballindalloch Edition No. 1 Seven Springs Collection
Single malt, 60.2% ABV
Cream, toffee, nutmeg, demerara sugar, peach, and fresh pastry on the spicy nose, while the palate offers figs, strawberries, cinnamon, and coffee, with a hint of chili.

BALMENACH

OWNER International Beverage Holdings

FOUNDED 1824

WEBSITE www.inverhouse.com

Situated in a remote location off the main road from Grantown-on-Spey to Aberlour, Balmenach dates back to 1824, when it was one of the earliest distilleries to take out a license in the wake of the landmark 1823 Excise Act, which made legal distilling in the Highlands a financially attractive proposition. The single malt is extremely rare, with the vast proportion of the output destined for the blending vats. The Deerstalker brand has bottled Balmenach for some years, and other independent bottlings may be found. The Caorunn gin distillery is open to the public, though the whisky distillery is not.

Deerstalker 12-Year-Old

TASTING NOTE

Deerstalker 12-Year-Old
Single malt, 43% ABV
A big nose of sherry and honey leads into a smooth, full-bodied palate, featuring dry sherry, honey, and ginger. Rounded and relatively lengthy finish.

BENRINNES

OWNER Diageo plc

FOUNDED 1826

WEBSITE www.malts.com

The distillery stands below the eponymous mountain that is a distinct Speyside landmark. The present plant dates from a mid-1950s reconstruction program. The relatively meaty spirit produced is used in a variety of Diageo blends, and its essential characteristics are created in part by taking a notably wide spirit cut and

by the use of worm tubs for condensing purposes. Benrinnes boasts two wash stills and four spirit stills and operates at full capacity, producing 925,000 gallons (3.5 million liters) of spirit each year.

TASTING NOTE

Benrinnes 15-Year-Old
Single malt, 43% ABV
Caramel, old leather, black pepper, and sherry on the nose. Full-bodied, with sherry, figs, and savory notes on the palate. Spice and delicate smoke in the complex finish.

Benrinnes 15-Year-Old

BRAEVAL

OWNER Chivas Brothers Ltd (Pernod Ricard)

FOUNDED 1973

WEBSITE www.secret-speyside.com

Originally christened Braes of Glenlivet, Braeval was constructed by Seagram's subsidiary Chivas Brothers to produce malt spirit for blending purposes. Like nearby Allt-a-Bhainne, it was built in a very modern style and is Scotland's highest operational distillery, situated in a remote location, not far from Glenlivet. The 1970s was a boom time for blended Scotch, and

Braeval was expanded from its original three stills to six during that decade. It now has an annual capacity of 1.1 million gallons (4.2 million liters) per annum. Proprietary bottlings are rare, but 2019 saw Chivas Brothers release 25-, 27-, and 30-year-old expressions in its Secret Speyside Collection.

TASTING NOTE

Braes of Glenlivet 25-Year-Old
Single malt, 48% ABV
Vanilla, honey, peaches, and hot chocolate on the nose, with flavors of fudge, milk chocolate, honey, and apricots, closing with soft spices..

Braes of Glenlivet
25-Year-Old

CRAIGELLACHIE

OWNER John Dewar & Sons Ltd (Bacardi)

FOUNDED 1891

WEBSITE www.craigellachie.com

Dating from 1891, and having had several owners in its lifetime, the distillery was most recently sold to John Dewar & Sons Ltd in 1998. Today, much of its output goes to Dewar's White Label and its stablemate, the William Lawson blend. Craigellachie single malt has a distinctive, heavy style, due in part to short fermentations, large stills, and the use of worm

tubs for condensing purposes. The core range of single malts comprises 13-, 17-, 23-, and 33-year-old bottlings. A Cask Collection range was introduced in 2022 beginning with a 13-year-old armagnac cask-finished expression.

TASTING NOTE

Craigallachie 13-Year-Old
Single malt, 46% ABV
An intriguing nose of apple blossom, treacle, and charcuterie, leading into an oily palate of malt, wood smoke, bacon, canned pineapple, and pine.

Craigallachie 13-Year-Old

DALMUNACH

OWNER Chivas Brothers Ltd (Pernod Ricard)

FOUNDED 2015

WEBSITE not available

The former late-Victorian Imperial distillery, near Aberlour, was demolished in 2013 to make way for Dalmunach. The new distillery was intended to provide Chivas Brothers with a state-of-the-art, environmentally efficient source of single malt for blending. The distillery is architecturally very attractive and has a capacity of 2.6 million gallons (10 million liters) per annum, provided by four large pairs of stills.

TASTING NOTE

Dalmunach 4-Year-Old Single Cask Edition
Single malt, 59% ABV
The nose offers grapefruit, cinnamon, pencil shavings, and cereal, while the palate offers peaches, lemon, vanilla, white pepper, and a closing hint of copper.

GLENBURGIE

OWNER Chivas Brothers Ltd (Pernod Ricard)

FOUNDED 1810

WEBSITE not available

Located near Forres, the current distillery was constructed in 2003–2004 and now has six stills. Via a convoluted series of takeovers and mergers, Glenburgie came into the Chivas Regal portfolio in 2005. It produces one of the "heart malts" of Ballantine's, the second bestselling blended Scotch in the world after Johnnie Walker, and 15- and 18-year-old expressions are now available.

TASTING NOTE

Glenburgie 15-Year-Old
Single malt, 40% ABV
The nose is lightly perfumed, with orange juice, vanilla, and Brazil nuts. Orchard fruits, vanilla fudge, and hot chocolate on the palate, with subtle spice and oak.

Glenburgie 15-Year-Old

DUFFTOWN

OWNER Diageo plc

FOUNDED 1896

WEBSITE www.malts.com/www.thesingleton.com

Dufftown has had a long association with the Bell's blend, and since 2006, the single malt has enjoyed a higher profile under The Singleton banner, which has proved a great success. Along with Glendullan and Glen Ord, Dufftown is classed as one of Diageo's "Recruitment Malts," intended to attract consumers to the category. The core range comprises Malt Master's Selection, 12-, 15-, and 18-year-old expressions.

TASTING NOTE

The Singleton of Dufftown 12-Year-Old
Single malt, 40% ABV
Apple pie, orange, and honey on the nose, while the palate gives orchard fruits, fudge, cinnamon, and spicy sherry.

GLENDULLAN

OWNER Diageo plc

FOUNDED 1897

WEBSITE www.thesingleton.com

Along with Dufftown and Mortlach, Glendullan is one of three Diageo distilleries in the malt whisky capital of Dufftown. The present buildings date from an early 1970s redevelopment. Along with Glen Ord and Dufftown, Glendullan became one of the trio of single malt brands embraced by The Singleton venture. Today, 12-, 15-, and 18-year-olds comprise the principal lineup.

TASTING NOTE

The Singleton of Glendullan 12-Year-Old
Single malt, 40% ABV
The nose offers spiced apple pie, sherry, and almonds, while the palate majors in sherry, hazelnuts, toffee, nougat, and a hint of black pepper and spice.

**The Singleton of
Glendullan** 12-Year-Old

GLEN KEITH

OWNER Chivas Brothers Ltd (Pernod Ricard)

FOUNDED 1957

WEBSITE www.secret-speyside.com

Located close to Strathisla in the town of Keith, Glen Keith was mothballed in 1999 due to a surplus of blending malt stocks but reopened in 2013, after a major refurbishment. It played a key role as an experimental distillery, and triple-distilled and peated malts were produced at various times. With a capacity of 1.6 million gallons (6 million liters) per annum, 21-, 25-, and 28-year-old single malts are available in the Secret Speyside Collection.

TASTING NOTE

Glen Keith 21-Year-Old
Single malt, 43% ABV
Toffee, honey, orchard fruits, vanilla, and spice on the soft, inviting nose. The palate is full and malty, with toffee apples, apricots, and sweet oak.

INCHGOWER

OWNER Diageo plc

FOUNDED 1871

WEBSITE www.malts.com

Situated just outside the port of Buckie on the Moray Firth coast, Inchgower was taken on by the local council in 1936 when its operators were declared bankrupt. Two years later, it was sold to Arthur Bell & Sons. Today, Inchgower remains an important component of the Bell's blend, and the distillery's two pairs of onion-shaped stills can turn out up to 845,000 gallons (3.2 million liters) per annum of robust, nutty, new-make spirit.

TASTING NOTE

Inchgower 14-Year-Old
Single malt, 43% ABV
Light and zesty on the nose, with cooking apples and wet grass. Subtle on the palate, with orange, ginger, and mild licorice. Medium length in the spicy, clean finish.

Inchgower 14-Year-Old

GLENLOSSIE

OWNER Chivas Brothers Ltd (Pernod Ricard)

FOUNDED 1876

WEBSITE www.malts.com

Located south of Elgin, Glenlossie shares its site with Mannochmore. It is also now home to a bioenergy plant, fueled by draff. The single malt—along with that of Mannochmore—is a core component of the Haig Gold Label blend. This was once one of the most popular in the UK but is now a shadow of its former self, with India as its most popular market.

TASTING NOTE

Glenlossie 10-Year-Old
Single malt, 43% ABV
A light, gristy nose, with vanilla and freshly planed wood. The full palate gives ginger, barley sugar, and spice. The finish is lengthy and mouth-coating, with developing oak.

KININVIE

OWNER William Grant & Sons Ltd

FOUNDED 1990

WEBSITE www.williamgrant.com

Kininvie shares a site with The Balvenie distillery and contributes spirit to the Grant's family of blends and also to the blended malt Monkey Shoulder. The initial Kininvie appeared in 2013. Six years later, three experimental releases were launched under the Kininvie Works label. They included a 5-year-old triple-distilled single malt.

TASTING NOTE

Kininvie 17-Year-Old
Single malt, 42.6% ABV
Coconut, vanilla, tropical fruits, and light tropical fruit aromas lead to a palate of pineapple, mango, flaxseed, and increasingly nutty notes, finishing with spice and drying oak.

Kininvie 17-Year-Old

KNOCKDHU

OWNER International Beverage Holdings

FOUNDED 1893

WEBSITE www.ancnoc.com

Knockdhu, near Huntly, markets its single malt under the AnCnoc brand, to avoid potential confusion with Knockando. According to manager Gordon Bruce, "Each shift is run by a single man with zero automation. They're kept busy the whole shift, not just sitting in front of a computer screen." Each year, up to 475,000 gallons (1.8 million liters) of spirit is produced, of which 53,000 gallons (200,000 liters is to some degree peated.

TASTING NOTE

AnCnoc 12-Year-Old
Single malt, 40% ABV
Delicate and floral on the nose, with oranges and white pepper. Palate of gentle peat, boiled sweets, and spice. More orange in the spicy, drying finish.

MACDUFF

OWNER John Dewar & Sons (Bacardi)

FOUNDED 1960

WEBSITE www.thedeveron.com

Located near the port of Banff, Macduff was bought by Martini Rossi in 1972. Two decades later, Bacardi acquired Martini Rossi. There are two wash stills with vertical condensers and three spirit stills with horizontal condensers. Much of the spirit finds its way into Bacardi's William Lawson blend. As a single malt, house bottlings carry the Deveron name, and 10- and 12-year-old expressions are available.

TASTING NOTE

The Deveron 10-Year-Old
Single malt, 40% ABV
Nose of planed timber, resin, and malt. Peanuts, spicy malt, and tangerines on the palate. Short-to-medium finish, with grist and wood.

The Deveron 10-Year-Old

LINKWOOD

OWNER Diageo plc

FOUNDED 1821

WEBSITE www.malts.com

This distillery in the suburbs of Elgin dates back to 1821, though only a warehouse and pagoda-roofed kiln survive from the Victorian era, and the site has been expanded on several occasions. The distillery boasts six pear-shaped stills, and its "make" has long enjoyed an excellent reputation for blending purposes, as well as a low-profile single malt.

TASTING NOTE

Linkwood 12-Year-Old
Single malt, 43% ABV
The nose is sweet, with soft fruit and almonds. Vanilla, spice, and marzipan on the rounded palate. Dry and citric in the finish, with a hint of aniseed.

MANNOCHMORE

OWNER Diageo plc

FOUNDED 1971

WEBSITE www.malts.com

Mannochmore shares a site with Glenlossie, near Elgin. Its four pairs of stills provide up to 1.6 million gallons (6 million liters) per annum of malt for Diageo blends, including Haig, but the distillery is probably best known for having produced the almost black "Loch Dhu" single malt, matured in double-charred casks. Loch Dhu divided opinion between those who loved it and those who hated it.

TASTING NOTE

Mannochmore 12-Year-Old
Single malt, 43% ABV
A floral, perfumed nose, with marshmallows and a hint of lemon. Sweet, malty palate, with ginger and vanilla. Almonds in the short-to-medium finish.

Mannochmore 12-Year-Old

MILTONDUFF

OWNER Chivas Brothers Ltd (Pernod Ricard)

FOUNDED 1824

WEBSITE not available

Along with Glenburgie, Miltonduff provides one of the key malts in Ballantine's, the world's second bestselling blended Scotch after Johnnie Walker. Near Elgin, most of the present plant was built in the mid-1970s. It currently houses six stills, but the continuing growth of Ballantine's has led to plans to create an entirely new distillery on the site, equipped with 18 or 20 stills, giving a capacity of 4.2 million gallons (16 million liters) per annum.

TASTING NOTE

Miltonduff 15-Year-Old
Single malt, 40% ABV
Subtle sherry, peaches, coconut, and ginger on the nose, while the creamy palate offers honey, cinnamon, vanilla, and red berries, closing with caramel, cloves, and oak.

TAMNAVULIN

OWNER Whyte & Mackay (Emperador)

FOUNDED 1966

WEBSITE www.tamnavulinwhisky.com

Established not far from Glenlivet, Tamnavulin was recommissioned in 2007 after a long closure. Much of the spirit has always been used for blending, but 2016 saw the release of Double Cask, with a sherry cask finish, and since then a number of others, including single malts finished in Grenache, Cabernet Sauvignon, Sauvignon Blanc, and Pinot Noir casks. Tamnavulin has become a fast-growing whisky in recent years.

TASTING NOTE

Tamnavulin Double Cask
Single malt, 40% ABV
Aromas of hazelnut, sherry, ginger, and milk chocolate lead into a palate of sweet, nutty sherry, plums, brittle toffee, and ultimately fruity oak.

Tamnavulin Double Cask

ROSEISLE

OWNER Diageo plc

FOUNDED 2009

WEBSITE not available

Sustainable technology is at the heart of Roseisle built by Diageo not far from Elgin. Next to the company's Roseisle Maltings, it has a capacity of 3.3 million gallons (12.5 million liters) per annum and is equipped with 14 stills. It can produce both light and heavy Speyside styles of blending spirit, with stainless steel condensers fitted to three wash and three spirit stills, to produce a heavier spirit when required.

TASTING NOTE

Roseisle 12-Year-Old (Diageo 2023 Special Releases)
Single malt, 56.5% ABV
The nose yields pears, peaches, light caramel, and vanilla, with poached pears, honey, almonds, and toffee on the palate, closing with lemon pepper.

TORMORE

OWNER Elixir Distillers

FOUNDED 1958

WEBSITE not available

From an architectural viewpoint, Tormore makes a lavish statement, but its principal role until now has always been to provide malt for blending. The distillery was in the hands of Chivas Brothers from 2005 to 2022, when it was sold to Elixir Distillers, headed by brothers Sukhinder and Rajbir Singh, who formerly owned The Whisky Exchange retail business.

TASTING NOTE

Tormore 14-Year-Old
Single malt, 43% ABV
Freshly cut grass, vanilla, and fudge on the nose, with a palate of orchard fruits, milk chocolate, marzipan, and cinnamon, plus mixed spices and soft oak in the finish.

Tormore 14-Year-Old

HIGHLANDS

REGIONAL STYLES
Insofar as it is possible to generalize about Highland single malts, they tend to be medium- to full-bodied, with a degree of substance; not often overly peaty, but with depth and complexity. Even the lightest examples are far from insubstantial whiskies.

AUTHOR'S CHOICE
DALMORE Traditional on the outside, situated in a great coastal location, with an idiosyncratic stillhouse and first-class visitor facilities. The whisky is a delight for lovers of sherried malts.

THE GLENTURRET This claims to be Scotland's oldest working distillery and boasts a picturesque Perthshire location. Tours and tastings are available. , Glenturret is now home to the only UK Lalique Boutique outside London and is the sole distillery to boast a Michelin-starred restaurant.

REGIONAL TRAILS AND EVENTS
There is no formal whisky trail for the Highlands, and in view of the scale of the area, it pays not to try to cram in too many distilleries. Ideally, spend several days savoring the scenery, distilleries, and drams. In terms of events, September's Highland Whisky Festival features nine participating distilleries (www.highlandwhiskyfestival. co.uk), while Aberdeen's Whisky Mash Festival (www. cascnation.com) and the Dornoch Whisky Festival in Sutherland (www.dornoch whiskyfestival.co.uk) both take place in October. The Stirling Whisky Festival is in November (www.stirling distillery.com/pages/spiritfest).

As the Highlands is geographically the largest of all the single malt regions, the landscape in which distilleries are located can vary dramatically, embracing farmland, moorland, mountains, lochs, and lengthy stretches of coastline. Much of the Highlands is sparsely populated, and distilleries often inhabit remote locations, chosen for the availability of pure, reliable water sources and sometimes occupying sites that were formerly home to illicit whisky-making operations. Distances between distilleries can be quite long, but one of the benefits of traveling from one to another is the opportunity to experience the natural beauty of the Highlands in every season, to appreciate its wildlife, and to meet the people who inhabit this distinctive and beautiful part of the world.

The Highlands region encompasses all of mainland Scotland, with the exception of Speyside, north of a theoretical "Highland Line" that follows the old county boundaries between Greenock on the Firth of Clyde in the west and Dundee on the Firth of Tay in the east. The first official geographical definition of a Highland region of malt whisky production occurred in 1784, when the Wash Act specified the division behind Highland and Lowland for the purposes of variable levels of excise duty. Lower excise duties were set north of the line to encourage the illicit Highland distillers to become licensed.

The sheer scale of the region and diversity of its physical features make it more difficult to specify a generic Highland style of single malt whisky than it is with other categories. What we pour from the bottle owes more to methods of production and maturation regimes than any geographical proximity between distilleries across the region. Glenmorangie and Dalmore stand little more than 12 miles apart on the same coastline, but the two malts produced vary enormously in character.

The Highland region is home to some 30 operational malt whisky distilleries, and while the area has not seen the same large-scale investment in major distillery expansions and new builds like Roseisle on Speyside in recent times, most of the distilleries produce malts that are of great importance for blending, while many also enjoy high profiles in their own right.

The Perthshire distillery of Aberfeldy is home to a range of varying visitor experiences.

GETTING AROUND

Perth and Inverness are the principal population centers in the Highlands, with the A9 road connecting the two and then heading on into Sutherland and Caithness, leading to Wick and Thurso. In the west, Fort William and Oban are the main towns, best reached from Glasgow via the A82. In the east, the A90 runs between Dundee and Aberdeen. Rail services connect Glasgow to Oban and link Perth, Dundee, Aberdeen, Inverness, and Wick with Edinburgh and England.

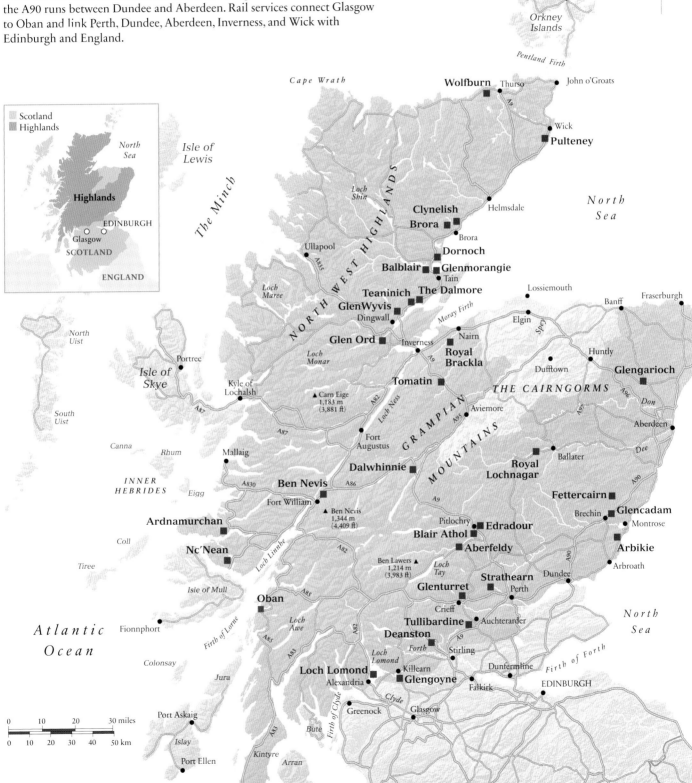

N

Orkney Islands

Kirkwall

Pentland Firth

Cape Wrath

Wolfburn · Thurso · John o'Groats

A9

Wick

Pulteney

Loch Shin

Helmsdale

Clynelish

Brora

Brora

Ullapool

Dornoch

Balblair · Glenmorangie

A835

Tain

Teaninich · The Dalmore

GlenWyvis

Dingwall

Lossiemouth

Banff · Fraserburgh

Moray Firth

Elgin · Spey

Glen Ord

Inverness · Nairn

Loch Monar

Royal Brackla

Huntly

Dufftown

Glengarioch

NORTH WEST HIGHLANDS

North Sea

North Uist

Portree

Isle of Skye

Kyle of Lochalsh

A87

▲ Carn Eige 1,183 m (3,881 ft)

Loch Ness

A82

Tomatin

THE CAIRNGORMS

Aviemore

Aberdeen

Dee

Don

A96

A97

South Uist

A87

Fort Augustus

GRAMPIAN

A95

Canna · Rhum

Mallaig

Dalwhinnie

MOUNTAINS

Royal Lochnagar

Ballater

Fettercairn

A90

INNER HEBRIDES

Eigg

A830

Ben Nevis

A86

▲ Ben Nevis 1,344 m (4,409 ft)

A9

Brechin · Glencadam

Coll

Fort William

Pitlochry

Edradour

Montrose

Ardnamurchan

Blair Athol

Arbikie

Tiree

Nc'Nean

Aberfeldy

A90

Arbroath

Ben Lawers ▲ 1,214 m (3,983 ft)

Loch Tay

Stratheam

Dundee

Loch Linnhe

Isle of Mull

Glenturret

Perth

North Sea

Oban

A85

Crieff

Fionnphort

Loch Awe

A85

Tullibardine

Auchterarder

Atlantic Ocean

Colonsay

A83

Loch Lomond

Deanston

Stirling

Forth

A9

Firth of Forth

Jura

Killearn

Dunfermline

EDINBURGH

Loch Lomond

Glengoyne

Falkirk

Port Askaig

Alexandria

Clyde

Islay

Firth of Clyde

Greenock

Glasgow

Bute

Port Ellen

Kintyre · Arran

0   10   20   30 miles
0   10   20   30   40   50 km

Inset map

Scotland
Highlands

North Sea

Highlands

EDINBURGH
Glasgow

SCOTLAND

ENGLAND

Isle of Lewis

The Minch

Loch Maree

ABERFELDY

OWNER John Dewar & Sons Ltd (Bacardi Ltd)

FOUNDED 1896

WEBSITE www.aberfeldy.com

Aberfeldy is one of those curious distilleries that has a physical profile higher than that of the single malts it produces. This is largely because Aberfeldy is home to Dewar's World of Whisky, an interactive visitor experience that set the bar high when it opened in 2000. Dewar's is one of the most iconic names in Scotch whisky, even if "Aberfeldy" has had less international cachet over the years. This has been changing, however, with the single malt brand growing significantly in terms of sales during the past decade.

Although the small market town of Aberfeldy is located about 10 miles west of the busy A9 road from the Central Belt of Scotland into the Highlands, it stands in the heart of an area that is notably popular with visitors to Perthshire. This ensures a steady stream of around 30,000 visitors a year from all over the world wishing to experience the various touch-screen displays, handheld audio guides, and the Brand Family Room, where they can pit their skills against a large-scale blender's nosing wheel.

Given all the interactive, crowd-pleasing aspects of the visitor center, it would be easy for the distillery itself to become overshadowed, but such is the timeless allure of a row of hot, hissing stills that Aberfeldy never becomes a visitor center with a distillery attached.

The distillery in question was built by the burgeoning Perth-based family business of John Dewar & Sons during 1896–1898. By this time, blended Scotch whisky was taking the world by storm, and the new distillery, like so many constructed at the time, was intended solely to provide malt whisky for the company's increasingly popular blends.

An advantageous location

A number of factors have informed the locations of Scotland's distilleries, and Aberfeldy was no exception to the usual criteria. All have been constructed with access to a guaranteed supply of pure water, so vital to whisky making, and in past times they were often situated comparatively close to the barley-growing

Aberfeldy 16-Year-Old

areas, which provide the main raw material of malt whisky, and near to the deposits of peat required to fire the furnace and dry the malting barley.

Many, however, were built in close proximity to the intricate network of railroads that covered Scotland during the second half of the 19th century and the first half of the 20th. Aberfeldy was one such distillery, being developed alongside the Aberfeldy-to-Perth railroad line, which provided a direct link into the sidings of John Dewar & Sons' vast bonding and blending facilities in Perth, from where blended Scotch whisky was subsequently transported to the thirsty markets of England and abroad.

New developments in a new century

Aberfeldy passed to the mighty Distillers Company Ltd in 1925 when the latter merged with Dewar's, but in 1998, it was one of four Scottish distilleries acquired by Bacardi Ltd, which subsequently increased the product range and gave the brand much more of a family ethos. It is easy to forget in these increasingly corporate times that Bacardi still remains a family-run company.

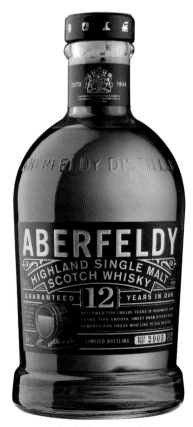

Aberfeldy 12-year-old

Aberfeldy distillery, with the 1970s stillhouse on the right of the original building.

The growth in sales of Aberfeldy single malt began after the range was relaunched during 2014, and the current lineup includes 12-, 16- and 21-year-old expressions, while a number of limited editions have been released, including a 15-year-old finished in Cadillac white wine casks and an 18-year-old finished in Napa Valley red wine casks.

With Dewar's occupying the number-one blended Scotch whisky position in the US, still one of the leading international markets for Scotch whisky sales, it is inevitable that most of the output of Aberfeldy finds its way into the blending vats. In total, John Dewar & Sons' five Scottish distilleries—Aberfeldy, Aultmore, Craigellachie, Macduff, and Royal Brackla—can distill 4.9 million gallons (18.4 million liters) of spirit per annum, and although the single malt offerings from these distilleries have achieved higher profiles and increased sales, much of their output inevitably is used for blending. Most of Aberfeldy's current production buildings date from a 1972 reconstruction program carried out by The Distillers Company Ltd to increase capacity, and Aberfeldy's four stills can produce up to 900,000 gallons (3.4 million liters) of spirit per annum.

WHISKY TALES
A Flamboyant Figure
Aberfeldy distillery was established by brothers John and Tommy Dewar, the latter renowned as one of the most flamboyant figures in Scotch whisky. An entrepreneur of the late-Victorian blended Scotch boom, "Whisky Tom" sailed yachts, bred racehorses, and worked tirelessly as the charismatic ambassador for the family business. He once declared, "A teetotaler is one who suffers from thirst instead of enjoying it."

TASTING NOTES

Aberfeldy 12-Year-Old
Single malt, 40% ABV
Sweet, with honeycomb, breakfast cereal, and stewed fruit on the nose. Quite full-bodied and sweet on the elegant palate, with malty notes. The finish is long and complex, becoming spicier and drying.

Aberfeldy 16-Year-Old
Single malt, 40% ABV
Floral aromas, with malt, ginger, and honey lead into flavors of heather honey, malt, stewed apricots, and nutty spice.

Aberfeldy 21-Year-Old
Single malt, 43% ABV
A nose of honey, soft fruits, vanilla, and lightly charred wood notes; full-flavored and sweet on the palate, with a suggestion of chocolate oranges. Long, spicy, and moreish in the finish.

BLAIR ATHOL

Blair Athol 23-Year-Old (Diageo 2017 Special Releases)

OWNER Diageo plc

FOUNDED 1798

WEBSITE www.malts.com

Like its Perthshire neighbors Aberfeldy and Glenturret, Blair Athol is better known as a distillery than it is as a single malt. Diageo's third-busiest distillery visitor center, after Talisker and Oban, stands on the outskirts of the bustling tourist center of Pitlochry, now bypassed by the A9 road between Perth and Inverness. The name is slightly confusing, as the village of Blair Atholl, with an extra "l," is located some 7 miles northwest of Pitlochry.

Blair Athol is one of Diageo's oldest distilleries, dating from the late 18th century, when it was established by John Stewart and Robert Robertson under the name of Aldour. The Allt Dour burn flows through the distillery grounds from the slopes of Ben Vrackie,and translates from the Gaelic as "Burn of the Otter," which explains the presence of an otter on the label of the 12-year-old "Flora & Fauna" expression of Blair Athol single malt. The Blair Athol name was adopted in 1825, when Robert Robertson expanded the distillery.

Just as Aberfeldy is the spiritual home of the Bacardi-owned Dewar's blend, and Glenturret performs the same function in relation to The Famous Grouse for The Edrington Group, so Blair Athol serves as the "brand home" of Bell's blended Scotch whisky.

Bell's blends

The Blair Athol distillery was purchased by Perth-based Arthur Bell & Sons Ltd in 1933 but, due to the prevailing economic climate, remained silent until 1949, when it was substantially rebuilt and reequipped prior to the recommencement of production. The rise of Bell's blend mirrored that of Dewar's and The Famous Grouse during the later decades of the 19th century, with all three subsequently bestselling brands being created by Perth wine and spirits merchants.

Today, Diageo uses Blair Athol distillery to relate the story of the blend, though compared to Dewar's World of Whisky, the Blair Athol visitor experience is altogether more traditional in its approach.

Blair Athol Distillery Exclusive Bottling

The central courtyard at the Blair Athol distillery.

WHISKY TALES

The Bells of Blair Athol
Arthur Bell joined T H Sandeman's Perth wine and spirits business in 1840, setting up on his own 11 years later from the same Kirkside premises. Using the expertise he had gained in blending tea, Bell began to blend grain and malt whiskies, using Blair Athol malt and the make of several other distilleries. By the time Arthur Bell died in 1900 and his son Arthur Kinmont "A. K." Bell took over the firm, the blend was on sale across the British Empire, with strong markets in Europe too. The story of the blend's slogan "Afore ye go" is rather mysterious. Some claim it derives from World War I when the men of the distillery were given a free bottle of Bell's whisky as they left for the front. Yet it was only adopted for the centenary in 1925, and the firm itself cites its origins in a "Gaelic war cry."

Although global sales of Bell's have fallen in recent years, and it tends to play a supporting role to Diageo's Johnnie Walker & J&B brands, it is still the company's sixth bestselling blended Scotch whisky, and number two in the UK after The Famous Grouse brand owned by Matthew Gloag and founded in 1896.

The Bell's blend gained a greater following when an 8-year-old age statement was applied to it in 1993, at a time when distillers had surplus stocks of older whiskies. Those days are long gone, however, and Diageo subsequently removed the age statement, declaring in 2008 that the revamped recipe for "Bell's Original" was closer to that first formulated by Arthur Bell.

As a company, Bell's retained its independence until taken over by the brewer Guinness in 1985, subsequently being absorbed into what was to become Diageo plc. In 1998, the Bell's brand lost its last connection with its "home" city of Perth when the Cherrybank sales, marketing, and distribution function was relocated hundreds of miles away to Harlow, Essex, in southern England.

In 2010, six new stainless steel washbacks replaced the existing four wooden and four stainless steel vessels at Blair Athol. Two pairs of stills are in place, the second being added in 1973, and the distillery operates on a seven days per week basis, turning out up to 740,000 gallons (2.8 million liters) of spirit per annum.

Single Malt

As most of the Blair Athol "make" is earmarked for blending, the single malt is a relatively rare beast, with a 12-year-old "Flora & Fauna" bottling now being augmented by a distillery-exclusive and 2017 saw the appearance of a 23-year-old expression matured in European oak butts as part of Diageo's Special Releases series.

Blair Athol spirit character lends itself particularly well to sherry cask maturation, and the percentage of sherry cask-matured spirit in Blair Athol 12-year-old is appreciably higher than in many other Diageo single malts.

TASTING NOTES

Blair Athol 12-Year-Old
Single malt, 43% ABV
The nose is moist, mellow, and sherried, with brittle toffee, sweet and fragrant. Relatively rich on the smooth palate, with malt, raisins, sultanas, and sherry. The finish is lengthy, elegant, balanced, and slowly drying.

Blair Athol Distillery Exclusive Bottling
Single malt, 48% ABV
Orange, caramel, honey, and a suggestion of smoke on the nose, while the palate offers fudge, milk chocolate, orange, vanilla, and a closing hint of chili.

Blair Athol 23-Year-Old (Diageo 2017 Special Releases)
Single malt, 58.4% ABV
The nose yields dried fruits, medium sherry, coffee, and orange marmalade, while flavors of butterscotch, plums, dark chocolate, and earthy sherry appear on the palate.

CLYNELISH

OWNER Diageo plc

FOUNDED 1819

WEBSITE www.malts.com

Clynelish stands close to the East Sutherland village of Brora, some 850 miles northeast of Inverness, and is the northernmost distillery in Diageo's portfolio. Only Pulteney, Wolfburn, and 8 Doors at John O'Groats have a more northerly location on the Scottish mainland. There are actually two distilleries on the Clynelish site, with the original stone structures built for the Marquess of Stafford, latterly the Duke of Sutherland, standing alongside their 1960s replacements. The Duke's distillery benefited from a supply of locally grown barley as well as abundant peat for fueling the malt kilns, while fuel was provided by the local Brora coal mine, which had been in use since the 16th century.

The changing fortunes of Clynelish

Clynelish had a number of owners before John Walker & Sons Ltd bought into it during 1916, and Walker's duly became part of the Distillers Company Ltd in 1925. Within five years, DCL owned the entire share capital of Clynelish, subsequently moving the distillery into the care of its Scottish Malt Distillers subsidiary. However, Clynelish was silent for most of the economically troubled 1930s, only resuming production just before the outbreak of World War II.

During the 1960s, DCL expanded and rebuilt many of its existing distilleries to cope with the increasing demand for blended Scotch whisky, and in the case of Clynelish, an entirely new modernistic plant was built during 1967–1968 alongside the old production buildings. The original distillery closed down in May 1968 but was revived the following year, renamed Brora.

During 1969–1973, Brora distilled relatively heavily peated spirit, with more batches being produced periodically in subsequent years, as DCL required additional stocks of Islay-style spirit for blending purposes. Today, bottlings of peaty Brora have achieved a cult status among connoisseurs, second only to those from the now defunct Islay distillery of Port Ellen. Bottlings of Brora ranging from 25–32 years of age have been issued in Diageo's annual Special Releases program

Clynelish 16-Year-Old
(The Four Corners of Scotland Collection)

Clynelish 14-Year-Old

Dunrobin Castle is a fine example of the Scottish Baronial style and remains the seat of the Dukes of Sutherland.

WHISKY TALES

Sutherland and the Clearances
The original Clynelish distillery was established by the 2nd Marquess of Stafford in 1819 to provide an outlet for the barley crops grown by tenants on his estate. The Marquess married Elizabeth, 19th Countess of Sutherland, and in 1833 was created Duke of Sutherland. At the time the Clynelish distillery was constructed the Dukes of Sutherland were the largest private estate owners in Europe, and the family is closely associated with the Highland Clearances, in which thousands of tenants were evicted from their homes. An imposing stone statue of the 1st Duke of Sutherland dominates the landscape from the summit of Ben Bhraggie, near Golspie.

to great acclaim. Brora closed in 1983, but its quirky pair of stills remained in place and the distillery became active once again in 2021

Waxing technical

Clynelish is unique in being the only Diageo distillery to offer spirit with a "waxy" profile, and it is an important component in many of Diageo's older blends, especially the Johnnie Walker range—most notably Johnnie Walker "Gold Label." There are undertones of "grassy" and "fruity" in Clynelish, but these are overwhelmed by "waxy," which contributes significantly to mouthfeel in a blend.

In most distilleries, there is one combined vessel for low wines and feints and foreshots, but Clynelish has a separate low wines receiver and a foreshots and feints tank. The low wines from the wash still are pumped into the low wines receiver, and from there into the spirit still via the spirit still charger. The foreshots and feints from the spirit still are collected in a receiver and then briefly added to the low wines in the spirit still charger. Because of the comparatively long time the liquid sits in the low wines and foreshots and feints tanks prior to being mixed to create the spirit still charge, there is a buildup of waxiness. The wash distillation is similar in technique to that required to make "fruity" character, but the use of the intermediate tanks ensures that low wines are converted into "waxy" as a result of the spirit still distillation.

The whiskies

While the most prominent Clynelish bottling is a 14-year-old, launched back in 2002, the distillery was represented in Diageo's Special Releases programs with a 12-year-old expression in 2022 and a 10-year-old in 2023. A no age statement cask-strength variant appeared under the name Clynelish House Tyrell in Diageo's Game of Thrones portfolio, and a majestic 26-year-old was launched during 2020 as part of Diageo's Prima & Ultima series. A 16-year-old bottling exclusive to the distillery and www.malts.com was released in 2021 to mark Clynelish becoming one of the "Four Corners of Scotland" distilleries, celebrated for its important contribution to the Johnnie Walker range of blends.

TASTING NOTES

Clynelish Reserve Game of Thrones House of Tyrell
Single malt, 51.2% ABV
Floral on the nose, with candle wax, honey, ginger, malt, and ripe apples, while the slightly viscous palate offers honey, sharp orange notes, black pepper, and cocoa.

Clynelish 14-Year-Old
Single malt, 46% ABV
The nose is fragrant and spicy, with candle wax, malt, and discreet smoke. Slightly waxy in the mouth, with honey, citric orange, spice, and peat. Brine and spicy tropical fruit in the finish.

Clynelish 16-Year-Old (The Four Corners of Scotland Collection)
Single malt, 49.3% ABV
The nose is almost shy initially, with developing gorse, white pepper, and sweet nutty notes. Oily on the palate, with tropical fruits, honey, and developing pepper and spicy oak.

THE DALMORE

OWNER Whyte & Mackay Ltd (Emperador Inc)

FOUNDED 1839

WEBSITE www.thedalmore.com

The Dalmore's transformation from a well-regarded single malt to one of the two most collectible and highly prized whiskies in Scotland has been a remarkable one. Along with The Macallan, The Dalmore is able to release extremely limited editions of very old whisky and sell them for the sort of sums many rival distillers can only dream of.

Record-breaking luxury

The Dalmore's dramatic move upmarket from respected Highland single malt to multiple record breaker began when the brand's owner, Whyte & Mackay Ltd, was acquired by the India-based company United Spirits Ltd in 2007, and it has continued in the hands of current owner Emperador Inc. Renowned master blender Richard Paterson OBE has been responsible for many of the most iconic Dalmore releases, and he now works in partnership with Master Whisky Maker & Blender Gregg Glass on exclusive Dalmore bottlings.

The early years of the United Spirits regime saw Dalmore undergo a major packaging makeover, a broadening of the range, and the start of an ongoing program of ultra-limited releases. These have included 40-, 45-, 58-, and 59-year-old whiskies, with just a dozen decanters of the 58-year-old from two sherry casks being released in 2010 under the Selene banner, followed by 20 decanters from the same cask in 2011, named Eos. Also, in 2011 came Astrum, distilled in 1966 and finished for 18 months in Gonzalez Byass casks. Rarest of all, however, was Trinitas, a 64-year-old expression of The Dalmore, in which some of the component whiskies had been maturing for more than 140 years. Just three bottles were filled, each with an asking price of $125,000 (£100,000).

The Dalmore began setting records for the price of its whisky in 2002, when a bottle of 62-year-old Dalmore changed hands for $39,200 (£25,877), then the world's most expensive whisky ever to be sold at auction. Just 12 bottles of the expression were produced, and more headlines were garnered in April 2005 when one of them was bought at the Pennyhill

The Dalmore 12-Year-Old

The Dalmore King Alexander III

Park Hotel in Surrey by an anonymous businessman who proceeded to share it with five of his friends during the course of the evening. Then, in September 2011, another record fell when the last bottle of "The Dalmore 62" was sold at Changi Airport in Singapore for $195,000 (£125,000).

In 2013, the Paterson Collection was offered for sale in Harrods department store, London, and this one-off collection of 12 bottles ultimately sold for $1.5 million (£987,500). In 2021 The Dalmore Decades collection—a one-of-a-kind set of six vintage single malts spanning 1951 to 2000—sold at Sotheby's in Hong Kong for HK$8,750,000 ($1.3 million).

More recently, a 48-year-old Luminary bottling has been launched, produced in association with V&A Dundee and aged in a combination of bourbon, sherry, and port casks and finished in Japanese and virgin Scottish oak. The year 2023 saw the first release in the Cask Curation Series.

Starting out

Such luxury is a very long way from The Dalmore's origins, with the distillery having been established beside the Cromarty Firth, close to Alness, in 1839 by Alexander Matheson, who had made a fortune in the opium trade. Matheson gave over the running of his distillery to various estate tenants, and in 1867 Andrew Mackenzie and his family took the reins. The Mackenzies eventually bought The Dalmore distillery from the Matheson family in 1891 for $72,500 (£14,500), by which time the number of stills had been doubled to four. The distillery remained in the Mackenzie family until 1960, when Mackenzie Brothers (Dalmore) Ltd merged with the Glasgow blending firm of Whyte & Mackay Ltd, who were longstanding customers for The Dalmore single malt. In 1966, with the Scotch whisky industry booming, another four stills were installed to double capacity.

That is the status quo today, but the stillhouse is one of the most quirky in Scotland, featuring four flat-topped wash stills of diverse shapes and sizes and four spirit stills with "boil balls" and distinctive cooling copper water jackets, while a section of "number two spirit still" dates back to 1874.

Sherried spirit

The Dalmore is characterized by its richly sherried house style and its ability to flourish during extended periods of aging. The principal casks used for maturation are first-fill ex-bourbon barrels and former sherry butts, with The Dalmore being the only Scotch

The Dalmore distillery lies beside the calm waters of the Cromarty Firth, a sea loch to the north of Inverness.

whisky distillery with access to matusalem oloroso sherry butts from the historic sherry house of Gonzalez Byass. Core bottlings of The Dalmore include 12-, 15-, 18-, 21-, and 25-year-old expressions, along with Port Wood Reserve, Cigar Malt Reserve—aged in 30-year-old oloroso sherry butts, American white oak, and premier cru Cabernet Sauvignon wine barriques—and King Alexander III. This expression takes its name from the fact that in 1263 an ancestor of the Clan Mackenzie saved Alexander III, King of the Scots, from being gored by a stag. The stag's head duly became the emblem of Clan Mackenzie and adorns all expressions of The Dalmore.

The Dalmore 25-Year-Old

TASTING NOTES

The Dalmore 12-Year-Old
Single malt, matured 50% ex-oloroso sherry wood and 50% ex-bourbon American white oak, 40% ABV
Malt, orange marmalade, sherry, and a hint of leather on the nose. Full-bodied and sherried on the palate, with spice and balancing citrus notes. The finish is long, with spices, ginger, and lingering oranges.

The Dalmore King Alexander III
Single malt, matured in vintage oloroso and Madeira butts, vintage bourbon barrels and Cabernet Sauvignon barriques, 40% ABV
The nose presents almonds, hedgerow berries, plums, brittle toffee, and treacle. Sherry and fresh berries merge with plum notes on the palate, plus vanilla and toffee. Oak, red wine, and black pepper in the finish.

The Dalmore 25-Year-Old
Single malt, 42% ABV
The nose offers Jaffa oranges, medium sherry, figs, and vanilla fudge, while the palate exhibits flavors of more sherry and orange, peaches and milk chocolate, closing with licorice and spicy, nutty oak.

DALWHINNIE

OWNER Diageo plc

FOUNDED 1897

WEBSITE www.malts.com

Dating from 1897–1898, Dalwhinnie was created just before the great, expansionist Victorian whisky bubble burst. It was developed for $50,000 (£10,000) under the auspices of the Strathspey Distillery Company Ltd by local businessmen John Grant, Alexander Mackenzie, and George Sellar and originally bore the name of Strathspey.

However, just a few months after production commenced in February 1898, the distillery's founders were forced to sell their new plant to AP Blyth & Son and John Somerville & Company, who changed the distillery name to Dalwhinnie.

Takeover bids
Dalwhinnie had the distinction of becoming the first Scottish distillery to fall into US hands, with Cook & Bernheimer of New York and Baltimore purchasing it at auction for a mere $6,250 (£1,250) in 1905. Dalwhinnie's decline in value reflected the collapse of confidence and activity in the Scotch whisky industry. Cook & Bernheimer operated Dalwhinnie as part of its James Munro & Son Ltd subsidiary, and this name was retained when ownership changed again in 1920, with Sir James Calder buying the distillery.

The Distillers Company Ltd (DCL), now part of Diageo, acquired Dalwhinnie six years later, and in February 1934, a major fire led to the closure of the distillery for four years while reconstruction took place. In the hands of DCL, Dalwhinnie was licensed to James Buchanan & Company Ltd, and to this day Dalwhinnie malt whisky is an important part of the Buchanan family of blends, which enjoy notably strong sales in South America.

Black & White whisky
The Black & White blend was established in 1884 by James Buchanan, a Canadian-born, Northern Ireland–educated individual of Scottish parentage. In 1879, he took his first steps into the Scotch whisky industry, when he moved to London to work as an agent for the Leith blenders Charles Mackinlay & Company. Five years later, he was in business for

Dalwhinnie 2022 Distiller's Edition

Dalwhinnie 15-Year-Old

Located on the edge of the Monadhliath and Cairngorm mountains, Dalwhinnie is one of the highest distilleries.

WHISKY TALES

On a Whisky High

At 1,072ft (327m) above sea level, Dalwhinnie is the second-highest operational distillery in Scotland after Pernod Ricard's Braeval, located south of Glenlivet. Its lofty situation makes it one of the coldest places in Britain, and the Met Office, the UK's national weather service, uses it as an official weather station. One of the duties of the distillery manager is to take readings from the on-site meteorological station. Still within sight of the main A9 Perth to Inverness road through the Highlands, before the village of Dalwhinnie was bypassed in the 1970s, it was located right next to the road. Dalwhinnie also used to be served by the adjacent Perth to Inverness railroad line courtesy of its own siding, but nowadays all transportation is by road.

himself, developing his personal blended whisky, which was designed to appeal to the discerning palates of English drinkers. After being known as House of Commons whisky and Buchanan's Special, the brand was finally christened Black & White, due to the eye-catching white label on a dark bottle.

The worms return

In 1987, the Dalwhinnie 15-year-old was chosen as part of Diageo predecessor United Distillers' Classic Malts range, and a visitor center opened four years later. The period 1992 to 1995 saw a $5.3 million (£3.2 million) refurbishment program, though just a single pair of stills remained at the end of the work. Dalwhinnie is one of comparatively few Scottish distilleries still equipped with worm tubs for condensing purposes, and in 1986, the existing two tubs were removed in favor of "shell and tube" condensers, but these altered the character of the Dalwhinnie "make" in a way considered undesirable, and a new pair of worm tubs was installed.

Cool character

Using worms rather than shell and tube condensers tends to create a complex spirit character. At Dalwhinnie, this is accentuated by icy cold water (often snow melt) used in the worm tubs. It allows spirit vapor to be cooled very quickly, reducing the copper contact to a minimum. This helps create a particular new-make spirit character that goes on to develop into a complex single malt.

At Dalwhinnie, around 1,500 casks are maturing on site, with the resultant whisky being earmarked for

bottling as single malt. Weather conditions can be severe and create challenges for living and working at Dalwhinnie. However, the character of the maturing whisky is not overly affected by the prevailing climate, although the "angels' share" of evaporated spirit is less than at other distilleries.

The Dalwhinnie lineup consists of a 15-year-old and a "Distillers Edition" variant, introduced in 1998, along with Winter's Gold—distilled between October and March and added to the range in 2015. A 30-year-old subsequently appeared as part of the 2019 Special Releases collection.

TASTING NOTES

Dalwhinnie 15-Year-Old
Single malt, 43% ABV
An aromatic nose, with pine needles, heather, and vanilla, plus delicate peat notes. Sweet on the smooth, fruity palate, with honey, malt, and a subtle note of peat. The medium-length finish dries elegantly.

Dalwhinnie 2022 Distiller's Edition
Single malt, matured for a secondary period in ex-oloroso sherry casks, 43% ABV
The nose offers medium-sweet sherry, sultanas, and sweet smoke. Big yet elegant on the palate, with malt, cloves, sherry, and fruit notes, plus muted honey and peat. The finish is long, smooth, and gently drying.

Dalwhinnie Winter's Gold
Single malt, 43% ABV
The nose is pleasantly floral, with toffee, malt, pineapple, and ginger, leading to a palate of heather honey, milk chocolate, and apricots, closing with cocoa, spice, and a hint of bonfire smoke.

Dalwhinnie Winter's Gold

GLENDRONACH

The GlenDronach 12-Year-Old Original

OWNER Benriach Distillery Company (Brown-Forman)

FOUNDED 1826

WEBSITE www.glendronachdistillery.com

The story of GlenDronach is an object lesson in how a niche operator can acquire a once-cherished whisky from a global company with an overlarge portfolio of brands and restore it to its rightful eminence. It is also the story of how another international organization can come along and embrace and build upon all the good work done by that niche owner.

Having been established in 1826 by James Allardice, who headed a consortium of local farmers and businessmen, GlenDronach was taken over in 1852 by Walter Scott, formerly manager of Teaninich distillery, who proceeded to expand the operation. On his death in 1887, the distillery was acquired by a Leith partnership.

Famous names acquire GlenDronach

A significant part of GlenDronach's subsequent heritage was intertwined with two famous Scotch whisky families, the Grants and Teachers. Captain Charles Grant, fifth son of William Grant, founder of Glenfiddich, bought GlenDronach in 1920, and it remained with the family until 1960, when it was acquired by William Teacher & Sons Ltd. Passing to Allied Breweries Ltd in 1976, GlenDronach fell sadly silent from 1996 to 2002. Until the 1996 closure, floor maltings were in operation—much later than at most Scotch whisky distilleries. It is also notable for being the last distillery in Scotland to operate coal-fired stills, though health and safety issues precipitated conversion to steam in 2005, when Allied (now Allied Domecq) was taken over by Chivas Brothers.

GlenDronach did not fit comfortably into the Chivas Brothers portfolio, which was overburdened with riches after the acquisition of Allied, and it was not surprising when, in August 2008, it was announced that The BenRiach Distillery Company had purchased GlenDronach. This distillery company had already done a fine job of giving the low-profile BenRiach single malt a whole new identity and impetus. Buying GlenDronach gave the consortium of owners, headed by Billy Walker, a heavily sherried single malt to complement BenRiach.

The GlenDronach
18-Year-Old Allardice

Reinventing GlenDronach

Walker proceeded to copy the BenRiach capitalization quirk, changing to upper case the central D in what had previously been known as Glendronach. Starting with just one expression, Walker and his associates proceeded to build an entire range of GlenDronach expressions and launch many limited editions. While some new-make spirit is filled into ex-sherry butts, a significant proportion goes into ex-bourbon casks before being transferred into sherry wood for a final maturation. Around 9,000 casks of whisky were acquired by Billy Walker and associates with the distillery, and a program of reracking up to 50 percent of the spirit into fresh oloroso casks has been undertaken. As a result, GlenDronach now competes strongly against the likes of Glenfarclas, The Macallan, and The Dalmore.

The attractive visitor center with the tasting bar at GlenDronach distillery.

The year 2016 saw GlenDronach, along with BenRiach and Glenglassaugh acquired by US firm Brown-Forman, owners of Jack Daniel's, the world's bestselling whisky brand (who then changed the spelling of BenRiach to Benriach). Happily, the care bestowed on the distillery and its whiskies continues in the hands of the highly experienced master blender Dr. Rachel Barrie, who grew up near the distillery.

The GlenDronach lineup

The core range includes Original 12-year-old, Revival 15-year-old, Allardice 18-year-old, and Parliament 21-year-old. The 21-year-old is named "Parliament" after the parliament of rooks that has been a feature at GlenDronach for centuries. The rooks were said to have provided advance notice of the approach of excise officers by their crowing, in the days when the GlenDronach area was a hotbed of illicit distilling. A limited edition 50-year-old bottling appeared in 2022, and 12 batches of NAS Cask Strength GlenDronach have also been released, along with many single cask expressions.

WHISKY TALES

Street Marketing
Soon after establishing GlenDronach distillery, James Allardice ventured to Edinburgh in search of markets for his whisky, taking with him copious amounts of the spirit. However, he failed to interest the many tavern landlords he approached with his new single malt. According to legend, while heading wearily back to his hotel, he was accosted on the Canongate by two prostitutes whom he invited to his room for a drink. When they left, he gave them the remainder of his whisky, only to find word of GlenDronach spreading on the streets, and being requested by name in the city's hostelries. The orders soon followed.

The GlenDronach 21-Year-Old Parliament

TASTING NOTES

The GlenDronach 12-Year-Old Original
Single malt, Pedro Ximénez and oloroso sherry casks, non-chill-filtered, 43% ABV
A sweet nose of Christmas cake. Smooth on the palate, with sherry, soft oak, fruit, almonds, and spices. Dry, nutty finish, ending with bitter chocolate.

The GlenDronach 18-Year-Old Allardice
Single malt, 46% ABV
Orange oil, Christmas spice, and walnuts feature on the rich nose, while the viscous palate exhibits flavors of Seville oranges, old leather, plums, spicy oak, and slightly smoky sherry.

The GlenDronach 21-Year-Old Parliament
Single malt, 48% ABV
The nose offers sweet sherry, fresh leather, and soy sauce, with flavors of spicy orange, sherry, leather, cloves, dark chocolate, and oak tannins on the full palate.

GLENGARIOCH

OWNER Morrison Bowmore Ltd (Suntory Global Spirits)

FOUNDED 1797

WEBSITE www.glengarioch.com

Glengarioch (pronounced "Glen-geery") is one of those lesser-known distilleries, being located some distance from a concentration of other whisky-making operations and even from a major distilling region. For the purposes of classification, it produces an Eastern Highlands single malt, like Fettercairn, and in common with that distillery Glengarioch is not on a major tourist trail either. It is, however, situated about 17 miles from Aberdeen on the outskirts of the historic town of Oldmeldrum, which is popular with commuters working in Scotland's oil capital and is in the Valley of the Garioch, sometimes known as "The Granary of Aberdeenshire" and renowned as the finest barley-growing area in Scotland.

Somewhat confusingly, while the distillery is known as "Glengarioch," the single malt it produces is always described as "Glen Garioch."

Early days

Glengarioch is one of the oldest distilleries in Scotland, the site originally incorporating a brewery and tannery also. As in so many cases, there's a degree of doubt about the actual date when distilling began on the present site, but the owners of Glengarioch have nailed their colors to the mast and declared 1797 to be its date of establishment, producing a "1797 Founder's Reserve" expression. It's widely accepted that in 1798 the distillery was in the hands of one Thomas Simpson.

What can be said with certainty is that in 1884, Glengarioch was acquired by the Leith blending firm J. G. Thomson & Company, with fellow Leith blender William Sanderson taking an interest in the distillery and its whisky. Sanderson had launched his Vat 69 blend in 1882 and Glen Garioch went on to become the heart malt of this brand.

Sanderson gained ownership of Glengarioch in 1908 through the Glengarioch Distillery Company Ltd, which was bought by Booth's Distilleries Ltd in 1933. Glengarioch then became part of the Distillers Company Ltd when DCL acquired Booth's Distilleries Ltd in 1937.

Glen Garioch Virgin Oak

Glen Garioch 1797 Founder's Reserve

Silent spring

DCL closed Glengarioch in 1968, claiming there was insufficient water available for distillation, but two years later Bowmore Distillery's owner, Stanley P. Morrison Ltd, purchased the Oldmeldrum distillery and recommenced production. The water issue was solved in 1972 when a spring was discovered on neighboring Coutens Farm, nicknamed "The Silent Spring of Coutens Farm" as it could not be seen or heard. This allowed distillery output to be increased tenfold. Under the Morrison regime, a third still was fitted in 1972, followed by a fourth in 1973, the same year in which the first official bottling of Glen Garioch took place. The floor maltings were in use until the comparatively late date of 1993. A year later, what was now Morrison Bowmore Distillers Ltd came under the total control of Japanese distillers Suntory Ltd, which had owned a 35 percent stake in the company since 1989.

The distillery was silent from October 1995 to August 1997, but then in 2004, a 1958 expression of Glen Garioch appeared—the oldest bottling of the whisky ever undertaken. The following year, a visitor center opened in the former cooperage, and around that time Glen Garioch sales peaked in the region of 250,000 bottles per year. In 2009, a radical revamp of the Glen Garioch range took place, with the distinctive Highlands "tartan and stag" packaging dropped in favor of a more modern and restrained appearance. The existing lineup of 8-, 12-, 15-, and 21-year-old expressions was replaced by "1797 Founder's Reserve," without an age statement, a 12-year-old, and an ongoing program of annual vintage releases. The older vintages display a significant difference in character to the younger bottlings, due to the influence of the more heavily peated malt made on the distillery's floor maltings until 1993. The maltings remain intact and the distillery's owners have not ruled out the possibility of reinstating them at some future date.

Back to the future

During 2021, Glen Garioch distillery underwent some significant modifications that effectively took the site back in time, as the wash still was converted from steam heating to direct-firing by gas, and the old floor maltings were restored and reinstated. The result of direct-firing has been to produce a more robust and full-bodied spirit, while the floor maltings now turn out around 25 percent of the distillery's malt requirements.

Glengarioch has been the most easterly distillery in Scotland since the closure of Glenugie in Peterhead in 1983.

According to distillery manager Kwanele Mdluli, "The reason we've undertaken these changes is all about spirit quality. We're aiming for as high a quality of spirt as we can get. With floor maltings, the quality of malt you get is different from that in commercial maltings—it gives you an extra dimension. You get greater control in commercial maltings than in floor maltings, in both germination vessels and during kilning.

"In floor maltings, we don't get quite the same level of control, so there is greater potential variation. You may get a degree of undermodification, meaning that more proteins get into the process, and when protein breaks down, you get amino acids. So you get more amino acids in the wash still, reacting and helping create elements of flavor."

WHISKY TALES

Leader in the Fields
The dramatic rises in fuel costs in the 1970s led several distillers to develop energy-saving projects that prefigured more recent innovations. At Glengarioch, a waste heat recovery system heated the malt kiln and preheated the wash prior to distillation, and greenhouses and polytunnels were used to cultivate tomatoes, cucumbers, peppers, and eggplants along with flowers. In 1982, Glengarioch also became the first Scottish distillery to use North Sea gas for heating purposes.

TASTING NOTES

Glen Garioch 1797 Founder's Reserve
Single malt, non-chill-filtered, 48% ABV
A nose of soft fruits (pears, peaches, and apricots), together with butterscotch and vanilla. Quite full-bodied, with vanilla, malt, melon, and light smoke on the palate. The finish is clean and medium in length.

Glen Garioch 12-Year-Old
Single malt, non-chill-filtered, 48% ABV
Sweet on the nose, focusing on fresh fruit—peaches and pineapple—plus vanilla, malt, and a hint of sherry. Full-bodied, with more fresh fruit on the palate, along with spice, brittle toffee, and finally quite dry oaky notes.

Glen Garioch Virgin Oak
Single cask, 48% ABV
Notably fruity on the nose, with peach, mango, honey, and vanilla. The same fruity noses are present on the palate, with toffee, new oak, and soft spices.

GLENGOYNE

OWNER Ian Macleod Distillers Ltd

FOUNDED 1833

WEBSITE www.glengoyne.com

Glengoyne could have reason to doubt its identity. Classified as being in the Highlands region for malt whisky-making, its production buildings do lie just that side of the theoretical Highland Line. Once distilled, however, the spirit is transported across the A81 road to be matured in warehouses on the other side of the Line, in the Lowlands. Until the 1970s, Glengoyne was categorized as a Lowland single malt, and the presence of three stills (one wash and two spirit) in the stillhouse points toward the potential for a Lowland-like triple-distillation tendency. Furthermore, the distillery boasts a long-standing use of unpeated malt and is sometimes compared with Auchentoshan in style.

Prolonged distillation

What really matters, of course, is the quality of the whisky being distilled. With single malt sales having grown significantly in recent years, the Glengoyne team prides itself on both its use of unpeated malt and the slow rate of distillation, saying "Glengoyne has always distilled slowly."

Stuart Hendry, Brand Heritage and Commercial Manager, says, "Glengoyne has always distilled slowly. There are different ways to impart flavor to your new-make spirit. You can add most of the flavor at the start through the addition of peat at the drying stage in the malting process, or you can dry your barley with warm air then use your stills to create flavor nuances in the unsmoked version. Most peaty distillers go at it hammer and tongs to get the spirit out of the stills as quickly as possible.

"Our way is to prolong copper contact for as long as possible, which strips out much of the sulfur. Copper also acts as a catalyst, which brings together the sugars and amino acids created during fermentation to give a new range of molecularly light, intense, sweet, estery flavors. These we call 'early boilers,' and they come across as soon as we start collecting. It's our desire to capture these flavor congeners that leads us to collect our middle cut so early."

Glengoyne 12-Year-Old

Glengoyne 15-Year-Old

Illicit origins?

Glengoyne sits just 12 miles from Glasgow, but despite its comparative proximity to the city, the location in a wooded glen at the foot of Dumgoyne Hill could hardly be bettered. It was first licensed in 1833, but it's believed that distilling on the site predated official sanction; certainly the area was once a hotbed for smuggling. The distillery was built by George Connell, who leased the land, and the license was held by members of the MacLellan family for many years. Originally christened Glenguin, the distillery was known as Burnfoot at the time it was bought by Lang Brothers Ltd in 1876. They changed the name back to Glenguin, or Glen Guin, and the present spelling was adopted around 1905.

Bottlers take charge

A modernization program followed the acquisition of Lang by the Robertson & Baxter Group in 1965, and a third still was added during reconstruction work in 1966–1967. Robertson & Baxter is now part of The Edrington Group, and under its ownership a great deal of Glengoyne found its way into Lang's Supreme and other blends. Then, in April 2003, the distillery, the Glengoyne and Lang's brand names, and a significant amount of maturing stock were acquired by Ian Macleod Distillers Ltd, old-established blenders and bottlers but never previously owners of a distillery. The new proprietors doubled the output and began to market Gengoyne energetically as a single malt.

Principal bottlings available include 10-, 12-, 15-, 18-, 21-, 25-, and 30-year-olds, along with a no age statement cask-strength expression, while 2022 saw the introduction into China of a 53-year-old, the oldest release from the distillery to date. The Spirit of Time Series is available in travel retail outlets, while the Teapot Dram, named after the copper teapot formerly used to dispense drams to the distillery workforce, is exclusively available to distillery visitors.

WHISKY TALES

Top Tours

A dozen miles north of Glasgow and within relatively easy reach of Edinburgh, Glengoyne attracts large numbers of visitors per year and offers five experience options. These include distillery tours, tutored tastings, and The Malt Master's Experience. This is described as "A guided tour of Glengoyne Distillery followed by extra special hands-on experience in our Sample Room, where you'll take on the role of the Malt Master and create your very own bottle of Highland Single Malt from single cask whiskies specially chosen from our warehouse."

Glengoyne 21-Year-Old

TASTING NOTES

Glengoyne 12-Year-Old
Single malt, 43% ABV
Malt and light honey on the nose, with nuts and citrus fruit; palate of spices, toffee, and orange chocolate. Consistent, medium finish with mellow oak and a hint of ginger.

Glengoyne 15-Year-Old
Single malt, 43% ABV
Floral on the nose with toffee apples and cinnamon, leading into a palate of vanilla fudge, apple pie, and allspice, closing with black pepper and cloves.

Glengoyne 21-Year-Old
Single malt, matured in first-fill European oak sherry casks, 43% ABV
The nose offers immediate and accessible sherry, spices, and black treacle. Mouth-coating, bold and sherried on the palate, with aromatic spice and nutty notes. Licorice and Caramac bars dominate the finish.

GLENMORANGIE

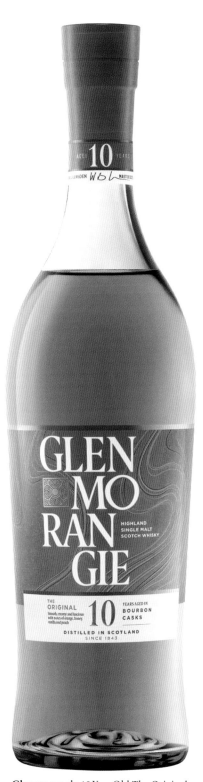

Glenmorangie 10-Year-Old The Original

OWNER The Glenmorangie Company Ltd (LVMH)

FOUNDED 1843

WEBSITE www.glenmorangie.com

Innovation is essential in a competitive commercial environment, although to an extent Scotch whisky distillers are limited by the very specific terms of the legal definition of Scotch whisky. However, that does not mean that within the industry clever minds are not coming up with innovative ideas and putting them into practice. A prime example of this is Glenmorangie's Dr. Bill Lumsden, Head of Distilling and Whisky Creation. Lumsden has a PhD in biochemistry, so he brings a solid science background to the business of creating whiskies that stand out from the crowd yet have total integrity.

The whys and wherefores of wood

One of Bill Lumsden's particular areas of interest is wood management, and he declares, "My philosophy on wood is that it doesn't matter how good your new spirit is if you don't fill it into good-quality wood, which is also sympathetic to the style of your whisky. No other company has gone into such detail with their wood policy as Glenmorangie." Indeed, the distillery has gone so far as to buy an area of woodland in Missouri's Ozark mountain region, from where the timber for "designer" casks is sourced. These are used to mature some of the spirit that finds its way into various Glenmorangie bottlings. Thanks in part to Lumsden's pioneering work with wood, Glenmorangie was the first single malt to offer its own bottlings of finished whisky, initially from ex-port casks, and it has remained at the forefront of the process, working with a wide range of finishes.

Early years

For the first 150 years of its existence, however, Glenmorangie offered one style of whisky, in common with every other distillery in Scotland, though it used— and continues to use—hard water for processing, while most distilleries use soft. Glenmorangie was developed between 1843 and 1849, when the first spirit flowed. Its founder was William Mathieson, who utilized existing elements of the defunct Morangie Brewery, and in 1887, the Glenmorangie Distillery

Glenmorangie The Nectar
16-Year-Old

Company Ltd was formed. The plant was entirely rebuilt at that time, and Glenmorangie became the first distillery in Scotland to use steam to heat its stills rather than coal. Macdonald & Muir Ltd, owners of the Highland Queen blended brand, took a majority share in 1918, and the distillery went on to survive a period of silence during the mid-1930s

Glenmorangie Signet

Rising capacity

The more recent history of Glenmorangie has been notably positive, with the complement of stills being doubled from two to four during a reconstruction program in 1979, and doubled again just a decade later. In 2004, Glenmorangie plc, as it had now become, was bought by Louis Vuitton Moët Hennessy (LVMH) for $555 million (£300) million, placing Ardbeg, Glen Moray, and Glenmorangie distilleries in the hands of the French-based organization. Today Glenmorangie is the third bestselling single malt in the UK and globally occupies the number four position.

Innovation continues

Early in 2022, a new production building, named The Lighthouse, opened at Glenmorangie. It is equipped with a pair of stills and will allow Dr. Lumsden and his colleagues the opportunity to be experimental, without disrupting everyday distillation.

As well as three wood finishes, Lasanta (sherry), The Nectar (Sauternes), and Quinta Ruban (port), notable among the current core lineup is Signet, one of Lumsden's proudest innovations. Twenty percent of its component whiskies is made from chocolate malt, matured for 10 years in a combination of ex-bourbon and new oak casks, then blended with other Glenmorangie whiskies, some up to 35 years old, from a variety of casks, including wine and sherry. Lumsden is also responsible for adding Glenmorangie X—designed for mixing with soda or ginger ale—to the core range in 2021. Recent limited editions have included four sherry cask–finished expressions in the Barrel Select Range and A Tale of The Forest, infused with botanicals during kilning.

WHISKY TALES

The Tallest Stills

Whisky stills come in all shapes and sizes, and their variations play a significant part in shaping the character of the spirit produced. Perhaps no distillery has placed more emphasis on the individuality of its stills than Glenmorangie. One print advertising campaign carries an illustration of the vessels in question and declares that "There are a lot of perfectly good single malts made in shorter stills. We have the tallest stills in Scotland." They are based on the design of the original ex-gin stills from London, installed when the distillery was founded, and contribute significantly to the light, fruity, floral character of Glenmorangie.

TASTING NOTES

Glenmorangie 10-Year-Old The Original
Single malt, 40% ABV
Fresh fruit, butterscotch, and toffee on the nose. Smooth palate of nuts, spice, vanilla honey, Jaffa oranges, and hard toffee. Fruity in the finish, with a hint of ginger.

Glenmorangie Signet
Single malt, 46% ABV
A nose of rich fruit, honey, marmalade, maple, sherry, sweet oak, and spice. Lots of fruit and spice on the palate, with dark chocolate, vanilla, and leather. The finish is spicy and medium in length.

Glenmorangie The Nectar 16-Year-Old
Single malt, finished in sweet white wine casks, 46% ABV
The nose is rich and sweet, offering fresh baking notes, apricots, honey, and almonds, leading into a full palate of gingerbread, custard, sweet orange, and contrasting lemon. Long in the finish, with soft spices, lemon curd, and subtle oak

THE GLENTURRET

The Glenturret Triple Wood

OWNER Lalique Group & Dr. Hansjorg Wyss

FOUNDED 1775

WEBSITE www.theglenturret.com

When it comes to offering hospitality to visitors, most Scottish distilleries content themselves with a simple café, ideally boasting some made-on-the-premises dishes and local treats. Head to the Perthshire venue of The Glenturret, however, and you find a Michelin-starred restaurant in situ. The beautifully appointed restaurant, presided over by head chef Mark Donald, is just one indication that The Glenturret is setting out its stall to do things differently from most of its rival distilleries.

The name Lalique is highly significant here, as The Glenturret is co-owned by Silvio Denz of the iconic French luxury glassmaking Lalique Group and Swiss American Dr. Hansjorg Wyss, who acquired it from The Edrington Group in 2019. As well as hosting the Lalique Restaurant, The Glenturret distillery is also home to the only UK Lalique Boutique outside London.

Oldest working distillery

The Glenturret served as the high-profile brand home of Famous Grouse from 2002 until 2019, but when owners Edrington decided to focus attention on its Macallan, Highland Park, and Glenrothes single malt brands, there was no shortage of potential purchasers for the Perthshire distillery.

After all, The Glenturret has the kudos of claiming to be the oldest working distillery in Scotland, with a foundation date of 1763, and prospective buyers gained a strong stock inventory plus former Macallan whisky-maker Bob Dalgarno to work with it. A price of $40 million (£31 million) was paid for the distillery and stocks, including in excess of 264,000 gallons (1 million liters) of maturing Glenturret single malt, the oldest of which was filled to cask in 1987, along with 2,400 cases of bottled whisky.

Famous heritage

The Glenturret name was adopted in 1875, and the distillery operated until falling silent in 1921. Eight years later, the equipment was dismantled, and the buildings were subsequently used for agricultural storage. The distillery remained closed until businessman James Fairlie acquired the premises in 1957 and reequipped it for distilling, with production starting two years later. Ownership passed to Rémy-Cointreau in 1981, with Highland Distillers taking over nine years later. In 1999, The Edrington Group and William Grant & Sons Ltd purchased Highland Distillers for $985 million (£601 million), operating as The 1887 Company, with Edrington owning 70 percent of the shares.

The production side of Glenturret remains much as it was under Edrington ownership, although the oft-admired open-topped mash tun, which was stirred by hand, has given way to a shiny new semi-lauter vessel in the interests of environmental future-proofing and increases in output. Fermentations in wooden washbacks are relatively lengthy, and distillation takes place slowly. The wash still dates back to the 1970s, while its spirit counterpart is a more youthful 30-something years of age. A very narrow "middle cut" of spirit is taken, and functions are manually controlled, being judged by strength, temperature, and clarity. The result is a light, floral, sweet, fruity, and elegant spirit.

Glenturret is currently producing around 57,000–58,000 gallons (215,000–220,000 liters) per annum, a figure that will increase in time, and of that annual output, some 9,200 gallons (35,000 liters) are made from peated barley. Some 15 or 16 casks are filled with spirit twice per week and the distillery operates with a production staff of seven.

The Glenturret single malt

The Glenturret core range is presented in eye-catching bottles designed by Lalique, and the lineup comprises

The Glenturret lies just east of the Trossachs, a gentle landscape of wooded hills and peaceful lochs.

Triple Wood (matured in American and European oak sherry–seasoned casks and bourbon barrels), 7- and 10-year-old peat smoked, 12- and 15-year-olds, while there are also 25-, 30-, and 35-year-old bottlings in the Limited Releases range. Perhaps uniquely, Glenturret's core range changes on an annual basis.

Highlight of the Glenturret portfolio is a single cask 50-year-old, distilled in 1972 and presented in 150 jet black crystal decanters, while well-heeled consumers are also likely to be attracted to the ongoing Glenturret by Lalique Trinity series of 33-year-old expressions.

An exclusive collaboration was undertaken in 2021 with Jaguar E-type to commemorate the 60th anniversary of the launch of the iconic sports car— 265 bottles were produced as 265 was the car's original horsepower.

WHISKY TALES

Distillery Cats

A bronze bust commemorates the achievements of Towser, the former Glenturret distillery cat, who earned a place in The Guinness Book of Records by accounting for 28,899 mice during her 24 years of service. Today, the feline tradition continues with Glen and Turret, who enjoy sleeping in the warmth of the stillhouse but are notably more relaxed about rodent control than their illustrious predecessor.

TASTING NOTES

The Glenturret Triple Wood (2021 release)
Single malt, 44% ABV
Charred oak and a slightly savory note on the nose, with developing nougat and orange aromas. The palate is delicately spicy, with vanilla, drinking chocolate, prunes, white pepper, and oak char.

The Glenturret 10-Year-Old Peat Smoked (2021 Release)
Single malt, 50% ABV
A nose of cigarette smoke, oatmeal, lemon, vanilla, and a hint of cloves. Earthy peat on the palate, with brittle toffee, coffee grounds, cinnamon, and smoky oak.

The Glenturret 12-Year-Old (2021 Release)
Single malt, 46% ABV
Old leather, figs, and orange on the nose, while the palate offers malt, toffee, aniseed, orange marmalade, and oak tannins.

The Glenturret 12-Year-Old

OBAN

OWNER Diageo plc

FOUNDED 1794

WEBSITE www.malts.com

John and Hugh Stevenson were local entrepreneurs in the Oban area, establishing a boat-building business, a tannery, and brewery, with the brewery being converted into a distillery by 1794. This places Oban among a historically elite group of working Scottish distilleries that have their roots in the 18th century.

The Stevensons' business ventures, which included slate quarries, made a significant contribution to paving the way for the development of Oban that was to take place over the next century, as Victorian steamers began to use Oban as a regular port of call, and the railroad arrived in the town during 1880.

Hugh Stevenson's son, Thomas, left Oban to farm in Buenos Aires but returned after the death of his father in order to purchase the distillery and slate-quarrying enterprise. He was also responsible for constructing Oban's grandiose Caledonian Hotel, but financial difficulties caused by supporting his brother's printing business led to a situation where creditors were paid in whisky and slates!

A change of hands

Oban distillery remained in the Stevenson family until 1866, when it was bought by Peter Cumstie, who sold it to James Walter Higgen in 1882. Higgen rebuilt the distillery between 1890 and 1894 but managed to continue producing spirit while doing so, due to its great demand. While many of today's most prestigious single malts spent much of their history as "blending fodder," Oban enjoyed strong sales as a single malt from the 1880s onward.

Ownership of Oban passed to Oban & Aultmore Glenlivet Distilleries Ltd in 1898, with the Oban Distillery Company Ltd, owned by Buchanan-Dewar, gaining ownership in 1923. Buchanan-Dewar went on to become part of the Distillers' Company Ltd two years later.

DCL days and onward

Oban was one of numerous Scottish distilleries to endure a period of silence during those economically depressed interwar years, closing from 1931 until

Oban 2022 Distillers Edition

Oban Little Bay

Traditional Oregon pine washbacks in the tun room at Oban distillery.

WHISKY TALES

Gateway to the Isles
Oban distillery stands proud right in the center of the town from which it takes its name, and this is no accident, for the town actually grew up around the distillery. *An t-Òban* or "The Little Bay" in Gaelic, Oban was originally a small fishing village before the founding of the distillery and arrival of the railroad turned it into a busy port, handling wool and slate shipments, as well as whisky. Today, Oban is the largest center of population in the West Highlands, a magnet for visitors, and also a busy ferry port in its role as "Gateway to the Isles." Oban is the principal ferry terminal for Mull, Coll, Tiree, Colonsay, Barra, and South Uist. Not surprisingly, Oban distillery is notably popular among visitors, receiving in excess of 30,000 per year.

1937. Between 1968 and 1972, however, the distillery underwent a major refurbishment program, with its floor maltings ceasing to operate at that time. Although the distillery had been refurbished, there was physically very little scope to expand operations due to the constricted nature of the site, and even if DCL had wanted to add more stills to increase production, this was not a feasible option.

Accordingly, today's distillery still has just one pair of lantern-shaped stills, among the smallest in Scotland, and Oban's output is the second-lowest in the Diageo portfolio after Royal Lochnagar. The stills are actually large enough to produce more spirit per annum than is currently being achieved but are unable to do so due to the fact that the character of Oban single malt is dependent on long fermentation times of up to 110 hours, which limits production to six mashes per week. The lengthy fermentation time ensures the required light character is achieved.

All of the Oban spirit is currently earmarked for single malt bottling, and a 14-year-old expression was one of the "founding fathers" of United Distillers' Classic Malts range in 1988, with a dedicated visitor center opening the following year.

In 1998, an Oban Distillers Edition was introduced, employing Montilla Fino sherry wood for a secondary period of maturation. Montilla Fino sherries are light in color and dry and salty in character, which makes them an ideal match for Oban with its salty, slightly peaty characteristics. As well as the 14-year-old and Distillers Edition, the

core lineup includes the popular no age statement Oban Litte Bay, while the 2023 Diageo Special Releases saw the appearance of an Oban 11-year-old with a Caribbean rum cask finish, following on from a 10-year-old 2022 Special Release with an amontillado sherry finish. A distillery-exclusive expression is also available.

If seeking out a bottle of the distillery-exclusive, the distillery itself is impossible to miss. Fronting Oban Bay, it is set into the base of a steep cliff, above which rises the unfinished folly of McCaig's Tower, the philanthropic venture of a local banker, constructed in 1897 to provide local employment and intended to resemble the Colosseum in Rome.

TASTING NOTES

Oban 14-Year-Old
Single malt, 43% ABV
The nose offers soft smoke, heather honey, toffee, and a whiff of seashore. Spicy, stewed fruits on the palate, with malt, oak, and a little smoke. The finish is rounded and aromatic, with spices and oak.

Oban 2022 Distillers Edition (1995)
Single malt, finished in ex-fino sherry casks, 43% ABV
Rich, spicy, confident, with caramel, milk chocolate, orange, and smoke on the nose. Spicy chocolate, malt, rich fruit, and brine on the palate. The fruit and salt linger through a long finish.

Oban Little Bay
Single malt, 43% ABV
Oily and nutty, with ripe apples and peaches plus white pepper on the nose. Malt loaf, cherries, cloves, ginger, and lingering oak on the palate, with a sprinkling of rock salt.

PULTENEY

OWNER Inver House Distillers Ltd (International Beverage Holdings)

FOUNDED 1826

WEBSITE www.oldpulteney.com

In the hands of current owners Inver House Distillers Ltd, Old Pulteney single malt has been a notable success story, rising from relative obscurity to become a global performer in little more than a decade, with significant sales increases both in the UK and key international arenas. Indeed, Old Pulteney is Inver House's bestselling single malt.

Maritime malt

Marketed as "The Genuine Maritime Malt," the Old Pulteney brand makes good use of its hometown's fishing heritage, given added relevance by the subtle briny characteristic present in most expressions of the whisky. The packaging of Old Pulteney is designed to reflect Wick's fishing history, bearing a prominent image of a herring drifter on both bottle and carton. While Scotland's northernmost distillery is always known as Pulteney, its single malt has long had the prefix of "Old" attached to it.

The distillery is in the Pulteneytown district of Wick, an area named after Sir William Pulteney, a governor of the British Fisheries Society, which created the settlement of Pulteneytown and a capacious harbor alongside the existing burgh of Wick during the early years of the 19th century.

Drunk as a herring

The herring industry may have made Wick its fortune, but it also contributed to a significant degree of drunkenness among the population. It was estimated that during the 1840s, a staggering 589 gallons (2,230 liters) of whisky was being consumed in the port per day during the height of the herring fishing season! Certainly some of that whisky was being supplied by Pulteney distillery, which had been established in 1826 by James Henderson, who had previously distilled at Stemster, near Halkirk. After almost a century of operation, Pulteney was acquired by the Dundee blending firm of James Watson & Company Ltd in 1920. Five years later, Watson's was absorbed into the mighty Distillers Company Ltd, and in

Old Pulteney 12-Year-Old

Old Pulteney Huddart

Old stone warehouses at Pulteney distillery.

1930 production ceased at Pulteney. Not only was the world in the grip of the Great Depression, but Pulteney had the added problem of being a whisky distillery located in the middle of an ostensibly dry town.

Pulteney revived

Pulteney was silent until 1951, when it was owned, along with Balblair, by Banff-based lawyer Robert "Bertie" Cumming. However, the lure of Canadian gold was too much for Cumming, who sold out to Hiram Walker, which was eager to expand its Scotch whisky interests in that postwar period. A comprehensive rebuilding program took place during 1958–1959, resulting in the external appearance of the distillery as it is today. Allied Breweries Ltd bought Pulteney in 1961 and operated it until what was then Allied Domecq sold the distillery and single malt brand to Inver House Distillers Ltd in 1995.

Two years later, a 12-year-old official bottling was released, and that remains the core bottling, along with 15-, 18-, and 25-year-olds and the smoky NAS Huddart. The Huddart expression is matured initially in second-fill American oak, ex-bourbon casks then finished in ex-bourbon casks that had previously held heavily peated whisky, while the 15- and 18-year-olds are aged in second-fill American oak ex-bourbon casks, followed by a period of further maturation in first-fill Spanish oak, ex-oloroso butts. The oldest expression currently available from the distillery is a limited edition 38-year-old, launched into the Chinese market during 2022.

The same year saw the appearance of the first bottling in an ongoing Coastal Series, inspired by coastal locations around the world, This was named Pineau de Charentes and, according to the distillers, "offers a lighter, sweeter taste layered on the classic Old Pulteney base."

Visitors to the distillery can personally fill, seal, and purchase a bottle of whisky from one of several unique single casks usually available, one of which is an ex-bourbon cask and another a former sherry cask.

While many start-up distilleries now boast biomass boilers for heating purposes, Pulteney was in on the act long before them all, with a plant being established in 2011–2012. The system supplies steam to the distillery and hot water to nearly 200 local domestic properties, a local hospital, and a meeting room–concert hall via the district heating network.

Sawed-off still

The distillery is equipped with a single pair of highly individual stills, with condensing taking place in a pair of stainless steel worm tubs. Both stills boast large boil balls, which encourage reflux, while the dramatically truncated, flat-topped appearance of the wash still is said to have resulted from an incident many years ago when a new still was fabricated for the distillery but turned out to be too tall to fit. The solution was to have a coppersmith remove the top and seal it. There seems to be no proof to this tale, but no alternative explanation for the still's appearance, either, and the roof of the stillhouse has since been raised in height.

The overall effect of the current regime is to produce a relatively oily new make spirit, some 95 percent of which is filled into ex-bourbon casks if being retained by the distillers, while approximately 40 percent is sold on for blending purposes and is removed from the site by tanker. Around 24,000 casks can be retained in five on-site warehouses.

WHISKY TALES

The Dry Town
Prohibition will forever be closely associated with the US and that 1920s period of bootleggers, speakeasies, and "the real McCoy," yet Scotland had its very own era of prohibition—or to be precise, the burgh of Wick did, being declared "dry" between 1925 and 1947. This ban resulted from opposition to the hard-drinking reputation of the town during the 19th and early 20th centuries, when Wick was at the center of the herring fishing industry, whose hard workers also tended to be hard drinkers. Wick may have officially been "dry," but at least one illicit still supplied the town with whisky, while a café on Bridge Street served it to diners in an ornate silver teapot!

TASTING NOTES

Old Pulteney 12-Year-Old
Single malt, 40% ABV
The nose presents fresh malt and floral notes, with a touch of pine. The palate offers a sweet whisky, with more malt, spices, fresh fruit, and a suggestion of salt. The finish is lightly drying and nutty.

Old Pulteney Huddart
Single malt, 40% ABV
Wood smoke, cinder toffee, apples, and crème brûlée on the nose. The palate is softly peated, with bananas, cinnamon, brine, and spicy oak.

Old Pulteney 18-Year-Old
Single malt, 46% ABV
The nose offers warming aromas of cinnamon, drinking chocolate, and honey, leading into flavors of dark chocolate, custard, citrus fruit, a suggestion of salt and soft oak.

BALBLAIR

OWNER Inver House Distillers Ltd (International
Beverage Holdings)

FOUNDED 1790

WEBSITE www.balblair.com

Attractively located overlooking the Dornoch Firth,
Balblair is one of the most northerly of the mainland
distilleries in Scotland. It also has a claim to being
one of the oldest surviving whisky-making plants in
Scotland, with the year of its founding given as 1790.
In reality, however, the present distillery actually dates
from the 1890s, with the 18th-century original being
located half a mile away.

Farm origins

That original was the work of John Ross of Balblair
Farm, and the distillery remained in the Ross family
until 1894, with major rebuilding taking place in

1872. Despite that program of reconstruction, when
Inverness wine merchant Alexander Cowan took on
the lease of Balblair distillery from its owners, the
Balnagowan Estate, the plant was relocated to its
present site during 1894–1895, taking advantage of
the adjacent railroad line to facilitate the import of
raw materials and the export of casks of whisky.
Despite relocating, Balblair has continued to draw
upon the same soft water source since its 18th-century
foundation, in the form of the Allt Dearg stream
(pronounced "Jerak" and meaning "Red Burn'"),
which flows down from the hills behind the distillery.

A dram back on track

Balblair was silent from 1915 until 1947, when Banff
solicitor Robert "Bertie" Cumming purchased it,
recommencing distilling two years later after
investing significantly in upgrading the distillery and
increasing output. When Cumming retired in 1970,
he sold it to the Canadian distiller Hiram Walker &
Sons Ltd. Hiram Walker merged with Allied Vintners
to become Allied Distillers in 1988, and Allied sold
Balblair to Inver House eight years later.

For some years, Balblair was sold with vintage
statements, but 2019 saw a reimagining of the
portfolio, and the introduction of age statements. The
current range includes 12-, 15-, 18-, 21-, and 25-year-
olds. There are three tour options, culminating in The
Definitive Tour, which offers participants the chance
to sample the wash and wort in the production area,
as well as the opportunity to bottle their own malt in
the warehouse, before sampling all four signature
expressions of Balblair.

Balblair 15-Year-Old

Balblair 12-Year-Old

TASTING NOTES

Balblair 12-Year-Old
Single malt, 46% ABV
Soft spices, figs, pears, malt, and delicate orange notes appear on the nose, while the palate
features honey, vanilla, and caramel, finishing on a note of black pepper and dark chocolate.

Balblair 15-Year-Old
Single malt, 46% ABV
The nose offers aromatic dark fruits, sherry, vanilla, and marzipan, leading into a palate of
sherry, spicy apple pie, caramel, orange, and walnuts.

Balblair 18-Year-Old
Single malt, 46% ABV
Spicy aromas, with toffee, sherry, and poached pears are followed by flavors of dried fruits,
caramel, vanilla, and juicy oranges, with chili and dry oak in the finish.

BEN NEVIS

OWNER Ben Nevis Distillery Ltd (Nikka)

FOUNDED 1825

WEBSITE www.bennevisdistillery.com

Ben Nevis distillery was established a short distance northeast of the West Highland town of Fort William in 1825, and it stands in the shadow of its namesake, Scotland's highest mountain. The distillery was founded by a farmer, "Long John" McDonald, who was famed for his great height, hence his nickname. McDonald's whisky was marketed as Long John's Dew of Ben Nevis, though the name "Long John" subsequently came to be applied to a blended Scotch whisky, now owned by Chivas Brothers. The distillery remained in the hands of the McDonalds until 1941, and between 1878 and 1908, the family operated a second distillery, named Nevis, which was then absorbed into the main Ben Nevis plant.

The Dubious Hobbs

The most colorful owner of Ben Nevis distillery was Joseph Hobbs, who bought the distillery from the McDonald family. He was born in Hampshire, England, during 1891, and migrated with his parents to Canada in 1900. There he made a fortune, which he subsequently lost during the Great Depression. Hobbs returned to the UK and proceeded to develop significant whisky-related interests in Scotland, where, among other distilleries, he owned Ben Nevis from 1941 until his death 20 years later. One of Hobbs's rather dubious innovations was the installation of concrete washbacks, and he also fitted a Coffey still in order to produce both grain and malt spirit and blend them on the premises.

A Japanese connection

Ben Nevis has had a number of owners during its lengthy existence and has endured several periods of closure, but its future was assured when the facility was purchased from the brewing giant Whitbread & Company Ltd by the Japanese Nikka Whisky Distilling Company Ltd in 1989. Today, some of the spirit made at Ben Nevis is shipped to Japan where it is a component in several Nikka blended whiskies, while the rest is used for blending in Scotland or is bottled as single malt.

The Ben Nevis distillery stands in the shadow of its namesake, Scotland's tallest mountain.

Notably old bottlings of Ben Nevis appear from time to time, but the core range comprises just three expressions. These are 10-year-old, the NAS Coire Leis—named after a popular route up Ben Nevis—and McDonald's Traditional Ben Nevis. Traditional is produced using peated malt and is matured for an unspecified period in fresh sherry casks.

TASTING NOTES

Ben Nevis 10-Year-Old
Single malt, matured in a mixture of refill casks, fresh bourbon barrels, and fresh sherry casks, 46% ABV
The initially quite green nose develops nutty, orange notes. Full-bodied, with coffee, brittle toffee, and peat, along with chewy oak, which persists to the finish, together with more coffee and a hint of dark chocolate.

McDonald's Traditional Ben Nevis
Single malt, 46% ABV
Initial starch on the nose, then buttery smoked haddock, a hint of chili, sherry, and wood smoke. Full-bodied, spicy on the palate, with hazelnuts and peat. Stewed fruit and lingering spicy cigarette ash in the finish.

Ben Nevis Coire Leis
Single malt, 46% ABV
The nose offers honey, lemon, malt, barley sugar, and wood spice, while flavors of toffee, honey, ripe pears, black pepper, and a hint of chili feature on the oily palate.

Ben Nevis 10-Year-Old

BRORA

OWNER Diageo plc

FOUNDED 1819

WEBSITE www.malts.com

Brora distillery was established under the Clynelish name in 1819 by local landowner the Earl of Stafford, later Duke of Sutherland, to provide an outlet for barley grown by his tenants. The whisky made there proved so desirable that, after visiting during 1896, the great distillery chronicler Alfred Barnard wrote that "…the make has always obtained the highest price of any single Scotch whisky."

Ultimately, Clynelish came into the ownership of the Distillers Company Ltd (DCL). During the 1960s, DCL expanded and rebuilt many of its existing distilleries to cope with the increasing demand for blended Scotch whisky. In the case of Clynelish, an entirely new modernistic plant was built during 1967 alongside the old production buildings, with the original distillery being renamed Brora. It closed in 1983, apparently forever.

Brora reborn
Happily, Brora was wakened from its lengthy slumber in 2021, after a major program of investment. "Waxy," "smoky," and "earthy" styles of spirit are produced at times in the distillery, and up to 211,000 gallons (800,000 liters) of spirit may be made each year. Having been silent since 1983, the distillery needed a significant amount of remedial structural work, which necessitated a complete rebuilding of the stillhouse. Fortuitously, the single pair of stills had remained in place and are now back in use after some refurbishment, allied to a replacement pair of "old-school" worm tubs, while an exact replica of the original rake and gear mash tun was commissioned, along with replacement wooden washbacks.

The whisky
Given the length of time for which Brora has been closed, and the fact that its whisky gained something of a cult status, bottlings are rare and expensive. A 34-year-old Special Releases bottling from 2017 is available along with a 1980 expression in Diageo's Prima & Ultima series.

However, the ultimate Brora is Triptych. Released in 2021, it comprises three 500ml bottles, named Elusive Legacy (1972), Age of Peat (1977), and Timeless Original (1982), presented in a beautifully crafted, custom presentation case. Just 300 have been created. As Diageo's Senior Global Brand Ambassador Ewan Gunn notes, "Triptych showcases the three styles of spirit for which Brora is known, and there will probably be no 'new' Brora for a long time as it was generally felt to get better with age."

The Brora distillery came back into production in 2021.

TASTING NOTES

Brora Triptych Elusive Legacy (1972)
Single malt, 46.3% ABV
Peaches and wood spice on the nose, with malt, smoked ham, and tobacco on the sinewy palate, closing with coal smoke.

Brora Triptych Age of Peat (1977)
Single malt, 46.3% ABV
The nose offers vanilla, green apples, and beeswax, while the viscous palate yields wood spice, ginger, and developing sweet peat, plus a hint of chili.

Brora Triptych Timeless Original (1982)
Single malt, 46.3% ABV
Lemon and freshly mowed grass on the nose. Flavors of honey, citrus fruit, and gunpowder smoke on the waxy palate.

Brora Triptych Elusive Legacy (1972)

DEANSTON

OWNER CVH Spirits

FOUNDED 1965

WEBSITE www.deanstonmalt.com

Deanston is one of those rare Scotch distilleries to have been developed within an existing structure, the former Adelphi cotton mill, an 18th-century listed building by the Teith River. Conversion work was carried out during the mid-1960s' whisky boom by the Deanston Distillery Company Ltd, formed by James Finlay & Company and Tullibardine owner Brodie Hepburn Ltd. Deanston was purchased by Invergordon Distillers Ltd in 1972, being bottled as a single malt two years later. The distillery then closed in 1982 as the Scotch whisky industry reined in production but was reopened in 1991, having been acquired by Burn Stewart Distillers.

After several years in the ownership of the South African Distell Group, Deanston—along with Bunnahabhain and Tobermory—is now owned by CVH Spirits.

Green traditions

Despite its relatively modern origins, Deanston is a notably traditional distillery, featuring a rare surviving open cast-iron mash tun, and no computerization of processes. It boasts the quirkiest maturation warehouse in Scotland, namely a vaulted ex-weaving shed constructed in 1836, and was operating in an eco-friendly manner long before "green" became such a hot topic, courtesy of a pair of water-driven turbines.

Deanston distills from 100 percent Scottish barley and was one of the first distilleries to make organic whisky, with regular batches being produced since 2000. In 2012, a 10-year-old bottling of organic Deanston was released, and a 15-year-old variant is now available.

Under the Burn Stewart regime, the quality of spirit improved, and the reputation of Deanston single malt was enhanced by opting for longer fermentation periods and a slower rate of distillation and then by increasing the strength and eschewing chill-filtration.

TASTING NOTES

Deanston Virgin Oak
Single malt, finished in virgin oak casks, non-chill-filtered, 46.3% ABV
Sweet and grassy, with vanilla and fresh oak notes on the nose. Light-bodied, youthful spice, and zest on the fruity palate. The finish is spicy and drying.

Deanston 12-Year-Old
Single malt, non-chill-filtered, 46.3% ABV
A fresh, fruity nose with malt and honey. The palate displays cloves, ginger, honey, and malt, while the finish is long, quite dry, and pleasantly herbal.

Deanston Organic 15-Year-Old
Single malt, 46.3% ABV
The nose offers ginger, white pepper, vanilla, lime, and cloves, while sweet orchard fruit, honey, and ginger feature on the palate, with black pepper and nutty, spicy oak at the finish.

Deanston Virgin Oak

Housed in an old mill warehouse dating back to the 18th century, Deanston was actually founded in the 1960s.

Deanston Organic 15-Year-Old

EDRADOUR

OWNER Signatory Vintage Scotch Whisky Company Ltd

FOUNDED 1837

WEBSITE www.edradour.com

Edradour is one of Scotland's most attractive distilleries, and if an incurable romantic were to paint a picture of a Highland distillery, they would surely paint something that looked very like Edradour. It comprises a cluster of lime-washed and red-painted farm-style buildings grouped around a burn in the hills two miles from the picturesque Perthshire tourist center of Pitlochry.

Heritage

Edradour boasts a fascinating heritage, receiving its first official mention in 1837 and operating as a farmers' cooperative before being formalized as John MacGlashan & Company in 1841. In 1922, William

Whiteley & Company Ltd, a subsidiary of American distiller J. G. Turney & Sons, purchased Edradour to provide malt for its blends, including King's Ransom and House of Lords.

In 1982, Edradour was acquired by the Pernod Ricard subsidiary Campbell Distilleries, which introduced Edradour as a 10-year-old single malt bottling four years later. But in 2002, Pernod Ricard declared Edradour surplus to requirements, following its acquisition of Seagram's extensive Scotch whisky operations. Andrew Symington of the independent bottling firm Signatory Vintage Scotch Whisky Co Ltd subsequently purchased Edradour and proceeded to offer a wide range of limited-edition bottling, including from single casks and with cask finishes, from what was then Scotland's smallest distillery.

Distillery doubled

One significant innovation of the Signatory regime has been the introduction of a heavily peated spirit (over 50ppm), named Ballechin after a long-lost nearby farm distillery, and 2018 saw the opening of a second distillery close to the existing plant. This mirrored the original by being equipped with an open-topped, cast-iron mash tun, Oregon pine washbacks, and a quirky pair of stills, operating with worm tubs. The distillery now has an annual capacity of 69,000 gallons (260,000 liters), and additional warehousing has been constructed on site. A few years ago, Edradour played host to as many as 80,000 visitors per year, but the distillery is now closed to the public.

Edradour 10-Year-Old Ballechin

TASTING NOTES

Edradour 10-Year-Old
Single malt, ex-sherry casks, 40% ABV
Cider apples, malt, almonds, vanilla, and honey on the nose, along with a hint of smoke and sherry. The palate is rich, creamy, and malty, with leathery sherry and persistent nuttiness. Spices and sherry dominate the finish.

Edradour 12-Year-Old Caledonia
Single malt, finished for 4 years in ex-oloroso sherry casks, 46% ABV
A plump, fruity nose, featuring figs, sultanas. and a hint of cloves. Rich and full-bodied in the mouth, nutty and orangey, with plenty of attractive spice and a slowly drying, well-balanced finish.

Edradour 10-Year-Old Ballechin
Single malt, 46% ABV
The nose is spicy, with earthy peat, leather, and subtle toffee, while the palate presents fruity peat, more leather, a hint of aniseed, and dark chocolate, finishing with ginger and ashy peat.

FETTERCAIRN

OWNER Whyte & Mackay Ltd (Emperador)

FOUNDED 1824

WEBSITE www.fettercairnwhisky.com

The distillery is located in the foothills of the Cairngorm Mountains, in an area once noted for illicit distillation, and dates back to 1824, when it was converted from a former corn mill by local landowner Sir Alexander Ramsay. It was first licensed to James Stewart & Company the following year. In 1830, Ramsay sold his Fasque Estate, including the distillery, to Sir John Gladstone, father of the future four-times British prime minister William Ewart Gladstone.

The distillery effectively remained in the hands of the Gladstone family until its closure in 1926, after which, in 1939, it was purchased by Ben Nevis owner Joseph Hobbs of Associated Scottish Distillers Ltd.

The whisky boom of the 1960s saw the number of stills at Fettercairn being doubled to four in 1966, and five years later the distillery was acquired by the Tomintoul-Glenlivet Distillery Company Ltd, which was purchased by Whyte & Mackay seven years later.

Unique stills
Fettercairn is unique in being equipped with two spirit stills that are cooled by the release of water externally onto the still necks. From there, it flows down the bodies of the stills before being collected and recycled. This has the effect of increasing "reflux," leading to a cleaner and lighter spirit.

Single malts
Having long had the status of something of an "ugly duckling" in the Whyte & Mackay portfolio, Fettercairn has emerged as a true swan in recent years, with an extensive range of expressions available, ranging from 12 to 50 years of age.

Fettercairn is at the center of Whyte & Mackay's groundbreaking Scottish Oak Program, headed by Master Whisky Maker & Blender Gregg Glass. Fall 2022 saw the release of an 18-year-old Fettercairn, finished in Scottish oak, which had previously only very rarely been used for whisky maturation. Whyte & Mackay is committed to expanding the employment of native oak not just through its own single malts but by encouraging other whisky producers to embrace its use, and 13,000 oak saplings have been planted close to the distillery.

The pretty, cream-painted distillery is one of the most attractive in the Highlands.

Fettercairn 12-Year-Old

TASTING NOTES

Fettercairn 12-Year-Old
Single malt, 40% ABV
A hint of charcuterie and damp earth on the early nose, with developing mango and malt. Orchard fruits, cloves, vanilla, and cocoa on the palate, closing with hazelnuts, orange, and oak char.

Fettercairn 18-Year-Old
Single malt, 46% ABV
Nutty on the nose, with grilled pineapple, salted caramel, and dark chocolate. The palate yields tropical fruit, spice, and malt, finishing with distinctive—and pleasing—tannic oak.

Fettercairn 22-Year-Old
Single malt, 47% ABV
Almonds, cereal notes, green apples, and unripe bananas feature on the nose, while the supple palate offers pineapple, milk chocolate, ginger, and hazelnuts, leading into a finish of baked apple, hot chocolate, cloves, and white pepper.

GLENCADAM

OWNER Angus Dundee Distillers plc

FOUNDED 1825

WEBSITE www.glencadamdistillery.co.uk

The old distillery buildings at Glencadam were originally built in 1825, and little has changed since then.

The historic Angus town of Brechin lies between the cities of Dundee and Aberdeen in the Eastern Highland region of malt whisky production. Until 1983, the former royal burgh was home to two distilleries, Glencadam and North Port, with the latter falling victim to the Distillers Company Ltd's severe round of plant closures during that troubled decade for Scotch whisky distilling. In 2000, it looked as though Brechin was losing its surviving distillery, when Glencadam's then-owner Allied Domecq Ltd closed it down. Happily, however, export blend specialist Angus Dundee Distillers plc came to the rescue in 2003, adding the Eastern Highland plant to its existing Tomintoul facility on Speyside. In addition to the actual distillery, Angus Dundee also operates a blending and bottling facility at Glencadam, which is capable of blending nearly 1.1 million gallons (4 million liters) of Scotch whisky per year. The site's six warehouses, two of which date back to 1825, have a capacity of around 20,000 casks, and some of the maturing stock at Glencadam is up to 30 years old.

Mellow spirits

The distillery is equipped with a single pair of stills, as it was when first constructed, and unusually their lyne arms run upward at an angle of 15 degrees, rather than sloping downward as in most Scotch whisky distilleries. This helps to produce a comparatively delicate and mellow "new-make" spirit. Process water is sourced from springs at The Morans, nine miles from Glencadam, giving it one of the longest water supply lines of any distillery in Scotland.

Glencadam is one of those relatively rare Scottish distilleries to have an urban location, and it boasts one potentially noisy neighbor and another very quiet one. Brechin City FC's ground is close to the distillery, while the site also borders the municipal graveyard!

Changing regimes

Glencadam was established in 1825 by George Cooper, and after changing hands several times, the distillery was purchased by Gilmour Thomson &

Company Ltd in 1891. That Glasgow blending company owned it until 1954, when it was acquired by Canadian distillers Hiram Walker & Sons (Scotland) Ltd, which undertook a major reconstruction program five years later. Through a series of takeovers, Glencadam came into the possession of Allied Lyons in 1987, with Allied Lyons later becoming Allied Domecq.

Under Allied Domecq and previous ownership regimes, Glencadam had been confined to a blending roll, but in 2005 Angus Dundee offered the first generally available bottling of Glencadam, namely a 15-year-old. Today, that has been joined by Origin 1825; Reserva Andalucia; American Oak; and 10-, 13-, 15-, 18-, 21-, and 25-year-old expressions.

Glencadam 15-Year-Old

TASTING NOTES

Glencadam 10-Year-Old
Single malt, 40% ABV
A delicate, floral nose with soft fruit, vanilla, and a slightly nutty note. Citrus fruit, malt, and spicy oak on the smooth palate. The finish is relatively long and fruity.

Glencadam 15-Year-Old
Single malt, 46% ABV
Spicy, with berries and malt on the nose, while the palate features more berries, a hint of salt, vanilla, and a closing note of spicy oak.

Glencadam 21-Year-Old, The Exceptional
Single malt, 46% ABV
The nose is floral, with citrus fruit notes, principally Jaffa oranges. The palate is elegant, with more orange and contrasting black pepper and oak. The finish is lengthy and drying.

GLEN ORD

OWNER Diageo plc

FOUNDED 1838

WEBSITE www.malts.com

Now little known in the UK and mainland Europe, Glen Ord has become something of a cult single malt in the Far East and especially Taiwan, thanks to reformulation and rebranding as The Singleton of Glen Ord in 2006. The Singleton name, first used in relation to Auchroisk Distillery during the 1980s, is now applied to Diageo's Glen Ord for markets in the Far East, and to Glendullan for the US.

Glen Ord distillery is located in fertile farmland to the west of Inverness and dates back to 1838, when it was established by Thomas Mackenzie. Through a number of owners, Glen Ord came into the possession of John Dewar & Sons Ltd in 1923, and when Dewar's joined the Distillers Company Ltd (DCL) two years later, the distillery was one of the assets transferred to DCL's Scottish Malt Distillers subsidiary.

Spirit of the Sixties

Along with many other DCL malt distilleries, Glen Ord was virtually rebuilt during the 1960s, when the stills were increased from two to six. There are now 14 stills, located in two stillhouses, giving the distillery an annual capacity of almost 3.2 million gallons (12 million liters). Glen Ord is an important

component of the Johnnie Walker family of blends and is brand home for the Singleton range of whiskies. From a blending perspective, the distillery produces spirit that is green, grassy, fruity, waxy, and oily in character. The stills are run slowly but very hot in order to capture pure, intense, grassy spirit.

TASTING NOTES

The Singleton of Glen Ord 12-Year-Old
Single malt, 40% ABV
Sherry, marzipan, plums, and peaches on the inviting nose, while the palate offers more sherry, malt, hazelnuts, and soft fruit, closing with gentle tannic oak.

The Singleton of Glen Ord 15-Year-Old
Single malt, 40% ABV
The nose is malty, with zesty fruit, nutmeg, and fresh leather. Figs, malt, and cinnamon on the palate, with citrus fruit and subtle, spicy smoke in the finish.

The Singleton of Glen Ord 18-Year-Old
Single malt, 40% ABV
Stewed fruits, malt, and ginger on the nose, while the palate yields pineapple, peaches, figs, and cinnamon, with a hint of menthol in the lengthy finish.

The Singleton of Glen Ord 15-Year-Old

The Singleton of Glen Ord 18-Year-Old

LOCH LOMOND

OWNER Loch Lomond Group

FOUNDED 1965

WEBSITE www.lochlomonddistillery.com

Despite the romance associated with the Loch Lomond name, the eponymous distillery is very much a no-nonsense whisky-making facility tucked away on an industrial estate at Alexandria, about five miles from the western shore of the famous loch itself.

Converted from a dye works during the mid-1960s, the distillery is now owned by the Loch Lomond Group, which also operates the Glen Scotia distillery in Campbeltown. Loch Lomond is rare among Scottish distilleries in producing both malt and grain spirit, with the latter stillhouse being commissioned in 1994.

The distillation regime is remarkably diverse and complex, as in addition to a pair of traditionally designed copper pot stills, Loch Lomond is also equipped with four stills with rectifying heads, which can be used to produce different styles of spirits by replicating varying lengths of still neck. There is also a Coffey still that has been used to produce Rhosdhu malt whisky, thereby causing category-related confusion within the ranks of the Scotch Whisky Association.

Eight distinct styles of single malt are produced at the Loch Lomond distillery, ranging from heavily peated through Speyside and Highland styles to a more Lowland-like spirit. The permanent range comprises the no age statement Loch Lomond Classic and Loch Lomond Original, along with 12- and 18-year-olds, plus Inchmurrin 12-year-old and Inchmoan 18-year-old.

The distillery also offers four grain whiskies, namely Single Grain, Single Grain Peated, Distiller's Choice, and Cooper's Choice. The year 2023 saw the release of Loch Lomond's oldest bottling to date, in the shape of a 50-year-old.

TASTING NOTES

Loch Lomond Classic
Single malt, 40% ABV
Feints on the slightly smoky nose, which sweetens into a porridge-like aroma. Medium-bodied, grassy, nutty, with unripe bananas. The finish is sweet, with raisins, bread, and butter pudding and oak.

Inchmurrin 12-Year-Old
Single malt, 46% ABV
Cereal, herbs, and floral notes on the relatively full nose. Pine nuts, honey, spice, and freshly planed wood on the palate, while the finish is quite short and spicy.

Loch Lomond 18-Year-Old
Single malt, 46% ABV
Soft spice on the nose, with a hint of sweet smoke and vanilla and ripe peaches. Citrus fruit, almonds, and cocoa on the palate, with coffee, allspice, and gentle peat smoke in the finish.

Loch Lomond distillery lies to the south of the popular loch, which is justifiably renowned for its beauty.

Inchmurrin 12-Year-Old

ROYAL BRACKLA

OWNER John Dewar & Sons Ltd (Bacardi Ltd)

FOUNDED 1812

WEBSITE www.royalbrackla.com

An identity as one of only two distilleries entitled to carry the "Royal" prefix might seem to offer huge promotional opportunities, but sadly for Brackla, it has been one of the unsung backroom boys of the Scotch whisky world for a long time. Now part of Bacardi's John Dewar portfolio, Brackla's attractive whisky is starting to receive more attention, but inevitably the bulk of the output will always be destined for the blending vats to satisfy demand for Dewar's "White Label," its bestseller in the US.

Fit for a king

Just three distilleries were ever given permission to claim royal association in their title: the now demolished Glenury Royal in Stonehaven, Diageo's Royal Lochnagar, and Brackla, the first of the trio to be granted a Royal Warrant, with King William IV bestowing the honor in 1834 for the brand named "The King's Own Whisky." Brackla had been founded more than two decades before gaining official royal approval and was the creation of Captain William Fraser, who at times seems to have fought a losing battle against the many illicit distillers located in the area south of the coastal town of Nairn.

The distillery today largely dates from a major reconstruction program undertaken by Distillers Company Ltd in 1966, and four years later, the number of stills was doubled from two to four. Brackla was one of many DCL distilleries to fall victim to the cull of the 1980s, closing in 1985, but unlike fellow casualties of that year, it reopened in 1991. DCL's successor company United Distillers & Vintners invested in a $3.3 million (£2 million) upgrade in 1997, but a year later it was sold to Bacardi.

The current core range was introduced in 2021 and comprises a 12-year-old, an 18-year-old with a Palo Cortado finish, and a 20-year-old finished in Palo Cortado, oloroso, and PX sherry casks. In 2023, the oldest bottling released by the distillery hit the shelves. It was a 45-year-old, finished in a single first-fill oloroso sherry cask, which yielded just 172 bottles.

TASTING NOTES

Royal Brackla 12-Year-Old
Single malt, 46% ABV
Toffee apples, ginger, figs, and a whiff of cloves on the nose, leading into a palate of butterscotch, sherry, milk chocolate, honey, and vanilla, with lingering sweet sherry in the finish.

Royal Brackla 18-Year-Old
Single malt, 46% ABV
The nose offers malt, toasted almonds, and pine, while pineapple, raisins, dark chocolate, and spicy orchard fruits appear on the palate, closing with soft oak tannins.

Royal Brackla 20-Year-Old
Single malt, 46% ABV
The nose features orange, honey, red berry fruits, vanilla, and wood spice, while flavors of tropical fruit, malt, cinnamon, and an herbal note develop on the palate, which finishes with sherry and black pepper.

Royal Brackla 12-Year-Old

Royal Brackla 18-Year-Old

ROYAL LOCHNAGAR

OWNER Diageo plc

FOUNDED 1823

WEBSITE www.malts.com

Lochnagar distillery was established south of the Dee River in 1845 by John Begg. It was built on the opposite side of the river to a distillery that had been created by James Robertson of Crathie in 1826 and was destroyed by fire in 1841, though that whisky-making operation was rebuilt the following year and remained in production until 1860. Following a visit by Queen Victoria, Prince Albert, and family while staying at their neighboring estate of Balmoral, John Begg received a Royal Warrant of Appointment as a supplier to the Queen, enabling him to style his distillery Royal Lochnagar.

Changing times

The plant was substantially rebuilt in 1906 and a decade later passed out of the Begg family, being acquired by John Dewar & Sons Ltd. When Dewar's became part of the Distillers Company Ltd in 1925, Lochnagar entered the DCL fold. Another major program of refurbishment and reconstruction took place in 1963, when the tun room was enlarged, the stillhouse altered, and a mechanical stoking system for the pair of stills was installed.

Remarkably, until that time, a steam engine and waterwheels had powered the distillery plant, but these were replaced by electrical equipment. In 1987, the old farm steading was converted into a visitor center, while 11 years later, a shop was developed in the center, providing a showcase for the whole Diageo Malts portfolio.

Royal Lochnagar is the smallest of Diageo's 28 malt distilleries and operates a cast-iron mash tun, complete with rakes, a pair of wooden washbacks, and cast-iron worm tubs to condense the spirit. In 2023, a special bottling of Royal Lochnagar was released to celebrate the coronation of King Charles III.

Much of the "make" of Lochnagar is destined for the more exclusive Johnnie Walker bottlings, while the principal single malt is a 12-year-old, along with Selected Reserve, which contains a vatting of whiskies around 20 years of age. A 16-year-old variant, matured in a combination of European oak refill and American oak casks, appeared in the 2021 lineup of Diageo's Special Releases program.

Royal Lochnagar 12-Year-Old

TASTING NOTES

Royal Lochnagar 12-Year-Old
Single malt, 43% ABV
Sherry, malt, vanilla, coffee, and oak on the aromatic nose, along with a wisp of smoke. Lots of spicy malt, grapes, molasses, and later oak on the palate. Drying oak and peat feature in the finish.

Royal Lochnagar Selected Reserve
Single malt, 43% ABV
Malt, sherry, green apples, and peat on the rich nose. The richness carries over onto the palate, which features flavors of fruit cake, ginger, malt, and fudge. The elegant finish showcases toffee and smoke.

Royal Lochnagar 16-Year-Old (**Diageo 2021 Special Releases**)
Single malt, 57.5% ABV
The nose is floral, mildly herbal, with ripe apples, oranges, and vanilla, while the palate features almonds, grapefruit, and peaches, closing with burnt caramel and oak.

TEANINICH

OWNER Diageo plc

FOUNDED 1817

WEBSITE www.malts.com

This distillery may be seen as the less glamorous relation of nearby Dalmore—the latter visually a very traditional Scottish distillery located on the shores of a firth, with its "make" acknowledged as one of the great single malts of the world, certainly in terms of its ultra-exclusive bottlings with price tags to match.

By contrast, only the most dedicated whisky fans have tasted Teaninich single malt, and the distillery itself is a relatively characterless early-1970s structure located on an industrial estate. In fact, of the two, Teaninich has greater provenance, being established in 1817, more than two decades before Dalmore began. Established by Captain Hugh Munro, Teaninich has belonged to Distillers Company Ltd and its successors since 1933. After an additional pair of stills was installed in 1962, a new production area was built in 1970, fitted with six more stills and known as "Side A." Both sides were shut down in the 1980s, but Side A reopened in 1991.

Green and oily spirit

At Teaninich, the aim is to produce spirit with a green and oily profile for blending purposes, adding to the textured mouthfeel of many Johnnie Walker expressions, and this is facilitated by the presence of a mash filter, rather than the usual mash tun. Although commonly used in the brewing industry, Teaninich is one of very few Scotch whisky distilleries operating such a filter. It allows the processing of grains other than malted barley, which mash tuns tend to find problematical. In recent times, Teaninich has produced rye spirit for use by Diageo's blenders, as well as up to 2.7 million gallons (10.2 million liters) of malt spirit per year.

Teaninich 10-Year-Old

TASTING NOTES

Teaninich 10-Year-Old
Single malt, 43% ABV
Fresh and grassy on the initial nose, with developing pineapple and spicy vanilla. Cereal notes on the palate, nutty and spicy, slightly herbal, and a suggestion of coffee. Drying in the finish, with cocoa powder and black pepper.

Teaninich 17-Year-Old
Single malt, 55.9% ABV
Citrus fruit, honey, nutmeg, and toffee apples on the nose. The palate yields lemon, vanilla, cinnamon, and poached pears, closing with a hint of white pepper, enduring fruitiness and oak.

Teaninich 17-Year-Old

TOMATIN

OWNER Tomatin Distillery Company Ltd

FOUNDED 1897

WEBSITE www.tomatin.com

Just as you should never judge a book by its cover, so you should never judge a single malt by the appearance of its distillery. Some very average whiskies are made in picture-postcard distilleries,

while a number of extremely fine malts are turned out from facilities that bear more than a passing resemblance to Soviet-era tractor factories.

While not wishing to compare Tomatin with the latter, the most fervent admirers of this distillery, set amid the bleakly beautiful moorland scenery of the Monadhliath Mountains, will surely concede that it is less than architecturally appealing.

Japanese giant

The three decades following World War II can be blamed for the rather industrial appearance of Tomatin. Expansion began in 1956, and by 1974, no fewer than 23 stills were in place, theoretically able to produce about 3.2 million gallons (12 million liters) of spirit per year, making it by far the largest distillery in Scotland in terms of capacity. However, Tomatin entered receivership in 1985, becoming the first Scottish distillery to be wholly owned by Japanese interests a year later.

Today, Tomatin's focus is very much on single malts, with a core range of Legacy, 12-, 18-, 30-, and 36-year-old expressions, plus a NAS cask strength bottling and a port cask-finished 15-year-old. Peated Tomatin malts have been offered since 2013 and are marketed under the Cù Bòcan banner.

Tomatin 12-Year-Old

TASTING NOTES

Tomatin 12-Year-Old
Single malt, matured first-fill bourbon barrels, refill American oak casks, and Spanish sherry butts, married in Spanish sherry butts prior to bottling, 40% ABV
Barley, spice, oak, and floral notes on the nose, along with a hint of peat. Toffee apples, cereal, malt, spice, and herbs on the reasonably full and nutty palate. Sweet fruitiness in the medium-length, oily finish.

Tomatin 30-Year-Old
Single malt, matured ex-bourbon casks, finished Spanish oloroso sherry casks, non-chill-filtered, 49.3% ABV
A sophisticated nose with apricots, raisins, and spicy leather notes. Big and very fruity on the palate, with oranges and delicate spice. The finish dries through fruit and bubble gum notes to acceptable oakiness.

Tomatin Cù Bòcan
Single malt, 40% ABV
Sweet, earthy smoke on the nose, with lemon and almonds. The palate offers smoky malt, cinnamon, and cloves, closing with peat and oak.

Tomatin Cù Bòcan

TULLIBARDINE

OWNER Terroir Distillers

FOUNDED 1949

WEBSITE www.tullibardine.com

The present distillery, built on the site of an ancient brewery, only dates from 1949, but whisky-making had previously been conducted under the Tullibardine name in this area of Perthshire during the late 18th and early 19th centuries.

Today's Tullibardine distillery was designed by William Delmé-Evans—who went on to create the Isle of Jura and Glenallachie distilleries—and it was operated by Brodie Hepburn Ltd from 1953 until 1971, when that Glasgow whisky-broking firm was taken over by Invergordon Distillers Ltd.

Tullibardine's capacity was subsequently increased by the installation of a second pair of stills in 1973, and when Invergordon was acquired by Whyte &

Mackay Distillers Ltd in 1993, the Perthshire plant was considered surplus to requirements, closing the following year.

Happily, for Tullibardine, however, a business consortium bought the site from Whyte & Mackay Ltd for $675,000 (£1.1 million) in 2003. Tullibardine became well known for releasing an apparently ever-widening range of cask-finished whiskies, while 2009 saw the appearance of the NAS Aged Oak expression.

A French Scotch whisky

After operating in the hands of a consortium of businessmen from 2003, Tullibardine distillery was purchased in 2011 by the third-generation family-owned French company Maison Michel Picard, based at the Château de Chassagne-Montrachet in the Côte de Beaune, Burgundy.

Maison Michel Picard was an existing customer for the distillery's "new-make" spirit, which it used for blending, and this continues to be the case, although a great deal of effort has been put into developing Tullibardine as a high-quality single malt brand. A bottling hall, additional warehousing, and even a cooperage were created at the distillery, which sits beside the busy A9 road, linking the Central Belt of Scotland with the Highlands.

The core Tullibardine range comprises NAS Sovereign, 225 Sauternes Finish, 228 Burgundy Finish, 500 Sherry Finish, and 15- and 18-year-old expressions. The Marquess Collection embraces a dozen limited-edition bottlings, with the 2023 addition being The Murray Triple Port, finished in white, tawny, and ruby port casks.

The stillhouse at Tullibardine distillery includes four copper pot stills.

Tullibardine 225 Sauternes Cask Finish

TASTING NOTES

Tullibardine 225 Sauternes Cask Finish
Single malt, 43% ABV
Cocoa, vanilla, toffee, and cinnamon on the nose, while the palate yields orange marmalade, coffee, and milk chocolate, finishing with allspice and black pepper.

Tullibardine 228 Burgundy Cask Finish
Single malt, 43% ABV
The nose offers malt, barley, and red berry fruits. Vanilla, hazelnuts, and malt on the palate, with a spicy jam finish.

Tullibardine 500 Sherry Cask Finish
Single cask, 43% ABV
Aromas of allspice, toffee apple, fall fruits, and demerara sugar, leading into flavors of cinnamon, honey, dates, and orange peel. The finish is long, full, and fruity.

ARBIKIE

OWNER The Stirling family

FOUNDED 2015

WEBSITE www.arbikie.com

As a single estate distillery, all ingredients are cultivated on the farm, near Arbroath in Angus, while distilling takes place in a pair of stills, equipped with a rectification column. Although single malt whisky is being distilled, its launch is still some time away. Arbikie has become known for resurrecting Scotch rye whisky. The first release came in 2018 under the 1794 Highland Rye Scotch label, and subsequent bottlings have included a Jamaican rum barrel finish.

TASTING NOTE

Arbikie 1794 Highland Rye (2022 Release)
Grain whisky, matured in new charred American oak barrels, 48% ABV
The nose offers newly mowed grass, nutmeg, and white pepper, while flavors of walnuts, cinnamon, black tea, and black pepper arrive on the oily palate.

ARDNAMURCHAN

OWNER Adelphi Distillery Ltd

FOUNDED 2014

WEBSITE www.adelphidistillery.com

Ardnamurchan distillery is located at Glenbeg, on the Ardnamurchan peninsula in Argyllshire, and is owned by independent whisky bottlers Adelphi Distillery Ltd. It is powered by hydro-electricity and a biomass boiler, which burns local harvested wood chips. Its single pair of stills turn out both peated and unpeated (30–35ppm) spirit. The distillery was fired up in 2014, and two years' later, the first spirit was bottled under the AD name. In late 2020, a 6-year-old expression of single malt was released, and further bottlings have followed, including AD Limited Edition Cask Strength and a 6-year-old unpeated expression finished in Champagne casks.

TASTING NOTE

Ardnamurchan AD/10.21:06
Single malt, 46.8% ABV
The nose offers fragrant peat smoke, toffee, and ripe peaches, while flavors of ginger, honey, orange rind, and more intense peat develop on the palate, closing with bonfire embers, brine, dried fruit, and dark chocolate.

Ardnamurchan
AD/10.21:06

DORNOCH

Dornoch Cask 54

OWNER Thompson Bros Distillers

FOUNDED 2016

WEBSITE www.thompsonbrosdistillers.com

Dornoch was developed by brothers Philip and Simon Thompson in a tiny former private fire station at Dornoch Castle Hotel in Sutherland. The aim was to produce whisky with character, using heritage barley varieties and brewer's yeast. Fermentations in the six wooden washbacks may last up to 10 days. The first casks of whisky were filled in 2017, and the initial bottling, in 2020, was from a first-fill oloroso sherry butt. More single cask bottlings have followed.

TASTING NOTE

Dornoch Cask 54
Single malt, 55.5% ABV
The nose is full and floral, with ginger, canned peaches, toffee, and marshmallows. The voluptuous palate features brown sugar, caramel, light citrus fruits, and milk chocolate, with lingering nutty toffee.

GLEN WYVIS

OWNER GlenWyvis Distillery Ltd

FOUNDED 2017

WEBSITE www.glenwyvis.com

The distillery name commemorates two "lost" local distilleries, namely Glenskiach and Ben Wyvis, and is Scotland's first community-owned distillery, operating entirely off-grid. It is located on a hillside near the town of Dornoch, and the first public release of its whisky came in 2021. A gin still is in situ along with a pair of Forsyth-made pot stills.

TASTING NOTE

Glenwyvis 2019 Batch 01/19
Single malt, aged in red wine, Moscatel, and Marsala casks, 46.5% ABV
Red grapes, orange blossom, and honey on the nose, with malt, apple pie, and wood spice on the palate, which closes with chocolate and oak.

STRATHEARN

OWNER Douglas Laing & Co

FOUNDED 2013

WEBSITE www.stratheardistillery.com

The small distillery was established by Tony Reeman-Clark. Since 2019, it has been owned by Glasgow-based Douglas Laing & Co, who have installed extra equipment and doubled capacity. In 2024, the Inaugural Release appeared, matured in a mix of ex-bourbon, sherry, and virgin oak casks and distilled with the distillery's signature Maris Otter malt.

TASTING NOTE

Strathearn Inaugural Release
Single malt, natural color, and non-chill-filtered, 50% ABV
The nose has soft caramel, new leather, porridge oats, and spicy orchard fruits, while the palate is voluptuous, with malt, honey, orange marmalade, sultanas, and chili, leading into dark chocolate, black pepper, and lingering dried fruits.

Strathearn
Inaugural Release

NC'NEAN

OWNER Nc'Nean Distillery Ltd

FOUNDED 2017

WEBSITE www.ncnean.com

Nc'nean, located within the Drimnin Estate on the remote Morven peninsula in the West Highlands, is the brainchild of Annabel Thomas and has been created with optimum sustainability in mind. Two different spirit types are produced from organic Scottish barley, one for relatively youthful drinking and the second for longer aging.

TASTING NOTE

Nc'Nean Organic
Single malt, 46% ABV
Spicy oak, citrus fruits, honey, and vanilla on the nose. The palate yields tropical fruit, cereal, vanilla, and milk chocolate, closing with oak and black pepper.

WOLFBURN

OWNER Aurora Brewing Ltd

FOUNDED 2013

WEBSITE www.wolfburn.com

Wolfburn is located on Thurso Business Park. While most Wolfburn spirit is unpeated, quantities of lightly peated whisky have been produced since 2014. Wolfburn's first release—named Northland—came in 2016, and 2017 saw the addition of a peated whisky, named Morvern, to the lineup, followed by the ex-bourbon barrel-matured Langskip in 2018.

TASTING NOTE

Wolfburn Northland
Single malt, 46% ABV
The nose offers cereal, orchard fruits, malt, and discreet wood smoke, while honey, licorice, and a hint of brine appear on the palate, closing with honey, black pepper, and oak.

Wolfburn Northland

ISLAY & THE ISLANDS

REGIONAL STYLES

Single malts from Islay are often categorized as peaty and medicinal, but Bruichladdich and Bunnahabhain have long made whiskies with low peating levels. Each island distillery has a distinctive style, from the smoky, heathery, sherried malt of Highland Park to the fruity, floral offerings of Arran.

AUTHOR'S CHOICE

BOWMORE Located at the heart of Islay and dating back to the 18th century, Bowmore still operates floor maltings and produces a range of medium-peated single malts that are highly respected all over the world. HIGHLAND PARK Another historic distillery, also malting on site, using sherry casks for single malt maturation and with a globally revered portfolio of expressions.

REGIONAL EVENTS

Islay boasts an extremely well-attended annual late-spring festival that goes by the name of Feis Islay, also known as the Islay Festival of Malt and Music (www.feisile.co.uk). All of Islay's working distilleries participate, plus neighboring Jura, with each having a day to showcase their operations. The Hebridean Whisky Festival is now staged each September (www.hebrideanwhisky.com). There are also many other events and attractions during festival week, with tours of Diageo's Port Ellen Maltings, not normally open to the public, and visits to Islay Spirits' rum distillery (www.islayrum.com).

The Highlands may be geographically the largest region for single malt whisky production, but Islay and the Islands are the most disparate in terms of distillery locations. Whisky is distilled on no fewer than seven Scottish islands, ranging from Arran in the southwest via Islay, Jura, Mull, Skye, and Lewis to Orkney, north of the mainland. The Hebridean Isles share a Gaelic heritage and culture, reflected in the place names and sometimes still in the speech of the people who live there. These are beautiful and often rugged places. In contrast to the Hebrides, Orkney's heritage is largely derived from Scandinavia, with place names reflecting the strong Norse influences that have shaped the story of this austere yet compelling group of islands.

The economies of relatively small island communities always have a sense of vulnerability about them, and the presence of distilleries on so many Scottish islands provides welcome regular and relatively well-paid employment, as well as bringing in "whisky tourists" eager to visit the places where their favorite drams are made. Island distilleries such as Tobermory on Mull, Talisker on Skye, and Highland Park on Orkney are all long-established ventures, rooted in their local communities, while the likes of Ardnahoe, Harris, Isle of Raasay, Lagg, and Torabhaig are relative newcomers. Potential new distilleries have been mooted for Barra and Shetland, but neither has come to fruition. In terms of new-build distilleries, choosing an island location adds significantly to production and transportation costs, making survival during those early years even more difficult. Of all island distilleries, those on Islay have the greatest collective cachet. The "whisky island" has 10 productive distilleries, including the revived Port Ellen, but that number is set to grow to 13 before too long. During recent decades, the peaty, medicinal style widely associated with Islay single malts has developed an international cult following. Islay's distilleries struggle to meet demand, and unless the world suddenly falls out of love with the Islay whisky character, which seems unlikely, the economic future of Islay's distilleries looks very promising.

Located in the island's tiny "capital," Isle of Jura malt is notably less peated than its Islay neighbors'.

GETTING AROUND

Be prepared for lengthy drives and ferry trips, or take the option of a flight where available. Edinburgh and Glasgow airports serve many Scottish islands, with Glasgow being the mainland terminus for flights to Islay. Ferries to the Western Isles are operated by Caledonian Macbrayne (*www.calmac.co.uk*) and those to Orkney are run by NorthLink Ferries (*www.northlinkferries.co.uk*). The Isle of Skye is now linked to the mainland by bridge. There is now a dedicated Hebridean Whisky Trail (www. hebrideanwhisky.com), which embraces Jura, Harris, Isle of Raasay, Talisker, and Torabhaig, and the website offers helpful itinerary options.

Westray
Rousay Eday Sanday
Stronsay
Orkney
Islands   Kirkwall
Scapa
Hoy   **Highland Park**
South
Ronaldsay
Pentland Firth
Stroma

Cape Wrath
Thurso   John o'Groats
Wick

North Sea

Port of Ness
Isle of Lewis
Stornoway

OUTER HEBRIDES

The Minch

Ullapool
Helmsdale

Harris Tarbert
Isle of Harris

Lochmaddy
North Uist
Benbacula
South Uist
Lochboisdale

Isle of Skye
Portree
Isle of Raasay

Talisker
Kyle of Lochalsh

Inverness
Moray Firth

NORTH WEST HIGHLANDS

GRAMPIAN MOUNTAINS

Fort Augustus
Loch Ness

Canna
Rhum
Torabhaig
Mallaig
INNER HEBRIDES
Eigg
A830

Fort William

Coll

A82

Atlantic Ocean

Tiree

Tobermory
Isle of Mull
Oban
Fionnphort
Firth of Lorne
Colonsay
Jura

Port Askaig
Isle of Jura
Islay
Port Ellen

Mull of Kintyre

Kintyre

Lochranza
Arran
Lagg
Campbeltown

Loch Lomond
Greenock
Bute
Firth of Clyde
Ayr

ISLAY & THE ISLANDS

North Sea

SCOTLAND

Glasgow ○ ○ EDINBURGH

Scotland
Islay & The Islands
ENGLAND

ISLE OF ISLAY

Bunnahabhain
Sound of Islay
Ardnahoe
Ardnave
Caol Ila   *Jura*
Sanaigmore
Port Askaig

Loch Gorm
A846
Kilchoman
Islay
Bruichladdich
Bridgend
Bowmore
Port Charlotte
Beinn Bheigeir
491 m
(1,611 ft)
Ardtalla
Rhinns of Islay
Loch Indaal
Glenegedale
A846
Port Wemyss
Ardbeg
Lagavulin
Port
Ellen   **Laphroaig**
The Oa

0   3   6 miles
0   5   10 km

0   10   20   30 miles
0   10   20   30   40   50 km

ARDBEG

OWNER The Glenmorangie Company Ltd

FOUNDED 1794

WEBSITE www.ardbeg.com

Distilleries do come back from the dead, and sometimes the experience can make them even stronger when they come to life again; Ardbeg is living proof of that. Long regarded as something of a cult whisky, even before Islay single malts became fashionable, the heavily peated Ardbeg is now one of the most highly regarded whiskies in the world. Yet as recently as the mid-1990s, the future, both as a distillery and a single malt, was in doubt.

Ardbeg 10-Year-Old

A checkered history

The story begins in 1794, when a distillery was first recorded at Ardbeg, though the current plant was actually established by John MacDougall in 1815. It operated in private ownership until 1959, when Ardbeg Distillery Ltd was formed, then in 1973 Ardbeg was jointly purchased by Hiram Walker & Sons Ltd and the Distillers Company Ltd, with the former assuming full control in 1977.

However, when blended whisky was truly king, a little of the powerful, assertive Ardbeg malt went a long way, and with the Scotch whisky industry facing a glut of maturing spirit, Ardbeg was silent between 1982 and 1989, during which period it became part of Allied Distillers Ltd when Hiram Walker was taken over by that company in 1987. Ardbeg reopened two years later, but production was limited and Allied finally closed the distillery once again during 1996. The future looked less than rosy for the run-down plant, but in 1997, it was acquired by the Glenmorangie Company Ltd (now themselves part of LVMH), who invested over $16.4 million (£10 million) in the purchase and refurbishment.

Ardbeg in action

The year 2000 saw the introduction of the Ardbeg 10-year-old expression, which is now the principal core offering. Along with the 10-year-old, Ardbeg embarked on an imaginative release program, with many products being exclusively previewed by the Ardbeg Committee, an organization for aficionados of the brand, established in 2000.

In 2004, the distillery took what was then the relatively bold step of releasing a 6-year-old Ardbeg under the name Very Young Ardbeg. The aim of this, and subsequent Still Young and Almost There bottlings, was to illustrate the changes that took place as spirit distilled in one particular year (1997) matured and was intended to engage consumers in the ongoing process that led to the release of the new 10-year-old variant.

Peat-freak portfolio

In addition to the 10-year-old, the permanent portfolio includes the cask strength Uigeadail, named after one of the lochs supplying water to the distillery and introduced in 2003. Also, permanently available are Corryvreckan, An Oa, 5-year-old Wee Beastie and

Ardbeg Corryvreckan

Ardbeg visitor center and Old Kiln Café are located in the distillery's former maltings.

WHISKY TALES

Ardbeg in Space
In October 2011, a vial of new-make Ardbeg spirit was sent to the International Space Station in a cargo spacecraft as part of a study into how micro-gravity would affect the behavior of terpenes, the building blocks of flavor for many foods, wines, and spirits. Another vial of the same whisky was kept at the distillery for comparison. The Space Station vial returned to earth in 2015, and Dr. Bill Lumsden, Ardbeg's director of distilling and whisky creation, declared that "The space samples were noticeably different. When I nosed and tasted them, it became clear that much more of Ardbeg's smoky, phenolic character shone through—to reveal a different set of smoky flavors, which I have not encountered here on earth."

a 25-year-old. Corryvreckan takes its name from an infamous whirlpool close to Islay. It carries no age statement but principally comprises spirit distilled during the period 1998–2000, along with some younger Ardbeg. A proportion of the total has been matured in new French oak casks.

An Oa takes shape in Ardbeg's Gathering Vat, where, according to the distillery team, "We gather together whiskies from several cask types—including sweet Pedro Ximénez, spicy virgin charred oak, and intense ex-bourbon casks, among others—where they familiarize themselves with each other."

Ardbeg is known for its many limited-edition expressions, the most recent of which include Bizzarebq and Heavy Vapours. The former is matured in double-charred casks, toasted PX sherry casks and heavily charred Brasero casks, while the latter is produced with the spirit still purifier disconnected to create a heavier style of spirit.

Ardbeg expands

Ardbeg's increasing popularity across many international markets led to a major expansion of the distillery during 2019 to 2022. This involved building a new stillhouse, fitted with two pairs of stills, while fermentation now takes place in 12 Oregon pine washbacks. As a result, capacity has increased from 300,000 gallons (1.2 million liters) per annum to 634,000 gallons (2.4 million liters).

Ardbeg is extremely popular with visitors to Islay, and an excellent café and retail space have been created in one of the former malting kilns.

TASTING NOTES

Ardbeg 10-Year-Old
Single malt, non-chill-filtered, 46% ABV
Sweet on the nose, with soft peat, carbolic soap, and smoked fish. Intense yet delicate palate, with burning peats, dried fruit, malt, and licorice. Long, smoky finish.

Ardbeg Uigeadail
Single malt, cask strength, matured ex-bourbon barrels and ex-oloroso sherry butts, non-chill-filtered, 54.2% ABV
Peat, coffee, barley, raisins, sherry, and asphalt on the complex nose; citrus fruits, malt, peat, treacle, and honey on the substantial palate. Caramel and peat in the finish.

Ardbeg Corryvreckan
Single malt, 57.1% ABV
Earthy on the nose, with smoked haddock, citrus fruit, ginger, and iodine. The palate is viscous and offers spicy, nutty flavors, charcuterie, licorice, and stewed fruits, closing with black pepper and peat.

BOWMORE

Black Bowmore 42-Year-Old

OWNER Morrison Bowmore Ltd (Suntory Global Spirits)

FOUNDED 1779

WEBSITE www.bowmore.com

Bowmore is not only the oldest licensed distillery on the island of Islay but one of the oldest surviving distilleries in Scotland. Built by farmer and distiller David Simson, the distillery passed through various hands before coming into the possession of whisky brokers Stanley P. Morrison Ltd in 1963. During 1989, Suntory Ltd, Japan's largest distiller, took a 35 percent share in what was by then known as Morrison Bowmore Ltd, and in 1994, Suntory assumed full ownership of Bowmore distillery, along with Auchentoshan and Glengarioch.

Bowmore is notable for being one of very few distilleries still making malt "in house," and about 40 percent of the plant's requirements are produced on its three malting floors, with the remainder being sourced from the mainland and peated to the same level of 25ppm. This places Bowmore in the middle ground of Islay single malts in terms of peating, though it is sometimes described as the smokiest of all the Islays.

At Bowmore, tradition blends with innovation, and a significant amount of time, energy, and money have been plowed into making the distillery more environmentally friendly. A process was developed to macerate and bake peat into "caff" for burning in the floor maltings, which generates increased peat flavor in the malting barley yet requires up to 75 percent less peat than was previously the case. In 1990, a warehouse was donated to the local community to create an indoor swimming pool, which is heated by hot water from the stillhouse condensers.

On-site maturation

Maturation is key to creating fine whiskies, and in particular, the type and quality of casks used and the location in which they are stored are vitally important when their contents are to be bottled as single malt. Bowmore currently fills around 20 percent of its output into ex-sherry casks, and the remainder into former bourbon casks, with the entire make now being destined for single malt bottling rather than blending. Some of the fresh spirit is transported to the

Bowmore 12-Year-Old

Bowmore stands on the shores of Loch Indaal, with the salty sea breeze blowing right into its warehouses.

WHISKY TALES
Black Bowmore
There are certain expressions of single malt whisky that cause a frisson of excitement among collectors and connoisseurs just at the mention of their names. One such expression is "Black Bowmore." The initial release of this 1964 spirit, filled into oloroso sherry casks, took place in 1993, and the notably dark color imparted during maturation led to the expression's name. It was soon considered a classic and bottles have been known to change hands for five-figure sums, having initially retailed for $150 (£100) each. In 2007, "Black Bowmore'" appeared again, with five casks from the same batch yielding 804 bottles of what was now 42-year-old single malt. A "final batch" appeared in 2016, though this was followed four years later by Bowmore D5 1964 (see left).

mainland, but the majority is matured on site. There is a contention that the place of maturation significantly affects the character of the spirit by the time it comes to be bottled.

Heavy sea air and a lack of pollution are put forward as reasons why the spirit displays different characteristics if aged on the island, rather than the Central Belt of the Scottish mainland, for example. Distillery workers will point out that casks on Islay are held together with hoops made of galvanized steel, because those made from mild steel rusted away due to the prevailing salt air.

Number 1 warehouse was the first warehouse to be built when the Bowmore distillery was established. It is partly below sea level, with very few temperature variations. It is mainly used to house sherry butts and is widely considered to be the optimum type of whisky warehouse, giving damp salt air evaporation, with lower maturation but less spirit loss than in large, modern racked or palletized warehouses

Rising sales
Sales of Bowmore have increased significantly since the entire range was revamped back in 2007, and in percentage terms, the brand has caught up with peaty Islay competitors, such as Ardbeg, which it outsold in 2022, claiming the second-place spot for bestselling Islay single malts behind Laphroaig.

Bowmore has offered many special releases over the years, and the current core range comprises 12-, 15-, 18-, and 25-year-old expressions, along with

limited quantities of 30- and 40-year-olds. For those keen on exceptionally old vintages, the distillery offers a 1965 52-year-old bottling.

Recent limited releases include the Timeless Collection—complete with particularly fine presentation that includes a working hourglass. Variants of 27- and 31-year-old appeared in 2021, followed by a 29-year-old bottling in 2023.

Eager to be associated with other luxury brands, Bowmore has partnered with prestige car maker Aston Martin to offer several extremely rare bottlings. These include Bowmore DB5 1964—a "Black Bowmore," described as "A striking concept which brings together an iconic whisky and a legendary car in a bottle of equal parts, featuring exceptional single malt and a genuine Aston Martin DB5 piston."

TASTING NOTES

Bowmore 12-Year-Old
Single malt, 40% ABV
An enticing nose of lemon and gentle brine leads into a smoky, citric palate with notes of cocoa and hard candy appearing in the lengthy, complex finish.

Bowmore 18-Year-Old
Single malt, 43% ABV
Soft sherry, ginger, hard candy, malt, and subtle peat on the nose. Stewed fruit, sherry, and walnuts on the rich palate, closing with lingering peat.

Black Bowmore 42-Year-Old
Single malt, cask strength, from five oloroso sherry casks, 804 bottles, non-chill-filtered, 40.5% ABV
Ginger, cinnamon, toffee, figs, and plain chocolate on the rich nose. The palate is notably full, with more toffee and chocolate notes, plus worn leather, coffee, and wood smoke. The finish is very long and satisfying.

BRUICHLADDICH

OWNER Rémy Cointreau

FOUNDED 1881

WEBSITE www.bruichladdich.com

Bruichladdich distillery stands on the western shores of Loch Indaal and was designed by 23-year-old engineer Robert Harvey. It was constructed for the Glasgow-based Harvey distillers. Unlike many other Islay distilleries, Bruichladdich was a modern, "courtyard" distillery, made with a new product called concrete, instead of being an extension of an existing agricultural enterprise, and it was designed with tall, narrow-necked stills to produce a relatively pure, elegant style of spirit.

Decline and revival

The Harveys operated Bruichladdich until it fell silent in 1929, a victim of the interwar Depression along with the nearby Port Charlotte distillery. Bruichladdich, however, was revived in 1936, then sold by the Harveys in 1938 to Ben Nevis distillery owner Joseph Hobbs and his associates. It was ultimately bought in 1968 by Invergordon Distillers Ltd, who doubled the stills from two to four.

After Whyte & Mackay Ltd won a fierce takeover battle for Invergordon, Bruichladdich was closed as surplus to requirements. The distillery remained almost entirely silent from 1993 to December 2000, when a private company headed by Mark Reynier of independent bottler Murray McDavid bought it at a cost of $9.9 million (£6.5 million). Reynier and his team, including veteran Islay distiller Jim McEwan and distillery manager Duncan McGillivray, inherited what was effectively an unreconstituted Victorian operation, with an open-topped, cast-iron mash tun and wooden washbacks, while one of the two wash stills in situ, now renovated, dates from the distillery's founding and is the oldest in Scotland.

A different approach

While distilling their own spirit, the company released a sometimes bewildering variety of often limited editions from existing stocks, and when distillation resumed in May 2001, the first batch of spirit produced was heavily peated, to around 40ppm. This variant was christened Port Charlotte and was

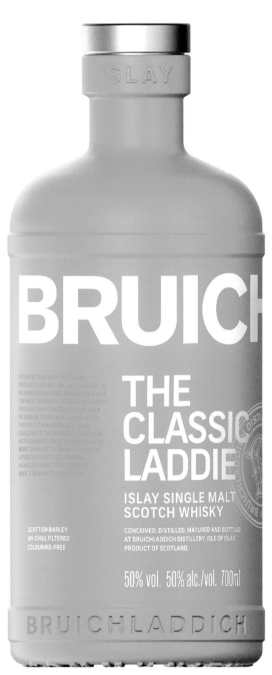

Bruichladdich The Classic Laddie

Bruichladdich
Port Charlotte 10-Year-Old

released as a limited edition on an annual basis, now part of the core range. Bruichladdich also produces Octomore spirit, described as "the most heavily peated whisky in the world," with phenolic levels of at least 80ppm.

In 2003, Islay's only bottling line was installed at the distillery, which means that some Bruichladdich

spirit is made with Islay-grown barley and is also bottled on the island. Along with the two pairs of conventional pot stills, the distillery now boasts the last fully functioning Lomond still in Scotland, rescued from Inverleven distillery at Dumbarton in 2004. "Ugly Betty," as the still was christened, now produces The Botanist gin.

New owners

In 2012, Bruichladdich was acquired by the French company Rémy Cointreau, which has continued to allow the distillery a great deal of independence, backed up by vital financial input. The use of Islay-grown barley pioneered by the Reynier regime remains key to the venture, and a Regeneration Project has been instigated.

According to Global Communications Brand Manager Amy Brownlee, "From just one farmer in 2004, Bruichladdich Distillery currently works with 20 local farming partners on Islay who grow over 50 percent of barley for total production. Giving whiskies total traceability, provenance, and the purest expression of terroir, it is also a way for the distillery to put value back into the community and support our farmers when it comes to looking for alternative, more sustainable farming practices." Organic barley and the ancient, low-yielding six-row landrace "bere" variety are also employed, while 2023 saw the release of Bruichladdich's first rye whisky.

The core range comprises The Classic Laddie, Port Charlotte 10-year-old, and Octomore Ten Aged Years, while recent annual releases include Bruichladdich Islay Barley 2014, Organic Barley 2012, and Bere Barley 2013.

WHISKY TALES

Under Surveillance
Bruichladdich is one of those distilleries just begging to be visited, due in part to its superb location on the shores of Loch Indaal. If you are unable to make the trip in person, the distillery website offers a range of webcams, so you can take a virtual tour and watch whisky making take place. On one occasion, the webcams were almost the distillery's undoing when it was discovered that the CIA in America was spying on the site via its webcams, having been convinced that the distillery equipment was so old it must be manufacturing some sort of chemical weapon.

Bruichladdich Octomore Ten Aged Years

TASTING NOTES

Bruichladdich The Classic Laddie
Single malt, 50% ABV
Floral, with barley sugar, lemon, orange, and honey on the nose, while subtle maritime flavors and red apples and cinnamon feature on the palate, which finishes with malt and vanilla toffee.

Bruichladdich Port Charlotte 10-Year-Old
Single malt, 50% ABV
Sea salt and ozone, wood smoke, and spicy orange on the nose. The palate yields iodine, more smoke, grilled meat, and sea salt, closing with fading tropical fruits and ashy peat.

Bruichladdich Octomore Ten Aged Years
Single malt, 56.3% ABV
Sweet tobacco smoke, vanilla, and orange on the slightly medicinal nose, leading into a palate of wood smoke, new leather, Brie, and dark berries. The lengthy finish features charcuterie, chili, and peat.

BUNNAHABHAIN

OWNER CVH Spirits

FOUNDED 1881

WEBSITE www.bunnahabhain.com

Bunnahabhain was established in the same year as fellow Islay distillery, Bruichladdich, with production commencing two years later in 1883. Although all of Islay's distilleries, with the exception of Bowmore, are isolated in location, Bunnahabhain takes remoteness to a whole new level, situated at the end of a long, unclassified road, just outside the northern ferry terminal of Port Askaig. Views across the Sound of Islay to neighboring Jura with its distinctive Paps are exquisite.

The distillery's spectacular site was chosen by founders William and James Greenlees and William Robertson for the availability of pure water and high-quality peat, along with its sheltered coastal location, which was important in the days when Islay's distilleries were served directly by sea.

It became part of Highland Distilleries Company Ltd in 1887 and remained in its control until 1999, when The Edrington Group took over. Edrington decided to concentrate its energies on a small number of high-profile single malt brands, such as The Macallan, and sold off Glengoyne and Bunnahabhain in 2003. Bunnahabhain was bought by Burn Stewart Distillers plc, along with the popular Black Bottle blended Scotch whisky brand.

Another change of ownership came in 2013, when Burn Stewart Distillers was bought by the South African Distell Group for $250 million (£160 million). Distell, in turn, was acquired by global brewing giant Heineken, and in 2023, the Scottish distilleries of Bunnahabhain, Deanston, and Tobermory came into the possession of CVH Spirits.

The power of the island

Bunnahabhain distillery is noted for the large size of its four stills, and because of their size, a great deal of copper contact occurs. Additionally, the stills are run very slowly, which allows for a significant degree of reflux. The heavy, oily compounds fall back into the stills instead of passing over into the condensers. This, along with lots of copper contact, makes for a gentle style of sweet, flavorful spirit.

Bunnahabhain 12-Year-Old

Bunnahabhain 25-Year-Old

Piling on the peat

Known as the "gentle spirit of Islay," Bunnahabhain single malt has been lightly peated during the past half century, but since Burn Stewart took over, the distillery has also produced heavily peated batches of spirit on an annual basis. There is strong demand for this spirit among blending customers, and around one-third of annual production is currently peated.

The peating level of Bunnahabhain malt is much the same as Laphroaig and Lagavulin, but because the stills are large and onion-shaped, giving significant amounts of reflux, it is less medicinal than some other Islays. The "cut" points during distillation of peated spirit also differ from those of "standard"

Bunnahabhain, because the rich, phenolic flavors appear later in the run, so the cut from the "heart of the run" is made at a later stage than normal. This also increases the oiliness of the spirit.

The whiskies

Peated expressions are evident in the core range, courtesy of the NAS Toiteach a Dha, matured in a combination of bourbon and sherry casks, and Stiuireadair, aged in first-fill and refill sherry casks. The permanent range also includes 12-, 18-, 25-, 30-, and 40-year-old expressions of "standard" Bunnahabhain, along with annual batches of a cask-strength version of the 12-year-old.

TASTING NOTES

Bunnahabhain 12-Year-Old
Single malt, non-chill-filtered, 46.3% ABV
Fresh on the nose, with light peat and discreet smoke. More overt peat on the nutty and fruity palate but still restrained for an Islay. The finish is full-bodied and lingering, with a hint of vanilla and some smoke.

Bunnahabhain 25-Year-Old
Single malt, non-chill-filtered, 46.3% ABV
Sweet and floral on the nose, with developing spices. The palate is sherried and elegant, with baked apple. The sherry lingers and dries in the long, pleasing finish.

Bunnahabhain Toiteach a Dha
Single malt, 46.3% ABV
The nose offers aromatic smoke, red berries, brine, and cloves. Jaffa orange, tobacco, sherry, and smoked fish appear on the palate, which closes with black pepper, sea salt, dark chocolate, and drying sherry.

WHISKY TALES
Visiting Bunnahabhain
To improve the public appeal of Bunnahbhain, a dedicated visitor center has been created, replacing two shoreside warehouses that were in a poor state of repair. According to CVH Spirits' Global Head of Brand Marketing Chiara Giovanacci, "Welcoming people into the distillery is of paramount importance. Getting people to explore Islay and to taste the drams is like nothing else. You can sit in the visitor center and enjoy your dram and take your time. You can just enjoy the center and the views if you wish. You can go as light or as deep as you want with the tours. It's all small-scale and hands-on with the distillery team."

Bunnahabhain distillery fronts the Sound of Islay, looking across to Jura.

CAOL ILA

OWNER Diageo plc

FOUNDED 1846

WEBSITE www.malts.com

In terms of capacity, Caol Ila is the largest distillery on Islay, having been expanded during 2012 to allow for the production of up to 1.7 million gallons (6.5 million liters) per annum. Upgrading at that time included the installation of a new full lauter mash tun and two new washbacks, taking the complement to 10. The distillery is equipped with three wash stills with descending lyne arms and three spirit stills with straight lyne arms. It operates seven days per week, undertaking 26 mashes and uses malt peated to 35ppm sourced from Diageo's Port Ellen Maltings. Caol Ila produces spirit that is widely used in Diageo's blends, notably the Johnnie Walker "family," to which it contributes rich, smoky characteristics.

As a single malt, Caol Ila enjoyed increasing popularity once the brand was re-launched during 2002, but sales have since plateaued, while the likes of local rivals Laphroaig, Lagavulin and Ardbeg have seen major levels of growth in recent years, coinciding with the apparently never-ending thirst for Islay whisky among consumers in a wide range of countries. Diageo is unworried by this state of affairs, however, as Lagavulin is its showpiece Islay distillery and single malt, soon to be joined by the revived Port Ellen operation, which fell silent in 1983, but has gained cult status among malt aficionados for its individualistic releases.

Between cliff and Sound

The distillery in its original form dates from 1846, when it was established by Hector Henderson, who also owned Glasgow's Camlachie Distillery. The location between a steep cliff and the Sound of Islay may seem an unusual choice, but it was close to an extremely good water supply, rising through limestone in Loch nam Ban and entering the sea at Caol Ila, and coastal locations were important for transportation when the needs of island distilleries were serviced by small vessels known as "puffers."

Caol Ila ultimately passed into the hands of Glasgow blender Bulloch Lade & Company in 1863, with rebuilding taking place 16 years later, but the

Caol Ila 2022 Distillers Edition

Caol Ila 12-Year-Old

most dramatic reconstruction at Caol Ila took place during 1972 and 1974. The distillery, owned by the Distillers Company Ltd since 1927, was totally rebuilt in somewhat stark, modernistic style at a cost of $4.9 million (£1 million), and the complement of stills was increased from two to the present six.

The characteristic 1960–1970s style of the DCL stillhouse, with a significant amount of glass, means that the Caol Ila stillman enjoys a superb view across the Sound of Islay to the neighboring Isle of Jura. Only the warehouse of the 19th-century distillery remains intact and in use, though today all the spirit produced at Caol Ila is transported by road tanker to the mainland for cask filling and maturation.

Although Caol Ila's spirit, peated to 30–35ppm, is now in great demand, there was a time not too long ago when Diageo had a potential overcapacity of it and accordingly an annual batch of unpeated "Highland-style" Caol Ila was made for some years.

Caol Ila's 1960s stillhouse has one of the best views of any Scottish distillery.

This was intended primarily for blending purposes, but in 2006 an unpeated eight-year-old expression was released in the annual Special Releases lineup, and 10-, 12-, 14-, 15-, and 18-year-old expressions have followed since then.

Core Caol Ilas

The range embraces the NAS Moch, 12-, 18-, and 25-year-olds, and a Distillers Edition, finished in Moscatel casks. A 35-year-old has been released in Diageo's Prima & Ultima range, and 2022 saw the appearance of a 14-year-old cask-strength "Four Corners of Scotland" bottling, matured in refill and freshly charred hogsheads and exclusive to the distillery and www.malts.com.

WHISKY TALES

Four Corners
Following on from Glenkinchie, Cardhu, and Glen Ord, Caol Ila was the last of Diageo's quartet of distilleries to receive the "Four Corners of Scotland" treatment. This involved totally reimagining the visitor experience, placing a greater emphasis on flavors and less on facts and figures, and putting Caol Ila in context as a key component of the Johnnie Walker blends. Tour options and facilities have been significantly enhanced, with a large retail area and also a popular "bottle your own" option.

Caol Ila 25-Year-Old

TASTING NOTES

Caol Ila 12-Year-Old
Single malt, 43% ABV
Iodine, fresh fish, and bacon on the nose, plus delicate, floral notes. Smoke, malt, lemon, and peat on the slightly oily palate, plus vanilla and a dash of mustard. Peppery peat in the drying finish.

Caol Ila 25-Year-Old
Single malt, 43% ABV
The nose is fresh and fruity, with sticking plasters, brine, and bonfire smoke. Relatively sweet on the palate, with more fruit notes, plus wood smoke, pepper, and some oak. The finish dries steadily, with mild smokiness.

Caol Ila 2022 Distillers Edition
Single malt, 43% ABV
The nose offers cloves, peaches, and iodine, with an oily palate featuring more overt peat and oranges, finishing with smoky orchard fruits, brine, and black pepper.

HIGHLAND PARK

OWNER The Edrington Group

FOUNDED 1798

WEBSITE www.highlandpark.co.uk

The Orkney Isles, to the north of mainland Scotland, have a character all their own—more Norse than Scottish in heritage, and closer to the Arctic Circle than to London. The islands actually belonged to Norway until 1472. Given the individualistic nature of the place and its independently minded people, it is appropriate that the whisky made in Orkney's best-known distillery, Highland Park, is equally individualistic.

Based in Kirkwall, Orkney's vibrant capital, Highland Park highlights five reasons why its whisky tastes the way it does—focusing on traditional floor maltings and the use of Orcadian peat and sherry oak casks, cold maturation, and cask harmonization.

Unique character

The peat burned in the Highland Park kilns is notably aromatic, and very different in character from that of Islay. Orcadian peat derives from heather, dried grass, and plants, rather than from trees, as there were no trees on Orkney 3,000 years ago, just as there are very few today, as a result of the frequent strong winds. The distillery owns about 2,000 acres of peat land on Hobbister Moor, annually cutting around 220 tons to fuel the distillery furnace and impart its unique flavor to the whisky.

Some 20 percent of the distillery's requirements are served by its own maltings, which produce malt peated to approximately the same level as that at Bowmore, while the balance of malt required is unpeated and is imported from the mainland.

About $12.5 million (£10 million) per annum is spent on casks, with all spirit destined for single malt bottlings being matured in ex-sherry wood. Nineteen of the 23 warehouses on site are of the old-fashioned "dunnage" variety, allowing for a relatively even and cool maturation. Each batch of Highland Park single malt is the product of a vatting of a combination of cask types. After vatting, the whisky is returned to casks for a "marrying" period of about six months, though this period may be longer for some of the older expressions.

Highland Park 18-Year-Old Viking Pride

Highland Park
12-Year-Old Viking Honour

Highland Park's heritage

The northernmost distillery in Scotland, Highland Park stands on the southern outskirts of Kirkwall, the largest settlement on Mainland island and the capital of the Orkneys. The distillery was constructed by David Robertson during the last decade of the 18th century, though the precise date of establishment has proved elusive, as is the case with so many of Scotland's older distilleries.

From 1826, various members of the Borthwick family ran Highland Park, and in 1895 James Grant purchased the distillery. Three years later, he doubled capacity by adding two more stills alongside the existing pair. In 1937, Highland Distilleries acquired Highland Park, and in 1979, the first official bottling of the brand took place, with the company investing

A range of traditional warehouses at Highland Park distillery

heavily to promote it, carving out an international profile for their prized single malt. Highland Distilleries was subsequently renamed Highland Distillers and in 1999 became part of The Edrington Group. Under the stewardship of Edrington, sales of Highland Park rose to 1.2 million bottles per year during the period from 2007 until 2013 and for the last few years, have been around the 2 million bottles mark. In terms of global bestselling malts, Highland Park occupies 20th place.

The whiskies

Principal bottlings include 12-year-old Viking Honour, 15-year-old Viking Heart, 18-year-old Viking Pride, along with 21-, 25-, 30-, and 40-year-old expressions. A popular NAS cask-strength variant is offered on a batch basis, and 2023 saw Dragon Legend join the core portfolio. According to Highland Park, its character is "Predominantly driven by slow maturation in sherry seasoned European oak casks, and a higher proportion of Orkney peated malt." In the same year, a 54-year-old bottling was launched—the oldest yet to appear from Highland Park distillery.

Highland Park 15-Year-Old Viking Heart

WHISKY TALES
Heavenly Spirits
By 1798, Highland Park distillery had been established on the site of a hut previously used by local beadle and smuggler/illicit distiller Magnus Eunson. According to legend, Eunson stored illicit whisky beneath a church pulpit, on one occasion moving it to his house in anticipation of a raid by excise officers. When the excisemen arrived at the house, they found Eunson and his family solemnly gathered around what looked like a bier but was actually the offending kegs of whisky, covered with a cloth. Eunson intimated to the officers that there had been a death, and utterance of the word "smallpox" was enough to send them scurrying away.

TASTING NOTES

Highland Park 12-Year-Old Viking Honour
Single malt, ex-sherry casks, 40% ABV
The nose is fragrant and floral, with hints of heather and spice. Smooth and honeyed on the palate, with citric fruits, malt, and wood smoke in the warm, lengthy, slightly peaty finish.

Highland Park 18-Year-Old Viking Pride
Single malt, ex-sherry casks, 43% ABV
Floral and aromatic on the nose, with heather, honeycombs, wood smoke, salt, and oak. The palate is sweet, with peat, nuts, honey, and stem ginger. The finish is spicy, drying, and long.

Highland Park 15-Year-Old Viking Heart
Single malt, 44% ABV
Crème brûlée, toffee apples, heather honey, and soft peat on the nose. Toffee, heathery peat, baked apple, and cinnamon on the viscous palate, closing with black currants and black pepper.

ISLE OF JURA

OWNER Whyte & Mackay (Emperador Inc)

FOUNDED 1810

WEBSITE www.isleofjura.com

Although separated from the Isle of Islay by only a narrow stretch of sea, in stylistic terms, the single malt from the Jura distillery in the island's tiny capital of Craighouse is generally much closer to the mainland whiskies of the Highland and Speyside regions. This is due to a conscious decision taken at the time of the distillery's creation in the early 1960s to produce a single malt that would have wider appeal than the heavily peated drams of Islay, which at the time were a long way from having the sort of cult status they enjoy today. Accordingly, tall stills were installed and a lightly peated malt regime was put in place.

Whisky once more

The style of spirit produced when Jura's pair of stills was first fired up in 1963 was very different from the original Jura distillery, which was probably established in 1810 and was first licensed during 1831 to William Abercrombie. Distilling continued under a number of different licensees until James Ferguson & Company took over in 1876, but the operation ceased in 1901, due to a dispute between Ferguson and his landlord, Colin Campbell. Ferguson stripped the distillery of its equipment, and Campbell removed the roofs in 1920 to avoid having to pay tax.

Distilling appeared to have been lost to Jura forever, but in 1960, as part of an attempt to stem depopulation and introduce new employment offers, Leith blenders and bottlers Charles Mackinlay & Company set out to restore whisky making to the island. The designer of Tullibardine distillery, William Delmé-Evans, was recruited to head the project to build a new Jura distillery at Craighouse, and some of the existing buildings were incorporated into the design. By the time the distillery came on stream in 1963, Mackinlay & Company had been taken over by Scottish & Newcastle Breweries Ltd, which ran the distillery until it was purchased by Invergordon Distillers Group plc in 1985. In 1993, Invergordon was acquired by Whyte & Mackay Ltd after a hostile takeover, and the Glasgow-based distiller continues to operate Jura today.

Jura French Oak

Jura Seven Wood

Jura style

Although stylistically and geographically separated from Islay, the Jura distillery participates fully in the annual Feis Ile, or Islay Festival of Malt & Music, and its visitor center, imaginatively upgraded in 2011, attracts an increasing number of people.

The whisky itself has been attracting a growing fan base, with Janice McIntosh, Whyte & Mackay Marketing Director UK, Europe & Global Travel Retail, explaining in 2023 that "For the past three years, Jura has held the position of the UK's number-one single malt by both volume and value—a considerable achievement for a whisky created by a remote island community of just 260 people. Our competitive pricing, with focused promotional activity and flavor led innovation are just three of the factors driving growth of the brand internationally as we continue in our ambition to become a top ten single malt globally."

Outside of the UK, Jura has developed a significant presence in Sweden, while The Netherlands, France, and Germany are other strong European markets. Further afield, the brand is growing in Tawain, China, and Australia, where it is driving the growth of single malt whisky as a category.

On a global scale, Jura 12-year-old has led the brand's commercial success to becoming one of the top 20 bestselling whiskies worldwide and the fastest growing single malt in the US, Scotch's biggest export market. Jura boasts an extensive portfolio, including Bourbon Cask, French Oak, 10-year-old, 14-year-old Rye Cask, Seven Wood, 15-year-old Sherry Cask, 18-year-old, and 21-year-old Tide.

Additionally, there are seasonal Cask Edition releases, which include Rum Cask, Pale Ale Cask, Red Wine Cask, and Winter Edition. A range of Rare Vintages is proving popular with experienced whisky consumers, and Janis McIntosh notes that "The Rare collection showcases Jura's old stocks, which have been perfected over years of our long whisky-making history. It comprises our most extraordinary, aged whiskies, including a single malt, which spent 48 years maturing to perfection before being finished in ex-bourbon barrels and tawny port pipes."

Jura 10-Year-Old

WHISKY TALES

Writers' Retreat

George Orwell wrote his futuristic novel *Nineteen Eighty-Four* while living in a remote cottage at Barnhill, in the north of Jura, during 1946–1948. Although his favorite tipple was dark rum, the Jura Malt Whisky Writers' Retreat program now gives authors the opportunity to spend a month living and writing on the island, based in the restored Jura Lodge. Literature and Jura single malt whisky had already been linked with the release of a limited edition sherry cask-finished 19-year-old "Jura 1984" bottling.

TASTING NOTES

Jura 10-Year-Old
Single malt, 40% ABV
Pine, white pepper, orange compote, and faint wood smoke on the nose. The palate delivers Jaffa oranges, ginger, and milk chocolate, with the chocolate darkening in the softly spiced finish.

Jura Seven Wood
Single malt, finished in six different types of French oak, 42% ABV
The nose comprises newly planed wood, peaches, and subtle charcuterie, while the palate yields tangerines, cinnamon, nutmeg, and toasted oak.

Jura French Oak
Single malt, 42% ABV
Spicy aromas, with pears and nutmeg, leading into flavors of sandalwood, caramel, and white pepper, closing with gentle smoke.

LAGAVULIN

OWNER Diageo plc

FOUNDED 1816

WEBSITE www.malts.com

The most evocative way to arrive on Islay is by ferry into the southern ferry terminus of Port Ellen. That way you sail past the three distinctive white-washed Kildalton distilleries of Ardbeg, Lagavulin, and Laphroaig—the big-hitting trio of the island. From the mainland, Lagavulin distillery boasts views across Lagavulin Bay to the ruins of Dunyvaig Castle.

Lagavulin is of similar vintage to its two distilling neighbors, first being licensed to John Johnston in 1816, when the area was a haven for illicit distillers. A year later, another distillery was constructed close by, carrying the Ardmore name and operated by Archibald Campbell. Ardmore survived for just four years before closing, at which time it was acquired by John Johnston, who ran it in tandem with Lagavulin until 1835.

Lagavulin's long and ongoing association with the White Horse blend of Scotch whisky effectively commenced in 1867, when the distillery was bought by James Logan Mackie & Company. Mackie's nephew, Peter, joined the company in 1878, and in 1889, he inherited the distillery on the death of his uncle.

Restless Peter

Peter Mackie has been described as "one-third genius, one-third megalomaniac, one-third eccentric," earning the nickname "Restless Peter" because of his enormous enthusiasm and appetite for innovation and the pursuit of excellence.

A year after he took over the distiller.y he launched White Horse into export markets; somewhat unusually, the brand didn't appear in the domestic arena until 1901. Lagavulin was a major component of the blend, and to this day, White Horse betrays a much greater Islay influence than most of its competitors. The name was taken from the White Horse Cellar Inn, located on Edinburgh's Canongate, and it in turn was named after the white palfrey ridden by Mary, Queen of Scots to and from the Palace of Holyrood.

Peter Mackie died in 1924, having been knighted for services to whisky, and in that year, the company was renamed White Horse Distillers Ltd in

Lagavulin 2022 Distillers Edition

Lagavulin 8-Year-Old

Lagavulin is one of four white-painted distilleries to line the southern coast of Islay.

recognition of its best-known product. In 1927, it became part of the Distillers Company Ltd. In 1988, a 16-year-old Lagavulin was chosen as the Islay representative in what had by then become United Distillers' Classic Malts portfolio. Until 2000, Lagavulin was the bestselling Islay single malt, but since then, Laphroaig has taken over that position, with Lagavulin falling to fourth place behind Ardbeg and Bowmore. The distillery works seven days per week and produces around 800,-000 gallons (3 million liters) of spirit per annum. Unusually, the two pairs of wash stills are smaller than the pair of spirit stills. Maturation takes place principally in ex-bourbon casks.

Making Lagavulin

Since the opening of DCL's large-scale commercial Port Ellen Maltings in 1974, Lagavulin has sourced its peated malt from that facility and slow fermentation of between 55 and 75 hours allows the full peaty character to shine through.

Lagavulin is equipped with four stills, two of which are in the same pear-shaped style as those transferred from Malt Mill back in the early 1960s. The same slowness of processing that characterizes fermentation continues in the stills, with the first run lasting for some five hours and the second for nearly twice that duration. Unusually, the spirit stills are filled almost to their full capacity in order to ensure minimal contact between spirit and copper, leading to the whisky's distinctively robust character.

Once distilled, Lagavulin is now transported to the mainland for maturation, though around 16,000 casks are currently maturing on Islay, in warehouses at

Lagavulin, Caol Ila, and the former distillery of Port Ellen. The stone-built warehouses at Port Ellen date back to the founding of the distillery in 1825 and, along with the listed malt kilns, are almost the only surviving structures.

A decade after the Lagavulin 16-year-old was selected as one of the founding whiskies of the Classic Malts range, it was joined by a Distillers Edition expression, finished in PX sherry casks. An 8-year-old is also now part of Lagavulin's core range, while a 12-year-old cask-strength expression is released annually as part of the Special Releases program. The 2023 edition was notable for having been finished in tequila casks.

TASTING NOTES

Lagavulin 8-Year-Old
Single malt, 48% ABV
The nose delivers spice, peat, iodine, and salted caramel, while the palate offers tropical fruits, caramel, brine, and earthy peat, closing with grilled meat and bonfire smoke.

Lagavulin 16-Year-Old
Single malt, 43% ABV
Peat, iodine, sherry, and vanilla come together on the rich nose. The peat and iodine theme continues onto the big, spicy, sherried palate, with brine and raisins. Peat embers in the long, full, spicy finish.

Lagavulin 2022 Distillers Edition
Single malt, finished in ex-Pedro Ximénez sherry butts after principal period of maturation, 43% ABV
Smoky and mildly fishy on the nose, with big, sherried, stewed fruit and raisin notes. Full-bodied and rounded, with peat smoke and sherry. The finish is long, softly smoky, and gently spiced.

WHISKY TALES
Malt Mill
Although you would never know it from looking at the distillery buildings today, the Lagavulin site once boasted a second, smaller-scale working distillery by the name of Malt Mill, which operated between 1908 and 1960; one of several lost distilleries from Islay's past. This partner plant was developed by Peter Mackie to produce a long-lost illicit style of "small still" spirit, and he made liberal use of peat rather than coal in his new facility. Malt Mill utilized some of the buildings of the erstwhile Ardmore Distillery, which had closed in 1835. In 1962, the pair of stills from Malt Mill was transferred into Lagavulin, and today the maltings of Malt Mill serve as the Lagavulin visitor center, where tours of the distillery end with a welcome dram.

Lagavulin 16-Year-Old

LAPHROAIG

Laphroaig 25-Year-Old Cask Strength

OWNER Suntory Global Spirits

FOUNDED 1815

WEBSITE www.laphroaig.com

It could be said that Laphroaig is the Marmite of the whisky world, since few consumers are noncommittal about its hard-core peaty, medicinal charms. Indeed, the marketing team behind the brand chose to make a virtue of this polarization several years ago with a campaign that declared "Laphroaig—love it or hate it." There was even a rather brave tagline to the effect that "Your first taste may be your last." High-profile aficionados of the distinctive style include the then HRH The Prince of Wales, who bestowed his Royal Warrant on the distillery in 1994. The continuation of in-house malting plays a significant part in the unique style of Laphroaig, and around 20 percent of the distillery's total malt requirements are made on the four malting floors. The overall phenolic level of all malt used at Laphroaig is around 60ppm, with third-party malt usually being blended with that from Laphroaig's own maltings before use. With Diageo having increased production at Caol Ila and with its revived Port Ellen distillery due on stream, the company is no longer supplying malt from its Port Ellen maltings to external customers, meaning that Laphroaig and other Islay distillers are increasingly having to turn to mainland suppliers.

Some of the unique salty, medicinal character of Laphroaig is derived from the floor maltings, with the malt being peated before it is dried, while most distilleries peat and dry it at the same time. Laphroaig peats at a low temperature and then dries the barley, which gives the spirit a wider range of phenol flavors.

The original two stills at Laphroaig were augmented by a second pair in 1923, with another pair added in 1968–1969, and the seventh still going in during 1974 to further increase capacity. The spirit distillation boasts the longest foreshots run of any Scottish distillery, a practice designed to eliminate the sweet esters that flow early from the spirit still and are not part of the Laphroaig character profile.

The owners of Laphroaig

Laphroaig is the world's bestselling Islay single malt, and the distillery that produces it was first licensed

Laphroaig Quarter Cask

As one of the few distilleries to retain its floor maltings, the rich aroma of peat smoke is common around Laphroaig.

WHISKY TALES
Fine Malt Friends
In 1994, Laphroaig devised a marketing innovation in the shape of the "Friends of Laphroaig," which now boasts around half a million members worldwide. Each Friend is given a lifetime's lease on a tiny portion of land at the distillery and the annual "rent" takes the form of a dram of Laphroaig. The scheme commemorates the Johnston brothers' struggle, after founding the distillery at the beginning of the 19th century, to secure the distillery's water supply. The brothers eventually purchased the land that the water flows through. In addition, the distillery offers a number of varied visitor experiences, including the Hunter's Hike, during which participants enjoy a dram at the distillery water source, cut peat, and then return to the distillery to tend the barley on the malting floors.

in 1815, to brothers Alexander and Donald Johnston, though it is thought that the Johnstons may have been distilling at Laphroaig for several years prior to receiving their license.

The distillery was operated by the Johnston family until the death of Ian Hunter in 1954, who was the last family member to be involved. Hunter was famously succeeded at the Laphroaig helm by the redoubtable Elizabeth "Bessie" Williamson, who had worked as Ian Hunter's personal assistant and became one of the very few women at that time to have a distillery role that extended beyond making tea or typing correspondence.

Bessie Williamson ran Laphroaig until she retired in 1972, though during the previous decade, ownership of the distillery had passed to Seager Evans & Company. The famous brewer Whitbread & Company Ltd bought Seager Evans in 1975, and in 1989 Allied Distillers Ltd took over Whitbread's spirits division. When the Allied empire was split up in 2005, Laphroaig, along with Ardmore distillery in Aberdeenshire and Teacher's blended Scotch whisky, was purchased by Fortune Brands. Today, the distillery is in the hands of global giant Suntory Global Spirits.

Laphroaig releases

Compared to fellow Islay distilleries Ardbeg and Bruichladdich, Laphroaig adopted a restrained releases policy for many years, but during the last decade or so, more expressions have been forthcoming. A Quarter Cask variant was launched under the Allied Distillers' regime in 2005 to keep the standard 10-year-old company. Quarter Cask draws its inspiration from the small casks often used to transport whisky on horseback from the distilleries during the 19th century, and as the smaller casks provide up to 30 percent more contact between the wood and its contents, the maturation process of the whisky is intensified.

Subsequently, principal additions to the core range have been the NAS Oak Select, 10-year-old Cask Strength, 10-year-old Sherry Oak Finish, the NAS Lore, and a 25-year-old Cask Strength. Laphroaig is also active in the travel retail sector, where the five-part Ian Hunter Story was developed from 2019 to 2023, closing with a 34-year-old bottling.

TASTING NOTES

Laphroaig 10-Year-Old
Single malt, 40% ABV
Old-fashioned sticking plaster, peat smoke, and seaweed leap off the nose, followed by sweeter and fruitier notes. Massive on the palate, with fish oil, salt, and plankton, though the finish is surprisingly tight and increasingly drying.

Laphroaig 25-Year-Old Cask Strength
Single malt, matured in a mix of ex-bourbon and ex-oloroso sherry casks, non-chill-filtered, 50.9% ABV
Sherry, sweet peat, and soft spices on the nose, with Germolene, smoke, and new leather. Full-bodied, with restrained sherry, more peat, spices, and apples. The finish is lengthy, with gentle smoke, sustained fruit notes, licorice, and iodine.

Laphroaig Quarter Cask
Single malt, initially matured in ex-bourbon barrels, transferred into 125-liter quarter casks for a final period, non-chill-filtered, 48% ABV
Sweet barley and profound smoky, medicinal notes, coal, and spice on the nose. Toffee, hazelnuts, powerful peat, and cigarette ash on the palate. The lengthy finish features digestive biscuits and chimneys.

LOCHRANZA/LAGG

OWNER Isle of Arran Distillers Ltd

FOUNDED 1993 and 2019

WEBSITE www.arranwhisky.com; www.laggwhisky.com

Lochranza and Lagg are situated at opposite ends of the Isle of Arran, with the former dating from 1993 and the latter being established in 2019. Both belong to Isle of Arran Distillers, and Lagg was created to increase capacity, with production there dedicated to making peated spirit. Lochranza was formerly known as Arran distillery but was renamed when Lagg came on stream.

Arran was one of the first new distilleries to be created after the boom Scotch whisky years of the 1960s and '70s, established in 1993 by former Chivas Brothers managing director and whisky industry veteran the late Harold Currie. He had long associations with the island and was attracted to the idea of restoring legal whisky-making after a gap of more than 150 years. Currie chose a site at Lochranza in the north of the island, after discovering an ideal water source there. The project was partly funded by the sale of 2,000 bonds, each of which entitled the bondholder to an amount of whisky once the distillery was in operation.

Arran in action

Lochranza is a four-still distillery, designed from the outset to be aesthetically pleasing, with mock pagodas and whitewashed buildings that blend well with the island's older architecture. As all the production processes take place within one room, it is also ideal for the reception of visitors. Although no longer owned by the Currie family, the distillery remains in independent hands.

The first bottling appeared as a three-year-old in 1998, followed by a four-year-old, and several single cask expressions without age statements, marketed as The Arran Malt A milestone came in 2006 with the launch of the distillery's first 10-year-old.

Today, the Arran range embraces 10-, 18-, and 25-year-olds, plus Quarter Cask The Bothy, Sherry Cask The Bodega, Barrel Reserve, and Robert Burns. A limited release of a 17-year-old appeared in 2023, and recent cask finished bottlings have included Amarone, Port, and Sauternes. Peated Arran

Arran 10-Year-Old

Arran 25-Year-Old

expressions appear under the Machrie Moor name and include Machrie Moor Cask Strength and a 10-year-old.

Lagg reborn

When it came to finding a site for expansion, initially for additional warehousing, a large plot of land at Lagg in the south of the island came on the market, and after acquiring it, a decision was made by Isle of Arran Distillers to build a small distillery there and dedicate it to peated spirit production. So it is that the new distillery stands just half a mile from the "original" Lagg—the last licensed whisky-making operation on the island, which operated from 1825 to 1837.

Lochranza distillery is one of the most visited attractions on the popular Isle of Arran.

All equipment was supplied by the renowned coppersmiths Forsyth of Rothes and includes a 4-ton semi-lauter mash tun, four 6,600-gallon (25,000-liter) Douglas Fir washbacks, and one pair of stills. The distillery has an annual capacity of 210,000 gallons (800,000 liters), compared with "original." Lagg, which could produce 6,600 gallons per year, and production began in 2019. Lagg is classified as a "Lowland" single (bourbon-cask matured) malt distillery, despite its island status, as it is located south of the Highland boundary fault line that divides Highland and Lowland regions of production. Lagg has the distinction of being the only Lowland whisky produced on an island. The first bottling of Lagg came in August 2022, and the following year saw the introduction of two core bottlings, Kilmory (matured in bourbon casks) and Corriecravie (sherry cask-finished).

WHISKY TALES

Scotland in Miniature
The Isle of Arran is one of the most southerly of Scotland's islands, situated between Ayrshire and the Kintyre peninsula. It is often referred to as "Scotland in miniature," since it embraces so many aspects of Scottish geography and topography, including pretty coastal villages; rugged mountains in the north; and soft, rolling hills and woodland in the south. Although Arran is less than 20 miles (32km) long and 10 miles (16km) wide, it's thought that as many as 50 distilling ventures were active during the 19th century. While most ran without the formality of licenses, three were officially sanctioned, with the last of these, at Lagg, operating until 1837.

Lagg Kilmory Edition

TASTING NOTES

Arran 10-Year-Old
Single malt, 70% from second-fill sherry casks, balanced mixture of ex-bourbon and some first-fill sherry casks, 46% ABV
Vanilla, apples, pears, malt, and gentle spice on the nose. Medium-bodied, with citrus fruits, soft cinnamon notes, digestive biscuits, and gentle oak on the palate. The fruity, malty finish fades slowly.

Arran 25-Year-Old
Single malt, 46% ABV
The nose is spicy, aromatic, and even savory, with aromas of sherry, while the palate offers raspberry jam, raisins, nougat, and more sherry, finally closing with a sprinkling of pepper and oak tannins.

Lagg Kilmory Edition
Single 46% ABV
Charcoal on the nose, with lemon, vanilla, and marine spice. Phenolic on the palate, with burnt oak and citrus fruit, closing with black pepper and peat.

TALISKER

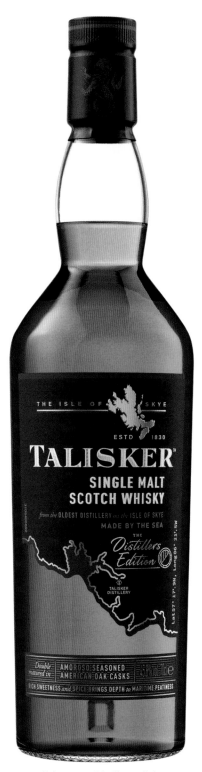

OWNER Diageo plc

FOUNDED 1830

WEBSITE www.malts.com

Talisker distillery was established in 1830 by brothers Hugh and Kenneth MacAskill. They had arrived in Skye just a few years previously from their native island of Eigg, purchasing agricultural land and the mansion of Talisker House, which had played host to Dr. Johnson and James Boswell during their famous 1773 tour of the Hebrides.

Subsequent owners of Talisker distillery included Anderson & Company, whose principal, John Anderson, was jailed in 1880 for selling nonexistent whisky to customers who assumed it was safely maturing in the Talisker warehouses! In the same year, ownership passed to Alexander Grigor Allan and Roderick Kemp, though Kemp was later to sell his shares and invest instead in a Speyside distillery by the name of Macallan.

"King o'drinks"

At a time when single malt whisky was a relative rarity outside the Highlands, Talisker was already highly regarded, with the novelist Robert Louis Stevenson writing in the same year that Anderson was imprisoned, "The King o'drinks, as I conceive it, Talisker, Isla, or Glenlivet!"

In 1894, The Talisker Distillery Company Ltd was founded, and four years later, Talisker merged with Dailuaine-Glenlivet Distillers and Imperial Distillers to create the Dailuaine-Talisker Distilleries Ltd. In 1916, that company was taken over by a consortium, including WP Lowrie & Company, John Walker & Sons Ltd, and John Dewar & Sons Ltd, and Talisker was one of the assets that passed into the hands of The Distillers Company Ltd in 1925. Three years later, the practice of triple-distillation was abandoned at Talisker, though the stillhouse configuration of two wash stills and three spirit stills that persists to this day harks back to the time of triple-distillation.

Talisker aflame

Those five stills were at the center of the most dramatic episode in Talisker's history, when, in November 1960, a valve on the coal-fired No.1 spirit

Talisker 2022 Distillers Edition

Talisker 10-Year-Old

The Campfire Bar in Talisker's beautifully appointed visitor center.

still was inadvertently left open during distillation. Spirit escaped from the still and caught fire, and the entire stillhouse burned down. The new stillhouse was equipped with five stills, exact copies of the originals. It is sometimes claimed that the fire actually saved the distillery, since it would have been an obvious candidate for closure during owner DCL's 1980s program of cutbacks due to its isolated location. In 1972, the replacement stills were converted to steam heating, and at the same time floor malting was abandoned, with malted barley being shipped in from the new Glen Ord Maltings in Inverness-shire. Talisker's malt is peated to 18–20ppm.

A 10-year-old Talisker was included in the new Classic Malts lineup in 1988, and a visitor center was created. Despite its remoteness, Talisker is Diageo's most-visited distillery, with around 75,000 people per year. After a major reimagining of its visitor offerings during 2021 to 2022, the distillery is now "future-proofed" to cope with up to double that number.

Today's Talisker

This interest in the distillery reflects the level of appreciation of the individualistic whisky made there, and sales top the 4.3 million bottles per annum mark, making Talisker the seventh bestselling single malt Scotch whisky. That "individual" character comes courtesy of a complex and unusual distilling regime.

The lye pipes on the tall wash stills, which lead off from the main necks, are U-shaped, designed to trap vapors from the first distillation before they reach the outside worm tubs. A small secondary "purifier"

copper pipe carries the vapors that are trapped back to the wash stills for a second distillation. The purifier pipe is said to add oiliness to the spirit, and relatively low levels of copper contact donate a sulfur note, while the generous amounts of reflux refine the fruity characteristics. Commenting on Talisker's unorthodox distilling setup, Diageo's Senior Global Brand Ambassador Ewan Gunn explains that "The U-bend in the lye-pipe and the 'reflux' pipe into stills make for lighter spirit, but the presence of the worm tubs pushes it into a meatier, heavier style. It's almost contradictory." The core Talisker range includes 10-, 18-, 25-, and 30-year-olds, along with NAS Skye and Storm, a Distillers Edition finished in ex-Amoroso sherry casks, and NAS Port Ruige, finished in ruby port casks.

Talisker 18-Year-Old

TASTING NOTES

Talisker 10-Year-Old
Single malt, 45.8% ABV
Pungent peat, brown sugar, and lots of spice on the nose. More peat and spice on the full, confident palate, with malt and black pepper. The finish is very long, with hot peat and chili.

Talisker 18-Year-Old
Single malt, 45.8% ABV
A powerful yet mellow nose, sweet and slightly smoky. The palate opens with sweet, fruity notes that deepen, with hints of a smoldering peat fire. The finish is rich, with a classic Talisker peppery kick.

Talisker 2022 Distillers Edition
Single malt, finished in ex-Amoroso sherry casks, 45.8% ABV
A nose of warm leather, pipe tobacco, black pepper, toffee, and prunes. Mouth-coating and luscious, with a palate of treacle, sherry, malt, and nutmeg. Slowly drying in a fruity, buttery finish, with pepper at the close.

TOBERMORY

OWNER CVH Spirits

FOUNDED 1798

WEBSITE www.tobermorymalt.com

Tobermory distillery is located close to the harbor in the eponymous fishing and tourist port that serves as the capital of the Inner Hebridean Isle of Mull. The town is characterized by its many brightly painted properties and gained wide recognition internationally, thanks to the children's television series *Balamory*, filmed among its primary-colored houses and shops.

The distillery is one of Scotland's oldest surviving whisky-making facilities, dating back to 1798 when it was founded by local merchant John Sinclair. He christened the new venture Ledaig, which translates from the Gaelic as "safe haven." However, during the ensuing two centuries, Ledaig was to be far from a safe haven for whisky making, as the distillery has actually been silent for more than half of its entire existence. It was first closed between 1837 and 1878, and then from 1930 until 1972, having been bought by the Distillers Company Ltd in 1916. Prior to its next bout of whisky production, the site served as a canteen for sailors and even as a power station!

In 1972, production began again, this time under the auspices of the Ledaig Distillery Ltd, formed by a Liverpool shipping operator and the Spanish sherry firm of Domecq. However, that company went bankrupt three years later. Yorkshire-based Kirkleavington Property Company Ltd bought Tobermory in 1979, but they also found profits elusive, committing the cardinal sin of selling the distillery's one warehouse for redevelopment into apartments and then closing the plant by 1989. Happily for Tobermory, Burn Stewart Distillers saw potential in the only licensed distillery on Mull and in 1993 spent $900,000 (£600,000) buying it, devoting a further $300,000 (£200,000) to maturing stock.

The complexities of maturation

Burn Stewart—now part of CVH Spirits—uses Tobermory and Ledaig in its Scottish Leader and Black Bottle blends and has strived to raise the profile and improve the image and quality of Tobermory single malt, turning a former tun room into a small

Tobermory 12-Year-Old

Ledaig 18-Year-Old

Tobermory's picture-postcard harbor front is famed for its row of brightly colored houses.

warehouse during 2007 so that at least some of the spirit being made could be matured in its place of origin. This initiative draws on the idea that there are subtle differences between the way whisky matures in varying microclimates, principally mainland locations away from the coast and maritime locations such as Tobermory.

In from the cold

Along with Bunnahabhain and Deanston, since 2010 Tobermory and Ledaig's principal single malts have been offered at a strength of 46.3 percent ABV and are no longer subject to chill-filtration, designed to ensure that lower-strength whiskies do not become cloudy at lower temperatures. This was the initiative of then Distilleries Manager and Master Blender Ian Macmillan, now working as a whisky consultant. "As a blender, you always work with non-chill-filtered samples, so I knew that those samples and the chill-filtered whisky that we bottled were totally different animals," says Macmillan.

"Tobermory and Ledaig were crying out to be non-chill-filtered, and now you have increased depth, weight of flavor, and complexity. They are much more structured and textured. The 'before' and 'after' were like two different liquids.

"When I took the sheets from the filter plates after chill-filtration, they were oily and greasy; they left a great intensity of aroma and texture on my hands.

This was part of the DNA of my single malts. Making the whisky 'pretty' by chill-filtering, it was at the expense of aroma and flavor. There was a part of the whisky missing, in effect. What was once seen as a flaw by marketing people is now being seen as a sign of integrity and quality."

At present, the lineup embraces a 12-year-old Tobermory bottling and 10- and 18-year-old Ledaig expressions, along with Ledaig Sinclair Rioja Finish. A new range of well-aged annual Tobermory releases named The Hebridean began to appear in 2021, and the 2023 edition was a 25-year-old, finished in oloroso and Gonzalez Byass casks.

WHISKY TALES

A Peaty Presence
While some distilleries producing unpeated or lightly peated single malt whisky also make occasional batches of more heavily peated spirit, 50 percent of Tobermory's annual output is now heavily peated spirit, bearing the Ledaig name. Ledaig was first introduced in 1996 and is peated to at least 35–40ppm. Due to the S-shaped lyne arms on Tobermory's stills, designed to give heavy reflux, the peated whisky produced is very smoky and sweet.

TASTING NOTES

Ledaig 10-Year-Old
Single malt, non-chill-filtered, 46.3% ABV
The nose is peaty, sweet, and full, with butter and smoked fish. Bold, yet sweet on the palate, with iodine, soft peat, and heather, developing spices. The finish reveals pepper, ginger, licorice, and peat.

Tobermory 12-Year-Old
Single malt, 46.3% ABV
A floral nose, with honey, tropical fruits, vanilla, and cinnamon, leading into a palate of malt, barley, cloves, and fresh oak, closing on licorice, dark berries, and an herbal note.

Ledaig 18-Year-Old
Single malt, 46.3% ABV
Salty peat on the nose, with red currants and sweet bonfire smoke. Sweet peat, smoked fish, cinnamon, and furniture polish on the palate, with sherry and worn leather in the finish.

ARDNAHOE

OWNER Hunter Laing & Co

FOUNDED 2017

WEBSITE www.ardnahoedistillery.com

When Ardnahoe came on stream in October 2018, it brought the complement of Islay's working distilleries up to nine. It was constructed on a spectacular site between Bunnahabhain and Caol Ila on the northeast coast of the island by Glasgow-based independent bottlers Hunter Laing & Co Ltd.

The distillery is manually operated and equipped with wooden washbacks, plus the longest lyne arms of any whisky distillery in the world. This is because Ardnahoe is equipped with worm tubs—the only ones in use on the island—and the long lyne arms help produce a sweet, fruity spirit from the single pair of stills. The principal output is heavily peated (40ppm) spirit, but some 10 percent is unpeated.

Ardnahoe means "height of the hollow" in Gaelic, and process water is sourced from Loch Ardnahoe, reputedly the deepest loch on Islay. Work on the distillery began in late 2016, and it has been designed with the visitor experience very much in mind. The operation is split over two levels, and standing in the stillhouse, the only land visible is the island of Jura, on the other side of the Sound of Islay.

Ardnahoe's founder Hunter Laing & Co Ltd was formed in 2013 by Stewart Laing and his sons, Scott and Andrew, though the firm has its origins in 1949, when Stewart's father, Fred, established a broking, blending and bottling company in Glasgow.

The family has long connections to Islay, with members of Stewart's maternal family living in Bowmore during the 18th and 19th centuries. Stewart undertook distillery training at Bruichladdich in the 1960s, followed by his son Andrew in the early 2000s.

The waiting period

While waiting for the first spirit to flow, Hunter Laing released six single cask Islay single malts at the 2017 Fèis Ìle festival to celebrate the start of building Ardnahoe. Named The Kinship, the six whiskies boasted a combined age of 181 years! The Kinship 2023 includes a 33-year-old Bunnahabhain and a 27-year-old Highland Park, and the combined age of the sextet is 163 years.

Ardnahoe, Islay's newest distillery, is located on the northeast coast of the island.

HARRIS

OWNER Isle of Harris Distillers Ltd

FOUNDED 2015

WEBSITE www.harrisdistillery.com

There is an understandable trend among start-up distillers to release their whisky as soon as it is legally old enough, but this distillery has taken a refreshingly different approach. Economic considerations often lead to three-year-old bottlings hitting the shelves, but at Harris, in the Outer Hebrides, the mantra has always been "our whisky is ready when it's ready."

Distilling commenced in 2015, and it was only on September 22, 2023, that 1,916 prepurchased bottles of The Hearach single malt were released, followed by seven batches for general sale.

"Hearach" is the Scots Gaelic term for a native of Harris, and the number of 1,916 bottles in the initial release is significant, as the 2011 census recorded that figure as the population of Harris. The 1950 census had counted around 5,000 inhabitants. This gradual depopulation was one of the reasons for the establishment of Isle of Harris distillery, enthusiastically promoted by Anderson Bakewell, a US musicologist with long-standing connections to the island.

The distillery is equipped with a pair of Italian-made Frilli stills, and the spirit still is named Eva after Eva Tenback-Biesta, who willed $1.25 million (£1 million) to the project, while a $2.4 million (£1.9 million) EU grant helped bring the venture to fruition. A purpose-built structure was erected close to the ferry terminal in the island capital of Tarbert, with warehousing being developed in the nearby village of Ardhasaig. Distillation of Isle of Harris Gin began in September 2015, followed soon after by the first flow of whisky. Today, just under 53,000 gallons (200,000 liters) of whisky are distilled each year.

The philosophy behind the whisky

As International Business Development Manager Peter Kwasniewski explains, "Because we have relatively few casks, there will always be slight differences between batches. We are celebrating those differences. We sell into 28 countries, and most markets will get part of one individual batch, but some may get two different ones.

"The bottlings don't carry an age statement but are a mix of 4-, 5-, 6-, and 7-year-old whiskies. The malt is peated to 15ppm and long (72–96 hours) fermentations give a lot of fruit flavors. We use Heaven Hill and Buffalo Trace ex-bourbon casks and oloroso and fino sherry casks. The Hearach is a blend of all four cask types. It's married for a minimum of 12 weeks in ex-sherry butts and the roundness and complexity after marrying is remarkable. It's a unique Harris whisky."

The Hearach

One of the Isle of Harris distillery's two stills, made by the Italian firm Frilli.

TASTING NOTE

The Hearach (Batch 00007)
Single malt, 46% ABV
Lime, subtle bonfire smoke, developing baked apple, caramelized nuts, and a hint of salt on the nose. The palate is earthy, with cereal, banoffee pie, and a mildly herbal note, finishing with soft peat and slightly tannic oak notes.

ISLE OF RAASAY

OWNER R&B Distillers

FOUNDED 2017

WEBSITE www.raasaydistillery.com

The island of Raasay is located off the west coast of Skye, in the Inner Hebrides, and boasts a population of around 120. In June 2016, work began to build a whisky distillery adjoining Borodale House, Raasay's Victorian former hotel, and in September 2017, the new distillery was officially opened. Borodale House itself has been converted into a visitor center and offers luxurious accommodation.

The idea of developing a distillery on Raasay came about when co-founder and entrepreneur Bill Dobbie learned that Borodale House was on the market. According to fellow founder Alisdair Day, "When I visited with Bill in May 2014, I was struck by the view (probably the best from any distillery in Scotland), the fact that there had been illicit distilling on the island in the past, and the geology that influences the

The Isle of Raasay distillery enjoys a beautiful location on this small Hebridean island.

water supply. There was previously a Celtic well on the site, and we now draw our water from the same source. Raasay and Borodale House looked like a great place to make Scotch whisky."

Day notes that "We filled our first cask on September 14, 2017, and went into full production of one mash (one ton a day) five days a week on September 27. The distillery has an annual capacity of 200,000 liters [52,800 gallons]."

Raasay's pair of stills was fabricated in Italy by Frilli, and a cooling jacket is fitted to the wash still, while the spirit still boasts an inclined lyne arm, to help create the desired spirit character. Production is split evenly between peated (48–52ppm) malt and unpeated malt, and cask filling, warehousing, and bottling all take place on the island in order to maximize local employment opportunities.

A somewhat unorthodox route is taken to create Raasay's house style, working with quantities of six styles of spirit, three peated and three unpeated. Both styles are filled into first-fill American oak, European oak, and Tuscan red wine casks.

The first Raasay release was launched in the summer of 2021, with maturation having taken place in a combination of Bordeaux red wine barriques, first-fill rye casks, and virgin chinquapin oak. Further releases followed in 2022 and 2023.

TASTING NOTE

Isle of Raasay RO2.1
Single malt, 46.4% ABV
Bacon, sweet peat, vanilla, and red berries on the nose, while the oily palate yields stewed apples, fruity peat, and chewy oak, finishing with licorice and black coffee.

Isle of Raasay RO2.1

KILCHOMAN

OWNER Kilchoman Distillery Company Ltd

FOUNDED 2005

WEBSITE www.kilchomandistillery.com

Kilchoman has established such a high-profile position among the ranks of Islay distilleries, it is easy to forget the first casks were filled only in 2005. This is partly a result of Kilchoman welcoming visitors right from the start. Perhaps more significantly, however, Kilchoman was one of the first distilleries to offer miniature bottles of its new-make spirit for sale, thereby embedding the Kilchoman name in the consciousness of Islay whisky aficionados. In 2009, it released a 3-year-old expression, and the succeeding years have seen many limited releases as well as the establishment of a core range.

These include Machir Bay—an NAS vatting of Kilchoman matured in both bourbon and sherry casks—and Sanaig—including a high proportion of

oloroso sherry cask–matured spirit. Also available are "batch" bottlings of Loch Gorm—matured in oloroso sherry casks—and 100 percent Islay, distilled from barley grown on the island, and matured and bottled at Kilchoman. November 2023 saw the appearance of a 16-year-old expression—the oldest Kilchoman released so far.

The distillery

Kilchoman was established at Rockside Farm, four miles from Bruichladdich, by Anthony Wills and family, and when it opened for business, it was the first new Islay distillery to come into being since the long-defunct Malt Mill plant was set up at Lagavulin in 1908. Anthony Wills explains that "We farm a variety of landscapes covering an area of 2,300 acres surrounding the ruined Kilchoman Church.... Our most fertile ground, 400 acres of rich soil surrounding the distillery, is reserved for our annual barley crop. Sown each spring, once Islay's 50,000 migratory geese have departed, the barley ripens over the summer months before being harvested in early autumn."

The distillery malts a percentage of its own barley and has expanded its maltings to increase the amount made in-house. The year 2019 saw Kilchoman's capacity doubled by the construction of a second production building to complement the first. Overall, the distillery now boasts two semi-lauter mash tuns, 16 stainless steel washbacks, two pairs of stills, and an annual output of 170,000 gallons (650,000 liters). Such is the global popularity of Kilchoman that there are also plans to further increase malting and distilling capacity.

Kilchoman 100% Islay

TASTING NOTES

Kilchoman 100% Islay
Single malt, peated to 10–20ppm and matured first-fill bourbon barrels from Buffalo Trace Distillery, non-chill-filtered, 50% ABV
Lots of brine, peat smoke, and overt citrus notes on the nose. Lemon pith and beach bonfires. Sweet, fruit notes on the early palate, then antiseptic and ashy peat. Relatively lengthy in the finish, with smoldering peat.

Kilchoman Machir Bay
Single malt, 46% ABV
A nose of peat, cigarette smoke, lemon juice, seaweed, brine, and iodine lead into flavors of medicine chests, ashy smoke, sea salt, and black pepper, closing on antiseptic and chili.

Kilchoman Sanaig
Single malt, 46% ABV
A sweet nose, with tropical fruits, toffee, sherry, and burning peat. The palate offers honey, red berry fruits, and dark chocolate, finishing with sea salt, allspice, and wood smoke.

SCAPA

OWNER Chivas Brothers Ltd (Pernod Ricard)

FOUNDED 1885

WEBSITE www.scapawhisky.com

A very fine single malt in its own right, Scapa has played second fiddle to its older and much better-known Orcadian neighbor, Highland Park, for as long as anyone remembers. Today, the distillery boasts a fine visitor center and offers tours and tasting options, with the latter being held in the distillery's striking cliff-top "Scapa Noust." Although there have been 14- and 16-year-old bottlings, the current core expressions are the NAS Skiren, matured in first-fill bourbon casks, and Glansa, which is finished in casks that formerly contained peated whisky.

A tradition maintained

The distillery is notable for its extremely long fermentation times (up to 160 hours), which tend to give a distinctly fruity character to the spirit when distilled, and for the fact that its wash still is of the "Lomond" type. This was installed at Scapa in 1959 in order to give the then-owners Hiram Walker a heavier and oilier style of spirit for blending purposes. Suitably modified for standard distillation, with its rectification plates removed, this idiosyncratic still is the only one of its kind making whisky in Scotland today.

Scapa dates back to 1885, when it was established on the shores of the famous anchorage of Scapa Flow by Glasgow-based Macfarlane & Townsend. Until recently, the owner who did most with Scapa was Hiram Walker & Sons (Scotland) Ltd, which acquired it in 1954 and largely rebuilt it in 1959. Further modernization followed in 1978, and a decade later Hiram Walker merged with Allied Vintners to become Allied Distillers. Then, in 1994, Scapa was mothballed, with sporadic production introduced three years later. It was thus a surprise when Allied decided on a program of much-needed investment, undertaking a $3.85 million (£2.1 million) upgrade in 2004, but the present Chivas Brothers regime is grateful to them for the money and effort they spent on Orkney's "second" distillery.

TASTING NOTES

Scapa Skiren
Single malt, 40% ABV
Lime, peaches, almonds, cinnamon, and a hint of salt on the nose, leading into a palate of canned pears, honey, vanilla, more subtle salt, and a spicy finish.

Scapa Glansa
Single malt, 40% ABV
Vanilla, honey, pears, roasted nuts, and caramel on the nose. The palate is fruity, with cocoa, caramel, and soft peat smoke, with the smoke increasing through a dark berry finish.

Scapa Skiren

Scapa Glansa

TORABHAIG

OWNER Mossburn Distillers

FOUNDED 2016

WEBSITE www.torabhaig.com

Torabhaig distillery was created in and around a derelict farmstead dating back to the early 19th century on the Sleat peninsula of southeast Skye. It is equipped with one pair of stills and has an annual capacity of 132,000 gallons (500,000 liters) of spirit.

Torabhaig uses the tagline "Well-tempered peat," with Global Brand Manager for Torabhaig's parent company Mossburn Distillers Ltd, Bruce Perry saying that "We're not trying to make a medicinal whisky; it's something of a non-Islay, island spirit.

We're looking for nuanced peatiness. Heavily peated, yet delicate and gentle."

Having commenced distillation in 2017, Torabhaig's first release came in February 2021, with the initial bottling in the Legacy series, matured in first-fill bourbon barrels. This was later followed by Allt Gleann (Gaelic for Glen of the Burn), named after one of the distillery's water sources and aged in a combination of first-fill bourbon and refill casks.

As Bruce Perry explains, "We were very happy with what we were making at the start, but felt that after 10 years in cask, it might not be quite what we wanted. So we spent nine months getting it exactly where we wanted it, and by this time, we had four 'foundations,' as it were.

"At the close of 2023, Allt Gleann ended, with a batch-strength release, and Cnoc na Moine (Hill of Peat) was then launched, which includes some sherry cask-matured whisky. Then, the fourth and final bottling in our Legacy series will be Allt Breacach (the Speckled Burn), named for our second water source, and the plan is to include some Madeira cask-matured spirit in that. We will sell that for two years and then we will have our first 10-year-old permanent expression."

Journeyman's Drams

A feature of Torabhaig is that staff members are each offered the chance to distill spirit to their own specifications for two weeks of the year. To date, eight such "Journeyman's Drams" have been created, and their releases will follow on from the initial two. Journeyman variations on the theme of whisky-making have so far included altering cut points, using chocolate malt, heritage barley, such as the Chevallier variety, malt peated up to 138ppm, and even totally unpeated spirit. Iona MacPhie and Niall Culbertson were the first two to do this, each producing 2,650 bulk gallons (10,000 bulk liters) of spirit—around 80 barrels— some of which is due be released in early 2025.

This device is called a **shuttlebox** *and sieves the milled product into its constituent size.*

Torabhaig Allt Gleann (The Legacy Series 2nd Edition)

TASTING NOTE

Torabhaig Allt Gleann (The Legacy Series 2nd Edition)
Single malt, 46% ABV
The nose is earthy, slightly savory, with baked apple and apricots, plus sweet pipe smoke. Flavors of fruity smoke, brine, lemon, and treacle feature on the palate, which closes with wood smoke and a suggestion of iodine and black coffee.

CAMPBELTOWN AND THE LOWLANDS

A port and former royal burgh located on the Kintyre peninsula in Argyllshire, Campbeltown is the historic capital of Scotch whisky. Whisky making thrived here during the 19th century, and it retains its identity as a classification of single malt, though today the streets are mainly filled with the ghosts of past distillers. The designated Lowlands region encompasses mainland Scotland below the theoretical "Highland Line," taking in many of the country's principal centers of population. However, the distilleries of the Lowlands tend to enjoy unspoiled rural locations to rival anything the Highlands and Islands can offer.

REGIONAL STYLES
Traditionally, Campbeltown whiskies were full-bodied, peaty, oily drams with a maritime influence, and that style remains part of the profile of the expressions now being distilled there. Lowland whiskies tend to be relatively gentle, delicate, floral, and subtle.

AUTHOR'S CHOICE
SPRINGBANK A superbly idiosyncratic distillery that embraces all stages of whisky production. Heritage in abundance.

AUCHENTOSHAN The last Lowland distillery to triple distil its spirit, Auchentoshan is conveniently close to Glasgow and offers visitors a warm welcome.

REGIONAL EVENTS
In Edinburgh, leading specialist retailer Royal Mile Whiskies runs The Whisky Fringe, a popular annual event held during the Edinburgh International Festival in August (www.royalmilewhiskies.com). The Scotch Whisky Experience (www.scotchwhiskyexperience.co.uk) is located close to the castle, and on the city's most famous thoroughfare, the Johnnie Walker Princes Street attraction (www.johnniewalker.com) serves as a spectacular brand home for the world's bestselling Scotch whisky. Popular annual festivals are held in the county of Fife in March (www.fifewhiskyfestival.com), Glasgow in November (www.glasgowswhiskyfestival.com), and Campbeltown in May (www.glenscotia.com).

During the late 19th century, Campbeltown was home to more than 20 distilleries, but today that number has dwindled to just three, with the Speyside region having usurped Campbeltown as the principal center of Scotland's whisky-making industry. However, the remaining Campbeltown distilleries are in responsible hands, and the old herring port's whisky heritage looks to be secure.

From the point of view of scale, the Lowlands region once far outstripped the Highlands in whisky making capacity and output. The establishment of a major commercial Lowland distilling industry dates from the 1770s and '80s, with no fewer than 23 distilleries being built there during those two decades.

The area boasted ready supplies of high-quality malting barley, coal to fire the kilns and stills, and a comparatively advanced transportation infrastructure, hence the prevalence of distilling operations in the region. As with Campbeltown, the Lowlands saw a major decline in its fortunes, but during the last two decades, the region has seen more new distilleries (18) than in any other part of Scotland.

The area classified as the Lowlands malt whisky-producing region is also home to four of the country's six grain distilleries, as well as most of its blending and bottling operations and administrative functions due to the region's location between the distilleries of the Highlands and markets to the south.

Campbeltown is the historic capital *of Scotch whisky and after a serious decline in the 20th century, with only three distilleries remaining, it is now undergoing a new lease on life.*

GETTING AROUND

Ideally, make the most of a visit to remote Campbeltown by taking in some of the spectacular coastal scenery around about, and perhaps even making the short ferry trip from Claonaig to Lochranza on Arran. Road access to Campbeltown is via the A83 from the Glasgow area. In the Lowlands, Glenkinchie is close to Edinburgh via the A68 and Auchentoshan is accessed from Glasgow by the A82, while in Galloway, Bladnoch enjoys a location almost as remote as Campbeltown. Glasgow and Edinburgh are linked by the M8 highway, and the county of Fife, so popular with start-up distilleries, is easily accessed from Edinburgh and the south via the M90 over the Queensferry crossing of the Forth River.

N

Dundee

Perth

Eden Mill

Lindores Abbey

St.Andrews

Daftmill

Kingsbarns

Glenrothes

InchDairnie

Kirkcaldy

North Sea

Alloa

Stirling

Dunfermline

Firth of Forth

Rosebank

Forth

EDINBURGH

Falkirk

M9

Scotland
Campbeltown
& The Lowlands

North Sea

SCOTLAND

Glasgow

EDINBURGH

Lowlands

ENGLAND

Greenock

Auchentoshan

Clydebank

Clydeside

Glasgow

Holyrood

Pencaitland

Glenkinchie

Paisley

Glasgow
Distillery

Motherwell

Cheviot Hills

Hamilton

Clyde

Kilmarnock

Peebles

Galashiels

Melrose

Selkirk

Kintyre

Arran

Firth of Clyde

Lochlea

Ayr

Doon

Hawick

The Borders

Glen Scotia

Campbeltown

Springbank
& Glengyle

AYRSHIRE

Annan

Moffat

Ailsa Bay

Girvan

Southern Uplands

Lockerbie

Dumfries

Annandale

Gretna

Annan

Newtown Stewart

Wigtown

Carlisle

Stranraer

Bladnoch

Kirkcudbright

Solway Firth

ENGLAND

Mull of Galloway

0   10   20   30 miles

0   20   40   60 km

AUCHENTOSHAN

Auchentoshan American Oak

OWNER Morrison Bowmore Distillers Ltd (Beam Suntory)

FOUNDED 1823

WEBSITE www.auchentoshan.com

Every single malt needs a point of difference, something unique to mark it out from the competition as special and worthy of note. In the case of the single malt from Auchentoshan Distillery, the marketing team at owner Morrison Bowmore Distillers Ltd are gifted with the fact that their whisky is one of only a handful in Scotland to be fully triple-distilled on a permanent basis. Triple distillation is principally associated with Ireland but was also a traditional characteristic of the Lowland Scottish style of production. So how does the process work in practice, and what differences in character result from it?

Three times distilled

Auchentoshan uses three stills—a wash still, an intermediate still, and a spirit still. Triple-distillation results in a new-make spirit that starts life at 81.5 percent ABV, while most other distilleries settle for a new-make spirit of 70 percent ABV, through double distillation. As a result of triple-distillation, a lighter, cleaner, and more delicate spirit is produced.

Starting out

That malt was first made at Auchentoshan in 1823— or, to be more precise, the first license to distill was taken out in 1823 by a Mr. Thorne, though it is thought that distilling may have been taking place on the site since around 1800.

Auchentoshan passed through various hands during the 19th century, being substantially rebuilt in 1875. In 1903, the distillery was acquired by John Maclachlan, better known as a Glasgow brewer. The distillery remained in the hands of the Maclachlans until 1960, when Maclachlans Ltd was bought out by its high-profile brewing rival J. & R. Tennent. However, Auchentoshan had been seriously damaged during the Clydebank Blitz of March 13–14, 1941, when the equivalent of a million bottles of whisky was lost, with contemporary reports describing a burn of flaming whisky stretching to the Clyde River. During the Luftwaffe's devastating attack on

Auchentoshan 18-Year-Old

Clydebank, around 1,200 people lost their lives, with a further 1,100 suffering serious injury, and of the 12,000 houses in the borough, it is said that only eight escaped damage.

If the postwar period saw some dramatic changes in distillery and whisky-brand ownership, this was nothing compared to the rate of consolidation

Auchentoshan Three Wood

prevalent in the British brewing industry, and Tennent's lost its independence to Charrington & Company in 1964, with Charrington morphing into Bass Charrington Ltd three years later.

Ownership today

Auchentoshan was bought out of the brewer's ownership by Eadie Cairns Ltd in 1969 for about $240,000 (£100,000), and an extensive program of modernization followed. The distillery then passed to Stanley P. Morrison in 1984, for slightly more than three times the previous sale price, and a decade later, Morrison Bowmore was acquired by the Japanese distilling giant Suntory Ltd and is now part of its Suntory Global Spirits subsidiary. Investment in a $1.8 million (£1 million) visitor center followed in 2004, and this stylish facility now attracts around 20,000 people per year.

A new core range of single malts was established, and today that embraces the NAS American Oak, 12-, 18- and 21-year-olds, as well as the NAS Three Wood, matured in ex-bourbon barrels, oloroso sherry casks and finally, Pedro Ximénez sherry casks. The brand is notably active in the duty-free market, for which Blood Oak, American Oak Reserve, and Dark Oak are exclusively produced. Recent special editions have included a Sauvignon Blanc–finished expression and Bartenders' Malt—which includes whisky from five different decades, matured in a diverse range of oak types, including American and European, as well as a variety of sherry casks, red wine barriques, and German Oak. From sales of around 300,000 bottles two decades ago, Auchentoshan passed the 2 million bottles mark in 2021.

WHISKY TALES

Glasgow Malts
Just as Glenkinchie in the east used to be promoted as "The Edinburgh malt," so Auchentoshan has been known as "Glasgow's malt whisky," since the distillery is situated just 10 miles from the center of Scotland's largest city. Auchentoshan once had a distilling neighbor in the shape of Littlemill on the north bank of the Clyde River at Bowling, until its closure in 1992 and demolition in 2006. With the creation of Glasgow and Clydeside distilleries in 2015 and 2017, respectively, whisky-making has returned to the city itself.

TASTING NOTES

Auchentoshan Three Wood
Single malt, matured principally in American oak ex-bourbon casks, then finished in Spanish oloroso sherry wood, and finally Pedro Ximénez sherry casks, 43% ABV
Butterscotch, dates, hazelnuts, and sherry on the nose. Sweet and sherried on the rich palate, with developing citrus fruits and almonds. Quite lengthy in the fruity finish, with a tang of oak.

Auchentoshan American Oak
Single malt, 40% ABV
The nose is floral, with pine, citrus fruit, and vanilla toffee. The palate features milk chocolate, coconut, and ripe peaches, closing with grapefruit and light pepper.

Auchentoshan 18-Year-Old
Single malt, 43% ABV
Spicy vanilla, honey, and almonds on the nose, while flavors of malt, ginger, and oak develop on the palate, which finishes with nutmeg, raisins, and drying oak.

GLENKINCHIE

Glenkinchie 27-Year-Old

OWNER Diageo plc

FOUNDED 1825

WEBSITE www.malts.com

Although Glenkinchie is situated in rolling East Lothian farmland some 17 miles southeast of Edinburgh, its proximity to Scotland's capital has led to it being known as "The Edinburgh Malt," though the arrival of Holyrood, Bonnington, and Port of Leith distilleries within the capital have somewhat discredited that claim.

Now one of more than 20 working Lowland malt distilleries, Glenkinchie was founded under the name of Milton Distillery in 1825 by the farming brothers John and George Rate, who grew their own malting barley. Glenkinchie's agricultural connection continued until relatively recent times, with the distillery manager running the distillery's own farm himself during the 1940s and 1950s, winning many prizes with his herd of pedigree Aberdeen Angus cattle.

The Glenkinchie name was first adopted in 1837, but after the Rates sold their distillery to a local farmer in 1853, he chose to use the premises as a sawmill and cowshed rather than a place to make whisky. However, in 1880, with blended whisky firmly in fashion, a consortium of Edinburgh businessmen purchased the site and subsequently began to distill again under the auspices of the Glen Kinchie Distillery Company, which became a limited company in 1890.

The distillery was refurbished and upgraded over the next few years, then in 1914, it was one of five Lowland distilleries (along with Clydesdale, Grange, Rosebank, and St. Magdalene), which merged to form Scottish Malt Distillers (SMD). Membership of SMD almost certainly ensured Glenkinchie's survival during the harsh economic climate of the next two decades. In 1925, SMD was acquired by the Distillers Company Ltd. While in the ownership of DCL, Glenkinchie was licensed to John Haig & Company Ltd, and to this day, the distillery provides malt for the Haig blend.

The Haig connection
From the 1930s to the 1970s, the Haig brand was Scotland's leading whisky, and by 1939, Gold Label

Glenkinchie 2022
Distillers Edition

had become the biggest seller in the DCL stable. The blend's origins lie in the 17th century, and claims have been made that Haig's is the oldest whisky distilling company in the world. During the 18th and 19th centuries, various members of the Haig family were at the very heart of large-scale Scotch whisky distillation. Most famously, Cameronbridge Distillery at Windygates in Fife was established by John Haig in 1824, and the plant is credited with being the first in Scotland to produce grain whisky. Cameronbridge became one of the six founding distilleries of DCL in 1877 and today is Diageo's flagship grain-producing facility, with a capacity of more than 265,000 gallons (100 million liters) of spirit per year.

Classic Lowland

In 1986, Glenkinchie was selected as the Lowland representative in the Classic Malts portfolio, and this choice may have played a major part in the subsequent closure of Rosebank at Falkirk in 1993. There are connoisseurs who claim that Rosebank was the superior single malt, but the distillery's situation on the outskirts of an industrial town were no match for the lush pastures of rural East Lothian when it came to creating a visitor-friendly environment. Rosebank's loss was Glenkinchie's gain, and today the latter has been known to play host to more than 40,000 visitors each year.

Glenkinchie is equipped with a pair of notably large stills, providing a relatively low level of copper

A handful of the barley used to produce the 345,000 gallons *(1.3 million liters) of malt whisky distilled annually at the distillery.*

contact for the spirit being distilled. Glenkinchie is known for producing clear wort, which is achieved by not back-stirring in the mash tun, but clear wort is only one factor in the character of Glenkinchie, along with the length of fermentations and the presence of worm tuns for condensation purposes.

The drams

A 12-year-old was selected as the core expression in 2007 and sits alongside a Distillers Edition, finished in amontillado casks. A limited edition 16-year-old appeared in 2020 when Glenkinchie became the first of Diageo's "Four Corners of Scotland" distilleries, and 2023 saw a 27-year-old, matured in refill American barrels and European oak butts, take its place in that year's Special Releases program.

Glenkinchie 12-Year-Old

WHISKY TALES

Four Corners
Glenkinchie's former maltings served as a museum of whisky production from 1969 onward, and the distillery has always enjoyed a high level of visitor footfall. However, 2020 saw its visitor offering transformed, when it was reimagined as the first of Diageo's Four Corners of Scotland, celebrating the important role its malt plays in the Johnnie Walker family of blends. Four tour and tasting options are available, including the Glenkinchie Flavor Journey—"A full-sensory tour and whisky tasting," while the Hidden Lowland Tour & Tasting is "Designed for the aficionado of extraordinary whiskies, great stories and adventure." Luxurious new bar and lounge areas have been developed, while a life-size statue of Johnnie Walker greets visitors at the distillery entrance.

TASTING NOTES

Glenkinchie 12-Year-Old
Single malt, 43% ABV
Fresh and floral nose, with spices and citrus fruits, plus a hint of marshmallow. Medium-bodied, smooth, sweet, and fruity, with malt, butter, and cheesecake. The finish is comparatively long and drying, initially rather herbal.

Glenkinchie 2022 Distillers Edition
Single malt, finished in ex-amontillado sherry butts after its principal period of maturation, 43% ABV
Rich and complex on the nose, with honey, vanilla, sherry, and new leather. Full-bodied palate, with stewed fruit and molasses, contrasting with drier, slightly smoky notes. The finish features toffee apples and nuts.

Glenkinchie 27-Year-Old (**Diageo 2023 Special Releases**)
Single malt, 58.3% ABV
The nose offers aromas of apple, vanilla, almonds, and new-mowed hay, while flavors of citrus fruit, oak spice, and more vanilla feature on the viscous palate, which dries in the lengthy finish.

GLEN SCOTIA

OWNER Loch Lomond Group (Hillhouse
Capital Management)

FOUNDED 1832

WEBSITE www.glenscotia.com

Having long played second fiddle to its slightly older
Campbeltown brother Springbank, Glen Scotia has
emerged in recent years as more than a match for its
sibling, in terms of whisky quality and distillery
profile. Glen Scotia was established by Stewart,
Galbraith & Company Ltd in 1832, and several
changes of ownership occurred before the distillery
fell silent between 1928 and 1933. Production
resumed courtesy of Bloch Brothers (Distillers) Ltd,
who sold the distillery to Hiram Walker (Scotland)
Ltd in 1954. Hiram Walker soon disposed of Glen
Scotia to the Glasgow blenders A Gillies & Company,
which became part of Amalgamated Distillers
Products (ADP) in 1970. Between 1979 and 1982
more than $2 million (£1 million) was spent
refurbishing Glen Scotia, but another period of
silence was just two years away. Whisky making
recommenced in 1989 under ADP's new parent
Gibson International, but a further change of
ownership saw the distillery mothballed once more
by Glen Catrine Bonded Warehouse Ltd in 1994.

Renaissance

Distilling recommenced five years later, and a major
factor in Glen Scotia' renaissance has been the
presence of manager Iain Macallister, who has
overseen a comprehensive refurbishment and
upgrading program, leading a team of dedicated staff
who had no intention of allowing Glen Scotia to
remain Campbeltown's "second" distillery. The good
work begun by Glen Catrine has been carried on by
Hillhouse Capital Management, which has owned the
distillery since 2019.

There is not a computer in sight in Glen Scotia's
production area, and the single pair of stills is
controlled by two hand-turned valves per still, with
the wash still having a capacity of 3,120 gallons
(11,800 liters), while the spirit still can hold 2,270
gallons (8600 liters). "The shape and height of the
stills will give heavy, robust, oily distillate," notes Iain
Macallister. "The wash still is wide at the base, short

Glen Scotia Victoriana

Glen Scotia 18-Year-Old

and stocky, with a long, wide lyne arm. We start to cut to heart of the run at 72–73 percent ABV and cut again at 63 percent ABV. We run relatively slowly, at 74–80 gallons (280–300 liters) per hour. The harder you run it, the more you burn off and lose positive character." He sums up the essential style of Glen Scotia as "Coastal, marine, with oiliness. Robust, with the potential for smokiness. 'Funk' sometimes—not quite in balance but an incredibly interesting flavor profile."

A Glen Scotia spokesperson adds that "we are delighted to be witnessing a real resurgence of interest across the globe for our style of whisky. Glen Scotia has doubled in size and is one of the fastest growing single malt whiskies in the world. We have a growing

At Glen Scotia, the cast-iron mash tun is more than 100 years old. During the mash, the temperature gradually increases to extract sugars from the mash.

group of passionate fans coming here from Asia to the US, from Europe to Australasia, and everywhere in between."

The whiskies

The core lineup consists of Double Cask, matured in first-fill bourbon barrels and finished in Pedro Ximénez sherry casks, Double Cask Rum Finish, 10-, 15-, 18-, and 25-year-olds, plus the cask-strength Victoriana, with whisky from heavily charred casks in its profile, along with the NAS lightly peated Glen Scotia Harbour. In 2023, the distillery's oldest release to date, a 42-year-old appeared, along with The Mermaid, the first installment in the Icons of Campbeltown series, 12 years old, finished in Palo Cortado sherry casks and bottled at cask strength.

TASTING NOTES

Glen Scotia Double Cask
Single malt, 46% ABV
Slightly smoky sherry on the nose, with peaches, apricots, vanilla, and caramel. Sherry, salted caramel, cinnamon, and wood spices on the palate, with a closing herbal note and sea salt.

Glen Scotia Victoriana
Single malt, 51.5% ABV
The nose is oily with barrel char, furniture polish, pineapple, and salt, while the palate offers crème brulée, salted caramel, sherry, and fennel, finishing on spice and charred briny oak.

Glen Scotia 18-Year-Old
Single malt, 46% ABV
Aromas of apple blossom, oranges, vanilla, wood polish, and ozone lead into flavors of sweet sherry, juicy orange, dark chocolate, and fondant, closing with spice and salt.

Glen Scotia Double Cask

SPRINGBANK & GLENGYLE

OWNER J. & A. Mitchell & Company Ltd

FOUNDED 1828 (Springbank); 2004 (Glengyle)

WEBSITE www.springbankdistillers.com;
www.kilkerran.com

Campbeltown stands close to the southern end of the remote Kintyre Peninsula and was once as notable for its herring-fishing fleet as it was for its whisky making. The fishing industry in Scotland is a shadow of its former self, and Campbeltown has suffered along with most other ports, while the great whisky industry that flourished there in the 19th century was dramatically diminished during the 20th. By 1925, only 12 Campbeltown distilleries were working, and 1935 saw just Glen Scotia and Springbank operational.

Heritage and survival
When it comes to whisky, Springbank Distillery is one of the great survivors, due in part to the fact that it is privately owned by members of the Mitchell family, with the late chairman Hedley G. Wright being a passionate advocate of Campbeltown's continuation as a center for whisky making.

Such was his passion that in 2000 he acquired the site and structures of the town's former Glengyle Distillery, and four years later, after almost eight decades of silence, it was back in production, becoming the first "new" whisky-making facility in Campbeltown for over 125 years. Glengyle whiskies are bottled under the "Kilkerran" name, as "Glengyle" is registered for an unassociated blended malt. A 3-year-old release appeared in 2007, followed by a number of "work in progress" expressions, until a 12-year-old bottling in 2016. Variants aged up to 17 years have been launched, along with several batches of "Kilkerran Heavily Peated." The distillery capacity is 200,000 gallons (750,000 liters) per annum, but the maximum usually distilled is around 26,500 gallons (100,000 liters).

Springbank and Glengyle distillery manager Gavin McLachlan reports, "The whisky itself is coming on well. It's sweet, floral, lightly peated, and maturing well. We bottle it as work in progress for people to try, and the current one is our third such bottling. It's seven years old and the component whiskies come from sherry, rum, and port casks as well as bourbon wood."

Hazelburn 10-Year-Old

Longrow

Glengyle's big brother, Springbank, was the 14th distillery to be established in Campbeltown, founded in 1828. It was founded by the Reid family, whose in-laws, the Mitchells, purchased it from them during a period of financial difficulty in 1837. It has remained with the Mitchells ever since and is the oldest family-owned distillery in Scotland.

Springbank 10-Year-Old

Idiosyncratic

One of the factors that make Springbank unique is that it is effectively two-and-a-half-times distilled. It is lightly peated and sweet. The sweet, fruity character comes in part from long fermentations—up to 110 hours—and Springbank is also unique in that 100 percent of the whole process, from malting to bottling, is carried out on the premises. Indeed, the distillery is almost a working museum. A significant number of people are employed compared to most distilleries these days, in line with the late Hedley Wright's desire to create as much local employment as possible.

In addition to making two-and-a-half-times-distilled Springbank in its one wash still and pair of spirit stills, the distillery has produced a double-distilled, heavily peated single malt by the name of "Longrow" since the mid-1970s, with a 10-year-old variant being released in 1985. Batches of unpeated, triple-distilled Hazelburn single malt are also made, while the wash still in which all these whiskies are created is singular in being heated both by internal steam coils and direct-firing by oil.

Springbank was silent from 1979 to 1987, and again during 2008–2009 when fuel and barley costs were high. Production has resumed since then, though on a relatively modest scale, with Springbank making up an average of 60 percent of annual output, while the remainder is split between Longrow and Hazelburn. Springbank is available in limited quantities at 10, 15 and 18 years of age, along with occasional batches of 21-, 25- and 30-year-olds. The standard Longrow expression is bottled without an age statement, though annual releases of an 11-year-old with a tawny port finish appear as Longrow Red, along with 18- and 21-year-olds. The core Hazelburn is 10 years old, but 14- and 21-year-old variants have also been released.

TASTING NOTES

Springbank 10-Year-Old
Single malt, matured in a mix of ex-sherry and ex-bourbon casks, 46% ABV
Fresh and briny on the nose, with citrus fruit and barley. Sweet on the palate, with developing brine and vanilla toffee. Long and spicy in the finish, with more salt, coconut oil, and peat.

Longrow
Single malt, 46% ABV
Brine, worn leather, and wood smoke feature on the nose, while the palate offers grapes, herbal and medicinal notes, and developing smokiness, finishing with salty peat.

Hazelburn 10-Year-Old
Single malt, 46% ABV
Tropical fruits figure on the nose, with apple pie, vanilla, and honey. Green apples and a hint of charcuterie on the palate, with ginger and salted caramel, closing with earthy, oily notes.

WHISKY TALES

Whisky City
Although only three distilleries operate in Campbeltown today, whisky making has actually taken place on approximately 35 sites in the Kintyre borough, with the first written reference to whisky in relation to the area occurring in 1591. When the writer Alfred Barnard visited Campbeltown in 1885, researching his epic tome *The Whisky Distilleries of the United Kingdom*, he toured no fewer than 21 distilleries and proclaimed Campbeltown to be "Whisky City." Among those he graced with his presence was Springbank, which had been built during the great distillery construction boom that saw a remarkable 24 new distilleries appear in Campbeltown between 1823 and 1835.

AILSA BAY

OWNER William Grant & Sons Ltd

FOUNDED 2007

WEBSITE www.ailsabay.com

William Grant & Sons Ltd is not a company that likes to make a fuss about its activities, and so it was that when the Ailsa Bay malt whisky distillery began producing spirit in 2007, many people did not even know that the facility had been under construction. It is located within Grant's vast Girvan grain distilling, blending, and bonding complex, close to the Ayrshire coast.

William Grant & Sons' vast Girvan grain distillery supplies grain spirit for the company's Scotch whisky blends.

The new distillery was developed within an existing structure, and it took just nine months to build. In that respect, it mirrored Girvan grain distillery, which was constructed and equipped to the same timescale back in 1963. Ailsa Bay was intended primarily to supply malt for William Grant & Sons' family of blends, and as such its stills were modeled on those at Balvenie. Having been doubled in size during 2013, the distillery now boasts two mash tuns, 24 stainless steel washbacks, and 16 stills, giving it an impressive annual capacity of 3.2 million gallons (12 million liters).

Freedom to experiment

One wash still and one spirit still are fitted with stainless steel condensers to allow for the production of a more sulfur-rich spirit. Overall, five styles of spirits are produced, including a sweet and relatively light variant, along with a sulfury type and three different peated versions.

"The whole place was set up to let us be experimental in ways we can't be with our more traditional distilleries," explains Master Blender Brian Kinsman. "Some 95 percent of the Ailsa Bay output is standard style, peated to less than 2ppm, while up to 5 percent comprises spirit that is lightly peated to 5–8ppm or heavily peated to 15ppm plus." The plant is geared toward making whisky for Grant's portfolio of blends, and Kinsman describes the template blend, Family Reserve, as "a Speyside-style blend with a sweet base of grain. Our own three malts of Glenfiddich, Balvenie, and Kininvie give it its essential fruity and floral style."

The whisky

In 2016, a peated single malt was released under the Ailsa Bay name, initially matured in 6.5–26 gallon (25–100-liter) Hudson Baby Bourbon casks, before maturation in virgin, first-fill, and refill conventional American oak casks. Two years later came 10-year-old Aerstone Land Cask and Aerstone Sea Cask, respectively matured inland and on the Ayrshire coast at Girvan.

TASTING NOTE

Ailsa Bay Release 1.2
Single malt, 48.9% ABV
The nose is fragrant, with tobacco smoke, vanilla, and lemon, leading into a palate of delicate, floral peat smoke, cinnamon, white pepper, and apple pie, closing with bonfire smoke.

Ailsa Bay Release 1.2

BLADNOCH

OWNER David Prior

FOUNDED 1817

WEBSITE www.bladnoch.com

Located in the village of the same name, near Wigtown in Dumfries and Galloway, Bladnoch is the most southerly operational distillery in Scotland. It was founded between 1814 and 1817 by Thomas McClelland, remaining in the family's hands until 1930, when it was acquired by the Belfast distilling company of Dunville. Since then, Bladnoch has experienced a somewhat checkered history, characterized by numerous changes of ownership and two decades of silence between 1936 and 1956.

Historically, triple distillation has been a common feature of many Lowland distilleries, and Bladnoch was a triple-distilled single malt until the 1960s. Bladnoch's owners have included Inver House Distillers, who acquired the site in 1973 and operated the plant for a decade. Another decade on, and now part of United Distillers, Bladnoch's remoteness in the far southwest of Scotland counted against it, and the last spirit flowed from its stills in June 1993.

The restoration of Bladnoch

That could well have been the end of Bladnoch, but Raymond Armstrong, a partner in the family construction business in Banbridge, County Down, Northern Ireland, acquired Bladnoch in 1994 and eventually persuaded United Distillers to allow him to recommission the distillery. By the end of 2000, Bladnoch had been reequipped and restored, and production recommenced on December 18, 2000.

A significant number of releases appeared under the Armstrong regime, but 2014 saw the distillery company liquidated, with ownership passing to Australian businessman David Prior the following year. Prior spent $41.2 million (£25 million) purchasing and totally refurbishing and upgrading the distillery, before production resumed in 2017.

Bladnoch is equipped with two pairs of stills and runs close to its annual capacity of 400,000 gallons (1.5 million liters) of spirit. A quartet of NAS expressions make up the core range, and these are Vinaya (matured in a combination of first-fill bourbon and first-fill sherry casks), Samsara (matured in ex-bourbon and ex-Californian red wine casks), the peated Alinta, and Liora (aged in bourbon and new oak casks). Additionally, 11-, 14-, 19-, and 30-year-old bottlings are available, along with Talia—matured in oloroso sherry and American oak red wine casks from the oldest stock in the Bladnoch warehouses.

Bladnoch 19-Year-Old

Bladnoch Vinaya

TASTING NOTES

Bladnoch Samsara
Single malt, 46.7% ABV
The initial nose is slightly savory, with peaches and cream, plus soft spices, leading into a palate of mango, passion fruit, and vanilla, closing with pears and spicy tannins.

Bladnoch Vinaya
Single malt, 46.7% ABV
Linseed oil, pears, vanilla, and butterscotch on the nose. The palate yields toffee, milk chocolate, honey, and sugared almonds, with malt and ginger in the finish.

Bladnoch 19-Year-Old
Single malt, 46.7% ABV
Molasses, overripe bananas, figs, and dark berries on the nose, while flavors of plus, cocoa, allspice, and dates appear on the palate, which closes with nutmeg and tannic oak.

ANNANDALE

OWNER Annandale Distillery Company

FOUNDED 2014

WEBSITE www.annandaledistillery.com

When Annandale fired up its stills in 2014, it was not so much the birth of a new distillery but the rebirth of an old one. The original plant had been established in 1836, near the Galloway town of Annan, and closed during 1918. The second-most southerly distillery in Scotland was revived between 2011 and 2014 by locally born businessman David Thomson, who spent some $18.5 million (€14.02 million) reconstructing Annandale, installing a copper-topped semi-lauter mash tun, three wooden washbacks, and two spirit stills and one wash still in the process.

Unpeated single malt is marketed as Founder's Selection Man O'Words (after the poet Robert Burns) and peated (45ppm) single malt as Man O'Sword

(after King Robert the Bruce). Core bottlings appear in the Founder's Selection range and are all from single casks—both bourbon and sherry—and are offered at cask strength. Other bottlings include Vintage and Rare Vintage, and these each consist of vattings of several casks. The Maltings Coffee Shop offers high-quality fresh food, craft beers and some rare bottlings of Annandale whisky.

TASTING NOTES

Annandale Founder's Selection 2017 Man O'Words
Single malt, 60% ABV
The nose is earthy, with freshly sawed wood, strawberry jam, and spice, while the palate offers red berries, salted caramel, cloves, and cinnamon, closing on red currants and lively oak.

Annandale Founder's Selection 2017 Man O'Sword
Single malt, 60% ABV
Peat, hay, white pepper, and chili on the nose. Malt, coconut, grilled meat, dark berry fruits, and coffee on the palate, ending with bonfire, black pepper, and dark chocolate.

Annandale Founder's Selection 2017 Man O'Sword

THE BORDERS

OWNER Borders Distillery Company Ltd

FOUNDED 2017

WEBSITE www.thebordersdistillery.com

Until the establishment of The Borders Distillery, the last whisky made on a legal basis in the Scottish Borders had been produced in Kelso during 1837. A disused former electric works on Hawick's Commercial Road that dated from 1903 was selected as the site, and a handsome conversion was undertaken to develop a facility that boasts two pairs of pot stills and can produce vodka, gin, and whisky.

Workshop whisky

Borders' first two whisky releases were highly innovative and were offered in the Workshop Series. WS:01 was Malt & Rye, with the Borders' team explaining that "In 2019, we distilled a small batch of rye spirit and matured it in the same fresh-fill bourbon casks as the malt, to create this remarkable and aromatic whisky. This is the first blended Scotch

whisky to leave the Scottish Borders since 1837." This bottling was followed by WS:02—The Long & Short of it. "Our distillers experimented with very short fermentations of 55 hours and very long ones of 150 hours," say the distillers. "Both batches were then distilled twice and matured in first fill ex-bourbon barrels, before being married with single grain." Additionally, the distillery retails a third-party blended Scotch named Clan Fraser Reserve and a blended malt called Lower East Side.

TASTING NOTES

The Borders Malt & Rye
Blended whisky, 63.8% single grain, 36.2% single malt, 40% ABV
Spicy orchard fruit and a hint of char on the nose, while the palate offers more fruit, vanilla, and marshmallows, closing with rye spice notes.

The Borders The Long and the Short of It
Single malt, 40% ABV
The nose yields aromas of barley sugar, pear juice, and white wine, while flavors of vanilla, peach, and toffee feature on the palate, which finishes on drying fruit.

The Borders The Long and the Short of It

CLYDESIDE

OWNER Morrison Glasgow Distillers

FOUNDED 2017

WEBSITE www.theclydeside.com

The former pumphouse of Queen's Dock on the River Clyde, not far from Glasgow city center, is home to The Clydeside distillery. The actual pumphouse, dating from 1877, has been converted into an attractive visitor center, while adjoining new buildings house the distilling apparatus.

The Clydeside operates two stills and has an annual capacity of 132,000 gallons (500,000 million liters). It is headed up by members of the illustrious Morrison distilling family, owners of independent bottler AD Rattray. In one of those quirks of fate, the great-grandfather of The Clydeside's founder Tim Morrison designed the pumphouse that used to power the gates of the Queen's Dock.

In late 2021, The Clydeside distillery launched its first single malt, named Stobcross after a historic feature that once marked the way to Dumbarton Rock on the Clyde. The whisky was made from 100 percent Scottish barley and matured in American and European oak casks. Five-year-old and cask strength variants have subsequently been released.

TASTING NOTES

The Clydeside Stobcross
Single malt, 46% ABV
The nose is floral, with honey and tropical fruits, leading into a palate of ginger, newly planed oak and fruit-and-nut milk chocolate bars, finishing with malt and citric oak.

The Clydeside 2023 Limited Edition
Single malt, 60.6% ABV
Rich tropical fruits, vanilla, and warm apple pie on the nose. Ripe peaches, crème fraîche, and ginger on the plate, which closes with citrus notes and oak spices.

The Clydeside 2023
Limited Edition

DAFTMILL

OWNER The Cuthbert family

FOUNDED 2003

WEBSITE www.daftmilldistillery.com

Daftmill was created by members of the Cuthbert farming family within disused agricultural buildings on their land near Cupar, in Fife. The first spirit flowed in December 2005, and the distillery's operation is fitted around the demands of the farming year, which include growing and harvesting their own malting barley—meaning that on average just 100 casks are filled per annum. A refreshing aspect of the venture, led by Francis Cuthbert, is that whereas so many "start-up" ventures are eager to release their spirit as soon as it is old enough to legally be termed "Scotch whisky," the Cuthbert family waited for 12 years before offering their inaugural release to the public in 2018.

Daftmill released
One of Scotland's smallest malt whisky distilleries, Daftmill's first release comprised just 629 bottles,

Daftmill uses ex-bourbon casks from the Heaven Hill distillery in Kentucky.

which were eagerly snapped up by aficionados eager to discover the qualities of this long-awaited single malt, and it was followed by a 2006 Summer bottling and a 2006 Winter bottling. Similar seasonal releases have continued, while the first 15-year-old bottling appeared in cask-strength format during 2022.

TASTING NOTE

Daftmill 15-Year-Old Cask Strength
Single malt, 55.7% ABV
Ripe green apples, vanilla, and nutmeg on the nose, while the palate offers grapefruit, guava, and orange marmalade, finishing on allspice and soft oak.

Daftmill 15-Year-Old
Cask Strength

EDEN MILL

OWNER Inverleith LLP

FOUNDED 2012

WEBSITE www.edenmill.co.uk

Eden Mill was developed from an initial brewing enterprise at Guardbridge in Fife, using distinctive "alembic" copper pot stills. Ownership passed from founders Paul Miller and Tony Kelly to the Innerleith investment company in 2022, and two years later, the distillery moved into new $10.1 million (£8 million) eco-friendly premises alongside its original home on the new St. Andrews University Eden Campus. This allowed for greater quantities of gin, vodka, and whisky.

In 2018, the first seven of 17 single cask expressions in 200ml bottles appeared under the "Hip Flask Series" label, after which the first 10 bottles of

"Eden Mill First Bottling—Limited Release" were offered for sale via Whisky Auctioneer. Bottle No. 1 sold for $9,220 (£7,296), breaking the world record for the first release from a distillery. In 2023, the distillery launched its Signature Single Malt Whisky collection, comprising The Bourbon Cask and The Sherry Cask.

TASTING NOTES

Eden Mill The Bourbon Cask
Single malt, matured in first-fill bourbon casks, 46% ABV
Apple pie, barley sugar, and toasted oak on the nose, while the palate yields salted caramel, ginger biscuits, and orchard fruits, closing with spicy oak.

Eden Mill The Sherry Cask
Single malt, 46% ABV, matured in sherry and bourbon casks, and finished in first-fill oloroso and first-fill Pedro Ximénez casks.
Aromas of toffee, dried fruit, and figs with flavors of dates, Jaffa oranges, and dark chocolate, closing with spicy sherry.

Eden Mill
The Bourbon Cask

GLASGOW

Glasgow 1770 Peated

OWNER Hughes & McDougall

FOUNDED 2015

WEBSITE www.glasgowdistillery.com

When Glasgow distillery started production in 2015, it became the first in the city to make single malt whisky since 1902. It is equipped with a pair of whisky stills made by Carl in Germany, along with a separate gin still. Makar Gin soon became a bestseller for the distillery, and Glasgow's whisky came of age in 2018, when 5,000 bottles of "1770" were released, being available by ballot via the distillery's website. The whisky in question had been aged in first-fill bourbon barrels and briefly finished in virgin oak casks.

Single malt

The initial single malt was released in 2018 and was named 1770 Glasgow Single Malt, with 1770 being the date when the original Glasgow Distillery Company was founded. A peated variant is also produced, and 2020 saw the third and final variant in its "Signature" range, namely 1770 Triple Distilled. Subsequently, an ongoing Small Batch Series has been

launched and, to date, releases have included a variant finished in tequila casks, a peated version finished in Cognac casks, and a bottling finished in a combination of Bordeaux red wine and port casks. For visitors to the distillery, there is also the exclusive Cooper's Cask Release.

TASTING NOTES

Glasgow 1770 The Original
Single malt, matured in virgin oak and bourbon casks, 40% ABV
Orange blossom, vanilla, and warm biscuits on the nose, with a palate of green apples, marzipan, and cloves, finishing with lime marmalade and lively oak.

Glasgow 1770 Peated
Single malt, matured in virgin oak and finished in Pedro Ximénez sherry casks, 40% ABV
Initially, fruity peat smoke, dates, and nougat, with the smoke becoming more tarlike, leading into a palate of earthy peat, bananas, and worn leather, closing on nutty peat.

Glasgow 1770 Triple Distilled
Single malt, matured in virgin oak and bourbon casks, 46% ABV
The nose offers vanilla, ginger, and cannned peaches, with flavors of pear juice and apples. Honey and brittle toffee appear on the palate, finishing on apricots, licorice, and drying oak.

HOLYROOD

OWNER Holyrood Distillery Ltd

FOUNDED 2019

WEBSITE www.holyrooddistillery.co.uk

When the first spirit flowed at Edinburgh's Holyrood distillery in 2019, it marked a return to malt whisky distillation in Scotland's capital city for the first time since 1925, when Glen Sciennes fell silent. Holyrood is based in the characterful "Engine Shed" building, which dates from 1835, when it was constructed as part of the Edinburgh & Dalkeith Railway.

The two stills stand 23ft (7m) tall, and the distillery boasts a capacity of 66,000 gallons (250,000 liters) per annum, with the onus being very much on experimental production. Heritage barley varieties are used—in 2022, no fewer than 23 different yeast types were employed in 99 varying mash recipes. Holyrood also boasts an innovative cask program, where participants may choose from a wide range of permutations relating to everything from yeast varieties to distilling "cut points" to size and type of cask.

Given its location close to Edinburgh's city center, Holyrood has set out its stall to attract visitors and is offering what is described as "A hands-on, sensory, educational experience." The year 2023 saw the release of Holyrood's first single malt whisky, named Arrival.

TASTING NOTE

Holyrood Arrival
Single malt, matured in oloroso and Pedro Ximénez sherry casks, bourbon barrels, and rum barriques, 46.1% ABV
The nose offers dried fruit, toffee, warm fruit cake, and a hint of leather, with flavors of vanilla, caramel, ginger, and raisins, and some charcuterie and sweet spice in the finish.

Holyrood Arrival

INCHDAIRNIE

Inchdairnie Ryelaw

OWNER InchDairnie Distillery Ltd

FOUNDED 2015

WEBSITE www.inchdairniedistillery.com

Rather like the Holyrood distillery, InchDairnie is far from being a conventional whisky-making venture. It is significantly larger than most of its independent, youthful contemporaries, boasting a capacity of 1.05 million gallons (4 million liters) per annum. It is equipped with a hammer mill, mash conversion vessel, and mash filter rather than a traditional mash tun, which makes for easier mashing when using nonmalted barley, To date, wheat, oats, and rye have been distilled at InchDairnie, as well as malted barley. In addition to a pair of copper pot stills, InchDairnie boats a Lomond-style still, which effectively comprises a column still with six plates above a pot.

Rye whisky

The Lomond-type still is used to produce RyeLaw rye whisky, launched in 2023, and the first product to emerge from InchDairnie as it was the earliest to reach maturity. Reflecting on InchDairnie's

Inchdairnie distillery is located on the outskirts of the Fife town of Glenrothes.

experiences with rye, distillery founder and managing director Ian Palmer observes that "US regulations state a minimum 51 percent rye content, and eventually we settled on 53:47 malted rye to malted barley. In the US, they specify using virgin oak casks, so we did the same."

TASTING NOTE

Inchdairnie Ryelaw
Single grain, 46.3% ABV
Sweet floral spices, increasing in heat, with honey, vanilla, and a lightly perfumed note on the nose. The palate is lightly oily and offers soft rye and spice, ripe bananas, and caramel, with lingering rye heat through the nutty, tangy fruit finish.

KINGSBARNS

OWNER The Wemyss family

FOUNDED 2014

WEBSITE www.kingsbarnsdistillery.com

Kingsbarns is located near the famous university and golfing town of St. Andrews in Fife and was constructed around a derelict 18th-century farmstead. It is owned by the Wemyss family, large local estate owners and entrepreneurs, who invested $4.75 million (£3 million) in 2012 to take on the distillery project and bring it to fruition.

The first casks of whisky were filled in March 2015, and the initial release—to Founders' Club members—came in 2018. The following year saw the launch of the distillery's flagship single malt Dream to Dram. It comprised 90 percent spirit from first-fill Heaven Hill ex-bourbon casks and 10 percent from first-fill STR wine barriques. Subsequent releases have included Distillery Reserve 2020 and 2021, and Balcomie, a 5-year-old expression matured in American oak oloroso sherry butts. In 2021 a limited edition comprising whisky aged in ex-bourbon and ex-oloroso sherry casks was introduced, named Bell Rock after a historic lighthouse located off the Scottish east coast. The year 2023 saw Dream to Dram replaced by Doocot, a variant twice as old as its predecessor.

TASTING NOTE

Kingsbarns Doocot
Single malt, 46% ABV
Red apples, banana, honey, and sharpened pencils on the nose, while the palate yields pineapple, raspberry, and cooked cereal, closing with kiwi fruit and soft oak.

Kingsbarns Doocot

LINDORES ABBEY

OWNER Lindores Distilling Company

FOUNDED 2017

WEBSITE www.lindoresabbeydistillery.com

The first spirit flowed from the stills of Lindores Abbey distillery on December 13, 2017, and the idea to create it came from Drew McKenzie-Smith and his wife, Helen, with the McKenzie-Smith family having owned the abbey ruins and surrounding farmland since 1913. With funds in place via three European investors, the $15.6 million (£10 million) project got under way in 2013, utilizing a 250-year-old farm steading opposite the abbey.

The distillery's mash tun and three stills were fabricated by famous coppersmiths Forsyth's of Rothes, while the wooden washbacks were made a few miles away by Joseph Brown Vats of Dufftown. Although Lindores boasts three stills, this does not signify a return to the old Lowland practice of triple distillation, rather one large wash still serves two relatively small spirit stills, ensuring a significant amount of copper contact, leading to a clean, delicate style of spirit.

The three copper stills were made by the famous coppersmith firm Forsyth's of Rothes.

The first release of Lindores single malt—named MCDXCIV—came in 2021, with maturation having been achieved in a mix of bourbon and sherry casks and wine barriques. Limited releases have followed.

TASTING NOTE

Lindores MCDXCIV (1494)
Single malt, 46% ABV
Gently spicy, with red berries, malt, sherry, and a hint of smoke on the nose. Dry fruits, nutmeg, and black pepper characterize the palate, which closes with licorice and subtle tannins.

Lindores MCDXCIV (1494)

LOCHLEA

OWNER Lochlea Distilling Company

FOUNDED 2018

WEBSITE www.lochleadistillery.com

Lochlea was developed by Neil McGeoch, owner of Lochlea Farm, located just eight miles from the Ayrshire town of Kilmarnock, famous as the "birthplace" of Johnnie Walker. The farm was once home to Scotland's national bard Robert Burns, who lived and worked there between 1777 and 1784, combining farming with penning some of his best-known poems.

In 2014, Neil McGeoch sold his herd of cattle and began the process of converting existing farm buildings for distilling use, using the farmland to grow barley that would be turned into whisky on site.

Spirit production began in spring 2018, and distilling is overseen by John Campbell, for many years the man at the helm of Laphroaig on his native Islay. Lochlea's first whisky was released in 2022, with maturation having taken place in first-fill bourbon and Pedro Ximénez sherry casks, though no fewer than 14 different cask types have been filled to date. The core Lochlea bottling is named Our Barley, and a cask-strength variant is also available, as well as seasonal releases.

TASTING NOTE

Lochlea Our Barley
Single malt, 46% ABV
Orchard fruits, light malt, and a hint of honey on the nose, leading into a palate of peaches and cream, almonds, and lively spice, closing with vanilla and white pepper.

Lochlea Our Barley

ROSEBANK

OWNER Ian Macleod Distillers

FOUNDED 1840

WEBSITE www.rosebank.com

Rosebank distillery is located beside the Forth-Clyde Canal at Camelon, on the outskirts of the industrial town of Falkirk, midway between Edinburgh and Glasgow. Its origins are confused, with claims being made for an establishment date of 1798, when the Stark Brothers were apparently running a distillery called Rosebank. The name crops up again in 1817 when a Rosebank distillery was in the hands of James Robertson. What is known for certain is that James Rankine constructed a distillery on the present site in 1840, based on the maltings of the Camelon distillery.

Rosebank produced triple-distilled malt through good and bad times for the whisky industry, before eventually being closed by owners United Distillers (now Diageo) in 1993. The late Michael Jackson described Rosebank as "The finest example of a Lowland malt…" and considered its demise "…a grievous loss." Happily, that loss has finally been reversed, with Ian Macleod Distillers having

The new Rosebank distillery has kept as much as possible of the old one with its Victorian red brick and towering chimney stack.

undertaken an ambitious reconstruction and reequipping project, having three stills fabricated to the original plans. Triple distillation is once again being practiced at Rosebank, where the first cask was filled during July 2023.

TASTING NOTE

Rosebank 31-Year-Old
Single malt, 48.1% ABV
Lemongrass, almonds, and vanilla on the nose, while the palate offers red berries, banana, chamomile, and soft leather, finishing with an herbal note and soft oak.

Rosebank 31-Year-Old

IRELAND

IRELAND

REGIONAL STYLES
Traditionally, Ireland has been known primarily for two styles of whiskey: the triple-distilled smooth and fruity Irish blend best represented by Jameson, and the rarer, rugged pot still-style such as Redbreast. Today, though, there is more variety available.

AUTHOR'S CHOICE
Once upon a time, Ireland had dozens of small distilleries due to the moderate climate and the abundance of grain, water and peat. BUSHMILLS Located near the Giant's Causeway on the beautiful Northern Irish coast, Bushmills is the oldest licensed distillery in the world and offers bags of old-world charm, with an emphasis on heritage, and a very warm welcome.

REGIONAL EVENTS
Irish Distillers, owned by Pernod Ricard and producer of Jameson, has visitor centers in Dublin and Midleton near Cork. You can also visit Bushmills in Northern Ireland and overall, more than 20 Irish whiskey distilleries are open to the public. Dublin boasts an excellent Irish Whiskey Museum (www.irishwhiskeymuseum.ie) and the brand home Jameson Distillery Bow St. (www.jamesonwhiskey.com). In terms of events, Whisky Live Dublin (www.whiskeylivedublin.com) is staged each May, while Belfast Whiskey Week (www.belfastwhiskeyweek.com) takes place in July, and Cork Whiskey Fest (www.corkwhiskeyfest.com) is held in March.

Where whiskey is concerned, no country in the world has turned around its fortunes more dramatically and successfully than Ireland. It could be likened to a boxer who, nine rounds into a 12-round fight, has been sprawled against the ropes, taking a pounding from both a weighty and bullish American whiskey industry and a sprightly and quick-punching Scotch one. Yet, incredibly, it has dragged itself back onto its feet and has come out of its corner fighting—and indeed since 2010 has become imperious, matching any other territory on the planet for world-class whiskey.

At the turn of the century, Irish whiskey in any abundance consisted of Jameson and a couple of under-funded Irish blends from the South, Bushmills blended and single malt whiskeys in the North, and a smattering of small-batch bottlings from Midleton and Cooley. Now the country is increasingly ditching the triple-distilled, unpeated, blended straitjacket and turning to lip-lickingly exciting whiskeys that are winning awards around the world.

There are many more brands of whiskey in Ireland than there are distilleries, but the number of distilleries is catching up fast, with some 30 currently in production and many more either at the planning or construction stage. Remarkably, there were only three distilleries little more than a decade ago. Whiskey-making has returned to both Dublin and Belfast after being absent for several decades in both cases, and there are now working distilleries from Bushmills on the north coast to Skibereen in the south, Achill Island in the west and Dundalk in the east. Innovation is the order of the day at some distilleries, with "old-style"' single pot still whiskey being made by the likes of Boann, Killowen, and Blackwater, using higher proportions of nonbarley grain in their mashbills. There's no doubt that Ireland has the swagger of a heavyweight champion.

Ireland's remote west coast *is now home to several distilleries, including Achill Island Distillery.*

GETTING AROUND

Developments in Irish road networks mean it's now easy to base yourself in Dublin and reach out to all the island's distilleries. The best motorway links Dublin to Belfast, with Bushmills a little farther on, while Midleton can be reached by the road or train down to Cork. A highway across country to the west coast passes Kilbeggan, so getting there and to nearby Tullamore is a much quicker and easier experience than it once was.

N

Atlantic Ocean

Bushmills & Causeway

Coleraine

Lough Swilly

Lough Foyle

Letterkenny

Londonderry Derry

NORTHERN IRELAND

Antrim

Titanic Distillers

McConnell's

BELFAST

Copeland

Omagh

Cookstown

Lough Neagh

Donegal Bay

Lower Lough Erne

Enniskillen

Armagh

Echlinville

Hinch

Rademon Estate

Sligo

Connacht

Killowen

Lough Conn

Lough Allen

The Shed

Dunalk

Cooley

Clew Bay

Achill Island

Great Northern

Lough Mask

Westport

REPUBLIC OF IRELAND

Drogheda

Irish Sea

Lough Corrib

Lough Ree

Slane

Boann

Galway

Athlone

Kilbeggan

DUBLIN

Galway Bay

Tullamore

Bray

Powerscourt

Great Britain
Ireland

Lough Derg

Wicklow Mountains

Wicklow

NORTHERN IRELAND

Belfast

Ennis

Lugnaquilla 925 m (3,035 ft)

DUBLIN

IRELAND

Shannon

Limerick

Kilkenny

Royal Oak

Celtic Sea

Barrow

Tipperary

Tipperary

Wexford

Cahir

Waterford

Dingle

Tralee

Blackwater

Waterford

Rosslare

Dingle

Killarney

Suir

Dingle Bay

Carrauntoohil 1,041 m (3,415 ft)

Midleton

West Cork

Cork

Clonakilty

0 10 20 30 40 miles
0 20 40 60 80 k

DUBLIN

Liffey

Roe & Co

USHER'S QUAY

TEMPLE BAR

Pearse Lyons

The Liberties

THE LIBERTIES

0 500 miles

Teeling

0 500 yds

PORTOBELLO

BUSHMILLS AND CAUSEWAY

Bushmills 21-Year-Old

OWNER Proximo Spirits

FOUNDED 1784

WEBSITE www.bushmills.eu

For many years, Bushmills was the sole operational whiskey distillery in Northern Ireland, though happily it has now been joined by several others. Legal distillation in the Bushmills area can be traced back to 1608, and the historic brand has been enjoying significant success in recent years, not only with its core Original, Black Bush, and Red Bush blends and triple-distilled single malts but also with its ongoing Causeway Collection of "finished" cask-strength malts and a variety of other innovative releases.

Having previously been in the ownership of Irish Distillers and then from 2005 to 2014 part of the Diageo portfolio, Bushmills now belongs to Proximo Spirits, best known for Jose Cuervo tequila, and the current owners have invested significantly in the Bushmills brand and its future. Bushmills is the third bestselling Irish whiskey globally, with volume sales rising by more than 10 percent in 2022, taking the brand over the million-case sales mark for the first time in its history.

A second distillery

To cope with the increase in demand, a brand-new second distillery was constructed alongside Bushmills, with the first spirit flowing in 2021. Named Causeway, after the famous landscape feature that is the Giant's Causeway, it comprises 40,000 interlocking basalt columns and is situated on the Antrim coast of Northern Ireland, just two and a half miles from the town of Bushmills. Constructing Causeway cost $46.8 million (£37 million) of the total $75.8 million (£60 million) Proximo has spent at Bushmills over the last five years, including construction of additional warehouses. The site is now home to 37 warehouses, with planning permission in place for another 15 to 20, and total spirit capacity is 3 million gallons (11 million liters) per annum.

The Causeway stillhouse contains exact replicas of the Bushmills stills in terms of number, shape, and size of wash, low wines, and spirit stills. The 10 large pots embrace a complex triple-distillation regime to produce Bushmills' characteristic single malt spirit,

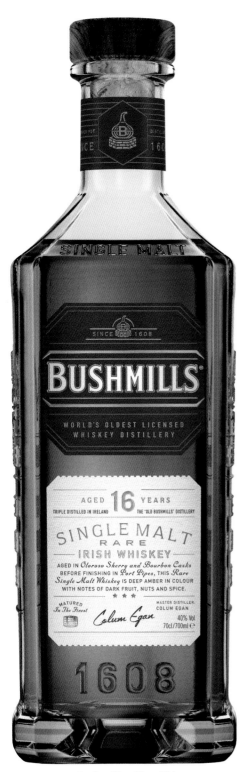

Bushmills 16-Year-Old

Bushmills' traditional "dunnage" warehouse, with casks stacked three high.

while thermal technology cuts energy usage by 30 percent. Causeway has been designed to allow the facility to be doubled in capacity as and when necessary.

Bushmills/Causeway boasts some of the most impressive cask management and wood policy in all Ireland, and the operation makes fine whiskey with dedication and care, combining innovation and tradition seamlessly and with panache. The whiskeys are never anything less than excellent. Indeed, the rich and sherried Black Bush has given Jameson a run for its money in the past. Drinking any Bushmills in the warmth of the distillery is one of the whiskey world's greatest pleasures. It is charm personified.

WHISKEY TALES

A Great Place to Visit
Bushmills is some distillery to visit. One of the greatest ironies about Northern Ireland is that while it was known for little else than the violence and terror of The Troubles for many, many years, to the north it boasts some of the prettiest shorelines in Europe, is an unspoiled delight, and has next to zero crime. Here, the Giant's Causeway is a natural phenomenon, and little villages nestle in a rural idyll. And it's here that you'll find the warmest of welcomes befitting an Irish distillery. The staff make a point of maintaining some of its old-world charm and focusing on the site's heritage and provenance as a renowned whiskey maker.

TASTING NOTES

Bushmills Black Bush
Blend, 40% ABV
As soft and silky as a jazz crooner and as fruity as whiskey gets, Black Bush is a classic mix of sherried berry fruits, stewed apple and pear, and some citrus notes, all delivered with an ordered, pleasant, and smooth package.

Bushmills 16-Year-Old
Single malt, 40% ABV
Maintaining the sweet, fruity triple-distilled character of many Irish whiskeys with 16 years of maturation as a single malt is a hard trick to pull, but this does it. A world-class whiskey, this is a complex stepping sequence between oak, spice, gooseberry and apple fruits, both sweet and drying at the same time. Delightful.

Bushmills 21-Year-Old
Single malt, 40% ABV
Twenty-one years is a lifetime for most Irish whiskeys, but this is by no means drowned in oak; far from it. It's beautifully ordered with rich, juicy raisin and black currant notes, a depth from the oak but no nasty sharpness, and some grape and citrus flourishes to make the overall experience a rewarding and complex one.

TEELING

OWNER The Teeling family and Bacardi

FOUNDED 2015

WEBSITE www.teelingwhiskey.com

The capital city of Dublin was once the powerhouse of Irish distilling, producing vast quantities of whiskey that sold all over the world. Jameson's Bow Street–distilled whiskey competed with that of the three other great distilling dynasties, George Roe & Company, John Power & Son, and William Jameson & Company.

But times change, and the overall Irish whiskey industry shrank to a shadow of its former self during the 20th century. The year 1976 saw the closure of Dublin's last whiskey-making operation, namely the

great John's Lane distillery of James Power & Son. Happily, that was not the end of the story for distilling in the city, and in 2014 brothers Jack and Stephen Teeling established its first new distillery for 125 years in former warehouses in the historic Liberties area. There are now four whiskey distilleries operating within Dublin.

The first Teeling spirit flowed in 2015, with the distillery being equipped with a 4-ton Steinecker full-lauter mash tun, two traditional pine 4,000-gallon (15,000-liter) washbacks and four 5,300-gallon (20,000-liter) stainless steel ones. The three pot stills were fabricated in Italy by Frilli, and both single malt and pot still spirit is produced.

Bacardi took its first step into Irish distilling by acquiring a minority shareholding in Teeling during 2017, and while waiting for its own spirit to mature, Teeling developed a popular range of whiskeys. These included its bestselling Small Batch, which is a blend with a high malt content, finished in rum casks, plus Single Grain and Single Malt. Some of these whiskeys are sourced from Cooley distillery, which had previously belonged to the Teeling family. Finally, in 2018, 6,000 bottles of Teeling Single Pot Still (made with half malted and half unmalted barley) were released to widespread acclaim, and that expression—triple-distilled and matured in a combination of American virgin oak, bourbon, and sherry casks—has now taken its place in the core portfolio.

Close to the world-famous Guinness Brewery and Dublin's other three distilleries, Teeling offers great visitor facilities, with fascinating insights into Dublin life past and present.

Teeling distillery as viewed from the street. Located in the center of Dublin city, it is well worth a visit.

Teeling Blackpitts

TASTING NOTES

Teeling Small Batch
Blend, 46% ABV
Spicy green apples and grain on the nose, with a palate of cloves, baked apples, rum, oak, and black pepper.

Teeling Single Pot Still
Pot still, 46% ABV
Floral on the nose, with grapefruit, honey, and cereal notes. Peaches, almonds, allspice, and black pepper on the palate.

Teeling Blackpitts
Peated single malt, matured in ex-bourbon and Sauternes casks, 46% ABV
Orange and vanilla, plus wood smoke and cloves on the nose, while the palate yields smoked apple, pineapple, charcuterie, and salted caramel.

THE LIBERTIES

OWNER Quintessential Brands and Stock Spirits

FOUNDED 2018

WEBSITE www.thedld.com

The Liberties distillery is located in a former 18th-century mill, which was once a tannery. It operates three pot stills that produce both double- and triple-distilled whiskey. While its own spirit matures, The Liberties offers a range of third-party whiskeys, with a number of expressions in The Dubliner range of blends. There is also a trio of Liberties-branded single malt bottlings, aged for 10, 13, and 16 years. The Liberties welcomes visitors, and tours include some good tales about the old lawless days in the area.

TASTING NOTE

The Dublin Liberties Whiskey Copper Alley 10-Year-Old
Single malt, non-chill-filtered, finished in ex-oloroso sherry casks, 46% ABV
Aromas of apple blossom, cinnamon, honey, and dried fruits, with flavors of plums, walnuts, raisins, and dark chocolate.

The Dublin Liberties
Whiskey Copper Alley
10-Year-old

PEARSE LYONS

OWNER Alltech Inc

FOUNDED 2017

WEBSITE www.pearselyonsdistillery.com

Pearse Lyons distillery is situated in the deconsecrated church of St. James in The Liberties, where the pair of copper stills occupy the position that formerly hosted the altar. The venture was the brainchild of the late entrepreneur, brewer, and distiller Pearse Lyons and his wife, Deidre. The couple undertook an epic $25.3 million (€20 million) transformation of the semiderelict church into a stunning whiskey-making venue. The finished distillery—complete with a landmark illuminated glass spire—is equipped with a lauter mash tun, two stainless steel fermenters, and two open wooden fermenting vessels, plus a pair of stills made by Vendome in Kentucky. Both single malt and pot still whiskeys are produced. Visiting the distillery is a joy.

TASTING NOTE

Pearse Founder's Choice 12-Year-Old
Single malt, 43% ABV
Ripe peaches, red apples, and pine on the nose, with flavors of butterscotch, orange, ginger, and cloves, and finally spicy oak.

Pearse Founder's Choice
12-Year-old

ROE & CO

OWNER Diageo plc

FOUNDED 2019

WEBSITE www.roeandcowhiskey.com

The creation of Roe & Co distillery in the former power station of the Guinness brewery represented Diageo's return to the Irish whiskey after selling Bushmills in 2014. It revives one of the great names from the heyday of Irish whiskey, with George Roe & Co's Thomas Street distillery, once being the largest in Ireland. From 2017, Diageo has sold a blended whiskey, sourced from a third party. Three stills are in situ and double- and triple-distilled whiskeys are produced. Tour options include a Cocktail Workshop.

TASTING NOTE

Roe & Co
Blend, 45% ABV
The nose is fragrant, with vanilla, mixed spice, and subtle oak, while the palate features spiced pears, more vanilla, ripe bananas, malt, and oak.

Roe & Coe

MIDLETON

Jameson

OWNER Irish Distillers (Pernod Ricard)

FOUNDED 1780

WEBSITE www.jamesonwhiskey.com

Irish whiskey finds itself in a very good place right now, but it wasn't always thus. Following its glory days in the 18th and 19th centuries, Irish whiskey suffered a long and undignified fall from grace. Its fate was in part self-inflicted; in part a consequence of social, economic, and political upheaval; and in part due to merciless business practice from its rivals, particularly in Scotland.

By the 1960s, the small number of surviving distilleries had clubbed together as Irish Distillers and defined themselves as a distinct entity from Scotch, stressing their characteristics as unpeated, triple-distilled, sweet, fruity blends. The tactic worked, and Jameson in particular managed to excel even when Irish whiskey had to take a back seat as first Scotch, then Japanese whisky, and finally a resurgent American whiskey industry cast it into the shadows.

The flourishing of Irish Distillers

Midleton became the base first for the entrenchment of Irish Distillers—now owned by Pernod Ricard—and then its fightback. The move to a new state-of-the-art plant, which has been expanded several times, is the most obvious manifestation of the flourishing of Irish Distillers, but the fact that land around the distillery has been occupied by an increasing number of warehouses is another clue. The site now has an overall annual capacity of 15.9 million gallons (60 million liters) of spirit. Irish whiskey is growing faster than any other whiskey category in the world, and after a belated entry into the new wave of innovation and diversity, Irish Distillers is firmly center stage.

In 2014, it sought to rejuvenate the Irish pot still category with the new definition of "single pot still," accompanied by an ongoing program of releases, and while the Jameson blend is by far the world's leading Irish whiskey brand, Irish Distillers also owns the historic Power's name, and the Power's lineup even includes an Irish rye whiskey. However, the Method & Madness collection is the ultimate expression of Irish Distillers' experimental side, with single malt, single grain, and single pot still offerings to its name,

Jameson Select Reserve Black Barrel

The Garden Stillhouse at Middleton opened in 2013 and is equipped with six pot stills.

including whiskey finished in mulberry, cherry, and chestnut casks. The highly unorthodox "Oats and Malt" limited edition comprises a mashbill of 60 percent oats and 40 percent malted barley.

Irish pot still whiskey

Pot still whiskey is unique to Ireland; it's made by taking malted barley and mixing it with another grain or grains, often unmalted barley, at the grist or flour stage—that is, before water is added and the wash fermented into beer. "It's a difficult trick to pull off because the mix becomes very gloopy and can block up the fermenting equipment," says one Irish whiskey expert. "It requires considerable time and effort to get right and demands a great deal of care and attention, but when it's done correctly, the results can be outstanding." Indeed, they can.

Pot still whiskey survived through the odd bottling of Midleton, through Green Spot—distilled by Irish Distillers for Dublin wine and spirit merchant Mitchell & Son—and through Redbreast, which was given periodic support by Irish Distillers. However, recent years have seen the expansion of the Redbreast range to include expressions from 12 to 27 years of age; a cask-strength variant; and Lustau, finished in first-fill oloroso sherry casks, while Green Spot has been joined by Yellow, Blue, and Red Spot— all recreations of historical "Spot" variants. Each year, Midleton's master distiller selects casks of single pot still and grain whiskey to create a vintage release of Midleton Very Rare. The first bottling took place in

1984, and component whiskeys are aged from 12 to 20 years, with maturation occurring in ex-bourbon casks. The appearance of each new release is one of the highlights of the Irish whiskey calendar.

New Midleton

If you pay a visit to Midleton, a short drive from Cork city, you are guaranteed to end up seeing double, though not (necessarily) because of a glass too many at the tasting session. For the site is, in fact, home to two distilleries sitting almost side by side. One is the new Midleton plant, which isn't open to the public but is the powerhouse of the current distilling operation of Irish Distillers.

WHISKEY TALES
Old Midleton
The second distillery is Old Midleton and which now offers visitors a great tour, courtesy of The Jameson Experience. Its solid, beautifully restored Victorian stone buildings lie alongside the Dungourney River, which still turns the giant waterwheel that once powered the distillery, and whose waters continue to be used in the production of whiskey at the new plant.

TASTING NOTES

Jameson
Blend, 40% ABV
Defines classic quality Irish whiskey at its best, with a healthy dose of oily, big-flavored, fruity pot still whiskey, some red berry, sherry notes, and lots of fruit, with milk chocolate in the mix.

Jameson Select Reserve Black Barrel
Blend, 40% ABV
A sharper, fiercer, feistier version of Jameson made up of older pot still whiskey and rare grain whiskey than is normal. There are lots of dark berry notes, some sharper green fruit flavors, and delicious woody, spicy, and dark chocolate notes.

Redbreast 12-Year-Old Cask Strength
Single pot still, non-chill-filtered, 58.1% ABV
As fine as Irish whiskey gets, this is rich, full, oily, and sherried, with Christmas cake, bitter orange, an array of berries and kitchen pantry spices, and some oak.

COOLEY

OWNER Suntory Global Spirits

FOUNDED 1987

WEBSITE www.thetyrconnellwhiskey.com;
www.connemarawhiskey.com

The Cooley distillery was created in 1987 by one of the shrewdest figures ever to be involved in the Irish whiskey industry, namely John Teeling, an academic and serial business entrepreneur who studied at Harvard Business School and who brought 12 companies to public listing on the London Stock Exchange, more than any other Irish person.

The Cooley distillery was established in a disused industrial alcohol plant on the east coast of Ireland, with Teeling adding a pair of pot stills to the grain-distilling apparatus in 1989. His aim was to offer an alternative to the monopoly that existed in Irish whiskey at that time, with Irish Distillers owning both Bushmills and Midleton, and he succeeded triumphantly.

The spirit produced by Cooley turned the Irish whiskey industry on its head. So threatened was the existing establishment by a small independent distillery, which refused to operate by conventional rules and set about playing with Irish whiskey styles, that it tried to close it down. But the Teelings—chairman John and sons Stephen and Jack—survived on cheap own-brand contracts for supermarkets and slowly but surely set about establishing new whiskeys in the then struggling Irish sector.

The year 1992 saw the release of Cooley's first single malt, reviving the old Locke's name, associated with Kilbeggan, and Teeling went on to acquire the silent County Westmeath distillery, restoring it to working order in 2007. Along with Locke's, Teeling launched a range of other whiskeys, including the single malt Tyrconnell, also named after a long-defunct whiskey brand; Kilbeggan blended whiskey; and Kilbeggan single grain whiskey, with the latter originally marketed as Greenore.

Cooley also developed the first peated Irish whiskey in many years, named Connemara, which is a mainstay of the distillery and has spawned a whole range of its own.

In 2012, Beam Inc acquired Cooley from the Teeling family, and with Beam subsequently being purchased by Japanese distilling giant Suntory, ownership is now in the hands of Suntory Global Spirits. John Teeling's sons, Jack and Stephen, had gone on to create Teeling distillery in Dublin, while their father proceeded to replicate his Cooley venture with Great Northern in Dundalk.

Kilbeggan Single Grain Whiskey

TASTING NOTES

Connemara 12-Year-Old Single Malt
Single malt, aged in American oak, 40% ABV
The traditional sweet green fruit and soft vanilla tones normally associated with the category are mixed here with growling, smoky notes that tease the taste buds.

The Tyrconnel 10-Year-Old "Sherry Finish"
Single malt, finished in ex-sherry casks, 46% ABV
The alcoholic strength gives a bite to this rich, toffeed single malt, and the sherry adds a depth of berry fruits and some orange citrus notes. There are some gentle spices at work here, too, preventing it from becoming too cloying. Very impressive.

Kilbeggan Single Grain Whiskey
Grain whiskey, 40% ABV
This single grain whiskey is a treat—its corn, candy, vanilla, and honey sweetness all in evidence, with spiciness, a hint of lime, and developing light oak notes.

ECHLINVILLE

OWNER The Braniff family

FOUNDED 2013

WEBSITE www.echlinville.com

The earliest of the "new wave" of Northern Irish distilleries to join the historic Bushmills operation was the Echlinville distillery, situated on the Ards peninsula, just over 20 miles southeast of Belfast. Established by Shane Braniff and his family in 2013, it was the first new distillery to be licensed in Northern Ireland in 130 years. Both single pot still and single malt spirit are produced, and the distillery boasts its own floor maltings, bottling facility, and a recently enhanced visitor center and café.

Significantly, Echlinville has been responsible for reviving the famous old Belfast Dunville's brand distilled in Belfast's vast, state-of-the-art Royal Irish Distilleries from 1869 until 1935. Today, blended Dunville's expressions under the 1808 and Three Crowns banners sit alongside a lineup of single malts of varying ages, finished in a range of different types of sherry cask.

Echlinville has also revived the Matt D'Arcy name with a premium blend, a 10-year-old with a port cask finish, and the Old Comber name with port and sherry-cask-finished pot still bottlings.

The strong whiskey portfolio will expand further with the launch of Echlinville Whiskey. The first field-to-glass release will feature liquid distilled, matured, and bottled at Echlinville from barley grown, harvested, and malted on the distillery farm.

*The **stillhouse** at the Echlinville distillery showcases statuesque column stills.*

TASTING NOTES

Dunville's PX 12-Year-Old
Single malt, 46% ABV
Orchard fruits and tropical spices combine with Christmas cake and oak on the nose, with a palate of banoffee pie, dried fruits, orange peel, and voluptuous sherry.

Matt d'Arcy & Co 10-Year-Old Port Finish
Blend, 46% ABV
The nose yields citrus fruit and oak spice, while malt and dark berries merge on the palate, with vanilla, oak, and black pepper.

Old Comber Irish Pot Still Whiskey
Pot still, 46% ABV
Vanilla, soft toffee, and sponge cake characterize the nose, with the palate offering a rich mouthfeel, apples, cinnamon, and lively spice.

Old Comber Irish Pot Still Whiskey

KILBEGGAN

OWNER Suntory Global Spirits

FOUNDED 1757

WEBSITE www.kilbegganwhiskey.com

Kilbeggan is an example of those one-street Irish towns comprising a couple of pubs, a couple of shops, and not much else—the sort of place where most of the time nothing happens and which you tend to pass through without stopping. Yet Kilbeggan has something that sets it apart from most small-time Irish towns and villages; it is home to Locke's Distillery, a stunning wood and wrought-iron piece of history in pristine condition.

Kilbeggan was established in 1757 and is the oldest productive whiskey distillery in the world. At various times, it has been known as Brusna distillery—after the local river—and Locke's distillery. In the ownership of John Locke and his sons between 1841 and 1893, it thrived, and during the mid-1880s, it was producing over 157,000 proof gallons (almost 600,000 liters) of spirit per year. It fell silent in 1953 but managed to avoid conversion or demolition due to the passionate efforts of townspeople who were determined that one day it would make whiskey again. Happily, Cooley's John Teeling shared their vision to bring whiskey back to this amazing and must-see distillery, and he did it, in 2007.

The big waterwheel turns once more, pistons shudder, and wheels whir, and while most of the main distillery's activity is for show only, you will find a fully operational micro-distillery producing all sorts of wacky, weird, and wonderful takes on what we know as Irish whiskey. A single malt was launched in 2010 and today—in the ownership of Suntory Global Spirits—the lineup of whiskeys produced at Kilbeggan includes a single pot still whiskey and a small batch rye. The latter was the first whiskey 100 percent distilled and matured at Kilbeggan distillery to be released since its restoration was completed in 2010. Featuring a heritage mash of malt, barley, and 30 percent rye, this whiskey recalls the 1890s when many large Irish distillers used rye in their mashbills.

Kilbeggan is one of the most photogenic of all Irish distilleries, and a tour highlights the long and fascinating history of whiskey-making on the site, along with the chance to see what is officially the oldest working still in the world in action. There is even an Irish Coffee Masterclass Experience.

Kilbeggan Single Pot Still

WHISKEY TALES

Still Lining Up

When businessman John Teeling mooted the idea of launching an Irish whiskey company when the category was struggling, more than a few people thought him crazy. For many, that view was reinforced when he decided to transport a huge copper pot still along rural roads. Kilbeggan used to be on the main thoroughfare from Dublin to the West Coast, and every weekend the *nouveaux riches* of the city headed west for some sailing. It was a Friday afternoon when Teeling and his team made the move, with a still so heavy the lifting crane nearly collapsed. For many hours the still blocked the route, causing a traffic jam stretching back miles.

Kilbeggan Rye

TASTING NOTES

Kilbeggan Single Pot Still
Single pot still, 43% ABV
Crisp apples on the nose, with hazelnuts and a hint of honey, while the creamy palate offers melon and lemon and lively pot still spice.

Kilbeggan Rye
Rye whiskey, 43% ABV
Milk chocolate, ginger, and red apples on the nose, with white pepper. A creamy mouthfeel and vanilla, cloves, and oily, peppery rye spice on the palate.

TULLAMORE

OWNER William Grant & Sons Ltd

FOUNDED 2014

WEBSITE www.tullamoredew.com

Sometimes history has a satisfying way of coming full circle. So it was that in the fall of 2014 production commenced at the new Tullamore distillery, half a century after the original one closed its doors forever.

That "original" had been established in 1829 by Michael Moloney, and one of the key attractions of the Tullamore location was its central position in Ireland, amid prime barley-growing countryside. Additionally, the distillery stood beside the Grand Canal, which facilitated the transportation of coal, barley, and casks of spirit. The railroad network also ultimately provided an important communications lifeline. The distillery survived through good times and bad before closing in 1954, having become the first Irish distillery to install a Coffey or grain whiskey still to facilitate the production of blended whiskey six years previously.

The new Tullamore

"New" Tullamore was created by William Grant & Sons, who purchased the brand from C&C Group plc, owners of Magners cider. A rebranding exercise was subsequently undertaken, which led to the whiskey being named Tullamore D.E.W. (the D.E.W stands for Daniel Edmund Williams, a great Irish distiller), and in keeping with Grant's passionate spirit of independence, it was decided to build an Irish distillery to secure the future of quality spirit supplies. No fewer than 48 potential sites were examined, and finally the choice was narrowed down to two, one in Clonmel, Tipperary, and another at Clonminch, on the outskirts of the town of Tullamore.

The Tullamore site was by far the more inconvenient from the point of view of construction, but the new owners were adamant that reuniting the whiskey with the town of Tullamore was the right thing to do. The work involved the removal of 275,600 tons of peat before construction could begin, and water had to be piped in for several miles from Clonaslee at the foot of the Slieve Bloom mountains, across the border in County Laois.

*The **imposing frontage** at the new Tullamore distillery.*

Architecturally, the new distillery makes a confident statement, and internally it boasts four pot stills, with one wash still being fabricated as a replica of its predecessor at the old Tullamore distillery, with a distinctive offset neck. A grain-distilling plant was constructed adjacent to the main distillery in 2017, along with a bottling hall. The core Tullamore range includes the NAS Original, plus 12-, 14-, and 18-year-old single malts. The brand is the second-bestselling Irish whiskey after Jameson.

Tullamore D.E.W.
18-Year-Old
New Distillery Image

TASTING NOTES

Tullamore D.E.W.
Triple-distilled and a blend of single pot still, single grain, and single malt whiskey, matured in ex-bourbon and sherry casks, 40% ABV
Whole wheat toast, walnuts, and brittle toffee on the nose. The palate offers green apples, honey, vanilla, and a hint of sherry. Warming, with a hint of char and toffee in the finish.

Tullamore D.E.W. 14-Year-Old
Triple-distilled single malt whiskey, finished in bourbon, port, Madeira, and oloroso sherry casks, 41.3% ABV
The nose offers strong aromas of orchard and tropical fruits, with vanilla and creamy oak. Spicy apples, pears, and pineapple are evident on the palate, with developing sweet oak. The relatively lengthy finish offers subtle sherry and oak tannins.

Tullamore D.E.W. 18-Year-Old
Single malt whiskey finished for up to six months in bourbon, port, Madeira, and oloroso sherry casks, 41.3% ABV
Toffee apples, sweet oak, sherry, and cinnamon on the nose. The palate yields red apples, Jaffa oranges, vanilla, sherry, and a hint of pipe tobacco. The finish comprises citrus notes plus rum and raisin milk chocolate.

WATERFORD

OWNER Renegade Spirits Ireland

FOUNDED 2015

WEBSITE www.waterfordwhisky.com

The quality of the barley from individual farms is of the utmost importance to the whiskey process at Waterford.

Waterford distillery started life as a Guinness brewery, the site having been home to beer-making since the establishment of Strangman's brewery in 1792. Guinness owner Diageo spent $50 million (€40 million) rebuilding the brewery during 2005, only to close it eight years later. Former Bruichladdich supremo Mark Reynier and his associates, trading as Renegade Spirits, were able to acquire it for only $9.5 million (€7.2 million) in 2014, spending a further $2.6 million (€2.4 million) converting the facility to produce *whisky*. Reynier insisted on that spelling, without the "e," declaring "This is whisky made in Ireland using Irish barley, rather than Irish whiskey." A pair of stills sourced from Inverleven distillery at Dumbarton on the Clyde River during Reynier's Bruichladdich days were refurbished and installed in what he calls "The Facilitator," though 2021 saw these venerable and well-traveled vessels replaced with identical copies.

With a background in the wine trade, Reynier was always going to do things differently at Waterford, and terroir was at the heart of the distillery's operations. Reynier recruited farmers to grow barley for him via grain brokers and suppliers Minch Malt. The integrity of each individual annual crop of barley is sacrosanct, and the grain is stored in one of 50 "bins" in what Reynier calls the "Cathedral of Barley" building in Kilkenny prior to malting.

At Waterford distillery, a week is devoted specifically to the distillation of each batch, and after maturation, the whisky in question is bottled in the Single Farm Origin series. That model has served the distillery well, earning praise from aficionados, and the variety of spirit character on display makes it difficult to argue that terroir is little more than a fanciful notion. However, Reynier always had something else in mind beyond this initial venture, and that was the creation of a Waterford Cuvée, inspired by the wine châteaux of France. As Reynier puts it, "We have celebrated and explored the singles, now we produce our more immersive concept album." Organic, peated, and biodynamic single malt whiskies are also produced.

The distillery welcomes visitors for tours and events and also offers webcams and a virtual distillery experience via its website.

TASTING NOTES

Waterford Single Farm Origin Ballymorgan 1.2 Bottling
Single malt, 54% ABV
Citrus fruit and malt on the nose, with developing cinnamon, while the palate offers toffee apples, white pepper, and oak.

Waterford The Cuvée
Single malt, 50% ABV
A nose of honey, peaches, vanilla, and light oak, with creamy oats, vanilla, malt, summer fruits, and white pepper on the palate.

Waterford Gaia Organic 2.1
Single malt, 50% ABV
Cereal, fruit salad, and orange on the nose, with a viscous palate, yielding salted caramel, hazelnut, licorice, and black pepper.

Waterford Gaia Organic 2.1

CLONAKILTY

OWNER The Scully family

FOUNDED 2016

WEBSITE www.clonakiltydistillery.ie

Nine generations of the Scully family have farmed near Clonakilty, on the Atlantic coast of County Cork, and now the dynasty has branched out into distilling. The building was destined to be a branch of the Royal Ulster Bank, until the financial crash of 2007–2008 brought completion to a halt. The family invested $14.7 million (€10 million) in turning it into a whiskey, gin, and vodka-producing operation, equipped with three pot stills, fabricated by Barison in Italy.

The first spirit flowed in March 2019, and there is a concentration on triple-distilling single pot still whiskey, which matures in a warehouse on the Galley Head peninsula, where the influence of the adjacent Atlantic Ocean is expected to be significant. Clonakilty offers a core trio of whiskeys, namely Double Oak Cask (a blend of single grain and Clonakilty's own single pot still whiskey, matured in ex-bourbon casks, virgin American oak, and shaved and retoasted European oak casks), Clonakilty Port Cask (a blend of single grain and Clonakilty single pot still whiskey), and Galley Head Single Malt. Visitors are welcome, and an entertaining tour and tasting "multisensory experience" awaits.

TASTING NOTE

Clonakilty Double Oak Cask
Blend, 43.6% ABV
Orchard fruits, wood spice, and cut grass aromas, with flavors of vanilla, ginger, and cinnamon.

Clonakilty Double Oak Cask

DINGLE

OWNER The Porterhouse Group

FOUNDED 2012

WEBSITE www.dingledistillery.ie

Dingle was established in the former Fitzgerald's sawmill on the outskirts of the most westerly town in Europe, located in the Irish-speaking Gaeltecht region on the popular "Wild Atlantic Way" in County Kerry. Dingle was in on the Irish distilling renaissance at an early stage, being the brainchild of Dublin-based Porterhouse Brewing Company, headed by the late Oliver Hughes, Liam LaHart, and Peter Mosley. According to its website, "The Dingle Whiskey Distillery came into being in the cold winter of 2012. Ireland was beginning to come out of the greatest recession in many people's memory. However unbeknownst to many, the most significant event in the Irish whiskey industry in decades was happening in a tin shed in the town of Dingle, Co. Kerry."

The distillery is equipped with a unique, manual, wooden mash tun, wooden washbacks, and a trio of Forsyth pot stills, along with two gin stills. The first casks were filled in December 2012, and three years later, in December 2015, the first triple-distilled single malt whiskey release appeared. Since then, numerous small batch releases of both single malt and single pot still have appeared. In 2017, Dingle became the first independent Irish distillery to release a single pot still whiskey in several decades. There is now a "core" single malt expression, matured in 39 percent ex-bourbon and 61 percent PX sherry casks, and a single pot still bottling, aged exclusively in Pedro Ximénez casks.

Guided tours lead visitors through Dingle's gin, vodka, and whiskey production and allow sampling of all three spirits, along with a "signature serve."

TASTING NOTES

Dingle Single Malt
Single malt, 44% ABV
Spicy toffee apple, almond, vanilla, and dark chocolate on the nose, with a palate of caramel, apricots, honey, and dried fruits.

Dingle Fifth Single Pot Still
Single pot still, matured in bourbon casks, 46.5% ABV
Milk chocolate, coconut, butterscotch, and orchard fruits on the nose, with the palate featuring ripe apples, fudge, almonds, and vanilla, closing with nutmeg and lively spice.

Dingle Single Malt

SLANE

OWNER Brown-Forman

FOUNDED 2017

WEBSITE www.slaneirishwhiskey.com

Slane distillery was created at the magnificent 18th-century Slane Castle, which stands at the heart of a 1,500-acre estate that has been in the hands of the Conyngham family since 1703. Slane has been as well known for its high-profile rock concerts as it has for its history, with the likes of Thin Lizzy, U2, Bruce Springsteen, The Rolling Stones, Guns n' Roses, and Madonna all performing there.

The Slane whiskey brand was launched by the Conyngham family in 2009, and plans were developed to create a distillery in the castle's stable block and grain store, taking water from the nearby

Boyne River and growing malting barley on the Slane estate. Then in 2015, Jack Daniel's distillers Brown-Forman acquired Slane Whiskey and went on to invest some $50 million (€45 million) in the distillery project, which took two years to complete. The distillery boasts three copper pot stills and six column stills, with single malt, single pot still, and grain spirit being produced. Slane boasts a Stalls Bar where tastings are conducted, along with a café and retail outlet. Combined castle and distillery tours are available.

TASTING NOTE

Slane Triple Casked
Blend, matured in virgin oak, seasoned Tennessee whiskey, and oloroso sherry casks, 40% ABV
Ginger, banana, caramel, and spicy oak on the nose, with a palate of banoffee pie, toffee, and orchard fruits, closing with raisins and toasted oak.

Slane Triple Casked

WEST CORK

OWNER West Cork Distillers

FOUNDED 2004

WEBSITE www.westcorkdistillers.com

West Cork Distillers, or WCD, was established in what was little more than a shed in the village of Union Hall, half a dozen miles from Skibbereen back in 2003 by research and development scientist Johnny O'Connell and his first cousins, former trawlermen brothers Denis and Gerard McCarthy.

The operation moved into an ex-Heineken lager bottling plant on Market Street in Skibbereen during 2014, where the idiosyncratic "Rocket" still was installed, allegedly the fastest still in the world. Two years later, WCD acquired a large site at Marsh Road on the outskirts of the town. Appropriately enough, given the founders' backgrounds, the latter had previously been a fish processing plant and was converted to house administration and bottling functions, along with warehousing. Four bottling lines are in place, and WCD undertakes third-party bottlings as well as carrying out contract bottling for other distillers.

The Marsh Street site now also houses the actual distilling function, with eight pot stills, two column stills, and an impressive annual capacity of 1.2 million gallons (4.5 million liters) WCD is the largest Irish-owned distillery in Ireland, exports to 70 countries, and employs around 80 staff in its operations.

There is a wide range of whiskeys, including "classic blends," single malts at varying ages, and single pot still bottlings, along with a number of finished and beer cask–matured offerings. Perhaps the most unusual expression is "Bog Oak Charred Cask," finished in casks heavily charred using bog oak harvested from the local boglands of Glengarriff Forest in West Cork.

TASTING NOTES

West Cork Single Malt Bourbon Cask Finished
Single malt, triple-distilled, 40% ABV
Vanilla, sweet spice, and grapefruit on the nose, with a palate of sweet malt, butterscotch, orchard fruits, and white pepper.

West Cork Black Cask
Blend, 40% ABV
Roasted nuts, honey, ripe banana, and almonds on the nose, while the palate yields malt, orchard fruits, cinnamon, and a whiff of smoke, closing with dark chocolate and char.

West Cork Black Cask

BLACKWATER

OWNER Peter Mulryan and Kieran Curtin

FOUNDED 2014

WEBSITE www.blackwaterdistillery.ie

Blackwater distillery is located in the small village of Ballyduff, County Waterford. It was established by former television producer and whiskey book author Peter Mulryan. The distillery is equipped with three stills fabricated by Frilli in Italy and produces single malt and single pot still whiskey, as well as gin, vodka, and rum. Mulryan is passionate about genuinely traditional Irish pot still whiskey, made with higher proportions of secondary grains such as oats, wheat, and rye, than are currently allowed under the 2014 definition of the genre.

TASTING NOTE

Velvet Cap Triple Cask
Blend, aged in bourbon, stouted rye, and port casks, 40% ABV
Banana, almond, honey, malt, and plum on the nose, with vanilla and tropical fruits on the palate.

Velvet Cap Triple Cask

BOANN

The Whistler PX I Love You

OWNER The Cooney family

FOUNDED 2016

WEBSITE www.boanndistillery.ie

The County Meath town of Drogheda in the Boyne Valley was once home to no fewer than 18 distilleries, the last of which closed in 1968. However, whiskey-making has returned to the area courtesy of Boann distillery, located alongside the Boyne Brewhouse craft brewery. Boann has been developed by members of the Cooney family, which boasts an impressive and extensive CV in the Irish drinks industry. Equipped with three pot stills and a gin still, maturation and bottling take place on site. The first single pot still spirit flowed in December 2019, and Boann has been eager to experiment with traditional pot still mash bills, along similar lines to Blackwater. Single pot still new-make spirit is on sale and a range of third-party whiskeys is marketed under The Whistler label.

TASTING NOTE

The Whistler PX I Love You
Single malt, finished in PX sherry casks, 46% ABV
Aromas of orange, sultanas, red cherries, and malt, with flavors of dried fruits, walnuts, and spicy dark chocolate.

CONNACHT

OWNER Connacht Whiskey Company Ltd

FOUNDED 2016

WEBSITE www.connachtwhiskey.com

Connacht distillery, at Ballina in County Mayo, close to the Atlantic Ocean, was established by master distiller Robert Cassell and associates, and the first whiskey distillation took place in January 2016, reviving a legal distilling tradition dormant in the region for 150 years. The three stills were fabricated in British Columbia, Canada, to Cassell's own design, and double- and triple-distilled spirit, single malt, and pot still spirit, is produced. In 2023, the first core whiskey, Spirit of the Atlantic, was launched. Regular tours and tastings sessions are available.

TASTING NOTE

Connacht Spirit of the Atlantic
Single malt, 44.8% ABV
Dried fruits, honey, fudge, and hazelnuts on the nose, with a palate of spicy vanilla, walnuts, and malt.

Connacht Spirit of the Atlantic

COPELAND

OWNER Copeland Spirits

FOUNDED 2019

WEBSITE www.copelanddistillery.com

Copeland distillery is situated in a former cinema and bottling plant at Donaghadee, 20 miles east of Belfast. The distillery was established by Gareth Irvine through a crowdfunding initiative and has a capacity of 10,500 gallons (40,000 liters) per annum. Five mashbills have been used to date, with double-distilled single malt and double-distilled pot still spirit being produced. Third-party bottlings appear under the Merchant's Quay name. The Copeland team wanted to wait and release its initial whiskey as a 5-year-old.

TASTING NOTE

Merchant's Quay
Blend, comprising grain whiskey and double- and triple-distilled malts and aged in four different cask types, 40% ABV
Vanilla, cloves, toffee apples, and blackberries on the nose, with flavors of honey, orchard fruits, and spicy oak.

Merchant's Quay

GREAT NORTHERN

OWNER The Irish Whiskey Company

FOUNDED 2015

WEBSITE www.gndireland.com

Having sold Cooley distillery to Beam Inc in 2011, entrepreneur John Teeling set out to replicate Cooley's role as supplier of whiskey for bulk private labels, contract distilling, retail own label, and other distillers awaiting maturation of their own spirit. He and fellow investors acquired the former Great Northern Brewery in Dundalk and set about converting it into a multipurpose distillery. It boasts three column stills to produce grain whiskey and nine pot stills to make single malt and single pot still spirit. Total capacity is 4.2 million gallons (16 million liters) per year. New-make spirit sales make up a large part of GND's business, and popular brands comprising GND whiskey include Burke's and Fitzwilliam.

TASTING NOTE

Fitzwilliam Irish Blended Whiskey
Blend, triple-distilled, matured in American rye whiskey and ex-stout casks, 40% ABV
Fresh on the nose, with citrus fruit and cereal while vanilla, spice, instant coffee, dark chocolate, and a hint of peat smoke feature on the palate.

Fitzwilliam Irish Blended Whiskey

HINCH

OWNER Dr. Terry Cross

FOUNDED 2020

WEBSITE www.hinchdistillery.com

Hinch is located on the historic Killaney Estate, just 15 miles south of Belfast. It was established by entrepreneur Dr. Terry Cross—owner of Château de la Ligne in Bordeaux—for $19 million (£15 million), and triple distillation is practiced. The location close to Belfast means that functions and visitor experiences are key activities. A range of third-party spirits is marketed, including Small Batch Blend, Single Pot Still, Aged 5 Years Double Wood blend, Peated Single Malt, and an 18-Year-Old Single Malt.

TASTING NOTE

Hinch Single Pot Still
Single pot still, 43% ABV
Aromas of allspice, cooked oats, lime, and cinnamon lead into voluptuous flavors of lemon, shortbread, and black pepper.

Hinch Single Pot Still

KILLOWEN

OWNER Killowen Distillery Limited/Brendan Carty

FOUNDED 2017

WEBSITE www.killowendistillery.com

The distillery was established in a converted barn in the Mourne Mountains, southeast of Newry, by architect Brendan Carty, who declares that "My aim has been to create an Irish whiskey from traditional techniques over flame," with Ireland's only operational worm tubs in situ for condensing purposes. Some malting is undertaken on site and fermentation takes place in open-topped vessels and lasts for a week or more. Carty has produced pot still Irish whiskeys with significantly higher proportions of "secondary" grains.

TASTING NOTE

Rum & Raisin Single Malt
Single malt, aged for five years and then finished in dark rum casks and PX sherry butts, 55% ABV
A richly aromatic nose of coconut, vanilla, cinnamon, green apples, and sherry, while the palate offers malt, sherry, figs, tropical fruits, cloves, and dark chocolate.

Rum & Raisin Single Malt

POWERSCOURT

OWNER The Powerscourt Distillery

FOUNDED 2017

WEBSITE www.powerscourtdistillery.com

Powerscourt distillery is situated within Powerscourt Estate, County Wicklow, 25 miles south of Dublin; the $21.4 million (€20 million) venture was the brainchild of local entrepreneurs Gerry Ginty and Ashley Gardiner, and Alex Peirce. The production building was constructed adjoining the 18th-century Old Mill House, which now has visitor facilities. The actual distillery with its three pot stills was a "turnkey" operation, fabricated and installed by Forsyth of Rothes in Scotland, with production commencing in 2018. Single malt and single pot still whiskeys are produced, and casks are filled and matured on site. A range of expressions has been created to fill the void until Powerscourt's own whiskey reaches maturity, in this case bearing the name Fercullen.

TASTING NOTE

Fercullen 18-Year-Old
Single malt, 43% ABV
The nose offers vanilla, honey, soft toffee, cinnamon, and dark chocolate, with caramel, ginger, and malt on the palate.

Fercullen 18-Year-Old

RADEMON ESTATE

OWNER The Boyd-Armstrong family

FOUNDED 2012

WEBSITE www.rademonestatedistillery.com

The distillery is situated 17 miles south of Belfast, and a range of visitor experiences is offered in a converted farm buildings. Gin and whiskey are marketed under the Shortcross name, and the first whiskey was distilled in 2015 on what was then Ireland's smallest copper pot still. Both single malt and single pot still spirit is produced, and between 200 and 300 casks are filled each year. The year 2021 saw the release of a highly regarded double-distilled single malt 5-year-old, aged in Bordeaux red wine casks, and finished in virgin chinquapin oak with a high char level.

TASTING NOTE

Shortcross Rye & Malt
Made from malted barley and rye, double-distilled, 46% ABV
Vanilla, milk chocolate, instant coffee, and apricot aromas, leading to flavors of orange marmalade, honey, and ginger.

Shortcross Rye & Malt

ROYAL OAK

OWNER Illva Saronno

FOUNDED 2016

WEBSITE www.thebusker.com

Royal Oak was initially known as Walsh Whiskey Distillery, as it was founded by Irish drinks entrepreneur Bernard Walsh, in association with Italian company Illva Saronno, best known for its Disaronno and Tia Maria liqueurs. In 2019, Illva Saronno took control of the distillery, while Walsh continued to bottle the popular Irishman and Writer's Tears brands that he had developed. Royal Oak is marketed as "A distillery like no other" and produces grain, single malt, and single pot still whiskeys. It is situated on an 18th-century country estate in County Carlow, is equipped with four column and three pot stills, and has an overall capacity of 660,000 gallons (2.5 million liters) of spirit per annum.

In 2020, The Busker brand was launched to market Royal Oak whiskey, and the range comprises Single Malt, matured and finished in bourbon and sherry casks, and Single Grain and Single Pot Still, both matured in bourbon and sherry casks. There is also a Triple Cask blend, made with a high percentage of single malt and single pot still spirit, aged and finished in bourbon, Marsala, and sherry casks.

TASTING NOTES

The Busker Triple Cask Triple Smooth
Blend, 40% ABV
Tropical fruit, vanilla, and malt on the nose, with a rich palate of malt, cinnamon, and chocolate fudge.

The Busker Single Pot Still
Single pot still, 44.5% ABV
An aromatic nose, featuring vanilla fudge, honey, and figs, leading into a palate of cardamom, black pepper, citrus fruit, and nutmeg, finishing with peppery oak.

The Busker Triple Cask Triple Smooth

THE SHED

OWNER The Rigney family

FOUNDED 2014

WEBSITE www.thesheddistillery.com

Drumshanbo Single Pot Still

When The Shed Distillery in the village of Drumshanbo, County Leitrim, opened in 2014, it revived an ancient tradition of whiskey-making in the Connaught region of western Ireland. It was the brainchild of drinks industry veteran and serial entrepreneur PJ "Pat" Rigney, who established it with International Brands Ltd. Rigney declares that "We were the first distillery in Connaught since the closure of Nun's Island in Galway around 1913."

Pat Rigney chose Drumshanbo for his distilling venture partly because it was where his parents were working when they first met, and also, as he puts it, "Drumshambo is in wild and remote country, and we wanted to be well off the main street."

The actual location of the distillery is The Food Hub, formerly Laird's jam factory, now transformed into 14 food production units after lying empty since 1998. Distillation equipment was sourced from the Arnold Holstein company in Markdorf, Germany, and comprises five pots and a gin still plus three column stills.

Although gin and vodka are also produced, the principal focus is on single pot still whiskey. Triple-distillation is practiced, and pot still mashbills include Irish oats. Maturation take place predominantly in ex-bourbon casks, along with around 20 percent oloroso sherry casks. The first distillation of whiskey occurred in 2014, and five years later, a single pot still whiskey was released. The Shed operates a popular visitor center, attracting around 25,000 people a year, and the overall operation now employs some 100 people. Close to $1.07 million (€1 million) was invested at the facility during 2023 to boost its capacity.

TASTING NOTE

Drumshanbo Single Pot Still
Single pot still, 43% ABV
Dried fruit, vanilla, and spice on the nose, while the rich palate offers figs, sherry, and creamy oak.

McCONNELL'S

OWNER The Belfast Distillery Company

FOUNDED 2020

WEBSITE www.mcconnellsirishwhisky.com

While Titanic has been developed in a former shipyard (see below), McConnell's is being created in a former prison. The Belfast Distillery Company is investing $27.8 million (£22 million) in the venture, based in A-Wing of the historic Crumlin Road Gaol in the north of the city, and expects to host over 100,000 visitors each year, with a range of tours and cocktail masterclasses, along with a tasting bar and shop. Three stills will produce triple-distilled single malt.

The J&J McConnell brand—which uses the spelling "whisky"—dates back to 1776 and is particularly associated with Belfast's Cromac distillery, which opened in 1899 and fell silent during the 1930s. McConnell's was revived in 2020 and achieved significant early success in Ireland, the US, Canada, Europe, Australia, and China. A 5-year-old blend and a sherry cask-finished blend from third-party distillers have been bottled while McConnell's own spirit matures. The distillery officially opened in spring 2024, and a spokesperson said that "While at the distillery visitors will be able to join us for whisky tours and premium tastings and see a working distillery in Belfast city center."

TASTING NOTE

McConnell's 5-Year-Old
Blend, aged in first-fill bourbon barrels, 42% ABV
Aromas of vanilla, lemon, and black pepper lead into flavors of butterscotch, berry fruits, pepper, and a hint of char.

WHISKEY TALES

The Friend at Hand
www.dukeofyorkbelfast.com
The Friend at Hand on Belfast's Hill Street is described as "A unique whiskey off-license combined with a mini-museum charting the whiskey-distilling history of Belfast. Browse and buy from the biggest collection of Irish whiskeys available anywhere and get exclusive access to our own brand 13-year-old whiskeys." Reopened in 2022 after a $2.5 million (£2 million) overhaul, this is now a fascinating new museum area and welcoming tasting room.

TITANIC DISTILLERS

OWNER Titanic Distillers

FOUNDED 2023

WEBSITE www.titanicdistillers.com

We tend to think of the city of Dublin as the historical powerhouse of Irish whiskey production, but the north of the island has had its fair share of significant distilleries, too.

Indeed, the whiskey output of Belfast in 1901 was 6.7 million gallons, which equated to 75 percent of the overall Irish whiskey market. By the late 19th century, Dunville's vast Royal Irish Distilleries on the Falls Road in Belfast was responsible for 2.5 of the total 14 million gallons of whiskey being produced in the whole country.

Dunville's fell silent in 1935, and distilling returned to Belfast for the first time since the company's demise with the opening of Titanic Distillers' facility in 2023. Titanic Distillers is named after the ill-fated ship, launched in May 1911, and is based in the pumphouse used during its construction, at Thompson Dock in the heart of Belfast's "Titanic Quarter" development.

The distillery has cost $12.6 million (£10 million) to create, and according to co-owner Peter Lavery, "We could have built on a brown field site, but I wanted something with a bit of history, with a story to it and the story of the Titanic is one that's known all over the world. You can look into the dry dock where it was built and launched from the windows of the distillery, and we offer tours of the dock and pumphouse, as well as tasting sessions."

Titanic Distillers began production in its new distillery in June 2023 and is making around 26,400 gallons (100,000 liters) of triple-distilled single malt per year. While Titanic waits for its own youthful spirit to mature, a Titanic Blend, called Premium Irish Whiskey, is on sale, produced in the Great Northern Distillery, just across the border in Dundalk. It comprises grain spirit and triple-distilled malt, with an element of peated spirit in the mix.

TASTING NOTE

Titanic Spirits Premium Irish Whiskey
Blend, 40% ABV
The rich nose offers aromas of sherry and subtle peat, while the palate features vanilla, black pepper, dates, and raisins.

Titanic Spirits Premium Irish Whiskey

NORTH AMERICA

UNITED STATES

The American whiskey industry has been booming over the past decade, with a huge growth in the choice of brands available to the drinker. The country now boasts a wave of new distilleries, both large and small, and a host of bottlers and non-producer distillers, which has led to a series of mergers and acquisitions and a super-premium trend that has elevated bourbon to new heights. Furthermore, the industry has admitted a new generation of entrepreneurs and innovators into the fold, propelling flavor creations to the next level through the use of finishing, blending, new mashbills, and innovative barrel maturation programs.

REGIONAL STYLES
Bourbon remains the dominant whiskey style and is unique to America. It must be made of at least 51 percent corn, though the proportion is normally far higher, with the mashbill topped off by other grains, usually malted barley and wheat or rye. The law dictates new white oak barrels must be used for maturation.

AUTHOR'S CHOICE
It's hard to beat WILD TURKEY, but the innovation taking place at HEAVEN HILL, BUFFALO TRACE, and JACK DANIEL'S is successfully capturing the attention of a new audience. WILLETT's Rowan's Creek and Noah's Mill and UNCLE NEAREST are worth seeking out. WESTLAND's approach to American single malt is creating great spirits with an authentic sense of place.

REGIONAL EVENTS AND TRAILS
Tourist authorities have helped drive the bourbon renaissance with an official Kentucky Bourbon Trail, as well as the Urban Bourbon Trail in downtown Louisville (www.kybourbontrail.com). For a celebration of local whiskey, the Kentucky Bourbon Festival (www.kybourbonfestival.com) held in September in Bardstown, the "bourbon capital," is an absolute must. Elsewhere, WhiskyFest is held in New York, Chicago, and Hollywood, Florida (www.whiskyadvocate.com/whiskyfest).

With its distinctive dark wood and red shutters, *Maker's Mark cuts a neat figure among distilleries.*

None of the long-established multinationals producing multiple brands can afford to sit still either, so they have been extending their lines with captivating new releases to keep the attention of their customers while hoping to catch the eyes of new drinkers. While many of the most eagerly anticipated releases never make it overseas and sell out quickly within the US market, a growing number of distillers are recognizing the worldwide appeal of their whiskeys and exporting to a greater number of countries.

Much is made of the need to use soft water for great Scotch, but in Kentucky, the opposite is true. The water is hard and calcium rich, great for breeding strong racehorses and making fine bourbon. In the southeast, Kentucky has long, very hot summers and

viciously cold winters, ideal for the accelerated maturation of bourbon.

Of course, bourbon isn't the country's only whiskey. Rye whiskey has made an enormous comeback, and while wheat whiskey and corn whiskey are all popular in pockets, the growth in American single malt (ASM) cannot be ignored as the country's most exciting emergent category. Distillers are eagerly awaiting a standard of identity to officially recognize the category. But while the picture continues to evolve, it remains the case that, just as with single malt whisky and Scotland, if you discover American whiskey anywhere, you will eventually be drawn to Kentucky, where traditional big-name bourbons are now being joined by exciting and innovative new styles.

GETTING AROUND

Every US state makes whiskey, so any trip can incorporate a distillery visit with a little effort. Louisville in north Kentucky is the perfect place to base yourself—it's a vibrant and stylish city with some stunning modern restaurants where bourbon is spotlighted. Rent a car or book transportation on a custom tour to get around. Nashville is a great location to visit, with Tennessee whiskey distilleries in the city and Jack Daniel's around 80 miles to the south.

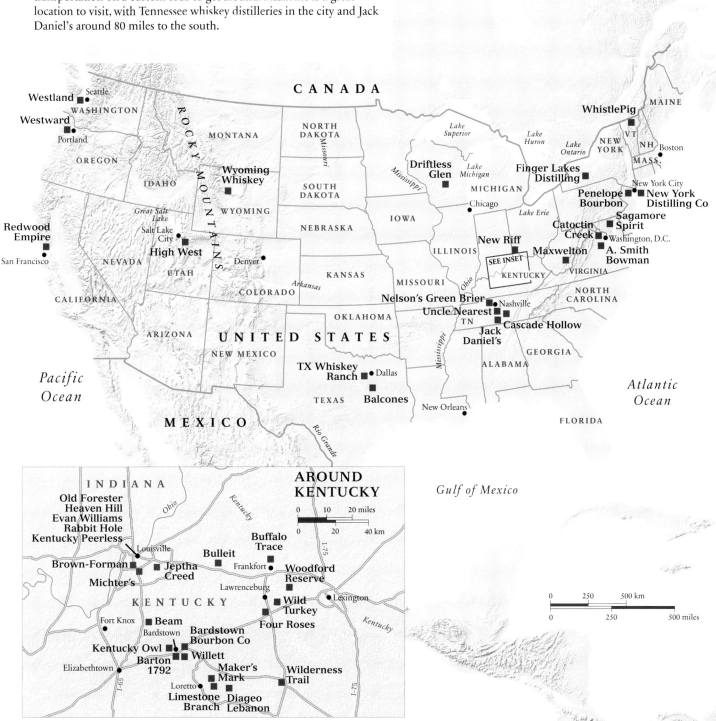

SUNTORY GLOBAL SPIRITS

WHISKEY TALES

Booker Noe
A number of Jim Beam's "Small Batch Bourbon Collection" whiskeys take their names from legendary bourbon characters, including the late Booker Noe, Master Distiller at Jim Beam for more than 40 years and father of Fred Noe and grandfather to Freddie Noe, the current father and son master distillers. Booker lends his name to the distillery's first-ever cask-strength bourbon and was well known for his generous hospitality. One visitor was told that if he were to turn up at Booker's house unannounced, he would be offered food, drink, and a place to stay. Amazed, he hesitated at first but was eventually persuaded to go. When he returned, the visitor was asked whether he had indeed been offered food, drink, and somewhere to stay. "No," he replied. "Booker offered me the drink first."

Suntory Global Spirits, a vast multinational drinks company, was founded in 2014 when Suntory purchased Beam for $16 billion. Its American whiskey brands include Jim Beam, Maker's Mark, Knob Creek, Basil Hayden's, Booker's, Baker's, Legent, Old Overholt, Clermont Steep American Single Malt, and many more.

JIM BEAM

OWNER Suntory Global Spirits

FOUNDED 1934

WEBSITE www.jimbeam.com

Jim Beam is the world's bestselling brand of bourbon, and for the first time in its history, it has two master distillers, with Fred Noe and his son Freddie Noe working side by side as the seventh and eighth generation master distillers, respectively.

Suntory Global Spirits has made significant investment into its production and visitor facilities in recent years. The refurbished James B. Beam Distilling Co. in Clermont, Kentucky, is the place to visit, and the enormous campus also encompasses the new Fred B. Noe Craft Distillery, which is where Booker's, Baker's, and Little Book will be produced. As the next generation to work on the site, Freddie Noe will develop the next line of experimental American whiskeys in the craft distillery. There are also production facilities at the Jim Beam Booker Noe Plant in Boston and the Jim Beam Old Grand-Dad plant in Frankfort, both in Kentucky.

Iconic bourbon brands

The core Jim Beam whiskies are iconic bourbon brands, with the Jim Beam white label being aged for four years while the black label version is extra-aged, though no longer carries the 8-year-old age statement. Jim Beam was one of the most successful pioneers of the flavored whiskey movement. While the products might not be to the taste of every whiskey purist, their line extensions of Honey, Peach, Orange, Apple, Vanilla, Red Stag, and Kentucky Fire, a variant flavored with cinnamon liqueur, have helped nudge people toward drinking whiskey who might have

never previously considered it. The whiskey line has developed over the past decade, too, and now encompasses Jim Beam Pre-Prohibition Style Rye, Jim Beam Single Barrel, and Jim Beam Double Oaked, where the process of filling a newly charred American oak barrel is repeated twice. With Jim Beam Devil's Cut, whiskey soaked into used barrels is extracted and blended with extra-aged Kentucky straight bourbon. They also draw on their own rich history for new limited editions such as the Jim Beam Repeal Batch, recreating the first batches of Jim Beam after the end of Prohibition, and Old Tub, based on a historic whiskey made by the Beam family before they made Jim Beam.

TASTING NOTES

Jim Beam Black Label
Kentucky straight bourbon, matured in new American white oak casks, 43% ABV
On the nose, there is blackened oak, leather, marron glacé, chocolate chip cookies, ginger, cinnamon, nutmeg, and peppermint patties. A great value bourbon with flavors of honey, vanilla fudge, caramel, buttered corn, and black cherry, and a finish of sweet brown sugar.

Jim Beam Single Barrel
Kentucky straight bourbon, matured in new American white oak casks, 47.5% ABV
A nose of honey, golden syrup, honeydew melon, green apple, white chocolate, and assertive oak. Extremely enjoyable with butterscotch, candied lemon, honey, vanilla, and clove, adding beeswax, roasted nuts, cinnamon, and orange with a finish of spicy oak, baked sugar, and barrel char.

Jim Beam Old Tub
Kentucky straight bourbon, matured in new American white oak casks, 50% ABV
Approachable with nougat, honey, macaroon bar, banana bread, s'mores, and cinnamon. Vanilla, creamed corn, coconut strips, pecan, and toasted oak, with a short finish of cedar spills, peanut, and spice.

Jim Beam Single Barrel

MAKER'S MARK

OWNER Suntory Global Spirits

FOUNDED 1953

WEBSITE www.makersmark.com

The legendary hand-dipped red wax seals may be iconic, the spelling of whisky on the label a nod to the family's Scottish ancestry, the continuance of the practice of hand rotating the barrels around the rickhouse quite traditional, but it's the soft, red winter wheat used as the secondary grain in the mashbill that gives Maker's Mark its signature approachability.

Bill Samuels founded Maker's Mark, a B Corp company just outside Loretto, Kentucky, with Margie Samuels, his wife, responsible for creating the distinctive bottle shape, labels, and red wax closures. The bourbon found traction as a premium spirit during the end of the 20th century. From 1958 until 2010, there was only one Maker's Mark expression, and while that is all changing now, they are still doing it in their own way.

Extending the range

Bill Samuels Jr. created Maker's Mark 46, where mature bourbon was finished in specialist barrels with 10 seared French oak stave inserts. Rob Samuels, son of Bill Jr., is now in charge and continuing to develop new expressions, following in his father's footsteps.

Since 2014, Maker's Mark Cask Strength has been available at barrel proof, and then there is Maker's Mark 101, named for its slightly lower proof strength. The Wood Finishing series ran from 2019–2023 in the US, an extension of the thinking behind Maker's Mark 46, using different barrel inserts to create a line of limited editions. The debut of Maker's Mark Cellar Aged in 2023 was the first release of an older aged whisky, a blend of 11- and 12-year-old whiskies, aged to taste, not time, from barrels of mature stock rotated into the cooler, stable climate of their limestone cellar.

The distillery at Star Hill Farm is equipped with copper column stills by Vendome Copper & Brass Works, but for visitors, there is as much important work going on outside the distillery as inside. The 1,100-acre site is now home to regenerative agriculture projects and Maker's Mark's important contribution to The White Oak Initiative, where they are growing a repository of different variants of the tree species to help the long-term sustainability of the oak that underpins so much of the spirits industry.

WHISKEY TALES

An Individual Approach
It may be a big distillery these days, but Maker's Mark still does things a little differently to its competitors. The grain is ground on a mill that uses a roller system rather than a hammer system, because the distillery believes that the heat from hammering makes for a more bitter taste. Also, the barrels are rotated in the warehouse for consistency, important for a bourbon that uses relatively few barrels in each batch and should not vary enormously in taste—something hard to avoid in Kentucky because of the huge temperature variations in the large, multifloored warehouses.

Maker's Mark Cask Strength

TASTING NOTES

Maker's Mark
Kentucky straight bourbon, matured in new American white oak casks, 46% ABV
Caramel and nutty on the nose, this classic bourbon has summer floral notes, creamy vanilla, sliced almond, bread crust, and a gentle herbaceous spiciness. Light and easy drinking, it has flavors of vanilla, caramel, brown, sugar, brioche, cinnamon, baked apple, and black pepper, a long finish of nutmeg-spiced dark caramels.

Maker's Mark 46
Kentucky straight bourbon, finished with French oak stave inserts, 47% ABV
Fresh, rich, and intense aromas on the nose, with vanilla, caramel, nutmeg, cinnamon, tobacco, and seasoned oak notes. It's smooth on the palate, delivering a greater level of flavor than the original through flavors of toffee, dark chocolate, cooked fruit, black cherry, and cinnamon and a flavorsome finish of peanut, cola, and almond with a hint of warm leather.

Maker's Mark Cask Strength
Kentucky straight bourbon, matured in new American white oak casks, 55.05% ABV
While variations are seen between batches, this example delivers an intense vanilla note, with caramel, pecan pie, cigar, and peanut with a slight oak astringency. Creamy chocolate praline, cherry, and black pepper as the spices crest at full strength, followed by digestive biscuit notes, with candied orange and hints of black tea. The finish is sweet with brown sugar, pecan, and dry oak.

BASIL HAYDEN

Basil Hayden Bourbon

OWNER Suntory Global Spirits

FOUNDED 1992

WEBSITE www.basilhaydenbourbon.com

Basil Hayden is the gentlest place to start with the Small Batch Collection, given its low proof and lighter style. Introduced in 1992 by Booker Noe, it was named after Basil Hayden and designed to reflect his high rye bourbon style from the late 18th century. Similar to other small batch releases, it's mainly the nonage stated flagship expression that's exported. The US market, however, enjoys a wider range of Basil Hayden variants, including Dark Rye, Toast, Malted Rye, Subtle Smoke, Red Wine Cask Finish, and a 10-Year-Old.

TASTING NOTE

Basil Hayden Bourbon
Kentucky straight bourbon, matured in new American white oak barrel, 40% ABV
Cedar, brown sugar, cinnamon cereal, toasted walnut, oak spice, and ground ginger aromas, this creamy bourbon has brown sugar, granola, butterscotch, buttery corn, and light spices, and a finish of vanilla and drying oak.

BOOKER'S

OWNER Suntory Global Spirits

FOUNDED 1988

WEBSITE www.bookersbourbon.com

Named after Jim Beam's grandson and sixth generation master distiller Booker Noe (1929–2004), Booker's bourbon was introduced in the 1980s and subsequently became the leading bourbon in the Small Batch Collection. It is rich and dark with notes of oak and tobacco, bottled uncut and unfiltered at barrel strength, just the way Booker drank it. It's the ideal bourbon to experiment with adding water or ice. Several batches are released annually, with full information about the sweet spots in the warehouse where each barrel came from.

TASTING NOTE

Booker's Pinkie Patch
Kentucky straight bourbon, aged in new charred American oak casks, 61.2% ABV
Honey, sweet peanuts, cinnamon, seasoned oak, and French cream puffs aromas with walnut whip and vanilla on first sip, while water releases beeswax, candied ginger, singed oak, and chocolate babka with a finish of vanilla, oak, and brown sugar.

Booker's Pinkie Patch

KNOB CREEK

OWNER Suntory Global Spirits

FOUNDED 1992

WEBSITE www.knobcreek.com

Part of the small batch bourbons that helped kick-start the bourbon revival, Knob Creek is a full-flavored Kentucky straight bourbon, bottled at 100 proof and aged for longer than most bourbons in new charred American oak barrels. It is also a brand developing exciting line extensions in the US.

TASTING NOTES

Knob Creek 9-Year-Old
Kentucky straight bourbon, matured in new American white oak barrels, 50% ABV
This should be on your repeat buy list with its nose of root beer, vanilla, pecan, dried stone fruits, citrus, cherry, and toasted cereals. A chewy toffee mouthfeel, the palate shows dark chocolate, blackened oak, allspice, and licorice with hot peppery spice to finish, showing dark chocolate, leather, and tobacco leaf.

Knob Creek Rye
Kentucky straight rye, matured in new American oak barrels, 50% ABV
A tantalizing nose of minty dark chocolate, cinnamon toast, rye spices, nutmeg, vanilla pod, charred oak, and a hint of treacle. On first sip, there's molasses, burnt sugar, and vanilla seed, then a wave of rye spices, walnut, clove, and dried herbs, and a spicy, fruity finish.

LEGENT

OWNER Suntory Global Spirits

FOUNDED 2019

WEBSITE www.legentbourbon.com

Called the bourbon that redefines bourbon, Legent is a Suntory Global Spirits collaboration between Fred Noe, seventh-generation master distiller, and Shinji Fukuyo, chief blender at the House of Suntory. Learning from each other, the two masters created this new blend and a new brand for the company in 2019. Blended whiskey has been a tainted term in the US, normally associated with low-grade products made from bourbon mixed with grain neutral alcohol. However, Legent is made of straight bourbon aged for four years blended with red wine-finished bourbon and a little sherry cask-finished bourbon—for the avoidance of doubt, grain neutral spirits were never part of the plan. Suntory Global Spirits has continued to innovate, with a related Scotch blend called Ardray resulting from a collaboration that takes a Japanese blender's approach to the art of blending Scotch whiskies. Far from being a one-off, a limited edition Legent Yamazaki Cask Finish Blend followed in 2023.

Master blender Shinji Fukuyo applied his Japanese blending skills to the world of American whiskey for Legent.

TASTING NOTE

Legent Bourbon
Kentucky straight bourbon, partially finished in wine and sherry casks, 47% ABV
Wine and sherry notes followed by peppery spices, cherry, red apple, citrus peel, and a stick of Wrigley's spearmint gum. Red apple, cranberry, black grape, butterscotch, and herbal notes on the palate, with black pepper, clove, vanilla cream, rye bread, and maple syrup. This complex blend evolves continually, departing with a fruity finish.

Legent Bourbon

OLD OVERHOLT

OWNER Suntory Global Spirits

FOUNDED 1810

WEBSITE www.overholtrye.com

Abraham Overholt founded A. Overholt & Co. in Pennsylvania, though these days it is made in Clermont, Kentucky, having joined the Beam family in 1987. When made in Pennsylvania, it was a robust style of Old Monongahela rye. It is said that it was the preferred whiskey of men such as President Ulysses S. Grant and dentist, gambler, and gunfighter "Doc" Holliday, known for his role in gunfight at the O.K. Corral in Tombstone, Arizona.

The classic expression is a bartending staple, but the affordable range has expanded to include higher-strength expressions, a bottled in bond version, and an extra-aged cask-strength expression that is aged for 10 years. In 2024, Freddie Noe released a new rye called A. Overholt, made with 80 percent rye and 20 percent malted barley, the same as the original recipe in 1810. They called this their Monongahela Mash, though it is made at the James B. Beam Distilling Co.

TASTING NOTE

Old Overholt
Kentucky straight rye, aged in new charred American oak casks, 40% ABV
Zested orange, lime, grapefruit peel, floral notes, and dusty grains with dabs of cinnamon powder and cocoa on the nose. That citrus theme continues on the palate, with citrus oil and lemon juice. Light bodied with an oily mouthfeel, the flavors develop to show vanilla, mandarin orange flan, and late glimpses of honey, nougat, and grain notes. The finish is short with lemon peel on a spicy base.

Old Overholt

BROWN-FORMAN

After more than 150 years in the beverage business, Brown-Forman produce some of the biggest names in brown spirits, such as Jack Daniel's, Old Forester, and Woodford Reserve, as well as Slane Irish Whiskey and Benriach, GlenDronach, and Glenglassaugh from Scotland.

JACK DANIEL'S

OWNER Brown-Forman Corporation

FOUNDED 1866

WEBSITE www.jackdaniels.com

Whiskey lovers tend to take Jack Daniel's for granted at best and at worst tend to distance themselves from it and condemn it for not being a "proper whiskey." This is insultingly simplistic and grossly unfair to a brand that has done more than any other to keep the world whiskey flag flying over the many years when it wasn't in vogue. And Jack Daniel's is actively participating in the American whiskey boom, using its platform to bring out intriguing new expressions for its vast audience to discover.

A good ol' success story
In fact, Brown-Forman, the brand's owners, have pulled off three marketing feats that deserve our total respect. One, they convinced younger people of legal drinking age that it could be cool to drink whiskey; two, they succeeded in making a brown spirit a success story when hardly any other dark spirit was selling very well at all; and three, they managed to convince drinkers that it was a small, good ol' boy brand when actually it's a commercial monster.

Pay a visit to the distillery and they're working overtime to protect that impression. Lynchburg itself is in a dry county where only the distillery is allowed to sell bottles, as you can't buy it in town. The site is a shrine to the distillery and when you wander through shop after shop selling "JD" merchandise from lapel badges to Harley-Davidson motorcycles, you get a sense of how big a brand it is—up there with Coca Cola and, indeed, Harley-Davidson. Not bad for a hard liquor.

Jack Daniel's celebrated its 150th anniversary in 2016, but it shows no signs of resting on its laurels. In fact, since its anniversary, Jack Daniel's has increased the pace of innovation and earned the No. 1 whiskey in *Whisky Advocate*'s Top 20 of 2022. Since the appointment of master distiller Chris Fletcher, grandson of Frank Bobo, the fifth Jack Daniel's master distiller from 1966 to 1988, Jack Daniel's has debuted Jack Daniel's Bonded and Jack Daniel's Triple Mash, 10- and 12-year-old age statement versions of its Tennessee whiskey, and a Jack Daniel's American Single Malt finished in oloroso sherry casks. This builds on the release of its Jack Daniel's rye products and flavored whiskeys over the past decade, which has only heightened the brand's appeal to the broadest possible audience.

How Jack Daniel's is made
Jack Daniel's Tennessee Whiskey such as Old No. 7 has a mashbill of 80 percent corn, 12 percent malted barley, and 8 percent rye, whereas Jack Daniel's Rye is 7 percent rye, 18 percent corn, and 12 percent malted barley. Obviously, its American single malt is made from 100 percent malted barley. The grains are cooked, then mixed with spring water drawn from Cave Spring Hollow, before 30 percent backset from the previous distillation is added to create a sour mash. They propagate their own yeast every week. The Jack Daniel's fermenters can accommodate up to 40,000 gallons.

Like most major American distilleries, Jack Daniel's distills through column stills, each attached to a doubler. Essentially, after the initial column still distillation, the vapors go through the doubler, which is like a copper pot still and where the second distillation takes place, before the vapors are condensed back into liquid.

The Lincoln County Process

Distilled to 140 proof, the new make then undergoes the Lincoln County Process where it is filtered through 10 feet of sugar maple charcoal, a process that takes about 24 hours and is practiced by almost all Tennessee whiskey makers. Three days a week, pallets of hard sugar maple are doused with new-make spirit and set alight. Once raked over and cooled, the charcoal is filled into vats for the charcoal-mellowing process that the new-make spirit undergoes before barreling, a distinctive step in making Tennessee whiskey. There are some bourbons that refer to charcoal filtering, but this is not the same as Tennessee whiskey; those whiskeys are filtered through charcoal after it has been matured in a cask,

The sun sets over a barrel warehouse at the vast Jack Daniel's distillery at Lynchburg in Tennessee.

and the process is mainly carried out to remove any floating impurities from the wood. For extra smoothness, Jack Daniel's Gentleman Jack undergoes charcoal mellowing before maturation and after.

Jack Daniel's has two cooperages and its own stave mill, so it is in complete control of its new charred oak barrels. Typically, they use a 13-minute toast ,which helps add color to the whiskey, followed by a 20–25 second char, equivalent to a level 3–4 char. Other than the recent age stated versions, Jack Daniel's is bottled when it's ready rather than when it's reached a specific age, though the consistency of the process gives the master distiller a reasonable degree of predictability for each product.

TASTING NOTES

Jack Daniel's Bonded
Tennessee whiskey, matured in new American oak casks, 50% ABV
Rich caramel, pecan, allspice, cacao, banana loaf, and dried herbs on the nose of this bottled-in-bond Tennessee whiskey. The palate delivers honey, brown sugar, dark chocolate, clove, and assertive peppery spices, then sweet cherry syrup, banana chip, and dried herbal notes that persist into an oaky finish. No wonder this was awarded No. 1 in *Whisky Advocate*'s annual Top 20 whiskeys of the year in 2022.

Jack Daniel's Single Barrel Barrel Strength
Tennessee whiskey, matured in new American oak casks, 64.5% ABV
Beautifully dark, yet balanced, the nose brings forth notes of vanilla pod, toasted cinnamon stick, blackened oak, treacle, clove, and eucalyptus, with melting dark chocolate puddings, syrupy sweetness, and crème brûlée. At this strength, a cask-strength sip shows cola, root beer, leather, and packs a lot of heat. Water brings out sweet caramel, cornbread, sweet citrus notes, granola, and dried orange slice, with cherry and fruit syrups as the texture gets a little sticky. Dried citrus and peach sweetness on the finish.

Jack Daniel's Sinatra Select
Tennessee whiskey, matured in grooved new American oak casks, 45% ABV
Made in tribute to Frank Sinatra using special grooved casks, the nose has heavy-hitting dry oak notes, with bitter dark chocolate, vanilla seed, cigar box, and dried orange slice. Sweet to taste, with orange peel, honey, clove, and dark oak, the texture oozes class with its exceptional smoothness, with additional flavors of plain chocolate and roasted hazelnut. Resinous oak and vanilla pod on a drying finish.

Jack Daniel's Bonded

WOODFORD RESERVE

OWNER Brown-Forman Corporation

FOUNDED 1996

WEBSITE www.woodfordreserve.com

If you're looking for a quaint distillery set in a stunning rural location and steeped in the past, then Brown-Forman's Woodford Reserve is the place for you. The old Labrot & Graham distillery is as historic as American whiskey gets, occupying a site where whiskey legends Elijah Pepper and James Crow fine-tuned the bourbon-making process, bringing to it a consistency and quality that ensured a bright future for this style of whiskey.

Brown-Forman own Jack Daniel's and the Brown-Forman Distillery in the city of Louisville, Kentucky, but Woodford Reserve couldn't be more different from them. To reach the distillery, you travel through some of the prettiest parts of the state, passing the huge stud farms where some of the world's finest racehorses are bred. The horses are here for the same reason that the whiskey is: a water supply drawn from calcium-rich hard-water basins that both produces great bourbon and enriches the grassland that the horses graze on, helping raise strong animals. Woodford Reserve sponsors the Kentucky Derby and releases an annual bottling with a commemorative label, perfect for sipping a Mint Julep while watching the race.

Triple-batch distillation

Master distiller Elizabeth McCall is in charge of Woodford Reserve. What is in the bottle is a combination of triple-pot-distilled whiskey and column-distilled whiskey from the Brown-Forman distillery in Shively, following a recipe developed by Chris Morris, master distiller emeritus. The bourbon is made from 72 percent corn, 18 percent rye, and 10 percent malted barley. Now, bourbon is normally produced on column stills with doublers, the mash passing through the columns with a consistency as thick as porridge, so triple-batch distillation in copper pot stills is an unusual process for Kentucky.

Woodford uses an "all grains in" mash process in the beer still, which is designed with a conical bottom to help drain the spent beer once the low wines have been distilled off. This hardworking still

has a much shorter working life than its neighbors, the high wines and spirit stills. This line of super-premium whiskeys has grown steadily, fed by innovations developed for the Woodford Reserve Master's Collection, their annual release bottling produced in limited quantities since 2006.

Beyond straight bourbon, the core lineup includes a rye, malt, and wheated expression in addition to double-oaked bourbon. In 2020, a Woodford Reserve Baccarat Edition was released; a luxury collaboration celebrated by an XO cognac cask-finished bourbon. You can also find a Batch Proof expression.

Those visiting the distillery or specialist Kentucky retailers can find their highly experimental Distillery series. These have included versions called Double Double Oaked, the Frosty Four Wood, a Five Wood expression, a Honey Barrel Finish, and a Chocolate Malt Whisper bottling.

TASTING NOTES

Woodford Reserve Double Oaked
Kentucky straight bourbon, finished in a secondary oak barrel, 43.2% ABV
Double chocolate muffins, box pressed cigars, vanilla seeds, cinnamon stick, toasted oak, and jellied dark fruits on the nose. Raisin, dark chocolate, mixed nuts, and vanilla seeds, getting slowly creamier until the heavy oak flavors increasingly dominate the flavors into the finish.

Woodford Reserve Straight Rye Whiskey
Kentucky straight rye, matured in new charred American oak casks, 45.2% ABV
Plenty of bite from the rye spices, with aromas of Williams pear, toasted oak, marzipan, crème caramel, and a dusting of cinnamon. Soothing and smooth on the palate, it shows flavors of dark chocolate, raisin, vanilla essence, coffee bean, and a kick of rye spices, faint dabs of mint and herbs, turning a touch leathery toward the end, with a finish of oak char, raisin, and chili flakes.

Woodford Reserve Master's Collection Batch Proof
Kentucky straight bourbon, aged in new charred American oak casks, 61.6% ABV
The nose is full of temptation, with aromas of toasted oak, vanilla seed, leather, fresh mint leaves, cinnamon stick, zested orange, beeswax, and cocoa powder. Caramel, toffee, chocolate, and oak on the palate, the spices slowly building up in intensity, followed by cherry, more chocolate and oak, and moist coffee grounds, with cocoa and glimpses of cherry on the finish. Water amps up the spices, adding ginger, pineapple cube, and chili flake notes.

Woodford Reserve Double Oaked

Woodford Reserve Straight Rye Whiskey

OLD FORESTER

OWNER Brown-Forman Corporation

FOUNDED 1870

WEBSITE www.oldforester.com

In 1870, George Gavin Brown created Old Forester bourbon, which became America's first bottled bourbon, a moment so important it has been trademarked by Brown-Forman. The importance lies in what qualities were guaranteed inside the bottle, when these were highly variable. Brown would batch bourbon from three different distilleries, Mattingly, Mellwood, and Atherton, bottle it at 90 proof, seal the bottles, and sign them as a guarantee of their quality. The bourbon was named after a local physician Dr. William Forrester (the second "r" was dropped later on) who gave it his approval, and it has become America's oldest continuously bottled bourbon.

The Bottled in Bond Act

In 1897, the Bottled in Bond Act required that the whiskey had to come from a single named distillery and distilled during a single season by a single distiller, aged for four years, and bottled at 100 proof, with the location specified if it was bottled elsewhere. Old Forester duly increased from 90 proof to 100 proof. During Prohibition, Old Forester was one of only a handful of distilleries in Kentucky granted a permit to continue distilling whiskey to be prescribed on medical grounds.

Old Forester has been made at the Brown-Forman distillery in Shively for many decades, usually bottled at 86 and 100 proof, with the Old Forester Birthday Bourbon released in September each year to mark the birthday of George Gavin Brown. In 2014, they launched the Whiskey Row series of historic Old Forester recreations from the early years of their 150 years of history. Old Forester Statesman was released as a movie tie-in in 2017. By 2019, Old Forester Rye had joined the lineup, followed by a new experimental line called the 117 series, akin to Woodford Reserve's Distillery series. These also have imaginative names, such as High Angels' Share made from a selection of low-yielding casks with high evaporative losses, Bottled-in-Bond, and Warehouse H celebrating the unusual microclimates found in this historic warehouse constructed in 1946.

A new working distillery

Old Forester returned home to Main Street in Louisville, Kentucky, in 2018 with the opening of the Old Forester Distilling Co., a working distillery that would add 10–15 percent production capacity for Old Forester as well as providing a brand home and quality visitor attraction.

Visitors can watch the sour mash process, see barrels being charred in the working cooperage, marvel at the casks in their temperature-controlled maturation facility, watch the bottles fly by in the bottling hall, and admire the 44-foot tall copper column known as Big Penny from the glass lift. The still produces around 100,000 proof gallons of alcohol every year. While the whole tour is built around the visitor experience giving it a theme park vibe, you're still witnessing a working distillery in action.

TASTING NOTES

Old Forester 86 Proof
Kentucky straight bourbon, matured in new charred American oak casks, 43% ABV
There are plenty of flavors to unpick from the glass, with charred oak, milk chocolate digestives, musty earthiness, tobacco leaf, warming oak spices, banana loaf, and potpourri. Light caramel, vanilla, baked apple, and musty chocolate, it has a soft mouthfeel with cocoa-dusted cornbread, rye crackers, chili flakes, and light oak, and a finish of vanilla seeds, drying oak, and rye spices.

Old Forester 1870 Original Batch
Kentucky straight bourbon, matured in new charred American oak casks, 45% ABV
Honoring the year that Old Forester became America's first bottled bourbon, this small batch brings together whiskeys produced on different dates with different barrel entry proofs and ages and matured in different warehouses. Dark toffee, saddle leather, dates, sultanas, tobacco leaf, vanilla pod, and some floral top notes. Dried citrus, tangerine peel, caramel, vanilla, clove, peanut, dried herbs, and brown sugar to taste with peanut and lingering dry spices to finish.

Old Forester 1920 Prohibition Style
Kentucky straight bourbon, matured in new charred American oak casks, 57.5% ABV
Fired oak, cherry jam, oak spices, and cacao on the nose, the spices gaining in intensity over time, adding vanilla pod, cinnamon stick, and dried herbal notes. At 115 proof, it's a heavy hitter with caramel, black cherry, clove, pepper, Maltesers, dry oak, and herbal rye spices and a malty sweetness on the finish. Water makes it smoother, boosting the maltiness and dialing down the herbal elements.

Old Forester 86 Proof

HEAVEN HILL

The Shapira family established Heaven Hill Distillery in 1935 with distiller Joseph Beam, who coincidentally, was Jim Beam's cousin. The distillery in Louisville, formerly the Bernheim distillery, is the largest single distillery in Kentucky, capable of producing 1,300 barrels a day, which help fill up nearly 70 rickhouses. Heaven Hill produces a multitude of brands and whiskey styles, and it welcome whiskey lovers to come to learn more about it at the Heaven Hill Bourbon Experience in Bardstown.

BERNHEIM

OWNER Heaven Hill Distilleries, Inc.

FOUNDED 2005

WEBSITE www.heavenhilldistillery.com

This wheat whiskey was introduced in 2005 and proclaimed to be the first new style of whiskey to be introduced since Prohibition. Heaven Hill uses 51 percent wheat, 37 percent corn, and 12 percent malted barley in their wheat whiskey mashbill. It is named after Bernheim distillery, which became the primary distillery for Heaven Hill after its Bardstown distillery burned down in 1996.

TASTING NOTE

Bernheim Original
Kentucky straight wheat whiskey, aged in new charred American oak casks, 45% ABV
Chocolate mint, buttered corn, fresh oak, toffee drops, green tea, and cinnamon on the nose, with minty milk chocolate, orange peel, cake mix, and creamy corn, and a dry, citrus finish.

Bernheim Original

ELIJAH CRAIG

Elijah Craig Barrel Proof

OWNER Heaven Hill Distilleries, Inc.

FOUNDED 1986

WEBSITE www.elijahcraig.com

One of Heaven Hill's best-known brands, Elijah Craig is named after a Baptist preacher, business owner, and enslaver who owned paper and wool mills. In 1789, he became the first distiller to age whiskey in new charred oak barrels. Heaven Hill is now actively engaged in academic research with the University of Kentucky's Commonwealth Institute of Black Studies and Central Kentucky Slavery Initiative in order to better represent the contribution enslaved people made to the bourbon industry.

Elijah Craig bourbon is made from 78 percent corn, 12 percent malted barley, and 10 percent rye, with Kentucky limestone water used in the mash, and matured in new oak barrels with a level 3 char. The most obtainable bottles are the small batch and barrel proof releases, but they also offer a toasted barrel expression, a mature Elijah Craig bourbon finished in a custom-toasted barrel, a straight rye, and an Elijah Craig 18-year-old.

TASTING NOTE

Elijah Craig Barrel Proof
Kentucky straight bourbon, aged in new charred American oak casks, 64% ABV
Dark chocolate, herbal notes, and black fruits on the nose with nutmeg, cinnamon, earthiness, espresso foam, and maple syrup popcorn aromas. Adding water reveals baked apple, cherry, red currant, milk chocolate, black pepper, clove, red licorice, and cinnamon balls, leaving a long, spicy finish. There's lots of depth here, so it's always worth pushing the boat out for the higher proof bottling when it's available.

EVAN WILLIAMS

OWNER Heaven Hill Distilleries, Inc.

FOUNDED 1957

WEBSITE www.evanwilliams.com

Named after Evan Williams, a Welshman who settled in Kentucky and started to distill in 1783, his namesake bourbons are made using the same mashbill as Elijah Craig. The black label is bottled at 43 percent while the white label is bottled in bond and therefore 50 percent proof. Aside from its flavored lines, there is also an extra-aged expression called 1783 Small Batch. Since the 1990s, the Single Barrel has

been one of the best bang for buck bourbons on the market but, latterly, has been available only at the Evan Williams Bourbon Experience in Louisville and a few select locations in Kentucky.

TASTING NOTE

Evan Williams Single Barrel 2014
Kentucky straight bourbon, aged in a single new charred American oak cask, 43.3% ABV
Aromas of vanilla and dark chocolate cake with singed oak, steamed ginger pudding, dates, fig, sultana, and licorice. Honey, caramel, apricot, dark chocolate, ginger, and chili flakes, with marmalade, toffee, hazelnuts, and Oreo cookies. Fired oak, hints of char, coffee grounds, and cocoa to finish.

Evan Williams Single Barrel 2014

HENRY MCKENNA

OWNER Heaven Hill Distilleries, Inc.

FOUNDED 1855

WEBSITE www.heavenhilldistillery.com/henry-mckenna.php

Henry McKenna was born in Draperstown in 1819, in what is now part of Northern Ireland. He moved to Kentucky in 1838. He opened a flour mill in 1855 and learned that he could distill the waste materials from the mill. He went on to build a distillery in Fairfield, Kentucky, and develop his brand, and it became an

ongoing family concern. Heaven Hill keeps the brand alive with a 4-year-old straight bourbon and a 10-year-old single barrel bottled-in-bond expression.

TASTING NOTE

Henry McKenna
Kentucky straight bourbon, matured in new charred American oak casks, 40% ABV
Aromas of cigar box, dark chocolate, black tea, vanilla seeds, brown sugar, and currants. Light and smooth with caramel, citrus peel, milk chocolate, hazelnut, plum, and tobacco and a finish of baking chocolate and oak spice.

LARCENY

OWNER Heaven Hill Distilleries, Inc.

FOUNDED 2012

WEBSITE www.larcenybourbon.com

The story goes that John E. Fitzgerald was a bonded US treasury agent who had the keys to the bonded warehouse and knew where all the best barrels were stored. The legend carries on with Larceny, which is made from a mashbill of 68 percent corn, 20 percent wheat, and 12 percent malted barley. Heaven Hill's

line of wheated bourbons includes Larceny Small Batch, Larceny Barrel Proof, and Old Fitzgerald Bottled in Bond.

TASTING NOTE

Larceny Small Batch
Kentucky straight bourbon, matured in new charred American oak casks, 46% ABV
An oily nose of sesame seeds, oak, cedar, sourdough crust, and dried stone fruits. Sweet caramel, with strawberry jam, clove, creamy corn, baking spices, toffee, black cherry, and peanut, with a finish of mint chocolate, cooked corn, and leather.

Larceny Small Batch

MELLOW CORN

Mellow Corn

OWNER Heaven Hill Distilleries, Inc.

FOUNDED 1945

WEBSITE www.heavenhilldistillery.com/mellow-corn.php

Corn is the main raw material used for most bourbons and Canadian whisky, but a corn whiskey is a niche style of drink with its own set of production rules. A straight corn whiskey must be made from 80 percent corn, but unlike bourbon and rye, it can be aged in used charred barrels as well as uncharred new oak barrels. Corn whiskeys often stand out from a packaging and price perspective, too, from Mellow Corn's vibrant yellow label to the homespun look of metal cans and jam jars. Bottles such as Balcones Baby Blue from Texas have helped bring new consumers to the corn whiskey category. While there are unaged and barely aged corn whiskeys on the market such as Georgia Moon and Stillhouse Original Whiskey, Mellow Corn is aged for a minimum of four years and bottled in bond.

TASTING NOTE

Mellow Corn
Kentucky straight corn, matured in new and refill American oak casks, 50% ABV
The nose has a big, happy wave of buttered corn, vanilla, toasted coconut, and white pepper, with slightly savory notes of roasted corn and banana skin. Sweet to taste with brown sugar, grain notes, vanilla essence, hazelnut, pecan, crème brûlée, and black pepper, evolving to show treacle toffee, sultanas, baked banana, and herbal elements, before a short finish of chocolate, cinnamon, and herbs.

PARKER'S HERITAGE COLLECTION

OWNER Heaven Hill Distilleries, Inc.

FOUNDED 2005

WEBSITE www.heavenhilldistillery.com/parkers-heritage-collection.php

Heaven Hill release this series of rare, limited-edition American whiskeys in tribute to their sixth-generation master distiller Parker Beam, who died at the age of 75 in 2017. Parker Beam launched the annual series in 2007, and it became noteworthy for its innovations as well as being a showcase for the different American whiskey styles produced by Heaven Hill.

The series has included well-aged bourbon whiskeys; examples of rye, malt, and wheat whiskeys to single-cask releases; the blending of different bourbons and mashbills; innovative cask finishes; and the flavor impact of heavily charred barrels on bourbon, rye, and wheat whiskey.

Many of the early examples personally selected and released by Parker Beam now fetch thousands of dollars at auction, and today, each year's latest expression stays true to being a unique whiskey with the capacity to teach something new to even the most experienced of American whiskey palates.

Parker's Heritage Collection 17th Edition

PIKESVILLE RYE

OWNER Heaven Hill Distilleries, Inc.

FOUNDED 2015

WEBSITE www.heavenhilldistillery.com/pikesville-straight-rye.php

Prohibition largely finished off the Maryland rye industry, with Pikesville Rye having been produced from the 1890s. A Maryland rye uses a mashbill made of predominantly rye with corn and malted barley or other small grains, based on what was grown in the state. This is distinct from the historic Monongahela Rye style from Pennsylvania (see below), which mainly used rye with malted barley as little corn was grown in the state then, and the distillers mashed and distilled their whiskey differently to elsewhere.

Pikesville is a suburb northwest of Baltimore. The last Pikesville Rye produced in Maryland was made in 1972 at Majestic distillery under Standard Distillers Products Inc., but the brand was kept alive, one of the few to survive when few drinkers cared about rye. Heaven Hill acquired the Pikesville Rye brand in 1982, and it may now be made in Kentucky, but Heaven Hill keeps the name alive.

TASTING NOTE

Pikesville Straight Rye 110 Proof
Straight rye, matured in new charred American oak casks, 55% ABV
The nose has notes of baking chocolate, rye bread, plum skins, toasted oak and clove, and charred oak. It's a little hard to handle at full strength, with notes of chocolate, malt, cherry, sizzling rye spice, red licorice candy, chili flakes, and root beer, getting creamier as it dilutes. With the addition of water, delicious black cherry and bramble notes emerge. A historically important and versatile rye, it's always worth having a bottle of Pikesville close at hand.

Pikesville Rye Straight Rye 110 Proof

RITTENHOUSE RYE

OWNER Heaven Hill Distilleries, Inc.

FOUNDED 1934

WEBSITE www.heavenhilldistillery.com/rittenhouse-rye.php

Named after Philadelphia's historic Rittenhouse Square, this was launched in the post-Prohibition era as a robust, full-flavored rye whisky (it doesn't use the "e" in its spelling of whisky), a spirit to capture Pennsylvania's historic Monongahela Rye whiskeys of the 18th and 19th centuries.

Once made by Continental Distillers Corp., Philadelphia, Heaven Hill acquired the brand in 1999. It flourished as a resurgent cocktail culture embraced this bottled-in-bond expression's ability to stand up in mixed drinks, and rye whiskey surged again in popularity. While rye whiskeys are no longer a rare sight in bars or liquor stores, this is an affordable and versatile bottled-in-bond option that is perfect for your next Manhattan.

Collectors now hunt the auctions for the 21-, 23-, and 25-year old Rittenhouse Rye bottlings that Heaven Hill released from 2005 onward.

Barrels stored high in a rickhouse at Heaven Hill Distillery.

TASTING NOTE

Rittenhouse Rye Bottled-in-Bond
Straight rye, matured in new charred American oak casks, 50% ABV
The nose has rye crackers, mild rye spices, caramel, toasted walnut, baked orange, dried apricot, and burnt sugar. A sip reveals brown sugar, rye bread, and a wave of rye spices, though it feels a little rough, settling down with dark chocolate, coffee grounds, toasted grains and a hint of mint. The finish shows drying oak and chocolate mints.

Rittenhouse Rye Bottled-in-Bond

SAZERAC

Founded in 1850, Sazerac owns three US distilleries, the best known of which is the historic Buffalo Trace distillery in Franklin County, Kentucky, but it also operates the Barton 1792 distillery in Bardstown, Kentucky, and the A. Smith Bowman distillery in Fredericksburg, Virginia. Sazerac distills and bottles some of the most collectible American whiskeys around, including the legendary Pappy Van Winkle.

1792

OWNER Sazerac Company, Inc.

FOUNDED 2002

WEBSITE www.1792bourbon.com

The oldest operating distillery in Bardstown, the Barton 1792 distillery is named after the year that Kentucky joined the United States. Although no longer open to the public, this working distillery produces a number of Sazerac brands, including the Thomas S. Moore bourbons, though the flagship brand is 1792.

The 1792 Small Batch expression uses a high rye mashbill, and the distillery has released a number of limited editions, including a sweet wheat expression, a 12-year-old, a port finish, a single barrel, and a bottled-in-bond version.

TASTING NOTE

1792 Small Batch
Kentucky straight bourbon, matured in new charred American oak casks, 46.85% ABV
This high rye mashbill recipe produces a nose of chocolate brownie, vanilla essence, wax cola bottle candies, pecan, cinnamon, singed oak, and hints of five spice. Dark sugared fruits, cola, pecan pie, toasty oak, leather with a nip of clove, and then grape jelly and black licorice, becoming increasingly oak driven through to the oaky dryness on the finish.

1792 Small Batch

BLANTON'S

OWNER Sazerac Company, Inc.

FOUNDED 1984

WEBSITE www.blantonsbourbon.com

When Blanton's was introduced in 1984, it was the first commercial release of a single barrel bourbon. Named after Albert B. Blanton, who rose to the position of Sazerac's company president in 1921, it was created by master distiller Elmer T. Lee who recalled how Colonel Blanton would handpick honey barrels from the center of the metaled Warehouse H.

It's a high rye mashbill bourbon, and the bottles are topped with one of eight collectible stoppers with a horse and jockey design. The Original is bottled at 46.5 percent, and Gold is 51.5 percent. There's a Straight from the Barrel expression, while some markets get the 40 percent Special Reserve.

TASTING NOTE

Blanton's Original Single Barrel
Kentucky straight bourbon, matured in a single new charred American oak cask, 46.5% ABV
Lots of toffee on the nose, with cooked corn, roasted nuts, vanilla sugar, honey, and pecan pie. Showcasing an attractive creaminess, there are aromas of chocolate-covered peppermint creams, cherry mousse, and a hint of singed oak. A sip unlocks flavors of caramel, creamy corn, and gentle baking spices, with heaps of brown sugar. There's vanilla essence, chocolate ganache, and fading chocolate orange with a long finish of rye spices, creamy corn, dark chocolate, and tobacco leaf.

Blanton's Original
Single Barrel

BUFFALO TRACE/BUFFALO TRACE ANTIQUE COLLECTION

OWNER Sazerac Company, Inc.

FOUNDED 1787

WEBSITE www.buffalotracedistillery.com

You could search the world over but find few distilleries that have such a great sense of history as the massive Buffalo Trace Distillery at Frankfort, Kentucky. In 1787, the distillery at Buffalo Trace, then known as Lee's Town, began shipping whiskey down the river to New Orleans. The whiskey business was brisk, and by 1810, there were no fewer than 2000 distilleries in the state of Kentucky.

Buffalo Trace distillery has been home to some of the greatest names of distilling, and in 1904, it was named after one of them, George T. Stagg, who had bought it in 1878. It survived Prohibition by gaining a permit to produce medicinal whiskey, and capacity steadily increased after Repeal, so by 1939, the distillery employed 1,000 staff members.

Buffalo Trace Antique Collection

Renamed Buffalo Trace in 1999, it has carved out a reputation for producing a range of world-famous and iconic bourbons, including the Buffalo Trace Antique Collection (BTAC) as well as the flagship Buffalo Trace brand. While BTAC has been delivering annual releases for more than 20 years, this remains their platform for showcasing the highest quality whiskeys they make. Demand now outstrips supply, and they are often attainable only on the secondary market, but every American whiskey fan should try to taste them at least once.

Typically, Buffalo Trace Antique Collection contains five staples: Eagle Rare 17-Year-Old, a straight Kentucky bourbon bottled at 101 proof like the original Eagle Rare from 1975; George T. Stagg, a powerful Kentucky bourbon bottled uncut and unfiltered; Sazerac Rye 18-Year-Old, an intense rye whiskey drawn from an incredible selection of older barrels; Thomas H. Handy, a barrel-strength rye whiskey aged for over six years named for the New Orleans bartender who first used rye in a Sazerac cocktail; and, finally, William Larue Weller, a dark, robust wheated bourbon bottled at cask strength.

TASTING NOTES

William Larue Weller
Kentucky straight bourbon, aged in new charred American oak casks, 66.8% ABV
Potent with dark intensity, the nose has cacao, vanilla seeds, and lots of leather, supported by blackened oak, black licorice, and stewed tea. Water is advisable to bring it down to drinking strength, lightening the chocolate notes to a creamy milk chocolate, with dark fruits, moist coffee grounds, black currant jam, chocolate wafers, and oak tannins with a finish of leather, chocolate icing, and toasted oak.

Eagle Rare 17-Year-Old
Kentucky straight bourbon, aged in new charred American oak casks, 50.5% ABV
The nose exudes dark chocolate, dried orange, vanilla essence, polished oak, coffee cake, allspice, and earthiness. The palate is solid and assured with dark chocolate, vanilla pod, and leather on the opening sip, with cherry and bramble following, then late notes of charcoal before a short, dry oaky finish. Water shakes up the fruit, coaxing out juicy cherry, red currant, and red licorice notes.

George T. Stagg
Kentucky straight bourbon, aged in new charred American oak casks, 67.5% ABV
A single, dark brooding aroma with notes of toasted oak, leather, dark chocolate raisins, oak spices, and vanilla essence. Lots of heat at cask strength, but with a good splash of water, there's plain chocolate, dried orange slice, clove, allspice, nutmeg and ginger loaf and a long, satisfying finish.

Thomas H. Handy
Kentucky straight rye, aged in new charred American oak casks, 62.45% ABV
Punchy rye spices on the nose with green herbal notes, fresh dill, spearmint gum, soft nougat, vanilla, and Kendall mint cake. Mouth-puckering at cask strength, with chocolate, raisin, and Brazil nut flavors, then leather, allspice, and dark fruits. It's so fantastically dense, you could eat it with a spoon. Adding water unleashes some high cocoa solids, chocolates, cherry, bramble, and grape jelly. A phenomenal drink.

Sazerac Rye 18-Year-Old
Kentucky straight rye, aged in new charred American oak casks, 45% ABV
Another epic Sazerac rye whiskey, this showcases polished oak, cola, brittle toffee, nutmeg, sweet cinnamon, roasted herbs, rye bread, halva, and grated dark chocolate. The texture is taut and supple, with rye grains, honey, citrus peel, and grapefruit, lifted by rye spices, to reach a higher plane with vanilla seeds, milk chocolate, currants, mixed peel, grape jelly, and dried cherries. A long finish of musty chocolate, leather, and oak ensues.

WHISKEY TALES
Buffalo Crossing
The distillery's name is a reference to the fact that the original settlement of 1775 was sited on a trail, or "trace," called the Great Buffalo Trace. This was a path carved in the land by one of the massive herds of American bison, or buffalo, which used to migrate in the hundreds of thousands across the great plains of America, the numbers so large that it took hours for them to pass. The bison would slow to cross the relatively narrow and shallow section of the Kentucky River here, making it an ideal location for the Native Americans to hunt them. White settlers found these wide, clear paths forged by the bison to be extremely useful transport routes, and the crossing an ideal place to found a settlement, laying the ground for a violent clash of cultures.

George T. Stagg

COLONEL EH TAYLOR

OWNER Sazerac Company, Inc.

FOUNDED 2011

WEBSITE www.sazerac.com

Edmund Haynes Taylor Jr. owned OFC distillery, now known as Buffalo Trace, and was instrumental in making the case to Congress to pass the Bottled-in-Bond Act in 1897. Buffalo Trace named this line after Taylor in 2011, beginning with the release of the Old Fashioned Sour Mash distilled in 2002, that within a

decade often surpassed five figures at auction. The line is an outlet for creativity, from small batch, single-barrel batches to amaranth and four grain mashbills.

TASTING NOTE

Colonel EH Taylor Small Batch
Kentucky straight bourbon, matured in new charred American oak casks, 50% ABV
Dried stone fruit, Wrigley's spearmint gum, rickhouse floorboards, stewed tea, and smokin' oak. Citrus, nectarine, apricot, and honey, with a finish of spiced orange and vanilla.

Colonel EH Taylor
Small Batch

EAGLE RARE

OWNER Sazerac Company, Inc.

FOUNDED 1975

WEBSITE www.sazerac.com

A former Seagram's brand, Eagle Rare is widely available as a 10-year-old expression, rumored to be made using their low rye mashbill. Aside from the highly prized 17-year-olds in the annual Buffalo Trace Antique Collection, Eagle Rare has been carving out a new niche in recent years as a high-end collectible. First, came limited annual quantities of Double Eagle Very Rare in 2019, which collectors quickly snapped

up, followed in 2023 by Eagle Rare 25-Year-Old, an extra-aged bourbon from its experimental Warehouse P. This enables Sazerac to engage with the growing ranks of high-end bourbon collectors.

TASTING NOTE

Eagle Rare 10-Year-Old
Kentucky straight bourbon, matured in new charred American oak casks, 45% ABV
The nose has leather, cocoa, wax cola bottles candies, and a dollop of honey. A velvety mouthfeel with brown sugar, cola, orange peels, fruitcake, and spice, with a finish of dark chocolate, dried cherry, and toasty oak.

SAZERAC RYE

OWNER Sazerac Company, Inc.

FOUNDED 2006

WEBSITE www.sazerac.com

Obviously, you need to buy a bottle of this rye whiskey to make your Sazerac, and pretend you are sitting in the coffee house on Royal Street, New Orleans. When rye whiskey came back into fashion, this was one of the most dependable and affordable ryes you could buy. Traditionally made with a rye mashbill of 51 percent

rye, there is still a gulf in the neat tasting experience between Sazerac Rye and the Sazerac Rye 18-Year-Old in the annual Buffalo Trace Antique Collection.

TASTING NOTE

Sazerac Rye
Rye whiskey, matured in new charred American oak casks, 45% ABV
Butterscotch, toasted rye grains, clove, and star anise aromas. Marmalade peels, gingersnap, mango syrup, aniseed cough sweets, and perky rye spices, with a citrus and dark chocolate finish.

Sazerac Rye

VAN WINKLE

OWNER Old Rip Van Winkle Company

FOUNDED 1972

WEBSITE www.oldripvanwinkle.com

There's no Old Rip Van Winkle distillery these days, but you can't tell the story of the modern bourbon industry without including Julian Van Winkle III and his son Preston, who occupy a unique position in Kentucky's whiskey output.

These days, Van Winkle whiskey is made at Buffalo Trace in extremely small quantities to the original wheated bourbon recipe, though the bottle codes tell collectors which of the older expressions were made at the now closed Stitzel-Weller Distillery and worthy of even higher bids. Though currently released once a year and available only through right-to-buy lotteries, lucky draws, and loyalty programs, it is notoriously subject to substantial markups once it leaves the Van Winkles' hands, which is a pity. The safest bet to own a bottle for yourself is to buy what you need at auction, where it is offered for sale every month. Pappy's needs no further hype, and meanwhile, the Van Winkle family continue to make fine bourbon so they can pass the traditions on to future generations of the family.

TASTING NOTE

Pappy Van Winkle Family Reserve 15-Year-Old
Kentucky straight bourbon, matured in new charred American oak casks, 53.5% ABV
Classic aged bourbon with sharp and astringent wood and chili spice battling it out with a softer, toffee nut sundae, and stewed peach, cinnamon, and sandalwood flavors. Full, spicy, and oaky on the finish.

Pappy Van Winkle Family Reserve 15-Year-Old

WELLER

OWNER Sazerac Company, Inc.

FOUNDED 1849

WEBSITE www.buffalotracedistillery.com/our-brands/w-l-weller.html

William Larue Weller traded in bourbon in the mid-19th century and is credited with devising wheated bourbon mashbills, switching out rye for wheat as the second grain to create a smoother bourbon. Notably, he also employed Julian "Pappy" Van Winkle (see above) as a salesman, and down the line, Weller's name was incorporated into the Stitzel-Weller Distillery with Pappy's company.

The Weller name is now reserved for a line of wheated bourbons from Buffalo Trace, ranging from the Special Reserve to the Antique 107, Single Barrel, and Full Proof to a superb 12-year-old, with the experimental Daniel Weller expression, named after W. L. Weller's grandfather, adding to the lineup in 2023. The line extensions to the Weller range have been one of the main beneficiaries of the global demand, and subsequent scarcity, of Pappy Van Winkle bourbons.

The historic Buffalo Trace distillery is the home of many world-famous bourbons, such as the Weller wheated bourbons.

TASTING NOTE

Weller 12-Year-Old
Kentucky straight bourbon, matured in new charred American oak casks, 45% ABV
Beautiful on the nose, with cinnamon, almond, creamy milk chocolate, black tea, clove, walnut, vanilla seeds, and cedar spills. Rich and thick-textured, it demonstrates flavors of maple syrup, caramel, oak, vanilla, cinnamon, and dark fruits, with dried cherry, clove, and stewed tea leading into a smooth, drying finishing with toffee, dried cherry, and oaky sweetness.

Weller 12-Year-Old

CAMPARI

Italian liqueur makers Campari own Wild Turkey distillery, a jewel in the Kentucky bourbon crown, and took a controlling stake in a start-up distillery called Wilderness Trail in 2022.

WILD TURKEY

OWNER Campari Group

FOUNDED 1855

WEBSITE www.wildturkeybourbon.com

If ever you wanted proof that American whiskey is in a good place, it's at the Wild Turkey distillery in Lawrenceburg, Kentucky. Campari invested $50 million in the site following the acquisition of the brand from Pernod Ricard in 2009, opening a new state-of-the-art distillery in 2011 to increase capacity and adding a magnificent visitor center in 2014.

The history of the brand and the place is a little complicated, from origins with Irish immigrants called the Ripy brothers in the 1840s to a succession of distillery openings, closures, and name changes over the next century or so to the established era of the Russell family.

The legendary Jimmy Russell

Jimmy Russell was born in 1934 during the Great Depression and started work at the distillery, not yet named Wild Turkey, before he was 20 years old. He worked in every position, learning the secrets of good bourbon from his seniors and gaining more responsibility. In 1967, Jimmy Russell became the master distiller, a position he has dedicated himself to ever since.

When bourbon sales slumped in the 1980s, Jimmy hit the road, meeting bourbon fans around the world, at tasting events and bars, spreading the word about Wild Turkey. Given his unwavering attendance, Jimmy Russell is likely to have attended more WhiskyFest events in the US than any other master distiller, and he would happily sit throughout the event chatting to Wild Turkey fans, answering questions, posing for photographs, and signing autographs. Behind the stand, you would find Eddie Russell, Jimmy's son,

pouring Wild Turkey 101 or Wild Turkey Rare Breed for the waiting line, dispensing his knowledge on the facets behind the latest releases. Eddie Russell started work at the distillery in 1981, and following in his father's footsteps, he was appointed master distiller in 2015. By 2018, Jimmy and Eddie Russell had garnered 101 years of experience in the bourbon industry, a memorable milestone for this Kentucky family who embody the brand and its American spirit. Now Jimmy's grandson Bruce is associate blender, and all three Russells collaborated for the 2023 release of Wild Turkey Generations.

For their loyal fans, Wild Turkey is not really about the non-GMO mashbill of 75 percent corn, 13 percent rye, and 12 percent malted barley, the proprietary yeast strain, the No. 4 alligator char barrels, or the barrels filled at a lower proof to preserve the gorgeous amber color by reducing the amount of water added at bottling. It's about the Russells, it's about the bird, and it's about the authenticity of the brand's roots and the pride in its Kentucky values.

WHISKEY TALES
Talking Turkey
Wild turkey shooting is a big sport in the American South, as is the sport of turkey calling—impersonating a female turkey to attract a male one so that you can shoot it. Competitions featuring turkey impersonators are even televised and attract good prize money. The Wild Turkey brand was conceived in 1940 and took its inspiration from an annual Kentucky turkey shoot. It was traditional for the local distiller to bring along a cask of special bourbon to the festivities. Thomas McCarthy, president of Austin, Nichols, the New York–based company that owned the distillery at the time, chose a quantity of 101-proof straight bourbon from company stocks to take along on the shoot. After a few years, people began to ask for the "wild turkey bourbon," and from there the brand was born.

Wild Turkey Distillery—Campari has invested heavily in new visitor facilities and upgrading the distillery.

A move to premium bottlings

Progress regarding Wild Turkey's standing has been swifter under Eddie Russell's tenure as master distiller. Wild Turkey Rare Breed and Russell's Reserve were launched by his father, matching the angles taken by competitor distilleries to court new drinkers. Eddie Russell's premium annual limited-edition expression, Wild Turkey's Master Keep, has showcased innovation, maturation, and finishing skills and a knack for savvy collaborations since it launched in 2015. With custom glassware and handsome presentation boxes for the series, Wild Turkey has been able to ride the crest of the wave of bourbon premiumization at just the right time. A partnership with Academy award–winning actor Matthew McConaughey between 2016 and 2022 led to the launch of Longbranch in 2018, an 8-year-old expression refined through Texas mesquite charcoal. The extra interest has helped propel a flourishing core line of bourbons, ryes, and flavored expression. In turn, that draws greater numbers of visitors to the Wild Turkey Distillery tours to marvel at the seven-story tall historic rickhouses.

TASTING NOTES

Wild Turkey Master's Keep Cornerstone
Kentucky straight rye, matured in new charred American oak casks, 54.5%
Made from 9–11-year-old rye whiskeys, the nose has honey, peppercorn and powdered sugar–dusted almond croissants. Hefty rye spices on the palate, with lemon curd, marmalade peel, powerful oakiness, red berries, and cranberry sauce, then as it dilutes, more grain notes come through with oak char and some late fudge sweetness, especially if you add a drop of water. Vanilla, tobacco, baked herbs, and oak make for a fantastic finish.

Wild Turkey Master's Keep Voyage
Kentucky straight bourbon, finished in Appleton Estate Rum casks, 53% ABV
Appleton Estate's master blender Joy Spence selected the finishing casks for Wild Turkey; barrels that had previously contained 14-year-old Jamaican pot still rum. Baked apple, cinnamon stick, ginger loaf, citrus, and Ceylon tea on the nose, with a rounded palate of honey, vanilla, toffee, red berries, dark chocolate, cola bottles, and baked orange. Dazzling spices on the finish, with just a hint of rum sweetness.

Wild Turkey Master's Keep Voyage

WILDERNESS TRAIL

OWNER Campari Group

FOUNDED 2013

WEBSITE www.wildernesstraildistillery.com

Shane Baker and Pat Heist, an engineer and a microbiologist, created Wilderness Trail distillery in 2013 on a farm outside Danville, Kentucky. Proponents of sweet mash, not a sour mash process, they also distinguish themselves with an unusually low proof, and costly, barrel-filling regime with the aim of coaxing out more water-soluble cask extractives from the staves.

Their whiskeys, ranging from wheated and high rye bourbons, bottled-in-bond rye, and single barrels to 6- and 8-year-old bourbons, are distilled either through an 18-inch beer column still standing 40-foot tall with a 250-gallon doubler or their 36-inch continuous beer still and 500-gallon doubler; the facility can produce 216 barrels per day. Small Batch, for example, is 64 percent corn, 24 percent wheat, and 12 percent malted barley and aged for at least four years in char level 4 barrels. The other bourbon recipe uses 64 percent corn, 24 percent rye, and 12 percent malted barley, while the rye mashbill consists of 56 percent rye, 33 percent corn, and 11 percent malted barley.

The Campari Group took a controlling stake in Wilderness Trail in 2022.

TASTING NOTES

Wilderness Trail Small Batch Bottled in Bond High Rye Bourbon
Kentucky straight bourbon, matured in new charred American oak casks, 50% ABV
This comes in hard and fast with baking spices, leather, charred oak, vanilla seeds, licorice, cocoa, and Brazil nuts. Vanilla, caramel, brown sugar, black cherry, and clove with creamy milk chocolate, mocha, and toffee apple and a finish of vanilla, digestive biscuit, and Cheerios.

Wilderness Trail Small Batch Bottled in Bond Rye
Kentucky straight bourbon, matured in new charred American oak casks, 50% ABV
Rye spice, toffee, granola, cinnamon stick, and almond aromas, with dusty damp earth. A fantastic, sippable rye, with chocolate, rye spices, cocoa, nut butters, and mocha latte, with a fruity finish with chocolate and a late minty note.

Wilderness Trail Small Batch Bottled in Bond High Rye Bourbon

DIAGEO

Most whiskey lovers associate Diageo with Scotch whisky, but the multinational drinks giant, founded in 1997, has smartly invested and built whiskey brands around the world. In the US, it owns the Diageo Lebanon Distillery, Bulleit Distilling Co., Cascade Hollow (the new name for George Dickel), and Balcones in Texas, as well as selling a number of old and new labels, including I. W. Harper, Blade & Bow, and Orphan Barrel, giving them a stake in the bourbon, rye, and fast-growing American single malt market.

BALCONES

OWNER Diageo plc

FOUNDED 2008

WEBSITE www.balconesdistilling.com

Chip Tate was the driving force behind the launch of this Texan craft distillery in Waco in 2008, creating waves with the likes of Balcones True Blue, a corn whiskey, and Balcones Brimstone, where the blue corn is smoked with Texas scrub oak. While founder Tate departed the business in 2014, the quality of the whiskeys has continued under the care of head distiller Jared Himstedt, now the recognizable face of Balcones. The attraction for Diageo, who bought the business in 2022, was the jewel of owning an American single malt, headed by Balcones Texas 1 Single Malt and their limited editions, through the acquisition of one of the brands in the vanguard of America's single malt revolution.

TASTING NOTE

Balcones Texas 1 Single Malt
Single malt, matured in new toasted and charred American oak casks, 53% ABV
Treacle, pecan pie, ripe banana, dark toffee, stewed fruits, ground cinnamon, and a musty earthiness. Pecan, baked orange, cedar, dark toffee, dried fruits, mango strips, and oak spices on the palate, with a milk chocolate finish.

Balcones Texas 1 Single Malt

BULLEIT

OWNER Diageo plc

FOUNDED 1987

WEBSITE www.bulleit.com

Tom Bulleit launched the Bulleit brand in 1987, resurrecting the name of a rye whiskey used by one of his forefathers in the early to mid-19th century for his new bourbon. The frontier whiskey styling was a hit, and the affordable high rye bourbon, sourced from another Kentucky distillery, took off in the new millennium. The brand has been owned by Diageo since 2000. More products followed—Bulleit Rye in 2011 helped forge a stronger link with their origin story, and Bulleit Bourbon 10-Year-Old in 2013 was an age statement for drinkers looking to trade up a level. Exclusive to the US, Bulleit Barrel Proof came out in 2015, and prior to her departure, blender Eboni Majors created Bulleit Bourbon Blenders' Select, a limited edition, 100 proof bourbon made from three of the Bulleit distillates and aged for a minimum of nine years.

Bulleit is not done with sourcing whiskey quite yet, as the return of Bulleit Rye 12-Year-Old in 2024 used stock sourced from MGP in Indiana and included some rye whiskeys aged up to 17 years. This expression surfaced first in 2019 and uses the same mashbill as Bulleit Rye, that is 95 percent rye and 5 percent malted barley. The best is yet to come. Diageo

Bulleit 10-Year-Old

has invested $115 million in a state-of-the-art distillery and visitor center in the Bulleit Distilling Co. Shelbyville, Kentucky, that opened in 2017 and produces Bulleit, I. W. Harper, and will bottle Orphan Barrel. The public tours and tasting experiences at the facility opened in 2019.

In 2021, the Diageo Lebanon distillery was opened, a 10-million proof gallon per year operation equipped with the very latest high-tech equipment, which will make Bulleit Bourbon and other bourbons and American whiskeys. The carbon-neutral distillery uses no fossil fuels on site and is designed to use resources, such as energy and water, as efficiently as possible. It fits into the sustainability initiatives, renewables, and low carbon future Diageo set out in its 10-year "Society 2030: Spirit of Progress" plan.

Further strengthening their hand in the American single malt category, Diageo announced the first Bulleit American Single Malt release in 2024, matured in new charred American oak barrels, just like the rest of the Bulleit range.

The former Bulleit Frontier Whiskey Experience at the closed Stitzel-Weller distillery in Shively, Kentucky, has reverted to a Stitzel-Weller Experience as a brand home for Blade & Bow and offers tours, tastings, and merchandise.

TASTING NOTES

Bulleit
Kentucky straight bourbon, matured in new charred oak barrels, 45% ABV
Zesty orange, plenty of corn notes, honey, vanilla cupcakes, and buttercream icing on the nose have always made Bulleit a great introduction for new bourbon drinkers. The palate has honey, vanilla, and buttered corn with orange jelly, pepper, caramel, red licorice, ginger, cherry candy, and cinnamon breakfast cereals, ahead of a finish of honey and gingersnaps.

Bulleit 10-Year-Old
Kentucky straight bourbon, matured in new charred oak barrels, 45.6% ABV
The nose has buttery corn, black pepper, vanilla essence, caramel, and fresh oak. Honey, citrus, pear, peppercorns, stem ginger, and pineapple cubes on the palate, and vanilla, hobnob biscuits, honey, and butterscotch. Lingering spices on the finish, with flavors of honey and dried apricots.

Blade & Bow
Kentucky straight bourbon, matured in new charred oak barrels, 45.5% ABV
Caramel, honey, and golden syrup aromas, with peach, popcorn, brown sugar, cinnamon, and dark chocolate. The palate is nutty with caramel syrup, cherry, grape jelly, and blueberry, with clove, vanilla fudge, dried pear, allspice, charred oak, and a finish of spiced vanilla cola and oak tannins.

Blade & Bow

CASCADE HOLLOW

OWNER Diageo plc

FOUNDED 1878 George Dickel

WEBSITE www.georgedickel.com

South of Nashville, Cascade Hollow is based in Tullahoma, Tennessee, and the home of George Dickel whiskies. George A. Dickel was a businessman, involved in marketing and distribution of his spirits rather than distilling. Diageo changed the distillery's name back from the George Dickel distillery to the original name of Cascade Hollow in 2018. It hasn't always been produced in Tennessee either, as it was produced in Kentucky for a couple of decades after the Repeal of Prohibition. The distillery, the second largest in Tennessee, has been in its present location since 1958, when it was under the ownership of Schenley Distilling Co., though it's not far from the original

distillery site where Dickel sourced his whiskies from. When Diageo was formed in 1997, it included Guinness plc, which had acquired Schenley in 1987.

While the full range of bourbon, single barrel, and rye whiskeys are not exported, the brand has received a steady stream of accolades at home for the whiskies released during the tenure of Nicole Austin, the director of George Dickel, including the *Whisky Advocate* 2019 Whisky of the Year for George Dickel 13-Year-Old Bottled in Bond.

TASTING NOTE

George Dickel Bottled in Bond 13-Year-Old
Tennessee whiskey, aged in new charred American oak barrels, 50% ABV
Aromas of rich corn, roasted peanut, blueberry jam, and oak on the nose, lead into a full-bodied Tennessee whiskey with cherries, chocolate, marron glacés, herbal notes, and plenty of oak. The long drying finish boasts plum and dark chocolate.

George Dickel Bottled in Bond 13-Year-Old

BARDSTOWN BOURBON CO.

OWNER Pritzker Private Capital

FOUNDED 2014

WEBSITE www.bardstownbourbon.com

Bardstown Bourbon Company has an impressive facility, described as the only Napa Valley–style destination on the Kentucky Bourbon Trail, with an additional visitor facility based at their Louisville Tasting Room on Whiskey Row. They offer distillery tours of their innovative Bardstown site for whiskey lovers of all levels, and have a welcoming kitchen and top-notch bar serving up plates of country hams, fried chicken with grits, and fried catfish tacos alongside cocktails and whiskey flights.

The company was co-founded by Peter Loftin and David Mandell and attracted former Maker's Mark master distiller Steve Nally to join the enterprise. Nally and his head distiller Nick Smith not only make bourbon, rye, and other whiskeys for their own brands but also offer custom distilling to other companies looking to source a high-quality product. Bardstown Bourbon Company can produce 40–50 different mashbills, servicing the needs of numerous nondistiller producer brands that account for the majority of their production.

Their own labels include their Origin series bourbon and bottled-in-bond wheated bourbon; their Fusion series, which blends their own products with older whiskeys; the Discovery series, which explores the art of blending; and the Collaborative series, which has a focus on finishing.

New ownership
In 2022, a private investment firm acquired Bardstown Bourbon Company. Some of the original team that moved on, including Mandell, have formed a new company called Whiskey House of Kentucky and unveiled plans for a similarly substantial distillery for custom-distilling purposes in Elizabethtown. Meanwhile, Bardstown Bourbon Company acquired Green River Distilling in Daviess County in 2022. This historic name, the 10th-oldest licensed distillery in Kentucky, dates back to 1885, but the modern distillery opened in 2016. Their bottlings returned in 2022 and include a straight bourbon, wheated bourbon, straight rye, and single barrel expressions.

Bardstown Bourbon Company is the only Napa Valley–style destination on the Kentucky Bourbon Trail.

TASTING NOTES

Bardstown Bourbon Co. Origin Series
Kentucky straight bourbon, matured in new charred American oak casks, 48% ABV
The nose has chocolate brownie, mocha, blackened wood, vanilla pod, toasted walnut, dried herbs, cinnamon stick, nutmeg, and a hint of citrus peel. Sweet to taste with chocolate orange flavors, peach, peppery spice, dried fruits, cinnamon, dill, and more herbals notes, and a finish of new leather, oak, and dried herbs. Perfectly fine as an introduction, but they have more tricks than this up their sleeves.

Bardstown Bourbon Co. Fusion Series #7
Blend of Kentucky straight bourbon, matured in new charred American oak casks, 49.05% ABV
Combining their own stocks with older 12-year-old bourbons, this has a nose of caramel, vanilla, dark chocolate, cigar box, and a hint of fresh mint. On the palate, there is brown sugar, baked cookies, ginger, and clove, but as the spices settle, flavors of chocolate, toffee popcorn, and cinnamon toast emerge. A dry finish with dark chocolate and blackened oak.

Bardstown Bourbon Co. Collaborative Series Foursquare
Blend of straight rye and bourbon, finished in Foursquare rum casks, 53.5% ABV
A welcoming nose of chocolate, bread dough, dried grasses, baking spices, poppy seeds, and red apple peelings. Good texture, and a real crowd-pleaser, this brings red apple sweetness, cherry, and peppery spice, followed by creamy milk chocolate, cinnamon, black currant jelly, and cookie dough with oak, musty chocolate, and tobacco on the finish.

Bardstown Bourbon Co.
Origin Series

CONSTELLATION BRANDS

This company started in 1945 and built its strength in sales and distribution of wine, taking the name Constellation Brands in 2000, by which time it was producing and marketing a strong portfolio of wine, beer, and spirit brands.

HIGH WEST DISTILLERY

OWNER Constellation Brands

FOUNDED 2006

WEBSITE www.highwest.com

Dave Perkins founded High West in Park City, Utah, in 2006, opening a saloon in 2009; the Blue Sky distillery and tasting rooms in Wanship, Utah, in 2015; and then sold the operations and brands to Constellation Brands for $160 million in 2016. Brendan Coyle stayed on as master distiller, responsible for the quality of the bourbon, rye, and limited editions going forward, such as A Midwinter Night's Dram, Bourye, and Campfire. High West was initially a sourced brand, but as their own stocks matured, their bottlings have gradually moved over to rely more on their own production and fit a more streamlined portfolio with international reach. Now they have American single malt too; High West High Country American Single Malt is distilled on the grain and matured in fresh and refill barrels.

TASTING NOTE

High West Double Rye
Blend of straight rye, matured in refill casks, 46% ABV
Containing High West distillate, the nose has caramel, pistachio shells, vanilla, and dry-roasted peanuts balanced with spicy rye and herbal notes. Delicious palate of vanilla, rounded citrus notes, caramel, grapefruit, and red apple, with glimpses of toasted cereal, raspberry, and tobacco notes and finish of rye spices, leather, and fruity sweetness.

High West Double Rye

NELSON'S GREEN BRIER

OWNER Constellation Brands

FOUNDED 2014

WEBSITE www.greenbrierdistillery.com

Brothers Andy and Charlie Nelson brought whiskey-making back into the family in honor of their late 18th-century whiskey-making ancestor Charles Nelson. They sourced whiskey to bring back Belle Meade Bourbon, a label lost to Prohibition, and then opened the Nelson's Green Brier distillery in Nashville, Tennessee, in 2014. The distillery is close to downtown Nashville, and the tour is fascinating and helps make the link with the family's past. As Belle Meade has been reined back to Tennessee only, the distillery is one of the best places to try and find a bottle. The flagship Nelson's Green Brier Tennessee whiskey arrived in 2019, the same year as Constellation Brands took a controlling stake in the company, the Nelson Bros. line of bourbon and rye arriving in the following years, with Charlie and Andy Nelson still at the helm and following their dreams.

TASTING NOTE

Nelson's Green Brier Tennessee Whiskey
Tennessee whiskey, aged in new charred American oak casks, 45.5% ABV
A nose of baked apple, cinnamon sugar, gingerbread, potpourri, spearmint, and a hint of shoe polish. Bright apple and citrus flavors, with brown sugar, vanilla, crème brûlée, herbal notes, cinnamon breakfast cereal, and milk chocolate, with a finish of cocoa, cinnamon, dried red berries, and citrus peel.

Nelson's Green Brier
Tennessee Whiskey

FOUR ROSES

OWNER Kirin Holdings Co. Ltd

FOUNDED 1888

WEBSITE www.fourrosesbourbon.com

Four Roses is the comeback kid of bourbon, especially as far as American drinkers are concerned. The rise and fall and rise again of this distillery in Lawrenceburg, Kentucky, formerly known as the Old Prentice distillery, is a tale of resilience, dogged commitment, and belief.

From the 19th-century roots of this Spanish mission–style distillery to the renaissance of the brand under current owners Kirin Holdings Co., the brand has been through some dark times. Seagram bought the distillery and the brand in 1943, and it stayed with them for the rest of the 20th century, but while the bottles exported to markets in Asia and Europe contained straight bourbon, the bottles sold in the US were not the same quality, or always from the same distillery, and it lost the respect of bourbon drinkers at home. In the fallout of the Seagram's breakup, Japanese beer giant Kirin stepped in to buy it to ensure it could maintain supplies of bourbon for its customers in Japan.

Rescuing its reputation

Longtime Seagram's employee Jim Rutledge is widely recognized for saving the brand, initially putting Four Roses yellow label on sale in Kentucky in 1996 and then rebuilding distribution following the Kirin takeover. Rutledge would attend tasting events like WhiskyFest, converting new drinkers to Four Roses one glass at a time.

The hook for aficionados was learning about the Four Roses methods of two mashbills and five yeast strains, which gave Rutledge and his successor Brent Elliott 10 different recipes to play with, each identifiable by a four letter code. These codes all start with O (for the Old Prentice distillery), and the third letter is always S, thought to be for straight. The second letter is either B or E and identifies the mashbill. They make a high rye mashbill (B) of 60 percent corn, 35 percent rye, and 5 percent barley, and a high corn mashbill (E) of 75 percent corn, 20 percent rye, and 5 percent barley, while the five yeasts nudge the flavors in different directions, creating

herbal notes (F), floral essence (Q), delicate fruit (V), rich fruit (O), and slight spice (K). Without tracking down a lot of different single barrel releases, tasting all 10 recipes was a pretty tall order, achievable to only the most committed Four Roses fan. In 2023, their prayers were answered when a tasting pack of miniatures containing all 10 recipes was introduced.

Four Roses doubled capacity in 2019, adding a second column still and doubler, 24 new fermenters, and extra warehousing. Four Roses is matured in single-story racked warehouses in Coxs Creek, 50 miles from the distillery, and by not having towering rickhouses like other distilleries, it limits the flavor impact of the region's seasonal fluctuations in temperature on the maturing spirit in the casks, avoiding the need to rotate the barrels.

The Four Roses range now includes Yellow Label, Small Batch, Small Batch Select, and Single Barrel releases. They run a private barrel program, but the greatest excitement is reserved for the annual barrel strength release of Four Roses Limited Edition Small Batch. This contains a blend of recipes of their older bourbons created by the master distiller. The Four Roses 135th Anniversary Limited Edition Small Batch Bourbon contained 12- and 16-year-old bourbons with the OESV recipe, 14-year-old OESK recipe, and some 25-year-old OBSV recipe.

TASTING NOTES

Four Roses Small Batch
Kentucky straight bourbon, matured in new charred American oak barrels, 45% ABV
Baking spice, brown sugar ,and a hint of star anise on the nose, evolving to show chocolate cookie, restrained oak, dried fruit, and toffee. Not too much bite on first sip, with brown sugar, baked apple, and stone fruits, then it thickens up nicely, with light pepper, clove, black grape, banana chip, and charred oak. Gentle heat with clove, oak, and hints of chocolate on the finish.

Four Roses Single Barrel
Kentucky straight bourbon, matured in new charred American oak barrels, 50% ABV
Lovely combination of cocoa, spice, and oak char on the nose, changing perceptibly to reveal baking chocolate, dried cherry, vanilla pod, peppermint tea, and menthol. Cherry caramel, blueberry, mint toffees, vanilla, and a hint of tobacco leaf, with crème caramel, Bananas Foster (a classic New Orleans dessert), cookie dough, peppermint, and herbal notes. A dash of water turns up the sweetness.

Four Roses Small Batch

MGP INGREDIENTS

MGP Ingredients—it stands for Midwest Grain Products—was founded in 1941. Its premium spirits have been the engine helping to power the acceleration in domestic brown spirit brands in the US market. Labels of sourced whiskeys distilled at Ross & Squibb distillery in Lawrenceburg, Indiana, were unlikely to have come from anyone else. MGP had been in partnership with Limestone Branch Distillery in Lebanon, Kentucky, since 2014, but since then, the company has broadened its approach, acquiring Luxco, Inc., and its bourbon brands, including Ezra Brooks, Blood Oath and Rebel, as well as Lux Row Distillers in Bardstown and Penelope Bourbon.

PENELOPE BOURBON

Penelope Bourbon Cooper Series 6-Year-Old Tokaji Cask Finish

OWNER MGP Ingredients

FOUNDED 2018

WEBSITE www.penelopebourbon.com

A young brand with a big future, Mike Paladini and Danny Polise founded Penelope in New Jersey in 2018, using whiskey sourced from MGP. The brand has differentiated itself from competitors by the use of blending, cask finishing, sleek presentation, and a wide choice of products, including some limited

releases. It's a formula that should ensure Penelope reaches new heights and expands its fan base under the ownership of MGP/Luxco.

TASTING NOTE

Penelope Cooper Series 6-Year-Old Tokaji Cask Finish
Rye, finished in Tokaji wine casks, 53.5% ABV
Aromas of black fruit pastilles, honey, granola, vanilla, and floral notes, with banana chip, cumin, and paprika. Baked sugary sweetness, with apricot, apple, blueberry fruit chews, and caramel with baked fruits lasting into the finish.

YELLOWSTONE

OWNER MGP Ingredients

FOUNDED Limestone Branch 2011; Yellowstone brand 2015

WEBSITE www.limestonebranch.com

Brothers Stephen and Paul Beam opened Limestone Branch distillery in Lebanon, Kentucky, in 2011 and can trace their lineage back to Jacob Beam. Yellowstone bourbon debuted in 2015, and the current version is made from an open-pollinated white heirloom corn, which makes for a slightly lighter flavor, with a mashbill of 75 percent corn, 13 percent rye, and 12 percent malted barley, with each grain type cooked at a specific temperature.

Additionally, Limestone has released an annual Yellowstone limited edition, and in 2023, they released Yellowstone American Single Malt Whiskey, using 100 percent malted barley and distilled and aged in Indiana, and an innovative debut in the Yellowstone Special Finishes collection.

TASTING NOTE

Yellowstone Select
Kentucky straight bourbon, matured in new charred American oak casks, 46.5% ABV
Vanilla, oak char, saddle leather, peppermint patties, seasoned oak, and fresh citrus. Chewy caramels, molasses, vanilla essence, rye spices, cherry, and oak char, with a burnt sugar finish.

Yellowstone Select

MICHTER'S

OWNER Chatham Imports Inc.

FOUNDED 2000

WEBSITE www.michters.com

Michter's is a well-respected name in American whiskey, with origins attached to the National Historic Landmark site of the distillery in Lebanon County, Pennsylvania, which can trace its roots back to the mid-18th century. Although the distillery carried many different names in different eras, it was here that the bourbon that would become the legendary A. H. Hirsch 1974 was distilled and left in cask for 16 years. Sadly, the distillery ran into financial difficulties when bourbon and rye were in a slump, and the stills ran cold in 1989.

Joe Magliocco subsequently acquired the Michter's brand and started buying up surplus stocks of maturing Kentucky bourbon and rye, bottling his first Michter's release in the year 2000. As he continued to bottle and release stock, Michter's sourced their own whiskey under contract, and the company grew to the size where it needed to be in charge of making its own whiskeys. Modern-day Michter's is based in Kentucky, not Pennsylvania, and the new Michter's distillery opened in 2012 in Shively, just outside Louisville, while their Fort Nelson distillery opened in downtown Louisville in 2019. The Fort Nelson operation is now home to a pair of pot stills, back in good working order, which were installed in the old distillery in Pennsylvania during the mid-1970s that Magliocco managed to track down and restore.

Six production differences

Michter's distillers insist on six individual production steps that they believe sets them apart from other distilleries. The staves for the barrels are air-seasoned for a minimum of 18 months, and the barrels are toasted before being charred. They fill the barrels at 103 proof, lower than the standard 125 proof, meaning less water is added when the barrels are dumped for bottling. They heat the maturing barrels during the colder winter months, simulating extra seasons of maturation. Each whiskey has its own custom chill-filtration technique, and they release only single barrel or small batch bottlings.

Michter's impressive Fort Nelson distillery opened in the heart of downtown Louisville in 2019.

Celebration sour mashes

Their core range, known as US*1, includes their Original Sour Mash Whiskey, straight rye, straight bourbon, and their unblended American whiskey, which is matured in used barrels rather than new charred oak barrels. There are bourbon and rye releases at 10 years old, and occasional releases at 20 and 25 years old, in addition to a variety of limited editions. Those sourced whiskeys and older parcels acquired by Magliocco, in particular, have helped Michter's compete in the top ranks of collectible American whiskies, with their rare triennial Celebration Sour Mash releases and their 25-year-old single-barrel bourbon and ryes fetching substantial five figure sums in the salerooms.

TASTING NOTES

Michter's US*1 Straight Rye
Rye, 42.4% ABV
Punchy rye spices on the nose, with aromas of grape jelly, musty earthiness, rye bread, cinnamon muffin, licorice, and oak char. Brown sugar, soft oak, chocolate shell topping, baked apple, and cappuccino, with a developing oakiness, chicory, roasted pecan, cinnamon, and hints of grape jelly returning. The finish has rye spices, chicory, and brown sugar.

Michter's US*1 Sour Mash
American whiskey, aged in new charred American oak casks, 43% ABV
On the nose, there's allspice, milk chocolate, leather, oak char, cinnamon, grated nutmeg, and caramel. Easy to love, the palate begins with flavors of creamy vanilla, milk chocolate, caramel, mocha latte, and supportive black pepper, with the smooth, medium body carrying forward cinnamon and cherry cough drops into the mouth-coating spicy finish with rye grains, soothing caramel, and milk chocolate.

Michter's US*1
Straight Rye

PERNOD RICARD

Founded in 1975, the French company Pernod Ricard has taken steps to invest in a growing portfolio of entrepreneurial American distilleries, though Smooth Ambler, Jefferson's Bourbon, and TX whiskey are not currently exported to the UK.

JEFFERSON'S BOURBON

OWNER Pernod Ricard USA

FOUNDED 1997

WEBSITE www.jeffersonsbourbon.com

Troy Zoeller built the reputation of Jefferson's Bourbon through bottling casks of aged bourbon produced at the Stitzel-Weller distillery, giving him the freedom to create expressions such as the marine mingled barrels used for Jefferson's Ocean. The whiskeys for Jefferson's Small Batch and Jefferson's Reserve are mostly distilled under contract, with some bourbon made at the Kentucky Artisan distillery. There is an active program of limited editions and finishes.

RABBIT HOLE

OWNER Pernod Ricard USA

FOUNDED 2012

WEBSITE www.rabbitholedistillery.com

This Louisville urban craft distillery opened in 2018, following founder Kaveh Zamanian's 2012 launch of the Rabbit Hole brand using bourbon and rye distilled under contract elsewhere. Pernod Ricard USA bought a majority share in 2019, which has enabled the brand to reach new markets.

TASTING NOTE

Rabbit Hole Dareringer PX Finish
Bourbon, finished in Pedro Ximénez casks, 46.5% ABV
Plum, Parma violets, blueberry muffin, dried herbs, and gentle spice. Toasted wood, caramel, blueberry, and black pepper, then cinnamon, cocoa powder, chewed pencils, and a finish of oak, dried fruits, plum, and mint tea.

SMOOTH AMBLER

OWNER Pernod Ricard USA

FOUNDED 2010

WEBSITE www.smoothambler.com

Co-founder John Little bottles sourced bourbon and rye under the Old Scout label and, for their Contradiction line, blends the whiskey from sourced barrels with their own production. The Founder's Cask Strength series contains whiskeys from their own distillery in West Virginia.

TASTING NOTE

Smooth Ambler Old Scout 10-Year-Old
Straight bourbon, aged in new charred American oak casks, 53% ABV
Delightful notes of cinnamon stick, cigar box, chocolate orange Matchmakers, nutmeg, and toasted oak on the nose. Surprisingly hot on the palate with peppercorns and clove, cinnamon, chocolate orange, and oak, a slug of water brings out cherry cough drops and aniseed ahead of a long, fruity finish.

TX WHISKEY

OWNER Pernod Ricard USA

FOUNDED 2010

WEBSITE www.frdistilling.com

Leonard Firestone and Troy Robertson joined forces to launch the Firestone & Robertson Distilling Co. to make a truly Texan bourbon. Outgrowing their initial setup, they now run a substantial distillery just south of Fort Worth, where they produce their flagship TX Straight Bourbon made from Texas-grown corn, wheat, and barley with their proprietary yeast cultured from a Texas pecan.

UNCLE NEAREST

OWNER Fawn Weaver

FOUNDED 2017

WEBSITE www.unclenearest.com

Fawn Weaver, CEO of Uncle Nearest, has been a force for change in the whiskey industry. Following diligent historical research, the brand and distillery she founded in Shelbyville, Tennessee, honors Nathan "Nearest" Green, an enslaved man born in Maryland around 1820, who became one of the founding fathers of Tennessee whiskey.

Nearest Green and Jack Daniel

In the 1850s, the African American distiller labored for Dan Call on his farm, and encountered a young Jasper Newton "Jack" Daniel, and the pair became friends. Over time, Nearest Green taught Daniel the craft of making whiskey. Meanwhile, Daniel showed a natural aptitude for selling whiskey as he grew older. Daniel grew up to buy Call's distillery, and even after emancipation, Nearest Green continued to work as the master distiller until his retirement. Similarities of using charcoal in West Africa to filter water to remove impurities have been likened to the origins of the Lincoln County Process. Subsequently, Jack Daniel needed a larger distillery, and operations moved to Lynchburg, though Jack Daniel employed Nearest Green's sons and grandsons.

Master blender Victoria Eady Butler is a fifth-generation descendant of Nearest Green, and she has been responsible for the whiskey range at the distillery since 2019. The Uncle Nearest line of premium whiskeys are sourced as they build up stocks and include Uncle Nearest 1856 Premium Whiskey, launched in 2017; the Uncle Nearest 1884 Small Batch; and single barrel releases. Although rye is not a particularly successful crop in Tennessee, they have managed to source and bottle a range of Uncle Nearest Rye whiskeys too.

Uncle Nearest has partnered with Jack Daniel's to launch the Nearest and Jack Advancement Initiative to increase diversity in the industry, and together they now host an annual Spirits on the Rise Summit to help underrepresented communities grow their businesses. In 2023, Fawn Weaver bought the Domaine St. Martin estate and cognac house in France from Martell.

There's plenty for whiskey lovers to do at the Uncle Nearest distillery in Shelbyville, Tennessee.

TASTING NOTES

Uncle Nearest 1884
Tennessee whiskey, aged in new charred American oak casks, 46.5% ABV
This small batch whiskey carries a nose of honey, caramel, citrus, bitter almonds, peach, white pepper, and floral notes. Lemon blossom honey, candied orange, black pepper, toffee, and hints of dark chocolate and vanilla, it signs off with notes of peanut butter, strawberry laces, and tangy marmalade. The finish has honey, spice, and a touch of green herbal notes.

Uncle Nearest 1856
Tennessee whiskey, aged in new charred American oak casks, 50% ABV
Fresh oak, black cherry, strawberry preserves, leather, and lots of dark fruits on the nose, with a scattering of peppercorns, barbecued cobs, and a hint of ginger. Nutty with caramel on the palate, its light texture carries flavors of apple pie, dark fruits, plain chocolate, clove, and hazelnut chocolate spread with a finish of dark chocolate gingers, cinnamon, and cocoa.

Uncle Nearest Uncut/Unfiltered Rye
Straight rye, aged in new charred American oak casks, 59.8% ABV
This impressive blend of sourced rye shows a wider range of characteristics than many rye whiskeys on the market. Floral top notes, lemon peel, spicy rye, vanilla sponge, chocolate milk puddings, cinnamon, and fresh herbal notes on the nose. Honey and lemon shortbread collide with a big swell of clove, chili, and rye spices, and with water, there's toffee, dried cherry, fire-toasted marshmallow, pink cotton candy, and mint chocolate on the finish.

Uncle Nearest 1856

WILLETT

OWNER Willett Distillery Ltd

FOUNDED 1936

WEBSITE www.kentuckybourbonwhiskey.com

The Willett family can point to a long legacy in the distilling business, but the modern story begins with Even Kulsveen, who married into the family and began buying barrels of surplus mature bourbon and rye to bottle for sale when the industry was close to rock bottom, operating under the name Kentucky Bourbon Distillers. Some casks he bottled for export, some for private clients, and some of the bottlings became legendary. These are now some of the most sought after collectible bottles of American whiskey ever released. Bottles of LeNell's Red Hook Rye have fetched close to $50,000, while bottles from the early Willett Family Estate single barrel bottlings private barrels have broken $40,000. While this was never Kulsveen's goal, he was also bottling small batch bottlings of the company's other brands with his sourced bourbon, such as Old Bardstown, Pure Kentucky, and Kentucky Vintage, and creating new brands, including Noah's Mill, Rowan's Creek, and Johnny Drum.

Thompson Willett, Even Kulsveen's father-in-law, opened the Willett distillery in Bardstown in 1936 shortly after the Repeal of Prohibition, and it operated until 1981. In 2012, the family completed renovations on the distillery, and it went back into production, returning their status to being one of legitimate distillers rather than nondistiller producers.

Willett's bourbons and ryes

Even's son Drew Kulsveen is now master distiller, and by 2016, Willett bottled their first 4-year-old Kentucky bourbon from their own production. These days, they bottle a Willett Family Estate 4-Year-Old rye, a Willett Family Estate bottled bourbon, and Willett Wheat, a wheated bourbon aged for eight years. Shaped in a bottle like their still, Willett Pot Still Reserve is bottled at 94 proof, and the family's other labels are all still in production. In 2022, Willett announced a $93 million investment in a new production facility in Springfield, Kentucky, that will include a new distillery and new warehousing for their maturing spirit.

Sour mash fermentation in action in Willett distillery's open-topped fermentation tanks.

TASTING NOTES

Willett Family Estate Bottled Small Batch Rye
Straight rye, aged in new charred American oak casks, 56.4% ABV
Citrus peel, lemon zest, and a firm array of rye spices, then an extra swirl opens up notes of spearmint, toasted fennel seeds, blackened bread crust, charred oak, baked orange, and black tea. Sweet caramel, dried fruits, vanilla, and rye spices, though it comes in pretty hot, with mint leaf, licorice, and fennel, with earthy spices and rye muffin notes to finish.

Noah's Mill
Kentucky bourbon, aged in new charred American oak casks, 57.15% ABV
Actively spicy on the nose with black pepper, aniseed, clove, cinnamon, cocoa powder, caramel, and roasted nuts, then return to the glass to find stone fruits, root beer, and Dr. Pepper. Cola, leather, pecan, and clove on first sip, with Red Hots, dark chocolate, digestive biscuit, brown sugar, Brazil nut, and mint to follow, with a finish of dried fruits, spice, and cinnamon buns. This is so good, yet still under the radar for many people, so track a bottle down.

Rowan's Creek Small Batch
Kentucky straight bourbon, aged in new charred American oak casks, 50.05% ABV
Sugar encrusted nuts, runny caramel, honey, vanilla, hay, jute sacking, toasted rye grains, and mint tea make for a pleasing nose. It's utterly charming, with butterscotch, caramel, vanilla, clove, and a distinct mintiness, with glimpses of herbal notes and oak, before a return to milk chocolate, brown sugar, and peppercorn, with caramel and vanilla joining the rye spices in the finish.

Willett Noah's Mill

AMERICAN SINGLE MALT

American single malt whiskey is arguably the most exciting story in American whiskey for the next decade. Westland's co-founder and master distiller Matt Hoffman is also a co-founder of the American Single Malt Whiskey Commission that argues and lobbies for official recognition of this style of whiskey, though it hasn't stopped hundreds of American distillers from making and selling it.

WESTLAND

OWNER Rémy Cointreau

FOUNDED 2010

WEBSITE www.westlanddistillery.com

Westland Distillery was founded in 2010, and its early success helped them expand and increase capacity over their first decade. Rémy Cointreau acquired the distillery in the industrial SoDo district of Seattle in 2016, recognizing the shared values with its Bruichladdich distillery on Islay in the pursuit of flavor, terroir, and a sense of place.

Championing the Northwest

Hoffman and his team take their own approach to making whiskey, particularly when it comes to the source and quality of their raw materials. That passion has evolved into a mission to express the Pacific Northwest in their bottlings, through a focus on the provenance of their barley, oak, and peat. This thinking coalesced into the Outpost Range, which encompasses a trio of expressions called Westland Garryana, Westland Colere, and Westland Solum. Working with Washington State University's Breadlab based in the Skagit Valley, they partnered with farmers, bakers, agronomists, and researchers to look into the best varieties of barley for flavor, while looking at ways to better care for the soil. After all, the climate of the Northwest is ideal for growing barley, and they began with using Washington State barley and roasted malts more commonly used by breweries for their standard expressions.

Pilot barley is now grown for Westland Colere, specifically sourced, matured, and bottled to showcase the flavor contributions of the barley, but the varieties will change with subsequent harvests. Westland Garryana is matured in *Quercus garryana*, a threatened species of oak native to the Northwest. Westland has joined restoration projects to plant acres of saplings, and partnered with foresters, loggers, sawmills, and cooperages in order to create a supply chain for this scarce oak; and so each annual Garryana release since 2016 has been limited by nature.

An early pioneer of peated American single malt, Westland initially had no other choice but to import peated malt from Scotland. Skagit Valley Malting in Washington helped develop peated malt using a soggy, fibrous vegetation quite different from the dense slabs of peat cut from peat bogs in Scotland. Brought to the surface from a Washington bog, the peat contains plants such as Labrador tea and needs to be artificially dried by the maltsters before they can use it to create smoke to flavor the malt used to make Westland Solum.

TASTING NOTES

Westland Garryana 8th Edition
Single malt, matured in Garryana oak casks, 50% ABV
Vanilla, heather honey, fragrant spices, salted caramel, and bran muffin on the nose. Rich, creamy vanilla with raisins, toffee, Fig Newton, black cherry, red apple, and lots of brown sugar notes. The finish is rich, creamy with oak char and dark chocolate.

Westland Colere 2nd Edition
Single malt, matured in refill casks, 50% ABV
The nose is attractive with lemon and lime zest, summer florals, green apple, creamy vanilla, grist, and marzipan notes. A satin mouthfeel with flavors of lemon, kiwi fruit, bright tropical fruit flavors, and gentle spices, evolving to show mango, papaya, and poached pear before an exceptionally long finish of vanilla and dried fruit.

Westland Colere
2nd Edition

WESTWARD WHISKEY

OWNER Westward Whiskey

FOUNDED 2004

WEBSITE www.westwardwhiskey.com

Christian Krogstad founded House Spirits distillery in 2004, in Portland, Oregon. Their international breakthrough came when actor Ryan Reynolds backed Aviation Gin, and it became the leading product from House Spirits; Diageo subsequently acquired the gin brand in 2020. Thomas Mooney became CEO in 2011, the distillery was renamed Westward Whiskey, and it has played an important part in the American single malt story as the category has gathered momentum across the country, though Krogstad moved on to other projects in 2022.

A brewer's approach to whiskey

Portland has an amazing craft beer culture and a renowned wine industry on its doorstep in the Willamette Valley and other parts of the state. Staffed by ex-brewers in a beer-loving city, they take a brewer's approach to the production of Westland Whiskey American single malt, taking malt from Great Western Malting and fermenting it at relatively low temperatures with ale yeast; essentially, making a great craft beer to distill into single malt. With the aim of preserving as many of the flavors as possible, distiller and master blender Miles Munroe uses small stills with little reflux and heavily toasted but lightly charred new American oak casks for maturation, and then mingles the mature stocks from the barrels to produce a balance of flavors in the bottled whiskeys.

Their range extends logically from Westward Whiskey Original to a Westward Whiskey Pinot Noir Cask, in tribute to the Willamette Valley vineyards, and a Westward Whiskey Stout Cask Finish, reflecting Portland's brewing culture. Approaching their 20th anniversary, Westward released their most ambitious whiskey yet, named Westward Whiskey Milestone. Styled as a masterpiece of American whiskey, Munroe created a 21-barrel solera system that includes their full body of work, including some of their most precious whiskeys. Each year, they will draw off and release the next edition, topping off the solera system with select whiskeys and leaving it to mingle for another year until the next limited release.

Westward Whiskey *takes a brewer's approach to the production of American Single Malt whiskey.*

TASTING NOTES

Westward Cask Strength
Single malt, matured in new charred American oak casks, 62.5% ABV
This impressive single malt has a nose of chocolate, vanilla essence, marron glacé, cracked black pepper, oak spices, waxy palm leaves, and sliced kiwi fruit. Baked orange, apricot, peach, tropical fruits, chocolate, coffee bean, and clove at cask strength, this has a lot to offer with a nimble flavorsome texture. The finish is spicy with chicory and chocolate notes.

Westward Pinot Noir Cask
Single malt, finished in Pinot Noir casks, 45% ABV
The nose has dark chocolate, plum, tobacco leaf, dried apricot, and banana chip. It's thick and velvety textured, with plum, damson, cranberry, pink grapefruit, and a hint of musty chocolate, developing lighter notes of lemon sherbet and white chocolate ahead of a finish of vanilla and gentle white pepper.

Westward Milestone Edition No. 1
Single malt, matured in a 21-cask solera system, 43% ABV
Toasted wood, almond, and a hint of blueberry emerge from the glass, with aromas of stewed fruits and gentle wood smoke. Cherry cough drops, oak, caramel, vanilla ice cream, peach, and some late peppermint on the palate. Nectarine and peach cola make for a fruity finish. It feels like the solera system blunts some of the individual character of the component whiskies.

Westward Cask Strength

CRAFT DISTILLING

The upswing in American craft distilling followed the craft beer revolution. These passionate distillers may work on a smaller scale, but their focus on ingredients, quality, and methods sends an appealing message to the curious drinker.

DRIFTLESS GLEN

OWNER Brian and Reneé Bemis

FOUNDED 2014

WEBSITE www.driftlessglen.com

Brian and Reneé Bemis founded and own this craft distillery on the river in Baraboo, Wisconsin. Driftless Glen has been filling barrels since 2014, producing a wide range of spirits from local Midwest grains, using pure water filtered through a natural sandstone aquifer. They double distill through a 44-foot tall column still and pot still, a setup designed by the late Dave Pickerell.

The range includes a small batch straight bourbon and rye, with single-barrel bourbon and rye bottled at 48 percent, and cask strength, and a 51 Rye, named for the percentage of rye in the mashbill. There is an active program of limited releases, and they are now making their own American single malt.

TASTING NOTE

Driftless Glen 51
Rye, aged in new charred American oak casks, 51% ABV
The nose has everything you're looking for in a rye whiskey. There's rye bread, rye spices, caraway seeds, pistachio, peppermint, clove, and shredded ginger, with hints of dark chocolate and dried apricot. Attractive palate of caramel, fudge, vanilla, chocolate, and baked orange, it grows creamier though underlying spice remain, shifting gears with brown sugar, chocolate muffin, and Red Hots, with a spicy, hot chili finish. Definitely worth a try.

FINGER LAKES DISTILLING

McKenzie Bottled in Bond Bourbon

OWNER Brian McKenzie

FOUNDED 2007

WEBSITE www.fingerlakesdistilling.com

Brian McKenzie drew on his Scottish heritage to build a distillery with whitewashed walls and a traditional-styled pagoda roof when he founded this New York State farm distillery in 2007. Overlooking Seneca Lake and deep in wine country, distillation began using their Holstein still with the first McKenzie bourbon release arriving in 2010, with a continuous still added to the setup in 2013.

Initially focused on single malt, their 10-year-old single malt was first released in 2019, though they have pivoted to making more bourbon over time. They make a straight bourbon with a 70 percent corn, 20 percent rye, and 10 percent malted barley mashbill; small batch bourbon; bottled-in-bond bourbon; and a wheated bourbon made entirely from grains grown in the Finger Lakes region. There is also a straight rye; a bottled-in-bond rye; a 10-year-old straight malt; a corn whiskey; a blended whiskey; and an Irish-inspired McKenzie pure pot still whiskey made from 80 percent unmalted barley, 15 percent malted barley, and 5 percent oats.

TASTING NOTE

McKenzie Bottled in Bond Bourbon
Wheated bourbon, aged in new charred American oak casks, 50% ABV
Marmalade peels, dark chocolate, sticky toffee pudding, and herbal notes. Honey, marzipan, and orange chews, with savory and herbal notes.

JEPTHA CREED

OWNER Joyce and Autumn Nethery

FOUNDED 2016

WEBSITE www.jepthacreed.com

The Nethery family founded their distillery on the home farm in the foothills of the Jeptha Knobs in Shelby County, Kentucky. With an abundance of raw materials from the farm, master distiller Joyce Nethery uses a 30-foot column still and doubler to distill her spirits, and she has been making grain-to-glass bourbons since 2019. Bloody Butcher corn, heirloom white corn, and blue corn are combined in their red, white, and blue straight bourbon.

TASTING NOTE

Jeptha Creed Red, White, and Blue Heirloom Mashbill
Kentucky straight bourbon, matured in new charred American oak casks, 50% ABV
Ginger loaf, nutmeg, cinnamon, digestive biscuit, and cedar aromas. Sweet caramel, citrus, stone fruit, and cask-strength spices, with a black tea and leathery finish.

Jeptha Creed Red, White, and Blue Heirloom Mashbill

REDWOOD EMPIRE

OWNER Derek Benham

FOUNDED 2015

WEBSITE www.redwoodempirewhiskey.com

This northern Californian distillery is located in the Russian River Valley wine country in Sonoma County, where it is run with sustainability at its heart. In fact, they plant a tree for every bottle sold. They use grains from the Midwest with some Californian grown grains, and master distiller Jeff Duckhorn and head distiller Lauren Patz use a variety of fermentation techniques and double distill in a continuous micro-column still built in Montana. Each label boasts a distinctive woodcut design, and the range includes the Pipe Dream and Grizzly Beast bourbons, Emerald Giant and Rocket Top ryes, and a bourbon–rye blend named Lost Monarch.

TASTING NOTE

Redwood Empire Emerald Giant Rye
Rye, aged in new charred American oak barrels, 45% ABV
Toffee, nuts, nougat, and cinnamon-dusted donuts on the nose, with dried flowers, freshly baked bread, lemon, and Cherry Bakewells. Brown sugar, cinnamon balls, and clove, with cherry, Lipton Iced Tea, and cinnamon to finish.

Redwood Empire Emerald Giant Rye

WYOMING WHISKEY

OWNER Edrington Americas

FOUNDED 2006

WEBSITE www.wyomingwhiskey.com

This distillery in Kirby, Wyoming, uses nothing but locally sourced grains that manage to thrive in the region's shorter summer seasons. Founded on the family ranch by Brad and Kate Mead, the Edrington Group took an 80 percent majority share in 2023. Distiller David DeFazio selects non-GMO corn, winter wheat and barley, and winter rye for their products; their standard mashbill is 68 percent corn, 20 percent wheat, and 12 percent malted barley. The bourbon is ready for bottling after five years.

TASTING NOTE

Wyoming Whiskey Small Batch
Bourbon, aged in new charred American oak casks, 44% ABV
Citrus, white peach, raspberry, vanilla, and floral aromas, with flavors of orange, vanilla, oak char, and clove, adding stone fruits, mango, nutmeg, brown butter, and orange buttercream icing, leaving a sparkling minty finish.

Wyoming Whiskey Small Batch

RYE WHISKEY

Rye whiskey rocketed back to its place as one of America's favorite whiskey styles after decades in the doldrums, fueled by the resurgence in cocktail culture and the search for new flavors in American whiskey.

CATOCTIN CREEK

OWNER Scott and Becky Harris

FOUNDED 2009

WEBSITE www.catoctincreekdistilling.com

Scott and Becky Harris founded this independent craft distillery in Purcellville, Virginia, in 2009, driven by their passion to make the best Virginia rye whiskey.

Chief distiller Becky Harris uses local organic ingredients and deploys numerous innovative finishes.

TASTING NOTE

Catoctin Creek Roundstone Rye Cask Proof
Rye, aged in new charred American oak casks, 58% ABV
Bramble, peppercorns, leather, citrus, and root beer floats. Fruity, creamy, and spicy with a cinnamon finish.

Catoctin Creek
Roundstone Rye Cask Proof

NEW RIFF

New Riff Straight Rye
Bottled in Bond

OWNER New Riff Distilling

FOUNDED 2014

WEBSITE www.newriffdistilling.com

Founded by liquor retailer and entrepreneur Ken Lewis and based in Newport in northern Kentucky, its goal was to be a new riff on old traditions as far as Kentucky sour mash bourbon was concerned. Family owned, their rye mashbill is 95 percent rye and 5 percent malted rye and aged for four years.

TASTING NOTE

New Riff Straight Rye Bottled in Bond
Rye, aged in new charred American oak casks, 50% ABV
Toffee, pine needles, mint, fresh cut grass, orange cake, and shortbread. Chocolate, baked orange, dried apricot, and rye spices on the palate, with mint chocolate on the finish.

NEW YORK DISTILLING CO

OWNER New York Distilling Co

FOUNDED 2011

WEBSITE www.nydistilling.com

Brooklyn Brewery founder Tom Potter and distiller and mixologist Allen Katz founded this craft distillery that is now based in Bushwick; it is a gin maker of renown and regional specialist of the Empire Rye style.

TASTING NOTE

Jaywalk
New York Heirloom Rye, aged in new charred oak barrels, 57.9% ABV
One of the tastiest rye whiskeys around, the nose has dark chocolate mint crisp, dried herbs, roasted nut, Rolos, dried red berries, and superbly integrated baking spices. It is wonderfully thick and chewy after more than seven years of aging, with dark caramel, taffy strawberry, cinnamon sugar, milk chocolate, and gentle oak, and a mouth-clinging finish of caramel and melted chocolate.

Jaywalk New York
Heirloom Rye

PEERLESS

Peerless Small
Batch Rye

OWNER KentuckyPeerless Distilling Co.

FOUNDED 2014

WEBSITE www.kentuckypeerless.com

Revived by fourth-generation Corky Taylor and his
son Carson, the Kentucky Peerless Distilling Co. name
can be traced back to the 1880s. They favor a sweet
mash process. Charred new oak barrels are filled at a
lower strength than most distilleries at 107 proof.

Master distiller Caleb Kilburn bottles barrel proof rye
whiskey, single barrels and finishes, with equivalent
expressions for their bourbon.

TASTING NOTE

Peerless Small Batch Rye
Rye, aged in new charred American oak, 55.2% ABV
Leather, strawberry, cherry cola, orange peel, rye, and herbal
notes. Strawberry mousse, cherry, rye bread, and chocolate
with a spicy, jammy finish.

SAGAMORE SPIRIT

OWNER Illva Saronno

FOUNDED 2013

WEBSITE www.sagamorespirit.com

Saviors of Maryland Rye for a new generation,
Sagamore Spirit's aim was to produce grain-to-glass
rye whiskeys on the ever-expanding Baltimore
waterfront. In 2023, Italian company Illva Saronno,
best known for Disaronno, acquired the business.
Initial releases used rye sourced from MGP in Indiana,
but the distillery now combines their own spirit into

the bottles. Their core collection combines high and
low rye recipes, a cask-strength rye, a bottled-in-bond,
and a Double Oaked version.

TASTING NOTE

Sagamore Spirit Rye
Rye, matured in new charred American oak casks, 41.5% ABV
Gentle rye grain notes on the nose with cornbread, roasted
hazelnut, dry oak, roasted chickpea, and a mix of herbs and
spices. Caramel, honey, pecan, and rye spices, followed by
fresh fruit, dried apricot, and pistachio macaroons, with
heaps of brown sugar to finish.

WHISTLEPIG

OWNER WhistlePig Whiskey

FOUNDED 2007

WEBSITE www.whistlepigwhiskey.com

You'll find WhistlePig distillery down on the farm in
Shoreham, Vermont. The company, founded by Raj
Bhakta, built its early reputation on bottlings of
sourced Canadian rye whiskies acquired by the late
Dave Pickerill. WhistlePig The Boss Hog was first
released in 2013, delivering an annual collectible
bottle of the finest rye bottled at cask strength that
continues to this day.

In 2015, the distillery was opened on the farm and
started making its own innovative rye whiskeys.
LVMH, owners of Ardbeg and Glenmorangie
distilleries, took a minority stake in 2020.

TASTING NOTE

WhistlePig The Boss Hog VIII Lapulapu's Pacific
Rye, double finished in Filipino rum casks, 52.4% ABV
Rye sourdough, musty earth, barnyard funk, dried vine fruits,
vanilla sponge, and rye spices. Creamy vanilla, toffee, herbal,
and spicy rye notes, with dark chocolate, nutmeg, cinnamon
stick, and malted milk balls and a finish of dark chocolate,
oak char, and rye spices.

WhistlePig The Boss Hog
VIII Lapulapu's Pacific

CANADA

REGIONAL STYLES
With plentiful harvests of corn, wheat, and rye, the Canadian style is sweet and spicy. For a symphony of variation on this style, there's one memorable source: Hiram Walker's distillery in Windsor, Ontario, Canada's longest-operating distillery. Although still comparatively tiny by volume, the number of Canadian single malt whisky producers is also on the rise.

Canada is undeniably huge. More than 3,700 miles (6,000 km) separate Shelter Point distillery, British Columbia, in the west from Glenora distillery, Nova Scotia, in the east—enough to convince anyone of this country's massive size. Between the two oceans, you cross a coastal delta; two gigantic mountain ranges; the flattest of prairies; rolling hills; rich, lush farmland; and the comparatively barren Canadian Shield, which stretches north from the Great Lakes to the Arctic Ocean and covers about half of the country's land mass. Driving from one Canadian distillery to the next often means traveling a greater distance than the entire length of Scotland. That's why, in Canada, talking "whisky regions" is impossible.

AUTHOR'S CHOICE
CORBY'S HIRAM WALKER
This Ontario distillery has plenty of history attached: its Detroit River waterfront, frequented by Prohibition-era rum runners, later afforded a berth for the Royal Yacht *Britannia* when Queen Elizabeth II and Prince Philip stopped by for a visit.

Typically, Canadian whisky is a mingling of a variety of whiskies made in one distillery, and it's commonly referred to as "rye." Confusingly, the first use of the word rye to describe Canadian whisky dates back to the time when most of it was made from wheat. Someone decided to add a small amount of rye grain to a wheat mash and a new whisky style was born. Customers soon demanded "rye" to be sure their whisky was made with a dash of rye grain.

Canada's great distilleries, the ones that produce the majority of Canadian whiskies consumed around the world, are giant, hulking industrial plants, typically built without any regard for visitor facilities.

In recent years, however, the country has enjoyed a wave of urban and micro-distillery openings, making a variety of artisanal spirits across the provinces based around local ingredients. Designed with distillery and tasting tours, merchandising, social media opportunities, and great food in mind, Canada has become a great destination for whisky tourism again, especially for those who love their craft spirits.

REGIONAL EVENTS
Canada's whisky season begins in January with the Victoria Whisky Festival (www.victoriawhiskyfestival.com), which includes the annual Canadian Whisky Awards, and the long running Spirit of Toronto event (www.spiritoftoronto.ca) with its big name masterclasses and live jazz. Elsewhere, from Whisky Ottawa to the Banff Whisky Experience and a host of smaller festivals, Canada offers fantastic events celebrating Canadian whisky side by side with Scotch, Japanese, and American whiskeys. New Brunswick, and Newfoundland fill out the balance of the whisky calendar.

Shelter Point *is a small distillery and farm on Vancouver Island and is typical of the new wave of micro-distilleries in Canada.*

GETTING AROUND

Known colloquially as "The Great White North," much of Canada is indeed cold in winter and so snowy that from October to April mountain passes are open only to vehicles equipped with tire chains. Maritime influences moderate the Atlantic and Pacific coasts. Across the land, though, spring is warm and summer hot. The Windsor-Montreal corridor, a 550-mile (885 km) hard day's drive, encourages travel by car; for the rest of the country, traveling any distance means boarding a plane.

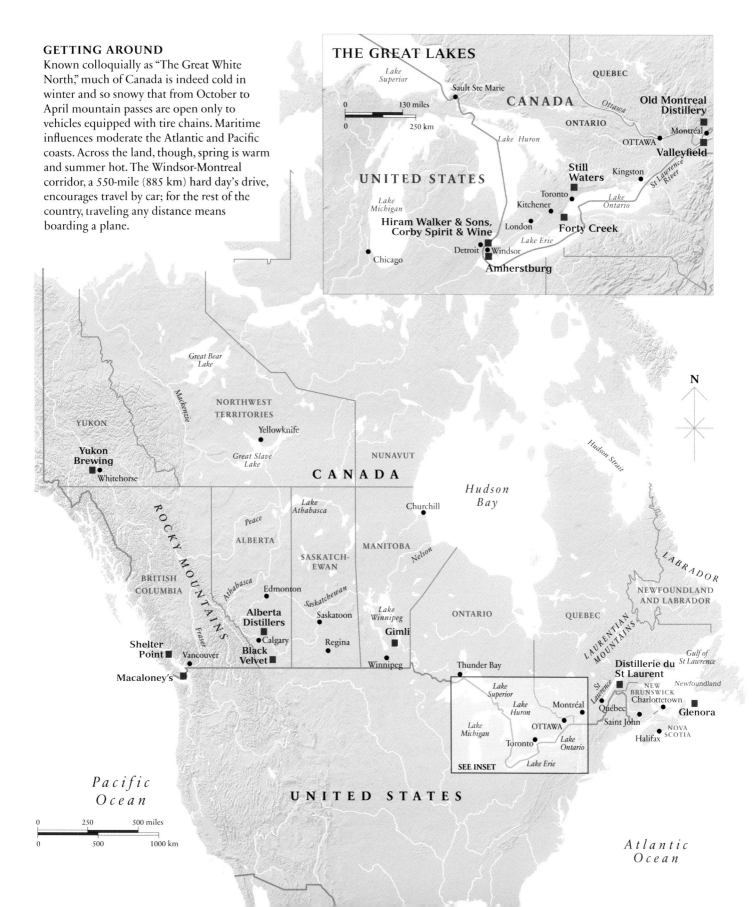

ALBERTA DISTILLERS

OWNER Suntory Global Spirits

FOUNDED 1946

WEBSITE www.albertadistillers.com

There are whisky lovers whose enjoyment is increased just by the knowledge that they are drinking whisky made from rye; perhaps its reputation prompts them to spend more time savoring its eccentricities. What makes rye so special is that certain flavor elements abound that are more subdued in other grains, and skilled whisky-makers know just how to highlight this distinctive rye flavor profile. Tasting the newly distilled spirit is most instructive.

While Alberta Distillers' corn spirits reveal woody, musty, corncob flavors, the peppery rye spirits are lavishly grainlike. After three years in new oak, both smell like whisky, but on the palate, the rye now sports its characteristic cloves, ginger, and hot, blistering pepper, the corn its creamy softness. Curiously, whiskies that declare a high percentage of rye tend to draw more favorable reviews than whiskies whose high content of rye grain is kept secret. No doubt the good people at Alberta Distillers in Calgary, the only major distillery in the world to make much of its whisky from 100 percent rye, recognize that response.

Canada loves its rye whiskey

They are also a major contract distiller, and their rye has gone into many well-known brands, such as WhistlePig when it's not made on the farm, and Masterson's 10-Year-Old, now owned by Deutsch Family Wine & Spirits, and Windsor Canadian, a former Alberta Distillers brand now owned by Prestige Beverage Group. Alberta Distillers Ltd is a subsidiary of Suntory Global Spirits, and their own bottlings include Alberta Premium and Alberta Premium Cask Strength Rye, both made from 100 percent rye, the rye blend Alberta Springs 10-Year-Old, plus the occasional special release.

When the distillery was built in 1946 on Calgary's ragged fringe, rye was the most common local grain, and the plant was designed specifically to process it. Alberta Distillers use plain, unmalted rye only, using the distillery's own grown enzymes to break down cell walls, carbohydrates, and the sticky beta glucans. While distilling rye grain is messy enough that other distillers will often shut down the plant for a thorough cleaning afterward, making rye is routine here. This is one of the reasons why the distillery can bottle nearly three times as much high-rye whisky as every other distillery in North America combined.

Alberta Premium Cask Strength Rye

TASTING NOTES

Alberta Premium Cask Strength Rye
Rye, matured in oak casks, 63.7% ABV
Ample rye spiciness on a background of toasty grains, oak char, and a hint of milk chocolate: there's a lot of heat if you drink this neat and water helps bring out the rye and flavors of honey, Sugar Puffs, spice, chili flakes, oak char, hazelnut, oak, maple syrup, pecan, praline, and peppercorns. The finish is dry and oaky, with burnt caramel and glimpses of citrus peel.

Alberta Springs 10-Year-Old
Canadian, matured in oak casks, 40% ABV
Aromatic spices, sour pickles, and dusty rye on the nose, with flavors of vanilla, butterscotch, maple syrup, and black licorice on the palate. A solid crisp Canadian oak backbone supports waves of heat and a vague fruitiness. The finish showcases cleansing citrus pith.

CANADIAN CLUB

OWNER Suntory Global Spirits

FOUNDED 1858

WEBSITE www.canadianclub.com

When Detroit grain broker and whisky rectifier Hiram Walker decided in 1858 to distill whisky, prohibition sentiments in the US made such a venture very risky there. Walker knew that the Windsor area, which lies just on the other side of the Detroit River in Canada, did not have a proper flour mill. And that's how Walker, an American citizen, gained a toehold in Canada.

Within months, grinding imported American corn for whisky accounted for half of his milling business. Hardy corn that would successfully thrive in Canada's climate was still more than a century of experimentation away. Back then, most distillers made whisky from wheat. Walker knew the American grain market well and became one of the first distillers in Canada to make whisky primarily from corn. Copying Canada's wheat distillers, he added small amounts of rye to increase the flavor, and his distillery eventually became the only one in Canada to use malted rye.

Barrel blending
Walker established a reputation for a high-quality product, rectifying it through tall wooden columns packed with charcoal and other materials. Soon, he switched to maturing it in white oak barrels, as many other Canadian distillers were already doing. Rather than using a mixed-grain mash, Walker experimented with adding new rye spirit to his corn spirit before filling barrels with the mixture. He felt that distilling the spirits separately then barrel blending them improved the flavor as the spirits married during maturation. To this day, Hiram Walker's best-known whisky, Canadian Club, is still barrel blended.

Prohibition and "Mad Men"
Canadian Club has a storied history during Prohibition, when bootleggers made it the most smuggled whisky to enter the US at a time when only a handful of American distilleries were permitted to produce whiskey for medicinal purposes. In fact, at the height of the popularity of HBO's Boardwalk Empire, Canadian Club capitalized on this infamy,

styling itself "the unofficial whisky of Prohibition." Conveniently made by the Detroit River, bottles were filled into jute sacks and loaded onto ships for the short crossing to the US. Jute sacks were preferable to wooden crates for packing whisky because they were lighter to lift but could sink without a trace if they had to be discarded overboard in a hurry.

Canadian Club reached a new audience as the preferred tipple of Jon Hamm's character Don Draper in the AMC series *Mad Men*. After all, this was a brand whose name was up in lights in Times Square, New York during the 1960s and '70s. The company now known as Suntory Global Spirits acquired the Canadian Club brand in 2011, though Pernod Ricard, the majority owner of Corby, owns the Hiram Walker & Sons Distillery where it is made. Each Canadian Club expression uses a different recipe and flavor profile, though they also market flavored whiskies and premixed expressions. Beyond the classic Canadian Club 1858 Original, there is a reserve 9-Year-Old and classic 12-Year-Old expression, and a Canadian Club 100 percent rye. In 2022, Canadian Club concluded the Chronicles series with the release of the oldest Canadian whisky to date, a 45-Year-Old Canadian Club made from corn in 1977, rounding off an annual series of aged expressions themed around Prohibition stories. Don't count them out from releasing something even older in the future.

TASTING NOTES

Canadian Club 1858 Original
Canadian, aged in bourbon casks, 40% ABV
The nose has molasses, peppery spice, vanilla seeds, clove, and blackened wood. Brown sugar, light vanilla cake, feisty spices, crème brûlée, chocolate brownie, granola, toffee, and charred barrel, with a finish of toffee and spice.

Canadian Club Classic 12-Year-Old
Canadian, aged in bourbon casks, 40% ABV
Sophisticated aromatic profile of vanilla pod, cinnamon, brown sugar, cola, toasted wood, walnut, and leather. The palate has pecan, honey, peanut, cola, orange peel, and gingerbread, with a finish of fading spices, Earl Grey tea, and dark chocolate.

Canadian Club Chronicles 45-Year-Old
Canadian, aged in bourbon casks, 50% ABV
Honeycomb, brown sugar, pecan pie, roasted corncob, black pepper, vanilla essence, and hints of new leather on the nose. Sweet sugared corn, vanilla, leather, black fruits, and lively spices, with dark chocolate, honeycomb, and vanilla to finish.

Canadian Club 1858 Original

CORBY SPIRIT & WINE LTD

OWNER Pernod Ricard

FOUNDED 1859

WEBSITE www.corby.ca; www.jpwisers.com; www.northernbordercollection.com

Owning brands like J. P. Wiser's, Pike Creek, Lot 40, and Gooderham & Worts, Corby is one of the largest producers and distributors of wine & spirits in Canada. Majority owned by Pernod Ricard since 2005, the whiskies are blended and bottled at the Hiram Walker & Sons Distillery in Windsor, Ontario.

A complicated heritage

Henry Corby was born in Hanwell, West London, and immigrated to Belleville, Ontario, where he created a number of businesses, including the H. Corby Distillery in 1859 and his own brand of whisky as his enterprise grew. Following World War I, the business was sold and the new owners also went on to acquire J. P. Wiser's distillery in Prescott. Ahead of Henry Corby, fellow immigrants from Britain, William Gooderham and James Worts were millers turned distillers who started in the 1830s in what is now Toronto. Businessman Harry Hatch acquired Gooderham & Worts and Hiram Walker in the 1920s, forming a joint company called Hiram Walker–Gooderham Worts that took a controlling share of the H. Corby Distilling Company in 1935.

Hiram Walker went on to develop substantial Scotch whisky interests. Corby was acquired by Allied Lyons plc in 1987, and the distillery in Corbyville was closed in 1989 as consumers turned to white spirits; it is now a craft brewery. The Gooderham & Worts Distillery suffered a similar fate to Corby's, closing in 1990. The site now accommodates the Mill St. distillery, which releases a single barrel of whisky every year.

Different grains and expressions

Hiram Walker & Sons master blender Don Livermore is a notable advocate for Canadian whisky. As well as being in possession of a fine scientific mind, he is adept at finding new hooks for consumers to engage with Canadian whisky, such as his Canadian whisky flavor wheel, and the various expressions in the Northern Border Collection. He knows how best to

Lot 40

express the character and profile of different grains through their distillation methods, even at this behemoth of a distillery. He is unafraid to make bold decisions, such as deciding to switch from malted rye to higher yielding hybrid rye varieties and industrial enzymes in 2015.

Pike Creek first launched in 1998 and is named after its maturation warehouse, which experiences extreme seasonal swings in temperature, leading to plenty of interaction between the spirit and the oak. Originally a 10-Year-Old Canadian whisky with a port cask finish, Pike Creek became a rum finish in 2016, and the brand is bolstered by occasional limited editions. Gooderham & Worts is known today for its Four Grain expression, which uses corn, barley, rye and wheat, and its limited editions, such as

Gooderham & Worts Little Trinity 17-Year-Old, a three-grain expression that eschewed the malted barley from the blend. Lot 40 had an earlier incarnation in 1998 like Pike Creek but returned in 2012. Dr, Livermore now makes it as a copper pot still-distilled product made from 100 percent unmalted hybrid rye aged in new American oak barrels. Think of it as the potent rye component used as the most powerful flavor driver in all the other whiskies produced at Hiram Walker. Lot 40 Dark Oak is matured in a new American oak No. 2 char barrel then finished in a new No. 4 char barrel and bottled at higher strength, which gives it an undeniable presence.

J. P. Wiser's 18-Year Old

TASTING NOTES

Gooderham & Worts Little Trinity 17-Year-Old
Canadian, aged in new oak, refill bourbon, and refill casks, 45% ABV
A recipe of rye, corn, and wheat, the nose has dried apple, poached pear, vanilla, fresh corncobs, and spun sugar, with a firm spicy edge. Brown sugar, cinnamon, peppercorns, and rye flavors on the palate, followed by clove, chocolate-covered peppermints, black tea, and maple syrup. A spicy finish with notes of tea, cinnamon, brown sugar, and rye.

J. P. Wiser's 10-Year-Old Triple Barrel
Canadian, aged in new oak, bourbon, and refill casks, 40% ABV
Sweet caramel, honey, vanilla, pleasant rye notes with spice, seasoned oak, and marmalade loaf. As well as the sweet taste of honey and candied citrus, it has a silky texture, with apricot, rye spices, tangerine, toffee, and nutmeg with a growing presence of deliciously creamy corn. Ridiculously easy to like.

J. P. Wiser's 18-Year-Old
Canadian, aged in new oak, bourbon, and refill casks, 40% ABV
The nose has stone fruit, rye spices, pear juice, and orange pith, creating a gently fruity aromatic profile. With flavors of nectarine, peach, butterscotch, honey, pear, and black pepper, it pays to keep swirling as a satisfying, thicker mouthfeel develops with apple, caramel, star anise, and that moreishly tasty late-breaking corn note, and a finish of dried fruit, creamy vanilla, and fine oak tannins.

Lot 40
Rye, aged in new oak barrels, 43% ABV
Dark aromas of plain chocolate, dark rye bread, scorched earth, oak char, cigar wrapper, cappuccino, and vanilla essence. On the palate, it packs a lot of flavor in, with notes of chocolate, rye, Brazil nut, aged tobacco leaf, black pepper, oak tannins, cinnamon stick, and grape jelly. The smooth satisfying finish has lingering black fruit and peppery spice.

Lot 40 Dark Oak
Rye, aged twice in new oak casks, 48% ABV
The nose is woody and earthy, with brown sugar, bramble jelly, dark chocolate, drying oak, and more rye spices than regular Lot 40. The higher ABV is noticeable, with flavors of dark chocolate ganache, vanilla essence, clove, burnt sugar, bramble jelly, and espresso, adding black cherry, tobacco, and leather on the finish.

Pike Creek 10-Year-Old
Canadian, finished in rum casks, 42% ABV
Black tea, with peppermint, pear, Seville orange peel, honey, black licorice, charred oak stave, and root beer on the nose. Orange, apricot, and honey on the first sip, the structure feels a bit loose, with a brief peak of rye spices, followed by toffee, buttered corn, caramel, and roasted hazelnut, with a caramelized sugar and drying oak finish.

Gooderham & Worts Little Trinity 17-Year-Old

CROWN ROYAL

OWNER Diageo plc

FOUNDED 1939

WEBSITE www.crownroyal.com

Crown Royal is North America's most valuable whisky brand. The clues to a connection with royalty are not difficult to spot for a bottle sitting snugly in a purple bag carrying this name, and indeed, it was created in 1939 as a gift to King George VI and Queen Elizabeth as they embarked on a royal tour of Canada by train. The whisky went on sale in Canada following the monarch's trip, then launched into the US and beyond in the 1960s. The range has been expanded significantly in the last decade or two to ensure there is a Crown Royal for every occasion, and for everyone, from novice to connoisseur.

Three sites and one more in the pipeline

Crown Royal is a blend of multiple different Canadian whiskies produced by brand owner Diageo at three sites: the main site being the Gimli plant in Manitoba. This is a huge industrial site, where row after row of regimented warehouses sit close to the shoreline of Lake Winnipeg. The Gimli plant passed to Diageo following the breakup of Seagram's in 2000, and Gimli had the colossal distilling power needed to supply sufficient liquid for Seagram's famous brands.

Valleyfield in Quebec also produces whisky for Crown Royal—a site built in 1945 by Schenley Distillers Corporation that came into Diageo's hands in 2008. Valleyfield makes huge volumes of whisky, too, mainly column still-distilled spirit made from corn, though they have a pot still, too. The blending and bottling of Crown Royal mainly takes place at Amherstburg, Ontario, other than the most precious stocks used for their Master series, which are handled at Valleyfield. Diageo St. Clair distillery will be the fourth site when it opens in southwest Ontario this decade. Offering the latest in distilling technology, the 400-acre site will run on renewable energy sources and produce zero waste to landfill from its direct operations, in line with Diageo's Society 2030: Spirit of Progress program.

The Crown Royal brand now encompasses Canadian whisky, flavored whiskies, and premixed ready-to drink cans. The Signature series is highly accessible and includes their Deluxe, Rye, and Black expressions, with plenty of affordable innovations for the connoisseur to try before the price bumps up for the age-stated versions from 18 to 30 years old.

Crown Royal Deluxe

Crown Royal Northern Harvest Rye

TASTING NOTES

Crown Royal Deluxe
Canadian, matured in white oak casks, 40% ABV
This blend has burnt sugar, oak char, vanilla essence, plain chocolate, rye bread, mild rye spices, and grain notes. Toasty, nutty rye bread flavors, with beeswax, vanilla essence, and chocolate on the palate. It feels like it could use a bit more body, but it levels out once it hits its stride with plenty of chocolate, baked orange, spices, and crème brûlée on the finish.

Crown Royal Black
Canadian, matured in charred white oak casks, 45% ABV
The nose has vanilla pod, cacao, charred wood, cocoa powder, black walnut bitters, and root beer. Dark maple syrup, chocolate, treacle tarts, and peppery spice on the tongue, with a good texture. It's warmer and sweeter than expected. Fruit syrup, vanilla essence, clove, and black pepper run through the finish.

Crown Royal Northern Harvest Rye
Rye, matured in white oak casks, 45% ABV
Rich with maple syrup aromas, rye sourdough, nutmeg, rye spices, and a little vanilla, with hints of chocolate and dried citrus peel. That maple syrup character develops on the palate, with honey and vanilla and a wave of black pepper, toasted nuts in caramel, milk chocolate, and dried citrus peel, with earthy notes, black pepper, and vanilla on the finish.

MACALONEY'S

OWNER Macaloney Brewers & Distillers Ltd

FOUNDED 2016

WEBSITE www.macaloneydistillers.com

Graeme Macaloney is a Scotsman making Canadian Island whisky and beer in Saanich, Greater Victoria, on Vancouver Island. The distillery opened in 2016 and was commissioned with the help of the late Dr. Jim Swan and Mike Nicholson, the retired Diageo distiller who also helped Vancouver Island's Shelter Point Distillery in its early days. Using barley from British Columbia, the distillery has a pair of Forsyth's Ltd copper pot stills, a 1,320-gallon (5,500-liter) wash still, and a 925-gallon (3,500-liter) spirit still with shell and tube condensers.

The distillery is now known as Macaloney's Canadian Island Distillery and Two Dogs Brewery. The Scotch Whisky Association (SWA) filed a lawsuit against the company when it was trading as Macaloney's Caledonian Distillery, over objections to the association of terms, which collectively, they regarded to be associated with Scotch whisky. The dispute was settled amicably in 2022, with Macaloney agreeing to slightly alter the names and phrasing on his products and distillery. This is not the first time a Canadian distillery with Scottish heritage has fallen foul of the SWA's role in protecting Scotch whisky.

Myriad different expressions

Dr. Jim Swan introduced Macaloney to his shave-toast-rechar, or STR, cask and shared his trade secrets to help them produce a more mature-tasting whisky in just three to four years, though Victoria does not enjoy the same subtropical climate as Kavalan in Taiwan, also helped by Dr. Swan.

Within a few short years, Macaloney was offering an array of young spirits, followed by a staggering choice of different whisky expressions. The best way to comprehend the range is by breaking it down by whisky style. First, the unpeated single malts, which include An Loy, Cath-Nah-Aven, and the St. Mallie single cask series. An Loy is their flagship expression, matured in bourbon, Spanish oloroso sherry, Portuguese red wine, and Spanish Pedro Ximénez casks; while Cath-Nah-Aven is a sherried single malt matured in Spanish oloroso and Pedro Ximénez casks. They make

three peated whiskies, named An Aba, Siol Dugall, and The Peat Project single-cask series.

The distillery can handle peat, smoking 2-ton batches of barley at a time. The Peat Project bottlings are the smokiest, with malt smoked to 54ppm using peat from Washington State. An Aba uses lightly peated malt and a wood bill similar to An Loy with the addition of new American oak casks. Siol Dugall uses peated malt at 27ppm and includes a marriage of whiskies matured in bourbon, new American oak, and Portuguese wine STR casks. Dr. Swan never got the opportunity to help launch a new Irish distillery, but he did help Macaloney make a triple-distilled single pot still range made from malted and unmalted barley. Named Kildara, Killeigh, and the single-cask series Kirkinriola, these pay homage to Macaloney's Ulster-Scots heritage.

In 2023, Macaloney spearheaded the launch of the Northwest Whiskey Trail, a cross-border route across the Pacific Northwest that takes in seven partner distilleries in British Columbia, Washington, and Oregon. In less than a decade, Graeme Macaloney is proving to be an influential figure in Canadian whisky.

TASTING NOTES

Macaloney's An Loy
Single malt, matured in bourbon, oloroso, Pedro Ximénez, and red wine casks, 46% ABV
Fruit-forward aromas, with peach, orange fondant cream, vanilla, red berries ,and coastal notes. Red apple, marmalade, and vanilla flavors, developing blueberry jam, oak spices, and milk chocolate. Peppery finish, with cocoa, citrus peel, and dry oak.

Macaloney's An Aba
Single malt, matured in bourbon, oloroso, red wine, Pedro Ximénez, and new American oak casks, 46% ABV
Light peat smoke aromas with lemon sorbet, vanilla cupcakes, and red licorice. Malty, with chocolate vermicelli, salted ham, and peat smoke, melting into chocolate, salted caramel, and raspberry. Lingering saltiness with a dry, musty chocolate finish.

Macaloney's Kildara
Triple-distilled pot still whisky, matured in bourbon, oloroso, Pedro Ximénez, and new American oak casks, 46% ABV
Barley sugar, fruit polos, dried apricot, brambles, and vanilla cream make for an attractive nose. Velvety texture with chocolate orange, plum, glacé cherry, forest honey, and sultanas, with a mouth-coating finish of chocolate, coffee, vanilla, and tobacco.

Macaloney's An Loy

SHELTER POINT

OWNER Nelson Investments Inc.

FOUNDED 2011

WEBSITE www.shelterpoint.ca

Shelter Point is a coastal distillery and farm based in Oyster River, British Columbia, a three-hour trip up the eastern edge of Vancouver Island from Victoria. Founded in 2011, the distillery's stone and timber building is built in the style of a traditional Canadian barn and sits nestled in a grove of trees on the edge of barley fields belonging to third-generation farmer and distillery founder Patrick Evans.

Shelter Point makes Vancouver Island single malt whisky first and foremost, though it also makes gin, vodka, and limited quantities of 100 percent rye whisky. Canadian single malt whisky is a growing category with a coterie of determined producers from the east to west coast driving it forward, and the style has inspired many whisky lovers to take a fresh look at Canadian whisky, challenging their assumptions shaped by the massive volume legacy brands of Canadian rye.

Single malt first and foremost

Head distiller James Marinus uses malted two-row barley grown in British Columbia for the Shelter Point production and patiently allows long fermentations to take place in the neat row of stainless steel tanks. Double distillation takes place in two indirect heated onion-shaped copper pot stills made by Forsyth's Ltd, Scotland, consisting of a 1,320-gallon (5,000-liter) wash still and 1,050-gallon (4,000-liter) spirit still with slightly downward sloping lyne arms leading to shell and tube condensers. Next to them is a small, third copper pot still, which is linked to columns and used for making hand-foraged botanical gin and other spirits.

The location close to the shore encourages a coastal influence on the maturing stocks in the warehouse. The single malt whisky is matured in a 2,640-gallon (10,000-liter) solera system, developing flavor through a series of bourbon casks and picking up nuances as it passes through new oak, wine, sherry, and port barrels. They bottle a cask strength version of their single malt, too. Montfort is the single estate expression named after Barrett Montfort, who

Built in the style of a traditional Canadian barn, Shelter Point distillery is sited in a rural location in northern Vancouver Island.

founded Shelter Point Farm. Since 2021, Shelter Point has released small batches of 10-Year-Old single malt. Ripple Rock is matured in alligator charred new oak casks and bourbon casks, while Smoke Point is matured in driftwood-smoked barrels, the timber coming from the shore and local woods, imbuing the whisky with beach bonfire and maritime notes.

In 2022, Patrick Evans sold a majority share of Shelter Point to Nelson Investments, and Stephen Goodridge, formerly of Goodridge and Williams Distilling, was appointed as their new general manager, leaving Evans to concentrate on the farm.

Shelter Point
Classic Single Malt

TASTING NOTES

Shelter Point Classic Single Malt
Single malt, matured in oak casks, 46% ABV
The nose is slightly grassy with orange peel oils, ripe apricot, honey, vanilla, and very gentle spices. Impressive with a beautiful texture, showing tangy orange, candied citrus, apricot, peach, and a light pepperiness, with a later phase of marmalade, walnut, plum, and hints of red wine. The satisfying finish wraps together citrus peel, vanilla, and pineapple cubes.

Shelter Point Ripple Rock
Single malt, aged in alligator char new American oak and bourbon barrels, 46% ABV
The nose is rich and earthy with notes of oak, vanilla pod, wood spice, treacle, oak char, and a hint of cigar. Nimble on the tongue, with its vanilla, caramel, and chocolate, it ramps up the spice profile with oak char, black pepper, and clove. The mouthfeel gets creamier, adding layers of toffee, toasted sesame, and tobacco to the finish.

Shelter Point Smoke Point
Single malt, aged in casks smoked with driftwood and native woods, 53% ABV
Their barrel-smoking technique is highly effective, and the nose has driftwood bonfire, fresh citrus, vanilla, and tobacco notes. Full-bodied and creamy, with orange toffee and chocolate, the trajectory of flavor is impressive. Salted caramel, wood smoke, black pepper, sea salt, and graham crackers dipped in tea, with a finish of menthol gum and salty smoke.

TWO BREWERS

OWNER Yukon Brewing Company

FOUNDED 1997

WEBSITE www.twobrewerswhisky.com

Yukon Brewing is the home of the Two Brewers whisky distillery in Yukon, northwest Canada.

Engineers Bob Baxter and Alan Hansen co-founded Yukon Brewing in 1997 following a canoe trip to the Yukon. Aptly, the distillery resides on Copper Road in Whitehorse, the capital of Yukon Territory. Distilling was legalized by the Government of Yukon only in 2009; the Yukon Liquor Act is still regularly reviewed and revised, and Yukoners still have very few distilleries in their area. Once the legislation was passed, however, Baxter and Hansen were quick to acquire a still and become micro-distillers so they could turn their own brews into whisky. Their extensive brewing background and the Two Brewers approach to flavor draws parallels with the beer culture–inspired methods of making whisky at Westward Distillery in Portland, Oregon.

Originality is the name of the day

To understand the Two Brewers process is to free your mind of notions of reproducibility, homogeneity, and flavor consistency. This is truly a place where nobody is telling them what they can or cannot do, and the whisky world sorely needs places like Two Brewers as a counterpoint to the slick, polished presentation of whisky by multinational brands.

Two Brewers uses malted grains, but not just malted barley; they have made whisky from malted wheat and rye, too. They make unpeated and peated whisky, though the peated malt comes from Scotland. A brewer's eye informs their mashing techniques and fermentation, always geared toward boosting the creation of different flavors at every step, sometimes by experimenting with temperature, and at other times, with different yeast types according to the needs of each batch. Distillation in their Carl hybrid pot and column still is tuned to preserve the flavor created in their distiller's beer. New oak barrels are treated to a variety of toasting and charring permutations, and the spirits are then moved from new oak to bourbon barrels or other finishing casks.

Broadly speaking, their expressions are grouped into Classic, Peated, Special Finishes, and Innovative categories, but the rest is up to you. Drawing on stocks of different ages, they have seasoned casks with green coffee beans; used maple syrup barrel finishing; brewed with dark roasted grains, hops, Munich malt, and other specialty brewer's malts; and even devised a Yukon sour mash process. Finishes have included fresh bourbon barrels, Moscatel, PX sherry, and port. Every numbered batch is unique, idiosyncratic, and unrepeatable, so there is always an excuse to go back and buy another bottle.

TASTING NOTES

Two Brewers Yukon Classic Single Malt Release 35
Single malt, matured in bourbon and new oak casks, 46% ABV
Baking spice aromas, creamed banana, floral notes, honey, fresh linen, and old exercise books. Citrus, bitter lemon, clove, pear, and orange fondant creaminess, and an unusual finish of melon rind and root vegetables.

Two Brewers Yukon Peated Single Malt Release 38
Single malt, matured in oak casks, 43% ABV
Fruity fragrant peat, tobacco leaf, and leather, it grows more smoky and ashy, revealing dried herbs, damp moss, and barnyard notes. The palate has citrus, vanilla, tangy peel, and peppery smoke, evolving to barley sugar, dried mango strips, crystallized ginger, and more tropical fruit flavors ahead of a mouthwatering finish of vanilla and cream soda.

Two Brewers Yukon Special Finishes Release 41
Single malt, finished in Pedro Ximénez casks, 43% ABV
Classic sherry notes of fruitcake, black cherry, and citrus peel, loaded with spice on the nose, plus peat-smoked figs and a touch of leather. Chocolate, spice, dark caramel, vanilla cream, and clove on the palate, with dark fruits of sultana, cherry, date, and prune, it has a smoky thread that runs through the sweet peat notes. This is the best of the bunch.

Two Brewers Yukon Peated Single Malt Release 38

BLACK VELVET

OWNER Heaven Hill Distilleries, Inc.

FOUNDED 1951

WEBSITE www.blackvelvetwhisky.com

Named for its velvety texture, distiller Jack Napier created this whisky in 1951. It is still the second-largest Canadian whisky sold in the US market.

Black Velvet is a blended at birth whisky made from corn, rye, and barley, produced at the Black Velvet distillery in Lethbridge, Alberta, owned by Heaven Hill since 2019. Like other Canadian whiskies, the whiskies are blended with a milder base whisky, which is then matured for three years and bottled.

TASTING NOTE

Black Velvet
Canadian, aged in oak casks, 40% ABV
Aromas of baked apple, caramel, vanilla, banana chip, roasted spices, and rye. Velvety smooth, with flavors of grain whisky, heavy vanilla, caramel, rye spices, and clove, with a baked apple return, and a finish of butterscotch, burnt sugar, and rye spices.

CARIBOU CROSSING

Caribou Crossing

OWNER Sazerac Company Inc

FOUNDED 2010

WEBSITE www.sazerac.com/our-brands/sazerac-brands/caribou-crossing

New Orleans Sazerac Company now owns some of Seagram's biggest Canadian whisky brands, such as Canadian Mist and Seagram's V.O. following a $550 million deal with Diageo. Sazerac recommenced distilling at the Old Montreal Distillery in 2018, the former Meagher Distillery from the 1920s that Sazerac acquired in 2011 and used as a blending and bottling plant. The distillery is being used to create and experiment around a variety of different styles. Caribou Crossing was launched in 2010, the first single barrel Canadian whisky brand.

TASTING NOTE

Caribou Crossing
Canadian, matured in a single barrel, 40% ABV
Caramel, dark toffee, milk chocolate, rye bread, white pepper, poached pear, and floral top notes on the nose. Chocolate caramels ooze over the tongue with creamy vanilla, hazelnut, praline, and gentle spices, followed by a long chocolate-laden finish rounding out a sublime whisky-drinking experience.

DISTILLERIE DU ST. LAURENT

OWNER Distillerie du St. Laurent Company

FOUNDED 2015

WEBSITE www.distilleriedustlaurent.com

In the salty air blowing in from the wide St. Lawrence River, Joël Pelletier and Jean-François Cloutier opened this craft distillery with a focus on local raw materials. They produce seaweed-infused gin, acerum, and whisky. They ferment their whisky on the grain, make a rye with an 80 percent rye and 20 percent malted barley mashbill and a three-grain whisky with a mashbill of 75 percent corn, 15 percent rye, and 10 percent malted barley.

TASTING NOTE

St. Laurent Whisky 3 Grains 3-Year-Old
Canadian, matured in char #1 and #5 new oak casks, 43% ABV
Rye spices with almond bar cookie, coconut strips, cornbread muffins, and vanilla aromas. Delicious corn fills the mouth, with brown sugar, rye bread, and baked fruits with a spicy rye and chocolate finish. Impressive for its age.

St. Laurent Whisky
3 Grains 3-Year-Old

FORTY CREEK

OWNER Campari Group

FOUNDED 1992

WEBSITE www.fortycreekwhisky.com

When John Hall brought his Forty Creek whiskies to market, he rapidly became the best-known Canadian whisky-maker in the country. In 1992, he bought the Rieder distillery in Grimsby on the shores of Lake Ontario, renaming it Kittling Ridge and, later still, Forty Creek. In 2014, Hall sold Forty Creek to the

Campari Group. Master blender Bill Ashburn remained at the distillery and continues the tradition of releasing annual limited edition expressions.

TASTING NOTE

Forty Creek Barrel Select
Canadian, 40% ABV
Dripping with honey notes on the nose, there are aromas of orange peel, peach pit, and gentle oak spices. Pulped fruit, raspberry, squeezed orange, caramel, and black pepper in the mouth, this adds flavors of rye crackers, pie crust, and sour patch sweets that grows in intensity. The finish is spicy.

Forty Creek Barrel Select

GLEN BRETON

Glen Breton Ice 10-Year-Old

OWNER Glenora Distillers

FOUNDED 1990

WEBSITE www.glenoradistillery.com

When Glenora distillery's first drops flowed in 1990, it was sweet, pure malt spirit, distilled from Scottish malted barley, mashed in water drawn from MacLellan's Brook. The distillery was founded by Bruce Jardine on Cape Breton Island and produced the first single malt to be released in North America. It now belongs to Lauchie Maclean; both have Scottish ancestry. Glenora was the first to release an

ice wine finish single malt whisky. The malt is now firmly Canadian, and this traditional distillery now boasts an impressive range of age-stated Glen Breton single malts up to 30 years old.

TASTING NOTE

Glen Breton Ice 10-Year-Old
Single malt, finished in ice wine casks, 40% ABV
Pear, melon, and white peach on the nose, with a gentle maltiness, apple slice, honey, faint cinnamon notes, and aromas of the ice wine. This is a well-judged wine finish, with soft, pulpy white fruits, star fruit, candied lemon, and apple, with the ebb and flow of wine notes at the end.

STALK & BARREL

OWNER Barry Stein and Barry Bernstein

FOUNDED 2009

WEBSITE www.stalkandbarrel.com

In Concord, Ontario, on the northern edge of Toronto, business partners Barry Stein and Barry Bernstein founded the Still Waters distillery in 2009. They are contract distillers of gin and vodka, and in addition to single malt, they distill corn—the creamiest of Canadian whisky grains—as well as rye,

Canada's spicy signature grain. In 2017, they released their first traditional Canadian blends, particularly designed as a mixer for cocktails, such as Red Blend.

TASTING NOTE

Stalk & Barrel Red Blend
Canadian, matured in oak casks, 43% ABV
Toasty grain notes, buttery corn, almond, panna cotta, and light maple syrup on the nose. Peach, malt, vanilla, green apple, caramel, rye spices, crème brûlée, hazelnut, and baked orange flavors, with a spicy finish of vanilla and stone fruits.

Stalk & Barrel Red Blend

ASIA–PACIFIC

JAPAN

REGIONAL STYLES
The nature of Japanese
whisky production is that
every conceivable style is
made in a very small number
of distilleries. Both Suntory
and Nikka, the principal
producers, go to great
lengths to make sure they
have a range of whiskies of a
wide variety of ages, peated
and unpeated, and available
in sherry, bourbon, and
mizunara oak barrels. New
producers are exploring
differences in distillation
styles, Japanese barley, and a
wide array of cask styles.

AUTHOR'S CHOICE
YOICHI Located on the
northern island of Hokkaido,
Yoichi takes a bit of effort to
get to but its well worth it for
the beautiful coastal scenery,
pretty distillery buildings,
and fascinating museum
exploring the life of the
distiller who brought whisky-
making to Japan.

REGIONAL EVENTS
Japan hosts numerous
whisky events across the
country each year, including
the Tokyo International Bar
Show (www.tokyobarshow.
com), the long-running
Chichibu Whisky Festival in
Saitama Prefecture, and
newer events such as the
Shizuoka Craft Beer and
Whisky Festival.

The dawn of the 21st century put Japanese whisky on a roller-coaster journey. On the one hand, the long overdue and well-deserved global recognition generated a vast international audience curious to discover everything about Japanese whisky and taste the exotic flavors of whiskies matured in rare mizunara oak casks, while on the other hand, the legacy of Japan's economic woes and domestic whisky slump during the late 20th century meant the industry did not have the inventory to slake their thirst. Demand outstripped supply, leading to a shortage of choice and steep price rises, followed by the allocation, and sometimes withdrawal, of high-quality stock with age statements, leaving a few nonage statement bottlings in their place.

The final years of the 20th century resulted in the closure of several distilleries, but astute businesses like Number One Drinks and Venture Spirits stepped in to manage and market the remaining closed distillery stock to collectors. Rare bottlings from Karuizawa and Hanyu soared in value, transformed from unwanted casks into some of the most expensive bottles of Japanese whisky ever to go under the hammer. With the collectors' market running rampant, getting your hands on affordable and delicious Japanese whisky to drink became somewhat problematic.

The vacuum attracted unfamiliar brands dressed in vaguely familiar packaging but with an absence of information about the contents, tasting notes, or whether it was distilled on Japanese soil. All too common, new brands appeared at premium prices that drinkers couldn't be sure were associated with a physical distillery. The spotlight was turned on the lack of robust regulations and transparency around Japanese whisky, and in 2021, a voluntary set of regulations on labeling standards was published.

By the time Japanese whisky was marking its centenary in 2023, sufficient time had elapsed for a new generation of whisky-makers, distillers, coopers, and blenders to enter the category, and there was a boom in new distillery openings. The industry is changing, too, with greater numbers of craft distillers and smaller companies stepping onto the international stage, a greater spirit of collaboration between the distilleries, a growing appreciation of koji whisky in the US, the arrival of whiskies made solely from Japanese barley, and the adoption of the mizunara cask for finishing whiskies from the US, Scotland, and Ireland. After all the highs and lows, Japanese whisky is finally on the up again.

Miyagikyo's high-tech operation contrasts with its tranquil location in the foothills of Miyagi prefecture.

GETTING AROUND

Japan has a highly efficient public transportation system, a superb high-speed rail system network and airlines like JAL and ANA, which offer domestic flight connections to a wide range of regional airports. Tokyo and Osaka make good bases for visiting the main distilleries, though given the distances between them, be realistic about the number of distilleries you can visit in one trip.

N

RUSSIA

La Perouse Strait

Sea of Okhotsk

Rebun

Rishiri

HOKKAIDO

Sapporo

Yoichi

Akkeshi

Uchiura Bay

Okushiri

Hakodate

Aomori

NORTH KOREA

Akita

Ou Mountains

Sea of Japan

Miyagikyo

JAPAN

Sendai

Niigata

Sado

Fukushima

HONSHU

Iwaki

Komoro

Chichibu

SOUTH KOREA

Oki Islands

Mars Shinshu

Hakushu

TOKYO

Yokohama

Yamazaki

Biwa Lake

Nagoya

Mount Fuji 3,776 m (12,388 ft)

Fuji Gotemba

Kobe

Kyoto

Shizuoka

Tsushima

Eigashima

Osaka

Shizuoka

Oshima

Hiroshima

Kii Mountains

Miyake

Pacific Ocean

Kitakyushu

SHIKOKU

Mikurajima

Fukuoka

Aogashima

Kumamoto

Nagasaki

KYUSHU

Kanosuke

Kagoshima

Mars Tsunuki

| 0 | 50 | 100 | 150 miles |

| 0 | 50 | 100 | 150 | 200 | 250 km |

CHICHIBU

Ichiro's Malt Chichibu The US Edition 2021

OWNER Venture Whisky Ltd

FOUNDED 2004

WEBSITE Not available

When Ichiro Akuto opened his own distillery in Japan, it wasn't just a realization of a dream; it was the fulfillment of a personal promise. His grandfather built Hanyu distillery in the 1940s, and when it was closed in 2000 and demolished in 2004, Ichiro Akuto was determined that should not be the last chapter of the family's distilling history.

Through his company Venture Whisky, he is also responsible for the Hanyu "Card" series, in which each bottling featured a different playing card on the label, launched because he wanted to make it possible for people to recognize their favorite malts on the back bar shelf without having to study labels, age statements, vintages, and so on. The whiskies were drawn from 400 casks of Hanyu single malt that Ichiro Akuto managed to obtain after the distillery was closed down, but given the huge sums these bottlings now attract at auction, you won't find them being poured in many bars any more.

The new distillery

Work began at Chichibu in Saitama Prefecture in late 2007, and they were granted a distilling license in early 2008, releasing Chichibu The First in 2011. Their small maltings handles a few tons of Japanese grown barley, a rare grain considering Japan isn't in the top 50 barley-growing nations on the planet. That means they can experiment with peat, rather than only importing peated malt from the UK.

The size of the distillery was modest, with its hand-stirred mash tun and small onion-shaped stills with narrow downward-angled lyne arms, even if the vision and possibilities of their work still reached the sky. There were mizunara washbacks, and they began coopering new mizunara oak casks in their cooperage, learning the craft of how to precisely cut the logs with the grain to reduce losses from the notoriously leaky wood. The warehouses began to fill up with an encyclopedia of cask types for maturation from the traditional bourbon and sherry casks to the unusual, such as small chibidaru casks that mature more quickly than full-size vessels. By their nature, early

Glorious fall color surrounds the Chichibu distillery, with its traditional-looking pagoda above the kiln.

Ichiro's Malt & Grain Blue Label

bottlings were small batches or single casks, annual releases, festival and bar show bottlings, retailer exclusives, or only released to specific markets, and many ended up on the secondary market. They also do fun collaborations with other Japanese distilleries, showing the rest of the world a new spirit of camaraderie and cooperation among the new generation of whisky-makers in Japan.

Another new distillery

By 2019, Ichiro Akuto had opened a second larger Chichibu distillery, installing direct-fired stills and increasing his production capacity considerably; the first site now handles more of the experimental runs, while the new site builds up the volume. And for their next trick, Venture Whisky is planning to build a grain distillery in Hokkaido.

TASTING NOTES

Ichiro's Malt Chichibu The US Edition 2021
Single malt, matured in bourbon, sherry, and new oak casks, 53.5% ABV
Stone fruits, vanilla, citrus, barley sugar, and oak spices on the nose of this small batch bottling of 11 casks, consisting of a variety of different cask types. Ripe peach, caramel, and cask-strength spices on the palate, with generous oak characteristics, this is a full-bodied dram with baked fruits carrying through into an oaky finish.

Ichiro's Malt & Grain Blue Label
Blend, aged in a variety of oak casks, 48% ABV
Chichibu is blended with imported whiskies, with every component aged for at least 10 years, with some up to 30–40 years old. The nose has barley sugar, charcuterie, smoked paprika, and aromatic spices. Sweet citrus and sherbet fountain notes on the palate, with shredded ginger and black pepper and a creamy finish of mango and orange peel.

MARS SHINSHU AND MARS TSUNUKI

OWNER Hombo Shuzo Company

FOUNDED Mars Shinshu 2011; Mars Tsunuki 2016

WEBSITE www.hombo.co.jp

Hombo Shuzo Company operates two whisky distilleries that make contrasting styles of whisky. Located 750 miles apart by road, Mars Shinshu sits at elevation in a valley surrounded by mountains in the Nagano Prefecture, while Mars Tsunuki is south of Minamisatsuma City in the Kagoshima Prefecture at the southern end of Kyushu, where the company has its headquarters.

The modern era of Hombo Shuzo whisky production is relatively recent, as Mars Shinshu has been operating only since 2011 and Mars Tsunuki since 2016. What makes the Mars distilleries stand apart from the new crop of 21st-century Japanese distilleries is the storied history of their parent company, Hombo Shuzo.

Three key dates in the 20th century were important in the development of their whisky business, as Hombo Shuzo Company is a beverage company with significant interests beyond whisky, especially in shochu, a traditional hard spirit distilled from grains and vegetables. In 1949, the company received the necessary license permitting them to distill, but this was put into use only in 1960 when they began to distill at the company's facility in Yamanashi Prefecture, an area better known for wine production, but the enterprise did not see out the decade. In 1985, the distilling equipment was relocated to the newly built Mars Shinshu distillery, but production ceased after only seven years. Distilling spirit for whisky at Mars Shinshu did not start up again until 2011.

Kiichiro Iwai mentored Masataka Taketsuru when he was his superior and both worked for Settsu Shuzo, the company that dispatched Taketsuru to Scotland, a decision that changed the course of Japanese whisky history. Iwai designed Hombo Shuzo's first stills, based on the sketches and writings of Taketsuru, the founder of Nikka Whisky. Taketsuru made copious notes when he traveled around Scotland as a young man where he learned about making malt and grain whisky and how to become a whisky blender.

Mars Komagatake 2023 Edition

Mars The Y.A. #02

Differing maturation sites

Hombo Shuzo has another trick up their sleeve, too. To explore the impact of differing environmental conditions on whisky maturation, casks from both distilleries are matured in any of their three warehouse locations. Mars Shinshu offers cooler warehouses at altitude, Mars Tsunuki enjoys a more temperate climate, while their Yakushima Aging Cellar, with releases labclcd "The Y.A.," is a cedar-clad warehouse built on a subtropical island.

Mars Tsunuki distillery has a distinctive tower that dominates the town.

Mars Tsunuki 2023 Edition

TASTING NOTES

Mars Komagatake 2023 Edition
Single malt, matured in bourbon, sherry, and port casks, 50% ABV
Distilled at Mars Shinshu for their premium Komagatake line, this delivers spiced citrus, ginger, orchard fruits, and persimmon, with mocha notes on the finish.

Mars Tsunuki 2023 Edition
Single malt, matured in bourbon casks, 50% ABV
This annual limited edition bottling from Hombo Shuzo's second whisky distillery has notes of cherry, pear, and treacle on the nose, with flavors of fruit syrups, goji berry, and spiced ham giving a slightly savory finish.

Mars The Y.A. #02
Blended malt, matured in bourbon and sherry casks, 49% ABV
A beautiful bounty of citrus, tropical fruits, and salinity on the nose, with a thick mouthfeel of white chocolate, banana, red grape, watermelon, sea salt, and black pepper, and a slightly spicy finish.

FUJI GOTEMBA

OWNER Kirin Brewing Company Ltd

FOUNDED 1973

WEBSITE www.fujiwhisky.com

Kirin's Fuji Gotemba is the closest distillery to Mount Fuji, affording breathtaking views of the sacred mountain. Formerly known as Mt. Fuji distillery, Kirin began distilling there in 1973 in a joint venture between Kirin Brewery Co. Ltd and Joseph E. Seagram & Sons. This is a distillery designed to deliver almost any style of whisky that whisky drinkers in Japan might desire, and it has unrivaled capabilities in grain whisky production. All the production water comes from snowmelt from Mount Fuji, and they also produce a light, fruity style of malt whisky in unlacquered pot stills with upsloping lyne arms, the copper having developed a deep chestnut brown patina over time.

Since 2003, Kirin has run the site where Jota Tanaka, one of Japan's most experienced master blenders, puts the whiskies together. He manages the stock and creates the modern Fuji range but also is the international face of the brand as he travels frequently to pour and talk about his whiskies. Overseas travel and culture are nothing new to him, however, as he worked as the director of quality at the Four Roses distillery in Kentucky, a sister distillery to Fuji Gotemba, and before that, he trained as a winemaker in California. Of course, the company connection also provides Fuji Gotemba with an ample supply of fresh Four Roses bourbon barrels to fill and store in their huge racked warehouses.

The Fuji range includes both nonage statement single grain containing the distillery's three different styles, and a nonage statement single malt Fuji whisky. They bottled an intriguing Fuji single blend, a combination of grain whiskies and single malt distilled at a single distillery. As well as marking the distillery's 50th anniversary with a special bottling, they have released stocks of beautifully aged single grain whiskies at 30 years old from stocks of their Canadian-style whisky produced in the kettle and column still set up and matured in first- and second-fill bourbon barrels.

Fuji Single Blend

Fuji Single Grain

TASTING NOTES

Fuji Single Grain
Single grain, aged in American oak casks, 46% ABV
Combining the Canadian, bourbon, and Scottish-style grain whiskies produced at the distillery, the nose has black tea, baking spice, hazelnut, apple, and orange peel. The palate has pear, apple, and orange zest, with black pepper, oak spices, and bitter oak with hints of oak and cinnamon stick on the finish.

Fuji Single Blend
Single blend, matured in bourbon casks, 43% ABV
Spicy aromas, floral perfumes, and maltiness with dried tropical fruits, dark chocolate, and clove in this tasty blend of malt and grains whisky.

Fuji Single Grain 30-Year-Old
Single grain, matured in bourbon casks, 46% ABV
Sweet vanilla toffee, blackberry pâtes de fruits, tropical fruit, soothing honey, and citrus peel in this Canadian-style whisky made in Fuji Gotemba's kettle and column stills.

HAKUSHU

OWNER Suntory Holdings Ltd

FOUNDED 1973

WEBSITE www.house.suntory.com

While it may be the lesser known of Suntory's Japanese distilleries, Hakushu is a fascinating one. The distillery, near Hokuto City, Yamanashi Prefecture, is in the Southern Japanese Alps, a couple of hours on the fast train from Tokyo, surrounded by natural forests with walking and cycling trails. Fueling the "salaryman" boom, Hakushu was built in 1973 in the 50th anniversary year of the founding of Yamazaki, when the company was riding a Japanese whisky boom that was in part its own creation.

This was once the most productive distillery in the world, built to supply the huge thirst for easy-drinking Japanese blends that grew during the mid-to late 20th century, but this momentum slowed in the 1980s and 1990s as a variety of economic factors began to bite. The distillery itself is effectively two distilleries close together, though only one, Hakushu East, is used. When that boom ended, Hakushu West was forced to close its doors. But Keizo Saji, son of Suntory founder Shinjiro Torii, also believed in a future for premium blends and single malts. To that end, the distillery was crucial in the development of Suntory's Hibiki range of premium aged blends, launched in 1989. Other than limited editions, the core lineup includes aged expressions at 12, 18, and 25 years old, plus a nonage statement bottling named Distiller's Reserve. As Suntory celebrated its 100th anniversary in 2023, it was the 50th anniversary of Hakushu distillery, and centennial labels were created for their existing Hakushu range.

With its cooler mountain location and soft water source drawn from a mountain spring, the standard style of Hakushu is fresh, clean, and fruity. Whether it's the full lauter tun, the 18 Douglas Fir washbacks each with a capacity of 19,800 gallons (75,000 liters), or the 18 working stills fashioned in a surprising variety of shapes and sizes, this place is a substantial distillery, designed for capacity and versatility and there's an on-site cooperage. In the 2010s, Suntory installed a grain distillery within Hakushu. As it marked its centenary, Suntory announced significant investment in its distilleries, setting out their intention to bring floor malting to Hakushu and the ability to cultivate their own yeast strains.

The Hakushu 18-Year-Old Peated Malt 100th Anniversary Limited Edition

The Hakushu 12-Year-Old

TASTING NOTES

The Hakushu Distillers Reserve
Single malt, aged in bourbon, European, and American oak, sherry, and mizunara casks, 43% ABV
Mint, cucumber, and white pepper on the nose, with creamy vanilla, green foliage, and glimmers of mizunara character. Changes from clean and fresh to a creamy texture, shifting from vanilla, peppermint, and grapefruit peel to mint chocolate and green herbal notes, with cilantro stalk, green tea, candied peel, and wood smoke on the finish.

The Hakushu 12-Year-Old
Single malt, matured in a variety of oak casks, 43% ABV
Herbal with a hint of smoke, this provides a moment of tranquility with its notes of basil, green pepper, pear, mint, kiwi fruit, and green tea, and a lasting finish.

The Hakushu 18-Year-Old Peated Malt 100th Anniversary Limited Edition
Single malt, matured in a variety of oak casks, 48% ABV
Like walking through a forest after a rainstorm, this is herbal, with green apple, well-integrated peat smoke, sharp citrus peel, Sencha green tea, and gentle woody base notes.

KANOSUKE

OWNER Komasa Jyozo Company Ltd

FOUNDED 2017

WEBSITE www.kanosuke-en.com

Situated by Hoiki City in Kagoshima Prefecture, Kanosuke is a young distillery bursting with ambition, still in the early years when it comes to its bottlings and its maturing whisky, but it is already being whispered about as having great potential.

Komasa Jyozo, the parent company, is a shochu maker with roots going back to 1883. Yoshitsugu Komasa is the current company president and master blender and comes from the fourth generation of the family. Following the commencement of whisky production in 2017, the company also launched a range of Komasa craft gins, including the Komasa Sakurajima gin, which has aromas of the komikan—a small local mandarin type of citrus—and Komasa Hojicha gin, boasting aromas of hojicha, the roasted Japanese green tea prized for its sweet, nutty flavors.

In 2021, Distill Ventures, Diageo's accelerator program, took a minority stake in the Kanosuke distillery. The Distill Ventures unit seeks out new founder-led drinks brands with exceptional potential, enabling these fledgling enterprises to receive support to reach the next level, whether that's improving capacity and production at the distillery, access to expertise on branding and marketing, or improving access to global distribution networks. These are carefully selected partnerships and enabled Kanosuke to join the ranks of other highly ambitious distilleries around the world under the wing of Distill Ventures, including Starward, Stauning, The Oxford Artisan Distillery, and Westward.

Kanosuke enjoys stunning views over the East China Sea, a pleasure clearly relished by Yoshitsugu Komasa when he is writing notes for each release for the back of the box. The distillery is situated beside the longest sandy beach in Japan, an important habitat for nesting and hatching sea turtles. Inside, the production area is equipped with a full lauter tun, 10 stainless steel washbacks, and, unusually for a craft distillery, three indirect-heated copper pot stills with worm tub condensers. The 1,600-gallon (6,000-liter) wash still normally supplies low wines for the 425-gallon (1,600-liter) spirit still, while the 800-gallon (3,000-liter)

The Kanosuke distillery has an unusual setup with three copper pot stills and worm tub condensers.

still in the middle can be deployed either as a wash still or spirit still depending on the run, as the distillery uses peated and unpeated malt in its production.

"Mellow Land Mellow Whisky"

The first single malt made its debut in 2021, a 3-year-old aged in Mellowed Kozuru casks, their pioneering cask-aged shochu brand launched in 1957. Kanosuke has released further limited-edition single malts, festival bottlings, and single cask exclusives, each with their own unique flavor profile. Kanosuke embraces the concept of "Mellow Land Mellow Whisky," and this exemplifies their work, taking a combination of single malt whiskies distilled using all three of their stills and matured in the Mellowed Kozuru casks. Later editions introduced new American oak, wine cask finishing, and bourbon and sherry cask maturation to the recipes.

TASTING NOTES

Kanosuke Mellow Land Mellow Whisky
Single malt, matured in Kozuru and American oak shochu casks, 48% ABV
This dram has zippy citrus notes, with honeydew melon and banana chews on the nose, then creamy vanilla desserts, toffee, candied citrus, and a little spice on the palate, with a finish of toffee and orange peel.

Kanosuke 2023 Limited Edition
Single malt, matured in shochu and sherry casks, 59% ABV
A peated single malt expression, this has plenty of peat smoke, spice, and soft yellow fruit aromas on the nose with honeyed pear, vanilla, and a hint of savoriness on the palate through into the finish.

Kanosuke Mellow Land Mellow Whisky

MIYAGIKYO

OWNER Nikka Whisky Distilling Company Ltd

FOUNDED 1969

WEBSITE www.nikka.com/eng/distilleries/miyagikyo

Miyagikyo was designed to help Nikka extend its output and was the result of a three-year search by master distiller Masataka Taketsuru for the perfect location to build a second distillery to make malts that contrast with those produced at Yoichi distillery. Two hours northeast of Tokyo by high-speed train, the distillery in the Miyagi Prefecture has a rural setting to the west of the city of Sendai. The region is beautiful, rich in green woodland and famous for its waterfalls, many hot springs, and the mountains that surround the distillery itself.

High tech and automated

Triple the size of Yoichi, Miyagikyo is a high-tech and largely automated distillery, where the production of

Single Malt Miyagikyo Peated

a diverse range of malts is controlled by state-of-the-art computers. Conventional distillation, similar to practice in Scotland, takes place in their four pairs of large copper pot stills, leading to a rich, elegant, and fruity spirit. Casks are stored in traditional cellars with just two floors—mainly because the distillery is situated in the middle of an earthquake zone but also partly because this emulates Scottish maturation methods in musty warehouses. The distillery also boasts Coffey stills, the paired analyzer and rectifying columns named after inventor Aeneas Coffey who changed the world of whisky when he introduced the equipment in 1832. To those making their first forays into Japanese whisky, Nikka's highly regarded Coffey Malt, made from 100 percent malted barley, and Coffey Grain are as educational as they are delicious, and the company has since added a Coffey gin and Coffey vodka to the range.

In addition, while Nikka removed age statements from their ranges in 2015, Miyagikyo offered a nonage statement expression. Furthermore, Nikka maintained expressions of Nikka from the Barrel, Nikka 12-Year-Old, Nikka Tailored, and Taketsuru Pure Malt over the dry spell in age statements, meaning drinkers still had plenty of options.

The Discovery series is a line of experimental releases from chief blender Hiromi Ozaki. Preceding the Discovery series, Nikka released a pair of Miyagikyo and Yoichi expressions finished in apple brandy barrels to mark the centenary of the wedding of Nikka's founder Masataka Taketsuru's and his Scottish wife, Rita, in 1920. Apple products were instrumental to the company's cash flow in the early days. Nikka's Hirosaki Cidery in Aomori Prefecture produces Nikka Apple Wine using apple brandy.

TASTING NOTES

Single Malt Miyagikyo Peated
Single malt, matured in a variety of oak casks, 48% ABV
Showcasing the versatility of the distillery, the peat is expressed in notes of sweet smoke, bonfires, and tarry ropes, and it's one of the chewiest drams in their Discovery Series with a palate of vanilla, cocoa, spice, cherry, and dried vine fruits.

Single Malt Miyagikyo Aromatic Yeast
Single malt, matured in a variety of oak casks, 47% ABV
This Discovery series release is full of floral and confectionery sweetness, with flavors of orange, peach rings, tropical fruit, cotton candy, and a growing sense of tart citrus notes that lasts into the finish.

YAMAZAKI

OWNER Suntory Holdings Ltd

FOUNDED 1921

WEBSITE www.house.suntory.com

The distillery at Yamazaki, between Kyoto and Osaka toward the south end of Japan's main island of Honshu, is where it all started for Japanese whisky in 1923. Not just the physical production of malted barley spirit but the philosophy that Japanese whisky should experiment, challenge the existing parameters, and strive to create new flavors. After celebrating 100 years of Suntory whisky, that quest to pursue perfection continues to invigorate and inspire distillers across Japan as this dynamic industry looks forward to the next 100 years.

Japan's first whisky distillery was built on land bought by Shinjiro Torii, who employed chemist Masataka Taketsuru to set about creating Japanese whisky. Since then, Yamazaki has grown into one of the biggest malt whisky–making institutions in the world and also one of the most intriguing. Japanese distillers at Suntory and Nikka don't trade their malts for making blends like distillery companies do in Scotland. In the pursuit of excellence, that means creating the ability to make a variety of different whiskies under one roof.

Equipment of all shapes and sizes

Yamazaki produces nonpeated, lightly peated, and heavily peated malts, using imported malted barley. The distillery is equipped with two full lauter tuns, with 20 washbacks on site to handle fermentation, 12 stainless steel, and 8 wooden vessels made from Douglas fir. The stillroom at Yamazaki, then, has stills of all shapes and sizes, creating the versatility to produce light and heavy styles of spirits. There's lantern-, onion-, and conical-shaped stills, with different lyne arm styles, among the six pairs of stills in the main stillhouse, plus the two newer pairs installed in 2005. As at Hakushu, the wash stills are direct fired while the spirits stills are steam heated. Shell and tube condensers are mainly used, but two of the wash stills have worm tubs fitted to produce a heavier style spirit.

With different yeasts and various combinations of stills working in tandem and an assortment of casks types, the number of permutations is seemingly endless. They fill casks of American white oak puncheons, sherry casks, mizunara casks, and butts, Bordeaux casks, Japanese cedar, and a lot more besides, with extensive maturation facilities on site, and an even larger complex at the Ohmi Aging Cellar in Shiga Prefecture. The wide variety of casks isn't just to provide sophistication in the single malt output— it provides the perfect platform for the House of Suntory to create the world-class blended whisky Hibiki, too.

The Yamazaki range

In 2021, the company released the Yamazaki 55-Year-Old, which has since become the most expensive bottle of Japanese whisky ever sold at auction. The Tsukuriwake Cask Collection released in 2022 showcased four of the most important elements that make up the flavors of Yamazaki whisky; puncheon, mizunara, Spanish oak, and peated malt. The Yamazaki range includes age stated expressions of 12-, 18-, and 25-year-olds, with a nonage statement whisky called Distiller's Reserve. For Suntory's chief blender Shinji Fukuyo, Yamazaki is a single malt story expressed through the art of blending.

TASTING NOTES

The Yamazaki 18-Year-Old Mizunara 100th Anniversary Limited Edition
Single malt, matured in mizunara oak casks, 48% ABV
Complex and layered with fresh pear, plum, sandalwood, and nutmeg with concentrated flavors of manuka honey, tropical fruit, cinnamon, chocolate, and incense. This is utterly spectacular.

The Yamazaki 25-Year-Old (2021 Release)
Single malt, aged in Spanish, American, and mizunara oak casks, 43% ABV
Adding greater subtly and complexity compared to the early heavily sherried 25-year-old, the nose has incense, pressed flowers, sandalwood, and vanilla on the nose. Creamy on the palate with vanilla, oak, sharp citrus notes, and green fruit, with a creamy finish with subtle oaky notes.

Hibiki 21-Year-Old Mizunara 100th Anniversary Limited Edition
Blend, matured in mizunara oak casks, 43% ABV
Stunning floral notes, with citrus and orchard fruit aromas, followed by a thick texture replete with mizunara oak characteristics, zested lime, and cocoa powder, finessed by a deliciously creamy finish. An incredible blend.

Yamazaki 18-Year-Old Mizunara 100th Anniversary Limited Edition

YOICHI

OWNER Nikka Whisky Distilling Co. Ltd

FOUNDED 1934

WEBSITE www.nikka.com/eng/distilleries/yoichi

Yoichi distillery is striking and impressive, with its bright red tile roof, traditional pagoda-style chimneys, and thick-walled stone gatehouse. The distillery is often depicted in winter marooned under a blanket of deep snow. Situated 31 miles west of Sapporo, it is the largest and best-known distillery on Hokkaido, the northern Japanese island where the climate is most similar to that of Scotland. It is also regarded by many as the prettiest in Japan, Yoichi being a small fishing village on the coast with mountains on three sides.

This is the distillery that Masataka Taketsuru, the first distiller at Yamazaki, built upon the formation of his company Dainipponkaju Company Ltd in 1934, which was renamed Nikka Whisky Distilling in 1952. Japan's Agency for Cultural Affairs has designated it for its cultural importance. Originally called Hokkaido distillery, it was making whisky by 1940, though the site has been expanded considerably since. Taketsuru had only a single still here until 1966, meaning it had to be cleaned between the first and second run; now they work with six onion-shaped stills, perhaps the only distillery to practice direct fired distillation using coal. The original still remains in the stillhouse at Yoichi, though it is no longer used.

Different malt styles

It wasn't until the 1980s that a single malt was released. Yoichi can make a spectrum of different malt styles, but the house style is a rich, oily, full-bodied, peaty whisky. Yoichi became a victim of its own success, with Nikka withdrawing their age statement range in 2015 due to the global demand for Japanese whisky, filling the gap with a nonage statement single malt until the age statement was brought back with a new Yoichi 10-year-old expression in 2023.

Chief blender Hiromi Ozaki recently completed a three-year program of experimental releases called the Discovery series, which included a nonpeated Yoichi and a fruity expression called Yoichi Aromatic Yeast, ahead of the company's 90th anniversary celebrations in 2024.

Single Malt Yoichi 10-Year-Old

Single Malt Yoichi Aromatic Yeast

TASTING NOTES

Single Malt Yoichi Aromatic Yeast
Single malt, matured in a variety of oak casks, 48% ABV
A sweet dram with a nose of candied orange, marzipan, and bubblegum, with clean flavors of boiled fruit lollipops, apple juice concentrate, apricot, and peppery smoke in the background.

Single Malt Yoichi 10-Year-Old
Single malt, matured in a variety of oak casks, 45% ABV
This new version heralded the return of the age statement to Yoichi whiskies in 2023. Lemon zest, peat, and vanilla give way to a fruity palate of green apple, ripening banana, and buttery vanilla, with salt and pepperiness.

AKKESHI

OWNER Kenten Jitsugyō Company Ltd

FOUNDED 2016

WEBSITE www.akkeshi-distillery.com

The island of Hokkaido has fewer distilleries than Honshu or Kyushu, but Yoichi is no longer the only distillery in the north of Japan. Akkeshi is a coastal distillery where they have been making whisky since 2016. Forsyth's Ltd of Scotland equipped the site with its distillation equipment, including a stainless steel semi-lauter tun, six washbacks, and a pair of pear-shaped copper pot stills comprising a 1,320-gallon (5,000-liter) wash still and 950-gallon (3,600-liter) spirit still.

They have their own malting facility and spread their casks between a number of local warehouses that offer differing environmental conditions. This leads to subtle differences in the final flavors as the spirit mellows inside the cask. This is a team following traditional Scotch whisky distillery practices, drawing inspiration from Islay but working toward creating whisky using raw materials from Hokkaido. These start with barley grown near Akkeshi, Japanese peat, their own proprietary yeast strain, production water from the nearby Homakai River, and casks made from local mizunara oak. The first single malt was released in 2020, but no date has been set yet for the release of their 100 percent Hokkaido whisky. Single malt bottlings have been released to reflect the 24 solar seasons of Japan's Sekki system, with Akkeshi blends created with imported grain whisky.

TASTING NOTE

The Akkeshi Peated Single Malt Kanro Season
Single malt, aged in sherry, wine, bourbon, and mizunara oak casks 55% ABV
A mellow proposition on the nose, with aromas of charcoal, cigars, vanilla seed, and espresso notes. Notes of baked orange, ginger loaf, dark chocolate, and berry fruit compote entertain the taste buds through to the finish.

The Akkeshi Peated Single Malt Kanro Season

EIGASHIMA

OWNER Eigashima Shuzo Company Ltd

FOUNDED 1984

WEBSITE www.ei-sake.jp

Located on the coast in Akashi City in Hyogo Prefecture, this distillery can trace its roots as a sake brewery back to the Edo period in the 17th and 18th centuries. It was granted a whisky license in 1919, though until the modern era of production, it was last active in the whisky world during the 1960s and '70s, just as the popularity of whisky was soaring at home in Japan.

Formerly known as the White Oak distillery until 2019, the distillery upgraded its equipment to focus on its whisky operations as Japanese whisky found international favor during the 21st century, though this is still a tiny whisky distillery by Japanese standards. It has a stainless steel semi-lauter tun, four stainless steel washbacks, and a pair of copper pot stills made by Miyake Industries, with chunky shell and tube condensers. They maintain a shubo-style yeast starter for their fermentation process, more through their familiarity with sake production than any other reason.

They have been releasing single malt whiskies since 2007. The distillery mostly matures their whiskies in bourbon, sherry, wine, and brandy casks. Bottlings appear under the White Oak brand, Akashi, and Eigashima, their premium line, though only those labeled single malts originate entirely from the Eigashima distillery as imported whisky is still sourced for blending.

TASTING NOTE

Akashi Sherry Cask 5-Year-Old
Single malt, matured in sherry butts and hogsheads, 50% ABV
This delivers on the nose, with its aromas of dark berry fruits, Bramley apple, and dark chocolate from the sherry wood. The palate is less assured, with flavors of sweet citrus peel, barley sugar, and strawberry jam and a finish of tobacco and plum.

Akashi Sherry Cask 5-Year-Old

KOMORO

OWNER Karuizawa Distillers Inc

FOUNDED 2020

WEBSITE www.komorodistillery.com

Master blender Ian Chang left Kavalan distillery, Taiwan, in 2020 and formed a new company named Karuizawa Distillers Inc. in partnership with businessman Koji Shimaoka. The first stage was realized in 2023 when they opened Komoro distillery in Nagano Prefecture, a sleek architectural design built up in the hills with floor-to-ceiling windows giving the outside world an unrestricted view of the copper pot stills and production area.

The new distillery offers public tours and educational classes for whisky aficionados of all levels. Like Chang's former stills at Kavalan, the Komoro stills were manufactured in Scotland by the famous firm of Forsyth's Ltd. The 10 washbacks will produce batches to feed the 1,320-gallon (5,000-liter) wash still, while the larger 1,900-gallon (7200-liter) spirit still will distill the combined low wines from two runs of the wash still.

Chang has years of experience with Kavalan's fast-maturing stock in a range of sherry, bourbon, port, wine, and STR casks, so Japanese whisky fans can look forward to high-quality Komoro whiskies matured at a cooler altitude in a variety of casks styles when Chang judges they have reached the perfect moment for bottling.

SHIZUOKA

OWNER Gaiaflow Company Ltd

FOUNDED 2016

WEBSITE www.shizuoka-distillery.jp

Situated halfway between Tokyo and Nagoya, Shizuoka distillery was built in a mountainous region by the banks of the Nakakouchi River. Founded in 2016 by

Taiko Nakamura, the distillery boasts washbacks made from Oregon pine and Japanese cedar and two contrasting wash stills. Referred to as pot still K and W, respectively, the first is a 925-gallon (3,500-liter) still formerly used at the closed, but now legendary, Karuizawa distillery; the other is a new wood-fired 1,320-gallon (5,000-liter) still. Forsyth's Ltd built the new wash and spirit stills, making this the only whisky distillery in the world employing a wood-burning, direct-fired wash still. The early output has been a dream for whisky lovers, with compare and contrast releases exploring the differences in spirits made using the different wash stills and the flavor impact of low-yielding Japanese barley versus imported malt.

Shizuoka has two wash stills, including one salvaged from the legendary but now closed Karuizawa distillery.

TASTING NOTES

Shizuoka Pot Still K 100% Imported Barley First Edition
Single malt, matured in a variety of oak casks, 55.5% ABV
Distilled in the former Karuizawa wash still, the nose has lemon, conversation hearts, and grilled peach, with a palate of tangerine, stone fruit, sanded oak, and vanilla ice cream.

Shizuoka Pot Still W 100% Japanese Barley First Edition
Single malt, matured in a variety of oak casks, 55.5% ABV
Like nectar of the gods, this whisky distilled in the wood-fired still has intense aromas of honey, dried mango, and floral notes, with full-bodied flavors of peach, golden syrup, papaya, and jellied fruits and a fruity finish.

Shizuoka Pot Still K 100% Imported Barley First Edition

TAIWAN

Given the huge economic growth across Asia and the growing demand for quality whisky, it was perhaps inevitable that an entrepreneurial nation such as Taiwan would start producing whisky, given the obvious and direct route to the growing Chinese market.

KAVALAN

OWNER The King Car Group

FOUNDED 2006

WEBSITE www.kavalanwhisky.com

The King Car Group is a sizable Taiwanese company that has been making food and drink for more than 60 years. Following the aim of the founder, Mr Tien-Tsai Lee, to own a whisky distillery, the company spent whatever it took to get a high-quality malt whisky to market in the shortest possible time. True to their word, it took only nine months to build the distillery and start producing the spirit, and after just two years, that spirit was being exported. The 20th anniversary of the first spirit run at Kavalan is in 2026.

Producing whisky in a hot climate

Kavalan is named after the first tribe to inhabit the region of Taiwan where the distillery stands and symbolizes sincerity, honesty, and cultivation. When the King Car Group decided to make whisky, it turned to the world's best, bringing in stills from Forsyth's Ltd in Scotland and employing global whisky consultant Dr. Jim Swan (1941–2017) to advise on the distillation and maturation of whisky in a subtropical climate.

There were considerable obstacles to overcome, not least the warm temperatures and high humidity, so the fermenters were fitted with cooling jackets, and Swan acknowledged that the whisky would reach peak maturation in a relatively short period of time, though at the cost of high evaporative losses from the casks. Unlike the cool, consistent musty warehouses of Speyside, there's a high turnover of casks in Kavalan's three warehouses, which in the summer months can be a sultry 84°F (29°C) on the

Kavalan Solist Oloroso Sherry Cask

Kavalan Solist Port Cask

Kavalan distillery was designed with two distinctive pagodas though it doesn't malt its own barley.

ground floor but reach a stifling 107°F (42°C) on the fifth floor where they roll their best sherry casks. Jim Swan was a specialist in overcoming the challenges of making whisky in hot climates and consulted on new distillery projects in India, Israel, Wales, and elsewhere during his illustrious career. He was a talismanic figure to Kavalan, starring in their TV ads, and he always had the longest line of fans waiting for him to sign a bottle and pose for a photo at the annual Kavalan Masters Dialogue event in Taipei. Swan trained Ian Chang (see Komoro, page 243) to run the distillery, and he became Kavalan's master blender and global brand ambassador and the recognizable face of Kavalan at home and abroad for 16 years. Chang commissioned Kavalan's second distillery on the site in Yilan County, substantially expanding their capacity, and he is credited with creating some of their masterpiece bottlings using the finest sherry and Bordeaux wine casks.

King Car operates dozens of Kavalan showrooms across the island, such as Taipei's Zhongxiao

Showroom, where their handsomely boxed whiskies are displayed, akin to the luxury Macallan boutiques and Johnnie Walker House embassies found in other major cities in Asia. Zerose Yang, Kavalan's new senior blender, is now responsible for their expanding range of refined single malt whiskies.

TASTING NOTES

Kavalan Solist Port Cask
Single malt, matured in port casks, 59.4% ABV
The wood interaction draws a lot of color and flavor from the port casks, and this dram basks in dark aromas of vanilla, black cherry, plum, and leather, delivering a high strength, single-cask tasting experience redolent of dark fruits and nuts in the way only a port cask whisky can deliver.

Kavalan Solist Oloroso Sherry Cask
Single malt, matured in an oloroso sherry cask, 58.6% ABV
A rich, syrupy sherry cask whisky with aromas of date, sultanas, nuts, chocolate, and box-pressed cigars on the nose, and lush sherry flavors of black cherry, leather, coffee grounds, and licorice running into a lengthy finish.

NANTOU

OWNER Taiwan Tobacco & Liquor Corporation

FOUNDED 2008

WEBSITE www.omarwhisky.com/tw

Nantou Winery includes a state-owned distillery in Nantou County, where they produce whisky using imported two-row barley from the UK. The distillery has four moderate-size copper pot stills, and they use a lower barrel entry proof to mitigate the climate's influence on maturation. They market the Omar and

Yushan nonage statement range of Taiwanese whiskies, including traditional cask strength, peated expressions, and some idiosyncratic finishes using lychee liqueur and orange brandy barrels from the winery.

TASTING NOTE

Omar Bourbon Cask
Single malt, matured in bourbon casks, 46% ABV
Banana chips, coconut, and cilantro, but some astringent oak notes detract from the overall olfactory experience. The palate is sweet and fruity, with bright citrus, stone fruits, crème caramel, and spice, with a finish of fruit chews.

Omar Bourbon Cask

NORTH KOREA

Sea of Japan (East Sea)

SEOUL ○ ■ **Three Societies**

Daejeon ○

Yellow Sea

SOUTH KOREA

○ Busan

Korea Strait JAPAN

SOUTH KOREA

Koreans have a strong drinking culture that exists between friends and co-workers. Soju, the Korean rice spirit, is the most popular liquor consumed, but a growing number of Koreans have discovered whisky in recent years, especially the allure of imported luxury blends and brands of high-status single malt Scotch. Now the country produces its own whisky, with a new distillery taking its first steps on the world whisky stage.

THREE SOCIETIES

Ki One Batch 3

OWNER Bryan Do

FOUNDED 2020

WEBSITE www.threesocieties.co.kr

When the Three Societies distillery opened in 2020, it became the first Korean craft distillery to make single malt whisky. The spirit of the distillery draws strength from three different cultures: Scotland, through master distiller Andrew Shand who brings his Scotch whisky experience from working at Chivas Brothers and elsewhere; South Korea, through the Korean distillery operatives; and from the US, through founder and CEO Korean American Bryan Do, a former Microsoft executive who escaped corporate life to follow his dream of making craft beer and spirits.

Forsyth's Ltd supplied the pair of copper pot stills for their airy stillhouse, and Shand and assistant distiller Byeongsu Kim distill by following the conventions of a traditional single malt Scotch distillery, using malted barley imported from the UK. The spirit is filled into bourbon and new American oak casks from Kentucky and oloroso and PX sherry casks from Europe. With no need to wait a minimum of three years before bottling, the early batches of Ki One and single cask releases have been bottled at a young age but show plenty of promise..

TASTING NOTE

Ki One Batch 3
Single malt, matured in oloroso sherry hogshead casks, 56.9% ABV
The sherry cask is successful at tempering the spicy young spirit. Here, the aromas swirl with nutty fruitcake, walnut, and strawberry licorice, with a balance of marmalade, date, and chocolate notes proving a great foil for the pepperiness.

CHINA

As a whisky market, China continues to grow in importance. Scotch whisky companies have invested a lot of resources to establish a strong position for their brands to attract the increasingly affluent Chinese consumer. The next phase is production, with both Chinese and international drink companies racing to make Chinese whisky at their own distilleries and cultivate a new spirit of whisky tourism and tasting experiences.

THE CHUAN DISTILLERY

OWNER Pernod Ricard

FOUNDED 2021

WEBSITE www.pernod-ricard-china.com

The Chuan distillery started production in Emeishan, Sichuan Province in 2021. Committing to a 1 billion RMB ($152 million) investment over a decade, Pernod Ricard became the first international drinks group to open a distillery in China. Master distiller Yang Tao uses malted Chinese and European barley and matures the new-make spirit in bourbon, Spanish sherry, and Chinese oak casks. The distillery uses 100 percent renewable energy and offsets emissions to reduce its carbon footprint. The Chuan Pure Malt was launched into the Chinese market just over two years after production started, a blend of their own young spirit and imported Scotch whiskies. No single malt has yet been released.

ERYUAN

OWNER Diageo plc

FOUNDED 2021

WEBSITE www.diageo.com

Diageo is building its first Chinese malt whisky distillery in Eryuan in Yunnan Province in high-altitude surroundings 6,900ft (2,100m) above sea level. The production water will come from a natural spring that flows into the beautiful Erhai Lake. In such natural surroundings, Diageo has put sustainability at its heart, promising a carbon-neutral, zero-waste site running on renewable energy. Aside from Scotland, Diageo makes whisky in Ireland, Canada, the US, and India, and through Distill Ventures, it invests in distilleries in England, Australia, and Japan. With Camus and Angus Dundee Distillers also building new single malt whisky facilities in China, Diageo has joined the race to define the signature style of Chinese whisky. Though no single malt from Eryuan distillery has yet been released, the competition to be the leader in this field is going to speed up significantly by the end of the decade.

GOALONG LIQUOR DISTILLERY

OWNER Goalong Group

FOUNDED 2011

WEBSITE www.goalongliquor.com

The first large-scale malt whisky distillery in China, Goalong is situated in Liyuang City, south of Wuhan. The current distiller Luo Feng has been maturing whisky in a variety of casks for the domestic market, though the long-term goal is to create an international-known whisky brand.

TASTING NOTE

Goalong 5-Year-Old Bourbon Cask Aged
Single malt, matured in bourbon casks, 40% ABV
Deliciously well made. Lemon meringue pie, sweet vanilla, florals, and fudge dominate the nose with a palate of sweet melon, lemon drops, vanilla cream, caramel sauce, citrus, black pepper, and lemon.

INDIA

India now commands a position as one of the most highly respected world whisky nations on the international stage. While the domestic market still demands imported Scotch whiskies and the more economic molasses-based Indian whiskies blended with imported whisky, the companies that opened up the international export markets have done so with Indian single malts.

AMRUT

Amrut Spectrum

OWNER Amrut Distilleries Ltd

FOUNDED 1948

WEBSITE www.amrutdistilleries.com

The best-known Indian whisky brand outside of India, Amrut single malt launched in 2004, making the company one of the leading pioneers of world whisky. The family-owned distillery was established in Bangalore in 1948 to provide inexpensive alcohol for the military and grew into a producer of molasses-based blended whisky for the Indian market. Amrut became known for its Indian brandy, however, made with grapes too rich in tannin to be sold as wine but the base for a full and tasty brandy.

Indian whisky goes global

The malt whisky resulted from Rakshit N. Jagdale, grandson of the distillery's founder, who assessed the UK as a test market for Indian whisky for his MBA thesis at Newcastle University, exploring whether it would be possible to take malts to Newcastle and sell Indian whisky in Britain. While studying, Jagdale persuaded his classmate to join the endeavor, and Ashok Chokalingam went to work to sell Amrut Indian single malt to the world. Given the respect for Amrut in the whisky community, it is hard to recall just how groundbreaking this was for world whisky.

Chokalingam was a one-man band back then, a hardworking brand ambassador traveling around the world spreading the word about Indian whisky using any means possible. One year at WhiskyFest, New York, during Amrut's early years, Chokalingam brought T-shirts branded with the Amrut logo to the stand and began to hand them out for free as people enjoyed a pour of Amrut whisky. Already armed with a Glencairn glass in one hand and a WhiskyFest program in the other, the grateful attendees chose to slip it over whatever they were wearing instead of carrying it around. As they circulated among the stands, others would come up to them to ask for directions to the Amrut stand so they too could grab a T-shirt and sample the whisky—Chokalingam was busy on the stand pouring whisky all night long. This genius move resulted in hundreds of whisky lovers walking around the ballroom promoting the Amrut brand for the duration of the event. Long before social media, Amrut went viral with textiles.

A stream of innovative new ideas

Chokalingam became Amrut's new master blender following the departure of Surrinder Kumar (see Indri, page 253), who trained him in the art of whisky-making. A steady stream of innovative ideas come to fruition in their new releases—from Amrut Spectrum finished in a chimeric barrel created by the coopering challenge of raising barrels from staves of multiple different types of wood to the citrus charms of Amrut Naarangi disgorged from sherry casks seasoned with wine and orange peel. Then there is their commitment to making peated whiskies, the joys of the Amrut rye and Amrut single grain expressions, their becoming an independent bottler with their curated Single Malts of India range, and finally, the intercontinental maturation program behind Amrut Two Continents. Amrut is not afraid to push the boundaries.

TASTING NOTES

Amrut Bagheera
Single malt, finished in sherry casks, 46% ABV
Enticing aromas of ripe banana with deeper notes of hazelnut, prune, and coffee, a theme that develops on the palate with deep, satisfying flavors of dried vine fruits, baked apple, plum, and leather, and an array of bright spices.

Amrut Spectrum
Single malt, finished in a spectrum cask, made of 4 stave types: new American oak, new French oak, oloroso sherry wood, and Pedro Ximénez sherry wood, 50% ABV
A melange of prune, fig, date, and black cherry with baked orchard fruits and punchy spices.

Amrut Rye
Rye, matured in American oak casks, 50% ABV
The aromas of cereals, bread crust, and nutty rye bread result from the malted rye used. Butter toffee popcorn notes provide a counterpoint to the rye spices, chocolate, and black tea flavors, leaving behind a lingering spicy finish.

WHISKY TALES

Environmental Concerns
Amrut distillery takes environmental responsibilities seriously and wastes almost nothing. It has cut its energy consumption significantly and recycles as much as it can. In a country where water is a precious resource, Amrut draws water from a deep aquifer and transports it to the distillery, and it has invested in water conservation equipment. TI has long-standing partnerships with its farmers to ensure the health of the soil, but the food miles for the malted barley harvested in northern India to the distillery is considerable, though it hasn't traveled as far as the peated malt that comes in from Scotland.

Amrut Bagheera

PAUL JOHN

Paul John Oloroso Select Cask

OWNER John Distilleries Ltd

FOUNDED 2012

WEBSITE www.pauljohnwhisky.com

John Distilleries Ltd was founded in 1996 and now produces a portfolio of wines and spirits in seven states across the southern half of India. They supply the substantial and competitive Indian market with Original Choice; a molasses-based Indian whisky and their biggest seller domestically.

The mission for malt

Company chairman Paul John had grander global ambitions in mind, however, and set out to make "The Great Indian Single Malt." The distillery is located in Cuncolim, Goa, close to Goa's stunning coastline, popular with tourists and backpackers for its world-class beaches and excellent cuisine. Paul John launched as a new single malt brand in the UK in 2012 and has grown strongly, picking up awards over its first decade of exports. US company Sazerac increased its interests to 43 percent of the company in 2019, though Paul John remains the company owner. With India whisky performing well both at home and abroad, John Distilleries announced plans to double production for Paul John single malt whisky in 2023.

Paul John's master distiller Michael D'Souza has a preference for using Indian six-row barley for the qualities the husks bring to the process, which he finds creates a richer, oilier spirit and worth the sacrifice of the lower alcohol yield relative to milling imported two-row barley. Their peated malts use imported malt from Scotland; however, the peats cut from commercially harvested peat mosses and bogs in Aberdeenshire and Islay. Paul John's production water pours into the stainless steel mash tun, drawn from the mountains of the Western Ghats and naturally filtered through the region's wetlands. In the stillroom, the wash still has a noticeable bulging boil ball relative to the plain design of the spirit still, with an upward-sloping lyne arm and shell and tube condensers.

D'Souza has been making whisky since 2009 and has mastered the fast maturation and high evaporation that occurs to the spirit inside the casks in the Paul John warehouse. While there have been single-digit age statements on independent bottlings

Paul John's wash still has a bulging boil ball and an upsloping lyne arm.

of their single cask releases, the climate in this part of India means drinkers waiting for age statements on the official bottlings are rather missing the point.

Whiskies at standard and cask strength

Their core line is bottled at 46 percent and includes Paul John Brilliance, an unpeated expression matured in bourbon casks; Paul John Edited, which includes a hint of peat in the recipe; and Paul John Bold, made using malt peated to 25ppm. Paul John Nirvana is an affordable and approachable entry-level whisky made from unpeated malt and bottled at 40 percent.

More experienced palates should take their time to work through the Paul John Select series of cask strength expressions for a more sophisticated pour. The Classic Select Cask is unpeated and bourbon cask-matured, and there are other Select Cask expressions to explore, matured in PX sherry and oloroso sherry, and a Peated Select Cask expression. Each year, they release a Christmas edition, often showcasing a different cask finish and variable amounts of peat smoke. Previous years have included an oloroso sherry finish, PX sherry finish, and recipes drawing on casks of Paul John matured in brandy, port, and Madeira barrels. Topping the range is their Zodiac series of limited editions, such as Kanya by Paul John, which was aged for around seven years in American oak and named for the counterpoint to Virgo, the sixth Zodiac sign. Mithuna by Paul John

was named after the third Zodiac sign of Indian astrology, and the counterpoint to Gemini, an unpeated expression initially matured in new American oak casks and finished in bourbon barrels. Indian whisky is attracting an attentive global audience, and Paul John is at the vanguard as one of the leaders in the field.

TASTING NOTES

Paul John Oloroso Select Cask
Single malt, matured in oloroso sherry casks, 48% ABV
The sherry cask delivers notes of blood orange, figs, sultanas, and spice on the nose, the palate reveling in flavors of fruitcake, citrus, and chocolate, ending on a creamy finish sprinkled with spices.

Paul John Classic Select Cask
Single malt, matured in bourbon casks, 55.2% ABV
This cask strength unpeated Paul John whisky showcases apple pie, chocolate, and honey, though do experiment with adding water, as it helps to conjure up the tropical fruitiness, coffee notes, and a hint of spice.

Paul John Christmas Edition 2023
Single malt, finished in tawny port casks, 46% ABV
Each year, Paul John serve up a Christmas treat, and 2023 was no exception. Christmas cake, vanilla, plums, citrus, plain chocolate, and baking spices on the nose, and a palate rich in red fruits, orange, milk chocolate, and dried fruits with coffee, chocolate, and black fruits to finish.

Paul John Classic Select Cask

RAMPUR

OWNER Radico Khaitan Ltd

FOUNDED 1943

WEBSITE www.rampursinglemalt.com

The Rampur Distillery in Uttar Pradesh makes large volumes of molasses-based extra neutral alcohol and grain whisky. The distillery is one of the oldest in India, dating from 1943, but in 1996, the company added a single malt distillery. In 2016, they judged it was time to launch their own Indian single malt whisky brand and export it to parts of the world that were already becoming excited about Indian single malt whiskies from Amrut and Paul John. The inaugural whisky was named Rampur Select and won many accolades.

Rampur Double Cask

A new venture: Indian single malts

The single malt is made from six-row barley from neighboring areas. The three yeast strains create floral, fruity, and even tropical fruit notes in the spirit. The long fermentation also helps bring out the pronounced fruitiness in the spirit. There are four copper pot stills and a spirit still with a wide boil ball, a conical neck, and the option of two condensers that can help switch to spirits lighter or heavier in character.

The company has made great strides in improving its processes in line with its sustainability goals, especially with regards to generating biogas from waste products to use to generate steam and power. They have focused on their water consumption and the impact on the environment and strive toward greater water stewardship through rainwater harvesting and other projects.

Their second whisky was Rampur Double Cask, named for the bourbon casks and European oak sherry casks used in its maturation, followed by Rampur Asava, which combined whisky matured in Indian Cabernet Sauvignon casks and bourbon casks to produce a highly satisfying dram with delightful aromatics. Entering the world of global travel retail, they launched Rampur Trigun, a harmonious triple cask expression that combines their fruity whisky matured in American oak bourbon casks, Champagne casks, and Sauternes barrels. The team also produce the Jaisalmer Indian Craft Gin and Rampur Sangam World Malt Whisky. Sangam is an East-meets-West blended malt that combines single malt whiskies from distilleries in Europe and the New World with their own Rampur single malt. The range continues to expand with carefully thought-out releases; Rampur is refined and unhurried, ensuring quality over quantity as they build a world-class portfolio.

TASTING NOTES

Rampur Asava

Single malt, matured in bourbon and Indian Cabernet Sauvignon casks, 45% ABV
Master distiller Anup Barik finds balance with the Cabernet Sauvignon wine cask influences serving up aromas of damson plum, blackberry, and dark vanilla with a charming palate with cherry accents and delightful notes of honey and candied orange.

Rampur Double Cask

Single malt, matured in bourbon and European oak sherry casks, 45% ABV
Rampur's innate fruitiness shines here, with citrus, apple, and tropical fruit aromas, which are realized on the palate with sweet toffee flavors, zested lime, and some spices adding support.

GODAWAN

OWNER Diageo plc

FOUNDED 2021

WEBSITE www.godawansinglemalt.com

Godawan is a new luxury brand named after the critically endangered Great Indian Bustard that makes its home in Rajasthan. The finishing casks are seasoned with Ayurvedic botanicals. United Spirits Ltd, a Diageo subsidiary, produce the whiskies from locally harvested six-row barley in Alwar, Rajasthan.

TASTING NOTES

Godawan Series 01 Rich and Rounded
Single malt, first matured in PX sherry casks with a portion finished in botanical seasoned bourbon casks, 46% ABV
A bold whisky. Aromas of fig, cola, and exotic spices, with flavors of prune, dried vine fruits, licorice, and leather.

Godawan Series 02 Fruit and Spice
Single malt, initially matured in a cherrywood cask, then finished in botanical seasoned bourbon casks, 46% ABV
Floral and fruity aromas of stone fruits, citrus, and nutmeg, with a palate of red fruits, orchard fruit, and spices.

Godawan Series 01 Rich and Rounded

INDRI

Indri Trini—The Three Wood

OWNER Piccadily Distilleries

FOUNDED 2012

WEBSITE www.piccadily.com

Indri, one of Piccadily's three distilleries in the north of India, sits in Haryana State in the Himalayan foothills. The international breakthrough whisky was Indri Trini (meaning "three wood"), created by master blender Surrinder Kumar, the former Amrut master distiller and master blender, and made from organic six-row local barley.

Piccadily is now the largest independent producer of malt spirits in India. Built in 2012, the distillery is equipped with three lantern-shaped wash stills and three onion-shaped spirit stills and can produce 1.05 million gallons (4 million liters) of spirit per annum. Impressively, it meets all of its energy requirements from renewables and doesn't burn any fossil fuels.

TASTING NOTE

Indri Trini —The Three Wood
Single malt, matured in first-fill bourbon, French wine, and Pedro Ximénez sherry casks, 46% ABV
Dive in to aromas of plum, black cherry, and chocolate on the nose, and then savor the harmony of flavors of vanilla, citrus peel, hazelnut, and cassis ahead of a dark, fruity mouth-coating finish.

KHODAYS

OWNER Khoday India Ltd

FOUNDED 1965

WEBSITE www.khodayindia.com

Khoday is a diverse manufacturing company based in Bangalore that produces a number of beers and distilled liquors. The company fought a long legal battle with the Scotch Whisky Association over their Peter Scot brand, launched in 1968, due to the labeling and the word "Scot" in the name. Khodays Black is the export name of the Peter Scot Black.

TASTING NOTE

Khodays Black
Single malt, matured in oak casks, 42.8% ABV
Muted notes of caramel, granola, flaky pastries, and ground ginger. Light-bodied with Bramley apple peelings, toffee, vanilla, and spice. Hard to see this switching experienced single malt lovers on to Indian whiskies.

AUSTRALIA

REGIONAL STYLES
Despite the overall diversity, there is a core style emerging—single malt whisky matured in casks previously used in the production of tawny, red wine, and apera. Across the country, the Australian whisky industry has acknowledged the First Nations Peoples and their elders and made efforts to show its respect for their living culture.

AUTHOR'S CHOICE
As a pioneer of Australian whisky that has stayed true to its roots, BAKERY HILL is producing one of Australia's great single malts, while the gentle spirit of HELLYERS ROAD is also highly recommended. With superior global distribution, STARWARD is the torchbearer for Australian whisky internationally; their expressions demonstrate a great deal of creativity. The early MANLY SPIRITS CO. bottlings also show a great deal of promise.

REGIONAL EVENTS
Australia has a packed calendar of whisky events that showcase a combination of Scotch, Japanese, and Australian whiskies. From Tasmanian Whisky Week, Whisky Abbey in Melbourne, Sydney Spirits Festival, and the Scotch Malt Whisky Society, to events such as Whisky Live and The Whisky Show that tour the country, there's plenty of opportunity to meet the people behind the whisky over a dram.

The vast country of Australia is known for its harsh and extremely hot climate, conditions totally unsuited for whisky production—or so it may seem. Fifty years ago, nobody considered it to be suited to decent wine production either, and look what happened. And, in fact, Tasmania, to the south of the mainland, is just about perfect for making grain spirit, with an abundance of water, a mild climate, lots of peat, and ideal conditions for farming grain. Victoria has also proved to be a garden for Australia, and whisky is flourishing here, too, using casks seasoned with native wine and spirits and taking full advantage of the climate to accelerate maturation.

The practice of making Australian whisky fizzled out toward the end of the last century, but the Australian distillery scene has welcomed a raft of new openings over the last decade. Many of them are small-scale operations without the inventory to supply stocks beyond the local market yet, but with the older pioneering distilleries celebrating their 20th and 25th anniversaries, there is now a spirited whisky culture in Australia, with some fantastic festivals, bars, and distillery visitor centers to see on Australian soil.

But it's been a bumpy ride for some distilleries, with few of the well-known ones still in the hands of their founders. With a lack of competitors exporting Australian whiskies to the US and Europe, Starward

and Morris currently stand out as the main Australian whisky available to drinkers there. Australian distillers also have access to substantial neighboring markets for whisky across Asia that are much closer to home. In whisky markets like the US and UK, Australian whisky imports arrive in small batches, and there can be gaps of many years without fresh supplies. Given their high retail prices relative to Scotch and bourbon, turnover has been slow, making retailers reluctant to restock. Increasingly, independent bottlers such as Berry Bros. & Rudd and That Boutique-y Whisky Company are recognizing the gap in the UK market and filling it with their own single cask bottlings of Australian whisky.

Starward is one of Australia's whisky success stories and takes a thoroughly modern approach to distilling.

GETTING AROUND

In view of the size of Australia, it's very difficult to find a suitable base for exploration of its whisky. The best place to start is the city of Melbourne, known for its vibrant food and drink culture, followed by a trip to Hobart, on the island of Tasmania. Hobart can be reached by flights from Sydney and Melbourne, and you'll need to rent a car, take an organized tour, or hire a private guide to take you on a custom tour of the places you want to visit.

N

Timor Sea

Indian Ocean

Darwin

Cape York

Gulf of Carpentaria

Coral Sea

Kununurra

Lake Argyle

Tanami Desert

Great Dividing Range

Derby

Cairns

Broome

Townsville

Port Hedland

Great Sandy Desert

AUSTRALIA

Mount Isa City

Mackay

Lake Mackay

NORTHERN TERRITORY

Gibson Desert

Alice Springs

QUEENSLAND

Uluru (Ayers Rock) ▲

Great Barrier Reef

WESTERN AUSTRALIA

Lake Eyre

Brisbane

Toowoomba

Great Victoria Desert

SOUTH AUSTRALIA

Gold Coast

Lake Gairdner

Lake Torrens

Darling

Macquarie

Nullarbor Plain

NEW SOUTH WALES

Perth

Murray

Lachlan

Newcastle

■ Manly Spirits
●
Sydney

Great Dividing Range

Albany

Great Australian Bight

Adelaide

Morris ■

Canberra

AUSTRALIAN CAPITAL TERRITORY

VICTORIA

■ **Gospel**

Melbourne

■ **Bakery Hill**

Geelong

■ **Starward**

Tasman Sea

Bass Strait

TASMANIA

Hobart

SEE INSET

Marrawah

Cape Barren Island

Hellyers Road ■

George Town

Devonport

A10

A5

Launceston

TASMANIA

Great Lake

Tasman Sea

Strahan

TASMANIA

Lake Gordon

Lark ■

Killara

Hobart ●

Lake Pedder

■ **Sullivan's Cove**

Overeem ■

Bruny Island

0	25	50 miles

0	50	100 km

0	100	200	300	400 miles

0	100	400	600	800 km

STARWARD

OWNER New World Whisky Distillery Pty Ltd

FOUNDED 2007

WEBSITE www.starward.com.au

David Vitale founded Starward, which is now an urban distillery in Port Melbourne, a coastal suburb of Melbourne, Victoria. Energized by the city's renowned food and drink culture, the distillery moved to its current location in 2016 following investment from Distill Ventures in 2015, and it has been upgraded and enlarged further since then.

A single malt distillery

Starward is first and foremost a single malt distillery, using Australian malted barley and freshly emptied Australian wine and fortified wine barrels. While cooperages supply wineries in the Barossa Valley and elsewhere with American and French oak barrels, the Australian whisky industry is not bound to the ubiquitous bourbon cask for its maturation needs as elsewhere. Starward favors full maturation in wine casks, in particular favoring red wine, tawny (the Australian equivalent of port), or apera casks (the Australian equivalent of sherry).

As the business has grown, Starward's distilling capacity has increased; production director Sam Slaney and his team now have 6,600-gallon (25,000-liter) fermenters and a fine pair of Italian-made copper pot stills at their disposal. Their production setup is designed to mitigate the vagaries of Melbourne's temperature swings, with cooling jackets fitted to the fermenters and the neck of the still. Turning on the cooling jacket encourages greater reflux during distillation, which results in a lighter spirit, but producing a heavier style of spirit with less reflux is equally straightforward—no jacket required.

This is a part of the country where whisky matures quickly and can be sold after two years in the cask, as the ABV climbs in the dry heat. The whiskies are matured for three years, though they develop much more color and flavor in cask in Melbourne than the equivalent cask would in the cooler climate of Scotland over the same time period.

The full effect of red wine cask maturation is best experienced through their core range bottlings of Starward Left Field and their signature Starward Nova expression. They also have an experimental side, showcased by Starward Two Fold, which uses malted barley and wheat, and Starward Ginger Beer Cask Finish, a combination of Starward Nova and Solera whiskies, which is finished in French and American oak casks seasoned with ginger beer.

Starward Solera

Starward 100 Proof

TASTING NOTES

Starward 100 Proof
Single malt, matured in Australian red wine American oak casks, 50% ABV
Strawberry preserves, ginger loaf, black currant, new leather, and light milk chocolate on the nose, like the dome of a newly unwrapped Mallowmars cookie. The mouthfeel is creamy, with cooked apple, pear, black pepper, and clove, the dense, flavorsome texture opening up with vanilla and red berries, notably red currant, strawberry, and raspberry, with a sticky, fruity finish, though water brings out a little chocolate, date, and dried fig.

Starward Solera
Single malt, matured in an apera solera system, 43% ABV
Well balanced on the nose, with plum, citrus peel, floral bouquets, raisin, dark chocolate, and vanilla cream. The best of their mainstream releases, this displays a beautiful balance of stone fruit, citrus, vanilla, red licorice, Red Hots, and a lingering trail of black pepper and summer red berries chased by cinnamon fireballs.

LARK

OWNER Lark Distilling Co. Ltd

FOUNDED 1992

WEBSITE www.larkdistillery.com

Lark was one of the founding names in the modern renaissance of Australian whisky, as Bill Lark campaigned to overturn a 150-year-old prohibition law in order to start making single malt whisky in Hobart, Tasmania. Fast-maturing, small barrel single-cask releases received positive reviews. Peat was dug and used to flavor barley that had been already malted, by wetting it again and smoking it with peat. Australian whisky became a hot topic. Bill Lark and

head distiller Chris Thomson's enthusiasm was infectious, Bill's daughter Kristy became the distillery's general manager, and it looked like Lark and its little distillery in Cambridge had the (whisky) world at its feet.

A difficult decade

The next decade didn't exactly go according to plan. The Larks sold the business in 2013, and after a while, Kristy was made redundant. With a strong brand but little inventory, Lark's new owners began to acquire other Tasmanian distilleries to build up their portfolio. Investment companies began pumping money into the industry to try and back a future winner, sensing the potential for Australian whisky to make similar inroads into the world of whisky as Australian wine had made on the wine world. Then in a complicated story, Nant Whisky collapsed amid a scandal that played out publicly in the press. With the subsequent boardroom dramas, uproar, and exposés in the holding company that owned Lark distillery, it felt like few people were talking about the whisky anymore.

New beginnings

Years later, Lark is now rebranded and repositioned as a luxury Australian whisky, under a publicly listed holding company renamed the Lark Distilling Co. Ltd, albeit one that operates from a different location from Lark's origins. The company's new main production and visitor facilities are in Pontville, 30 minutes north of Hobart, after the company purchased the Shene Estate and Distillery. Lark Distilling Co. still has the Cambridge facility from Bill Lark's days, as well as the Bothwell distillery, formerly Nant, and it has used the stocks in their inventory to create blends of Tasmanian whiskies.

TASTING NOTE

Berry Bros. & Rudd Lark 2015
Single malt, matured in a tawny cask, 60.1% ABV
This independent bottling of Lark, one of the rare bottlings available in the UK, feels tightly wound at cask strength with aromas of rose hip, rowan jelly, crab apple, pretty floral notes, cracked black pepper, five spice, and ramen broth. Chocolate and baked fruit with nippy peppery and clove spices at cask strength, dilution helps to produce flavors of fruit chews and portlike flavors with quince jelly on the finish. It's slightly austere until more sweetness emerges in the latter stages, so be liberal with the water to unlock the cranberry sweetness, nectarine, and milk chocolate flavors.

Berry Bros & Rudd Lark 2015

BAKERY HILL

OWNER David Baker

FOUNDED 1998

WEBSITE www.bakeryhill.com

David Baker founded this distillery in Bayswater, Victoria, in 1998 on the eastern edge of Melbourne. After 24 years, David and his son Andrew crossed the city to a more central location in Kensington, where they added a second still to their operations. Now, there are tours of the new distillery and the bottlings have been updated with a fresh new look. Independent and family owned, Bakery Hill eschew the full wine cask maturation style practiced at many contemporary Australian distilleries.

The signature range of Classic, Double Wood, and Peated (using peated malt from Scotland) are aged for 6–8 years and have stood the test of time, with Classic and Peated also available at cask strength. There are also popular seasonal releases and rare bottlings sold locally, but these tend to sell out quickly.

TASTING NOTES

Bakery Hill Classic Malt
Single malt, matured in bourbon casks, 46% ABV
Lemon curd, honey, vanilla sponge, candied orange, pears in syrup, and baked sugar on the nose. Delicately spiced. It's divine, reminiscent of old Rosebank and Littlemill, with flavors of *tarte au citron*, clotted cream, vanilla, peppercorn, pie crust, custard, and lime and orange peel notes.

Bakery Hill Double Wood
Single malt, finished in French oak casks, 46% ABV
Apricot, floral, Chantilly cream, Strawberry Hubba Bubba, and baking spice on the nose. The palate brings fresh raspberries in cream, clove, black pepper, cherry jam, creamed banana, orange water, and plum mousse. Creamy finish with zesty highlights.

WHISKY TALES

The Cost of Gold
Bakery Hill distillery is named after the gold miners' uprising in 1854 and the bloody aftermath that saw at least 22 miners and 5 soldiers killed when the military stormed the Eureka stockade. The area had become a magnet for miners in the gold rush, who were forced to buy expensive licenses for relatively small plots of land irrespective of whether they actually found gold. Without voting rights, the miners felt this practice was an unjustifiable tax. Finally, a group of miners rebelled under a blue Southern Cross flag, but after days of standoffs, order was restored by government.

GOSPEL

OWNER Ben Bowles and Andrew Fitzgerald

FOUNDED 2015

WEBSITE www.thegospelwhiskey.com

Australian distilleries are mostly making single malt whisky, but there are distillers trying their hand at other styles such as Hunter Island and Transportation Whiskey, both in Tasmania, and their single pot still whiskeys, a style associated with Irish whiskey. Belgrove distillery, in Tasmania; Archie Rose Distilling, in New South Wales; Backwoods Distilling, in Victoria: and Great Southern Distilling Co., in Western Australia, are making rye whiskey, which is usually associated with whiskey from the United States. Master distiller Ian Thorn, a former Starward distiller, makes Gospel straight rye whiskey from single farm 100 percent unmalted Australian Mallee-grown rye on a continuous column still, matching all the US legal requirements for straight rye whiskey. He fills it into heavily toasted charred new American oak casks and lets it mature in the changable north Melbourne climate where the temperature swings encourage plenty of oak contact.

Gospel operates a solera maturation system to create their Gospel Solera Rye and occasionally bless the world with their experimental limited releases.

TASTING NOTE

That Boutique-y Whisky Company Gospel Rye 3-Year-Old
Rye, finished in Australian red wine casks, 58.6% ABV
This independent Gospel bottling made with 51% unmalted rye and 49% malted barley has a nose of nutty rye bread, herbal notes, chocolate muffin, spicy tobacco, leather, and vanilla seeds. It revels in a thick, velvety texture with flavors of dark toffee, rich fruit syrups, prune, fruit flans, chocolate, black cherry, allspice, and clove, with a spicy finish of oak tannins and black licorice wheels.

That Boutique-y Whisky Company Gospel Rye 3-Year-Old

HELLYERS ROAD

OWNER Hellyers Road Distillery Pty Ltd

FOUNDED 1999

WEBSITE www.hellyersroad.com.au

Hellyers Road is a large distillery in Emu Valley that has the advantage of being able to print age statements on their northwest Tasmanian whiskies. It's named after Englishman Henry Hellyer who surveyed Tasmania's interior in the 1820s, and their inspiration comes from his determination and spirit. The distillery uses Tasmanian barley and now does its own mashing. They practice double and triple distillation, using curious stainless steel stills, where only the necks and lyne arms provide the necessary copper contact.

Hellyers Road is a soft whisky with gentle stone fruit aromas, typically matured in bourbon, sherry, tawny, and wine casks. They also make peated and slightly peated expressions, and there are some beautifully labeled limited editions.

TASTING NOTES

Hellyers Road Double Cask
Single malt, finished in French oak Pinot Noir casks, 46.2% ABV
Picking up plenty of color and aromas from the secondary maturation, the wine cask serves up black grape, cherry, plum, and attractive floral notes, with hints of zested orange and white pepper. There's a beautiful fresh fruit delivery, with citrus zest, light honey, tangy peels, rolling cask spices, red apple, pear, and cherry, leaving a smooth, polished finish.

Hellyers Road Twin Oak
Single malt, matured in bourbon and French oak port casks, 48.9% ABV
Vanilla, black pepper, lemon biscuits, and candied orange aromas, with a palate of vanilla, dried apricot, cherry clafoutis, orange peel, peppercorn, butter caramel, and cinnamon fudge. A spicy finish with golden baked fruit.

Hellyers Road Slightly Peated 15-Year-Old
Single malt, matured in new charred American oak casks, 46.2% ABV
Mild smoke, lemon drops, and dried seaweed on the nose, with barley sugar, gingersnap, cinnamon, and vanilla on first sip, though mouth-drawing, followed by orange peel, smoky spices, and heather honey, with aromatic peat smoke and citrus on the finish.

Hellyers Road Double Cask

KILLARA

OWNER Kristy Booth-Lark

FOUNDED 2016

WEBSITE www.killaradistillery.com

Kristy Booth-Lark founded her own boutique distillery in 2016 to make single malt whisky, gin, and other premium spirits. As the daughter of Bill and Lyn Lark, she is a second-generation distiller with years of experience. Killara is situated in Richmond, north of Hobart. Distillation takes place in a compact copper pot still with the condenser at the top of the still, rather than at the side. Killara is small scale, handcrafted, and independent, with a strong focus on single cask bottlings.

In common with the early days of Tasmanian distilling, many whiskies are matured in smaller volume casks than is typical practice in Scotland, Kentucky, or Japan. Consumers are able to purchase 5¼-gallon (20-liter) Killara casks of new-made spirit, which will mature quickly. In 2024, Booth-Lark released her oldest whisky to date with KD19, a 6½-year-old single malt, matured in a port cask.

TASTING NOTE

Killara Distillery Single Cask KD60
Single malt, matured in a tawny cask, finished in an Australian rum cask, 50% ABV
A dark amber whisky with a reddish hue, it's slightly herbal on the nose, with cumin, red chili flakes, dried cherries, and aromas of new leather. Beautifully smooth on the palate, with plum, creamy vanilla, tropical fruit sweetness, and gentle spices.

Killara Distillery Single Cask KD60

MANLY SPIRITS CO.

OWNER David Whittaker and Vanessa Wilton

FOUNDED 2017

WEBSITE www.manlyspirits.com.au

David Whittaker and Vanessa Wilton founded Manly Spirits Co. in a northern suburb of Sydney, where they make whisky, gin, and vodka inspired by the coastal lifestyle that can be enjoyed beside the New South Wales shoreline. Their whisky, Coastal Stone, was launched in 2021 and is made in a pair of copper pot stills named after their sons. Whiskies are matured up to 5 years old, and they produce their Nor'Easter signature bottling, an Elements series showcasing whiskies from different 26–52-gallon (100–200-liter) cask types, and an Italian Luxe series matured in

Montepulciano, Aglianico, and Sangiovese casks. This is an environmentally conscious outfit with solar panels, a refill program at the cellar door, and upcycling of their bottles. The contemporary look and feel of their bottles encapsulates the weathered texture of the local sandstone cliffs.

TASTING NOTE

Manly Spirits Coastal Stone Nor'easter
Single malt, matured in charred red wine, American, and French oak casks, 46% ABV
A beauty. An invigorating nose—apricot, peach, sea spray, black pepper, Golden Delicious apple, vanilla custard, and floral notes. Well-developed fruit flavors on the palate, with panna cotta, pear, and five spice, it remains as thick as double cream with notes of apple peelings and a lengthy mouth-coating finish of rich, creamy vanilla and spice.

Manly Spirits Coastal Stone
Nor'Easter

MORRIS

Morris Single Malt Muscat Barrels

OWNER Casella Family Brands

FOUNDED 2016

WEBSITE www.morriswhisky.com

Based in Rutherglen, Victoria, halfway between Melbourne and Canberra, Morris has been making wines and fortified wines since 1859 and branched out into whisky in 2016.

Making full use of the used barrels from the winery, they use a reconditioned hybrid pot and column still system from the 1930s to produce their spirit. Two core bottlings were exported initially, which they have bolstered through an active program of cellar door exclusives and limited edition releases such as the Morris Smoked Sherry Barrel and the Morris Smoked Muscat Barrel.

TASTING NOTE

Morris Single Malt Muscat Barrels
Single malt, finished in Morris fortified Muscat casks, 48% ABV
Deep, fruity aromas of plum, strawberry, and dried vine fruits in dark, sweet syrup, with a palate of prunes, baked fruit, fig, cinnamon, and treacle.

OVEREEM

OWNER Jane and Mark Sawford

FOUNDED 2007

WEBSITE www.overeemwhisky.com

Casey Overeem operated the Old Hobart distillery from his garage from 2007, with his daughter Jane joining him in the business to help with sales. It was sold in 2014 to the new owners of Lark distillery when Casey retired, and the stills were transferred to Lark to increase their capacity. In 2020, Jane Sawford (née Overeem) bought back the Overeem brand name and some stock. Having established the Sawford distillery with her husband, Mark, in 2016 in Huntingfield, south of Hobart, they renamed it Overeem distillery. The core range includes bourbon, sherry, and port cask–matured expressions.

TASTING NOTE

That Boutique-y Whisky Company Overeem 5-Year-Old
Single malt, matured in an apera cask, 50% ABV
An independent bottling from the new Overeem distillery, formerly Sawford distillery, the nose has dark chocolate, dried apricot, peach, grapefruit peel, vanilla essence, and dusty spices. Thick-textured with a delicious range of flavors, it's very drinkable at this strength with lemon, lime peel, sweet candied citrus, and clove, shifting subtly to deliver chocolate ganache, mixed peel, dried vine fruit, and hazelnut latte notes with a resounding spicy finish.

That Boutique-y Whisky Company Overeem 5-Year-Old

SULLIVAN'S COVE

OWNER Sullivan's Cove Distillery Pty Ltd

FOUNDED 1994

WEBSITE wwwsullivanscove.com

Founded by Robert Hosken in 1994, Sullivan's Cove was brought to prominence by Patrick Maguire, a contemporary of Bill Lark, who became co-owner and master distiller until the distillery was sold to the current owners in 2016. Originally known as Tasmania distillery, the first distillery was built in Sullivan's Cove in Hobart's docks area, and the distillery moved to a bigger site in 2003, though only took on the name of the Sullivan's Cove distillery with the sale in 2016. Heather Tillott is the current head distiller, and until 2023, she managed with Myrtle, their single still and worm tub, but now two further stills have been added, which should make life easier. Double Cask includes whisky from French and American oak casks, and there are single cask American Oak and French Oak expressions, special editions such as apera, and a growing use of refill casks, which give Sullivan's Cove's oak a softer profile.

Steam rising from the still nicknamed Myrtle, which until 2023, was Sullivan's Cove's only still.

TASTING NOTE

Sullivan's Cove Double Cask
Single malt, matured in French oak tawny and American oak bourbon casks, 40% ABV
A sweet fruity nose, with plenty of vanilla, and clean, refreshing barley notes show off the influence of the bourbon cask. Red berries, soft toffee, mince pies, sultana, and sweet spices combine on the palate to indicate the flavors added from the tawny casks, leaving a medium length sweet and fruity finish.

Sullivan's Cove Double Cask

NEW ZEALAND

New Zealand is now a spirits nation to follow. The formation of Distilled Spirits Aotearoa has led to consensus guidelines and definitions on New Zealand whisky, the formation of a NZ Spirits Trail, NZ Spirits Awards, and a Distillers Conference. More brands are exporting internationally, and multinational drinks companies have started to explore adding New Zealand whiskies to their portfolios. These are all positive indicators of an industry in good shape producing innovative creations.

CARDRONA

OWNER International Beverage Holdings Ltd

FOUNDED 2015

WEBSITE www.cardronadistillery.co.nz

Desiree Reid-Whitaker founded this artisan distillery in the Wanaka Valley, by New Zealand's Crown Range Mountains, after studying to make single malt whisky in Scotland. The distillery is named after Cardrona, a mining town during the 1860s gold rush in Otago on the South Island.

The distillery started making spirit in 2015, though production is only sufficient to fill one cask per day. The barley is grown on the Canterbury Plains, toward the north end of the South Island. Fermentation runs for more than 70 hours. The spirit is distilled using a pair of copper pot stills built by Forsyth's Ltd in Speyside and modeled on smaller versions of the Glenfarclas stills. Named Roaring Meg, a 530-gallon (2,000-liter) wash still, and Gentle Annie, a 340-gallon (1,300-liter) spirit still, both have small boil balls and shell and tube condensers. They source high-quality casks of oloroso sherry butts from Jerez, bourbon barrels from Kentucky, and New Zealand Pinot Noir barrels from Central Otago on South Island.

With such a naturally beautiful setting, it would be hard not to build sustainability into the heart of the project, and Cardrona has done just that. The distillery draws cool water from an aquifer to cool the vapors back into spirit and returns 95 percent of the volume back to the Cardrona River when it's cool enough. The visitor center and warehouse, known as The Barn, have an underfloor heating system supplied by the warm water leaving the condensers. Draff is collected and fed to the animals on nearby farmland. Cardona chooses to ship its products to distant markets like the US and the UK.

For a distillery of this size, the releases have been generous with good availability, enabling whisky lovers to follow their progress. Bottled at cask strength in 350ml bottles, the ABVs were often well above 60 percent and pack quite a punch. Cardrona Just Hatched was a glimpse into the developing whisky at just three years old, with Cardrona Growing Wings giving a progress report on the whisky at five years old. Cardrona Full Flight is aged for seven years in oloroso and bourbon casks, though there are single cask versions of each. The ornithological theme of the whisky names relate to a New Zealand falcon that frequents the distillery.

In 2023, International Beverage acquired Cardrona distillery and its brands. The company already owns Pulteney, Balblair, Knockdhu, and Speyburn distilleries, and its ownership will help Cardrona benefit from its distribution channels.

Cardona The Falcon

TASTING NOTES

The Cardrona The Falcon
Single malt, matured in oloroso sherry butt, Pinot Noir, and bourbon casks, 52% ABV
Caramelized sugar, nectarine, black pepper, clove, and marmalade peel on the nose, though more floral notes emerge with water. Caramel flavors on first sip, with nectarine, apple, and sultanas, it develops to show bramble, marzipan fruits, and peppercorns on the palate, with spice and baked fruit on the finish.

The Cardrona Full Flight
Single malt, matured in oloroso sherry butts and bourbon casks, 65.6% ABV
Unless you have a hardy palate, dilute this to your desired strength. Steeped in dark fall fruits, mixed peel, and nutty toffee on the nose, the sherry cask influence shines with red berries, orchard fruit, ginger, and a lingering spicy finish. When diluted, there's honey, vanilla, tangy citrus, melon, and crystallized ginger to explore.

NEW ZEALAND WHISKY COLLECTION

OWNER Greg Ramsay

FOUNDED 2010

WEBSITE www.thenzwhisky.com

Dunedin's Willowbank Distillery closed in 1997, shutting the door on the last operating distillery in New Zealand. The remaining casks were sold off, while a Fijian rum maker acquired the redundant stills. Though there were hardly any world whiskies around in those days, and even fewer drinkers seeking them out, the Willowbank stock was a hard sell. The wider export markets didn't miss New Zealand whisky very much, and those primrose yellow tubes of Lammerlaw and Milford bottles with their giant red "M" labels would sit on shelves and back bars for many years to come.

A new era

In 2010, Greg Ramsay bought the remaining aging stock of Willowbank casks and set about relaunching it under the New Zealand Whisky Company name, backed by a group of investors and a couple of Australian associates.

Sensibly, New Zealand red wine barrels were used to finish some of the whiskies, bringing some attractively dark-colored whiskies with new fresh fruity flavors on to the market, which they named Double Wood, a character that hadn't been associated with the old incarnations of Willowbank stock. It also brought in an additional home-grown element that helped it ride on the back of New Zealand's wine export success.

The whiskies were well packaged, seriously tasty, and helped bridge the gap to today's flourishing New Zealand spirits scene. Given how long the distillery has been closed for, our tasting notes come from two vibrant early expressions. These are now sold out as, latterly, some aging whiskies were taken out of the barrels to preserve their qualities instead of leaving them to mature any further. There is a diminishing number of barrels younger than 30 years old among the last remaining barrels.

Today, the company is looking to the future as a distiller, and has released the first of its own whiskies. In 2021, they brought distilling back to Dunedin, installing a pair of stills in the Speight's Brewery and

Switching from bottlers to distillers, the company now distills wash made at Speight's Brewery.

started whisky sales and tastings through Speight's cellar door. Cyril Yates, who had worked for Wilson's Distillers at Willowbank distillery, joined head distiller Michael Byers in the new distilling venture. Speight's make the wash to the company's specifications, with distillation taking place in Dunedin with casks maturing in their bonded warehouse in Oamaru.

TASTING NOTES

New Zealand Whisky Collection 1988 23-Year-Old
Single malt, aged in oak casks, 56.4% ABV
Lemon curd, white chocolate, and dry roasted spices on the nose, particularly cumin, with aromas of vanilla cupcakes and banana chips. Candied lemon, rich vanilla, banana, with threads of tangy citrus peel over some spirited pepperiness and hints of clove, then hints of cherry cola and red licorice when diluted.

New Zealand Whisky Collection Double Wood 15-Year-Old
Single malt, finished in New Zealand red wine casks, 40% ABV
The New Zealand red wine cask influence envelops the whisky with aromas of plum jam, dried prune, vanilla essence, malt loaf, and a smudge of aromatic spice. Jammy but unsweetened fruits on the palate, with a tartness reminiscent of cranberries, dried goji berries, cooking apple, and crimson-colored drupelets on ripening blackberries with texture from the oak and a lift of brown sugar sweetness to finish.

PŌKENO

OWNER Pōkeno Whisky Company

FOUNDED 2018

WEBSITE www.pokenowhisky.com

Thirty miles south of Auckland, in the Waikato District of the North Island, you'll find the Pōkeno distillery (pronounced paw-que-no), which was founded by Matt and Celine Johns in 2018. Distiller Rohan McGowan sources barley from farms in the Canterbury region of the South Island, and the distillery draws mineral-rich water from an underground aquifer. Pōkeno is designed as a light, fruity spirit, which is achieved through a fermentation time of 72 hours and a slow double distillation through their copper pot stills with upsloping lyne arms. The distillery is located in an area that experiences a subtropical climate, like Kavalan in Taiwan, so single malt whisky maturation occurs at a much faster rate than in a traditional musty warehouse in Scotland. The core expressions include a first-fill bourbon cask expression called Pōkeno Origin, and a more complex recipe is used for Pōkeno Discovery, which marries whiskies matured in first-fill bourbon, oloroso, and Pedro Ximénez casks.

More experimental whiskies

The second wave of Pōkeno whiskies, called the Exploration series, were much more experimental, and showcased new directions in raw materials, distillation, and maturation. Pōkeno Totara Cask took a fully mature whisky from first-fill bourbon casks and finished it in 53-gallon (200-liter) light toast/light char Tōtara barrels, the first time this hard-grained tree indigenous to New Zealand had been used to create casks by a whisky-maker. The Māori has favored Tōtara for building waka, their traditional canoes, as well as houses, carvings, and weapons. Pōkeno Winter Malt was created using a mixed mashbill of manuka-smoked malt, chocolate roasted malt, toffee malt, and Laureate distilling malt and matured in first-fill bourbon barrels. Pōkeno Triple Distilled used a third distillation to concentrate the alcohol and the light, fruity flavors that associate with this fraction. Pōkeno distillery has only two stills, so they used the spirit still twice to complete the second and third distillations, in the same way Benriach distillery creates its triple distilled single malt Scotch.

Pōkeno Discovery

Celine and Matt Johns, founders of the Pōkeno distillery.

TASTING NOTES

Pōkeno Discovery
Single malt, matured in first-fill bourbon, oloroso, and Pedro Ximénez casks, 43% ABV
The aromas are appealing with raisin bread, citrus peel, vanilla, black cherry, and oak spices, with a delicious pour that tastes of black cherry truffles, dried vine fruits, and toffee, with a good delivery of maltiness and spice as it dilutes.

Pōkeno Exploration Series No. 01 Tōtara Cask
Single malt, finished in Tōtara casks, 46% ABV
Strips of toasted coconut, honey, cinnamon, lemon lozenges on the nose combine distillate- and cask- derived characteristics. Light-textured with flavors of lemon, dried apricot, mango, and creamy caramel with some white chocolate notes turning to milk chocolate as the mouthfeel thickens up.

SCAPEGRACE DISTILLING COMPANY

OWNER Scapegrace Distilling Co.

FOUNDED 2014

WEBSITE www.scapegracedistillery.com

Daniel McLaughlin and Mark Neal are brothers-in-law and the founders of Scapegrace Distilling Co., one of the most ambitious distillery ventures taking place in New Zealand at the moment. While they have been in business since 2014, the whiskies followed the launch of Scapegrace vodka and gin. The distillery is currently being constructed on the shores of Lake Dunstan in the Southern Alps of Central Otago, which they expect to be the largest in the country.

The early releases were young whiskies matured in virgin French oak, making use of smaller cask sizes for faster maturation and sold as limited editions. These liquids were contract distilled for Scapegrace at the Spirits Workshop in Christchurch, a few hundred miles northeast. Both Scapegrace Rise and Scapegrace Chorus were matured in virgin French oak casks. Scapegrace Revenant and Scapegrace Fortitude both brought in manuka-smoked Laureate barley, while Scapegrace Timbre's twist was the three years spent in Bulgarian oak casks. Both Scapegrace Fortuna and Scapegrace Dimensions were matured in virgin French oak casks for three years. These limited editions may or may not end up being representative of the final distillery profile once their own distillates are mature, but regardless, big things are expected from Scapegrace.

TASTING NOTE

Scapegrace Rise I
Single malt, matured in new French oak casks, 46% ABV
Banana bread, cinnamon bark, dark toffee, and clove on the nose, as well as other intriguing notes of dried porcini, walnut oil, and old woodworking tools. It has depth and personality, with dark honey and brown sugar sweetness hitting the taste buds, with hints of cherry, raisin, and baked citrus, and cappuccino notes to finish.

Scapegrace Rise I

THOMSON

OWNER Matthew and Rachael Thomson

FOUNDED 2014

WEBSITE www.thomsonwhisky.co.nz

Matt and Rachael Thomson started Thomson whisky as a hobby in 2009, selling their own independent bottlings of stock from the closed Willowbank distillery. Their success enabled them to open a craft distillery in 2014 so they could develop their own spirits. Here, they can apply innovative techniques such as smoking barley with manuka wood smoke, a native wood that gives a unique character to the spirit and is used in New Zealand for smoking fish and other foods. Think of it as similar to the post-malt smoking process pioneered in Tasmania. The early runs were distilled with a 238-gallon (900-liter) Portuguese-built copper pot still that they installed at the Hallertau Brewery, in Riverhead, northwest of Auckland. Now they have two hand-beaten stills at their distillery: a 500-gallon (1,900-liter) wash still and a 265-gallon (1,000-liter) spirit still. Working mainly with bourbon and New Zealand wine casks, their core range includes the use of a smoker on Manuka Smoke Single Malt and South Island Peat Single Malt, while their Two Tone Blend combines whiskies from American white oak and European oak New Zealand red wine casks. The Thomson Two Tone name was originally coined when they were using Willowbank stock. Beyond these, they make a Thomson Rye and Barley using malted grains with an 80 percent rye content, and occasionally put out single cask and limited editions.

TASTING NOTE

Thomson South Island Peat
Single malt, matured in bourbon barrels, 46% ABV
The nose is briny with smoked fish, iodine, peat smoke, bitter orange, and grapefruit peel. Warm honey and marmalade notes in the mouth, this shows good structure, with peat smoke, a little black pepper, vanilla essence, dark toffee, and chocolate brownie flavors. The finish has dark chocolate, clove, and peat smoke.

Thomson South Island Peat

EUROPE

EUROPE

REGIONAL STYLES
Single malt, rye, and grain styles predominate, distilled in a variety of still types, shapes, and sizes, and then matured in a world of different cask types and sizes encompassing different growing conditions for European oak species. This diversity results in a remarkable spectrum of aromas and flavors to explore.

AUTHOR'S CHOICE
DOMAINE DES HAUTES GLACES in France, EIFEL WHISKY in Germany, HIGH COAST in Sweden, KYRÖ DISTILLING COMPANY in Finland, THE LAKES in England, and PENDERYN in Wales.

REGIONAL EVENTS AND TOURS
Whisky festivals are common across Europe, with shows in London, Paris, Stockholm, and Limburg running for several days and attracting large international crowds, though their focus still centers on Scotch to pull in the crowds. Each February, the Viking Line cruise sets sail from Sweden packed with whisky fans. For a true festival vibe, European distilleries often throw open their doors for open days in summer, where there is access to special in-depth tours led by the distillers, stalls serving regional artisan cuisine, and exclusive bottlings to acquire.

On the surface, European whiskies appear to defy categorization. But to dismiss variety of style and technique for drive and intent would be to do it an injustice. Far from being in the shadow of Scotch whisky or taking a steer from the restoration of the industry in Ireland, the rest of Europe has become a cradle of distilling innovation, embracing the freedom to make whiskies in whatever way it pleases. If you seek commonality across these countries, it can be found if you know what to look for. Aspects such as multigenerational family businesses, close ties to agriculture and the land, care for the environment, organic and sustainable practices, and respect for local regional specialties, be that brewing, wine making, or distilling, make connections between seemingly unconnected distilleries on different parts of the map.

There are nascent world-beating companies being built on the one hand, while on the other, passionate amateurs are honing their craft as they go along and give whisky fans unprecedented access to their activities as they follow their dreams. Single malt whisky is the leading style, both in peated and unpeated forms, but it is far from the dominant style as rye whisky production now has a firm footing in many European countries. The most conspicuously absent style is the blend. The territory is largely independent of the involvement of multinational drink companies and lacks the circumstances that historically led to the boom in blends, so there is little reason for European distillers to pursue this category in this phase of its development.

Wherever you live, your local distilleries need your support, but for European distillers, cultivating the wider support of whisky drinkers in other countries or other continents takes deep pockets, a great story, and the ability to build the right partnerships to access importers, distributors, and retailers. The hard sell is convincing whisky drinkers fixed on a regular brand or favorite style to take a risk outside of their comfort zone and pick up an unfamiliar bottle from a new country. The onus is on whisky drinkers who share a passion for world whisky to spread the word and tell others the stories behind the whiskies, and of the distillers who make them. There's no question that European whisky has made impressive advances in the first quarter of this century.

Founded in 2010 in the South Tirol, northern Italy, *Puni is one of the most spectacular-looking distilleries in Europe, with a cube-shaped building of offset latticed brickwork inspired by the traditional local style.*

GETTING AROUND

Europe's whisky distilleries tend to be in colder climes, in rural locations near plentiful sources of grain and cold water, but the continent is perhaps uniquely well connected by air, rail, road, and sea, making whisky tourism a comfortable prospect.

NORDIC COUNTRIES

0   250   500 miles
0   250   500 km

ICELAND

REYKJAVÍK

Eimwerk

Atlantic Ocean

North Sea

Aurora

Myken

NORWAY   **SWEDEN**   **FINLAND**

Feddie Ocean
Bergen   OSLO

High Coast   Vaasa   Kyrö
Mackmyra   Teerenpeli
HELSINKI   The Helsinki Distilling Co
STOCKHOLM

Spirit of Hven

200 miles
0   200 km

N

UNITED KINGDOM

North Sea

DENMARK   **SWEDEN**

Stauning
COPENHAGEN   Malmö

Baltic Sea

Ad Gefrin
Yarm
The Lakes   Spirit of Yorkshire
Cooper King
Aber Falls   Weetwood
IRELAND
DUBLIN   Henstone   White Peak   The English Distillery
Dà Mhìle   Ludlow   Adnams
In the Welsh Wind   Cotswolds
Coles   **NETHER-LANDS**   Hamburg   *Elbe*   BERLIN
Penderyn   Oxford Artisan   LONDON   Amsterdam
Circumstance   Copper Rivet   *Rhine*   Stork Club   **POLAND**
Dartmoor   Bimber,   Zuidam   **GERMANY**
East London   Filliers   Pirlot   Ziegler
Hicks & Healey   Liquor Company   **BELGIUM**   Eifel Whisky
BRUSSELS   Wave   The Belgian   **CZECH REPUBLIC**
Distil   Owl   Frankfurt

Warenghem   PARIS
Celtic Whisky   Distillerie   Waldviertler
Distillerie   Rozelieures   Munich   Reiset-   VIENNA
Distillerie des   Santis   bauer   Ruotker
Menhirs   Langatun   Malt   Slyrs   **AUSTRIA**   **HUNGARY**
BERN   **SWITZ.**   Puni
Atlantic   **FRANCE**   **SLOVENIA**
Ocean   Distillerie   *Ebro*   **CROATIA**
Bercloux   *ALPS*
Bay of   Bordeaux   **SERBIA**
Biscay   *Rhine*   Domaine des   **ITALY**
Hautes Glaces   ROME   **ALBANIA**
Bilbao
Destilerías   **SPAIN**
Acha   DYC   Barcelona
PORTUGAL   *Douro*   MADRID   **GREECE**
Segovia
LISBON
SPAIN

Granada

Mediterranean Sea

FINLAND

Finland has a small but growing band of companies exporting their single malts and ryes to other countries. Teerenpeli had a significant head start, but add to this Kyrö's sharp eye for marketing and social media and Helsinki's willingness to experiment, and the door is open for other Finnish distillers to make a name for themselves.

TEERENPELI

OWNER Teerenpeli Group

FOUNDED 2002

WEBSITE www.teerenpelidistillery.com

The biggest distillery operation in Finland is well known among Nordic whisky explorers. Teerenpeli was founded by Anssi Pyysing in 2002 and follows the traditional methods of a single malt Scotch whisky distillery. The company already operated a busy chain of restaurants stocked with beers from their own brewery when they added the distillery to Taivaanranta, their city center restaurant in Lahti.

A second distillery connected to the brewery in Lotila was added in 2015, equipped with a larger 800-gallon (3,000-liter) wash still and two 240-gallon (900-liter) spirit stills made by coppersmiths in Scotland. The still shapes are based on the dimensions of the stills from the original distillery, which can still be seen and now serves as a pilot distillery and provides additional distilling capacity.

A Nordic whisky pioneer

The range and quality have developed impressively over the years. The nonage statement whiskies include Kaski, matured in 100 percent sherry casks; Savu, a gently peated malt made from mixing imported Scottish malt peated to 55ppm with local Finnish malt; and Portii, which is finished in port casks for its final 18 months. There are age statements, too, with a Teerenpeli 10-year-old matured in 85 percent bourbon and 15 percent sherry casks, and the sherry cask–matured Kulo bottled at seven years old. For their 20th anniversary, they released Palo, a peated expression matured in sherry casks, and a 14-year-old Teerenpeli matured in bourbon and sherry casks.

Beyond that, there is a now a program of limited editions, with an interesting Amarone cask finish trilogy following an earlier trio of rum cask finishes.

Water is drawn from a huge underground aquifer of glacial meltwater to supply the main Teerenpeli distillery with 26,400 gallons (100,000 liters) per annum capacity. A power plant burning wood pellets from waste wood from local sawmills supplies the energy needs, which helps reduce their carbon footprint by 90 percent. Local Finnish barley is used to reduce the need to transport raw materials over great distances, and the grains can be malted locally, too. Whisky casks are stored in insulated shipping containers, which might sound unconventional but has its advantages. The temperature and ventilation inside can be adjusted, which can help to protect the full-size and smaller casks, even during the harshest of Finnish winters.

Teerenpeli Portti

TASTING NOTES

Teerenpeli Kaski
Single malt, matured in sherry casks, 43% ABV
The sherry cask lends a sophisticated nose of citrus peel, plum, dried vine fruits, ginger, and aniseed. The wonderful mouthfeel shows real presence, with plenty of maltiness, assisted by flavors of raisin, prune syrup, fig, walnut, and clove.

Teerenpeli Portti
Single malt, finished in port casks, 43% ABV
Achieving a divine balance between the port cask influence and distillery character, the nose brings tantalizing aromas of plum, cherry, and pomegranate, with a touch of honey and herbal notes. The flavors revolve around baked citrus and the sweetness of fudge, with the port cask adding bright cherry and juicy apple notes.

Teerenpeli 10-Year-Old
Single malt, matured in bourbon and sherry casks, 43% ABV
Vanilla, honey, butterscotch, and creamy notes suggest the influence of the bourbon cask, with some additional sesame oil, minerality, and pepperiness on the nose. The palate is warming and well rounded with flavors of baked apple, malt, currant, and ground pepper, settling down to a satisfying wave of boiled fruits, walnut fudge, and almond, with a hint of aniseed on the finish.

THE HELSINKI DISTILLING COMPANY

OWNER The Helsinki Distilling Company

FOUNDED 2014

WEBSITE www.hdco.fi

This urban distillery, bar, and kitchen sits squarely in Teurastamo, a popular Helsinki food court and meeting place. Founded in 2014 by Mikko Mykkänen and Kai Kilpinen, now master distiller and master blender, respectively, the pair operate a second site in Tahkovuori called the Tahko distillery.

Their Rye Malt whiskey and 100 percent Rye Malt whiskey are made in their narrow hybrid pot and column still system and aged for five years. They also make single malt whisky and a Pioneer Corn whisky from Finnish-grown corn.

TASTING NOTE

Helsinki Whiskey Rye Malt
Rye, matured in bourbon and new American oak casks, 47.5% ABV
Pumpernickel, hazelnut, golden syrup, 50% cocoa chocolate, granola, and a hint of dill makes for an interesting nose. It's really good, with tasty fruit loaf flavors supplemented by flavors of cherry, plum, sultana, clove, and malty chocolate. The finish is drying, with bourbon biscuits and a hint of dill.

Helsinki Whiskey Rye Malt

KYRÖ DISTILLERY COMPANY

OWNER Kyrö Distillery Company

FOUNDED 2012

WEBSITE www.kyrodistillery.com

Kyrö distillery, like Stauning and Mackmyra, was formed by a group of friends who had a light bulb moment and decided to get together to make 100 percent malted rye whisky. Obviously, being Finnish, the guys had the idea while sitting in the sauna. Their origins are retold in hilarious fashion in an online video called "Kyrö Distillery: The Whole Story."

After surmounting the usual distillery birthing pains of trial runs, financing headaches, and the hunt for suitable premises, Kyrö moved into an old dairy building constructed in 1908 in the village of Isokyrö beside the Kyrö River. Rye is the fourth most grown crop in Finland, after barley, oats, and wheat, and the Finnish rye crop was mainly turned into rye flour and breads until the distillery opened.

Aside from their gin and cream liqueur, the whisky side of the Kyrö operation mills malted rye for mashing and pumps it into one of their eight fermenters for a lengthy six-day fermentation. Kalle Valkonen, the head distiller, uses a large pair of lantern-shaped copper pot stills powered by renewable biogas. They are installed in a linear arrangement, with the two shell and tube condensers, looking as thick as tree trunks, meeting in the middle of the still room. In addition to their popular unsmoked Kyrö Malt and Kyrö Malt Oloroso expressions, Kyrö Wood Smoke uses alder wood to smoke the malt in another nod to Finnish sauna culture, while Kyrö Peat Smoke uses the same dry smoking method but with freshwater Finnish peat, just like the post malt smoking process used at distilleries in Tasmania. Kyrö joins a wave of contemporary distilleries, from Adnams and Stauning to Zuidam and the Oxford Artisan Distillery, making some of the finest rye whiskies in Europe.

TASTING NOTES

Kyrö Malt Rye Whisky
Rye, matured in new white oak and bourbon casks, 47.2% ABV
The nose is complex with notes of worn leather, musty floors, dill, forest honey, rye bread, and moderate spices. The key is to let it breathe. Molten chocolate pudding, black currant, dill ,and oak on the palate, with rye bread, Brazil nut, and caramel.

Kyrö Malt Rye Kyrö Peat Smoke
Rye, matured in bourbon, new American oak, and refill casks, 47.2% ABV
There's a proper fug of aromatic peat smoke swirling over aromas of plain chocolate and rye spices. Under the smoke, there's sultana, prune, rye bread, cherry, honey, and strawberry jam on scones with delicious nutty chocolate notes on the finish.

Kyrö Malt Rye Whisky

SWEDEN

Known for its active whisky club scene and passion for Islay's peated malts, it was only natural that Sweden would grow to become arguably the best-known whisky-producing country in the region. Little wonder the list of Swedish distilleries is still growing. Mackmyra, High Coast, and Spirit of Hven have shown the world a meticulous approach to whisky recipe-building while engaging with whisky fans from the beginning and letting them feel part of the fun as the distilleries have grown in size.

MACKMYRA

OWNER Mackmyra Svensk Whisky AB

FOUNDED 1999

WEBSITE www.mackmyra.com

Mackmyra is the best known of the Swedish distilleries, having gone from a twinkle in the eyes of a group of college friends to one of the most active single malt producers in Europe. The idea was born from a skiing trip when the friends rented a mountain lodge and each brought a bottle of Scotch to stock the bar. Over drinks, they started musing about why there was no Swedish whisky, given the ideal environment and climate. Subsequently, they set up Mackmyra in 1999 and began operating out of a converted mill and cattle shed in a rural part of Sweden, 97½ miles (157km) north of Stockholm. After a decade of successfully serving their exceptionally well-made Swedish single malt whisky to a domestic audience, they reaped the benefits of a stock market listing, and construction started on a brand new distillery in 2010, capable of quadrupling their former output.

The 12ft (35m) tall gravity distillery opened in the Mackmyra Whisky Village just outside Gävle, about 1½ hours from Arlanda Airport. It's no longer the only gravity distillery since the Port of Leith distillery opened in Edinburgh in 2023 with distilling starting in 2024, but this clever design enables the water, malt, and yeast to be lifted up to the top of the building only once, saving time, energy, and effort. Floor by floor, the process is revealed, descending from mashing to fermentation and down to the Forsyth's copper pot stills on the distillation floor, until the new-make spirit runs into the receiver. Their water is

heated by biofuels next to the distillery, and the heat generated by production keeps the distillery building warm. Viking Malt in Halmstad, in the southwest of Sweden, malts the unpeated barley for the distillery's needs. Mackmyra makes smoked Swedish whiskies, too, using a white moss peat from Karinmossen that is crammed with forest matter, which they burn topped with twigs of freshly cut juniper to make a smoked malt. Years later, Dr. Bill Lumsden would adopt a similar technique when he kilned woodland botanicals to flavor the malt used to make Glenmorangie A Tale of the Forest.

Forget about clouds of smoke billowing from a whimsical pagoda chimney, however, as the Mackmyra malting facility is nothing less than a customized shipping container. But it works. After the 36-hour-long smoking process, they achieve the equivalent phenol levels of 50–60 ppm, and their smoked malt adds herbal and forest notes to the whiskies, wrapped in an oily, barbecue smoke.

Cask maturation on a huge scale
Mackmyra has many aspects that make it distinctive, but the distillery's approach to cask maturation takes everything to another level. Slow-growing Swedish oak is capable of imparting significant flavor to maturing whiskies, such as star anise, coriander seed, ginger, cedarwood, and tobacco. It is more similar in style to French oak, delivering less sweet notes than American oak.

Mackmyra built a loyal following with their cask program in their early years, with many individuals and clubs buying one of their fast-maturing 8-gallon (30-liter) Swedish oak casks, and the program continues today. Casks of varying sizes are now filled

Mackmyra Jaktlycka

Mackmyra Limousin

with Mackmyra spirit for their whiskies and stored across their many maturation facilities, including the Skybar in Lofsdalen and the Bodås Mine. This former iron ore mine opened in 1857, and the numerous underground chambers are filled with hundreds of Mackmyra casks, which are kept at a stable and naturally cool temperature throughout the year.

From juniper smoked malt to Japanese green tea

Mackmyra released their first whisky in 2006 and have released whiskies up to 20 years old, though they are not big on age statements. The core range includes Svensk Ek, in which 10 percent of the recipe is matured in virgin Swedish oak casks; and Svensk Rök, made from their juniper and peat smoked malt. Beyond that, there is a vast array of creative whisky-making to explore, not just because they were the first distillery to use AI to create a whisky but also because their use of casks is like nowhere else. Where else but Mackmyra would you find wood seasoned with cloudberry wine, birch sap wine, lingonberry, and blueberry wine or Japanese green tea? Each expression transports you to a different frame of mind or takes you to a moment in a different season in the Swedish landscape. Their high output of releases means only the real devotees will have tasted more than a fraction of their enormous back catalog. But still, there's always something fun to try.

TASTING NOTES

Mackmyra Svensk Rök
Single malt, predominantly aged in bourbon casks, 46.1% ABV
Aside from the bourbon casks, there is a small contribution of oloroso, American, and Swedish oak casks. Using malt smoked with peat and juniper, the nose has creamy lemon notes, pine, Turkish delight, and gentle smoke. Honey, vanilla, lemon, and creaminess on the palate with layers of peat smoke make this very approachable, leaving a subtle finish of smoked lemon peel.

Mackmyra Jaktlycka
Single malt, matured in Swedish berry wine casks, with Swedish and American oak casks, 46.1% ABV
This limited edition uses casks seasoned with Grythyttan Vin's lingonberry and blueberry wine, which leads to soft pear, ginger, and grassy notes on the nose. Fruity and honeyed, with a hint of blueberry, a ginger spice kick, and a nutty, oaky finish.

Mackmyra Limousin
Single malt, matured in French oak cognac, oloroso sherry, bourbon, Swedish oak, and raspberry wine casks, 46.1% ABV
That Mackmyra pear and ginger combination steals the show, with aromas of fragrant citrus peel, dried apple, and nutmeg. Caramel, vanilla, candied orange, and raspberry to taste, developing the texture of melted chocolate, and ending with notes of white grape and grated ginger.

HIGH COAST

OWNER High Coast Distillery AB

FOUNDED 2010

WEBSITE www.highcoastwhisky.se

High Coast's red brick distillery building was a former power station constructed in 1912. The distillery opened in 2010, though it was originally called Box distillery, named after the days when the building was the AB BOX sawmill that handled the timber that was floated down the Ångerman River to build billets for boxes destined for export. This spectacular part of Sweden is known as the Höga Kusten or High Coast and is a designated UNESCO World Heritage site. The Ångerman Rriver is wide yet fast flowing by the distillery, the water passing at a rate of 128,000 gallons (485,000 liters) per second. The ice-cold water is used to cool the vapors in the shell and tube condensers of High Coast's two pairs of stills, making it one of the coldest cooling waters of any distillery. This forms a connection with the natural environment that genuinely helps shape the character of their distillate.

Local conditions are challenging

High Coast distillery has a capacity of 79,250 gallons (300,000 liters) per annum and makes peated and unpeated single malt whiskies. They source their unpeated malt supplies from Viking Malt in the south of the country and peated malt from Scotland or Belgium. The warehouse conditions are their secret weapon, and the other reason for the distillery's location. The warehouses experience huge temperature fluctuations of up to 140ºF (60ºC) over the year, which forces the spirit in and out of the oak. From the heat of high summer when the black warehouse roof radiates the heat inside the warehouse, the temperature can drop to –22ºF (–30ºC) or lower in the depths of winter. That's so cold, that the warehouse team sometimes have to scrape off the crust of ice and frost that forms on the surface of the casks. They also need to be especially vigilant for leaking casks, both when the pressure drops suddenly in a big freeze and when the spirit expands as the temperature rises again.

Then there's the oak, which is a big deal here. Situated on the 63rd parallel north, the distillery is too far north for local Swedish oak to grow, but they do source Swedish oak casks using wood from farther south. Virgin American, Japanese, French, and Hungarian oak casks have also been used. The majority of spirit is matured in bourbon and sherry casks, but across their whole wood program, they are meticulous about experimenting with four specifications: toasting levels, charring levels, barrel entry proof, and small cask sizes, which all help them deliver their complex recipes.

The releases during the Box distillery years were well received as their early experiments came to fruition, and it helped steer them toward today's core range of internationally exported High Coast whiskies called Älv, Berg, Hav, and Timmer. In addition, there are regular drops of distillery exclusives and new limited editions for the domestic market, some of which make it to their best performing overseas markets.

High Coast has an excellent reputation for being meticulous about the details as their route to make the best whisky, and every detail of their recipes are published on their website. For example, High Coast Cinco II is finished in five different sherry woods, namely fino, amontillado, palo cortado, oloroso, and Pedro Ximénez, and the whiskies were aged for 8.59–8.91 years. If immersing yourself in the details of making great whisky is your thing, then High Coast distillery is the place for you.

TASTING NOTES

High Coast Hav
Single malt, matured in Hungarian oak, Swedish oak, and bourbon casks, 48% ABV
Named after the sea, this core expression is designed to show off its oak spices. Joining the wood spices on the nose is citrus peel, vanilla, and a hint of peat smoke. The palate has sweet stone fruits, honey, and ginger with a spicy finish.

High Coast Älv
Single malt, matured in first-fill bourbon casks, 46% ABV
Named for the Älv River, this is an easy sipper with an attractive nose of bright florals, vanilla, and lemon mousse, and a creamy texture of honey, tablet, orange peel, and fruit gummies, with lashings of vanilla on the finish.

High Coast Berg
Single malt, finished in Pedro Ximénez casks, 50% ABV
A rich sherry flavor full of red and black fruits, enlivened by plenty of spice. The flavors dance on the tongue, with cherries and red berries, toffee, and peppery spice.

High Coast Hav

SPIRIT OF HVEN

OWNER Spirit of Hven Backafallsbyn AB

FOUNDED 2008

WEBSITE www.hven.com

Between Denmark and Sweden, there's a little distillery on an island in the strait of Öresund that's an enterprise unlike any other distillery. Founders Anja and Henric Molin commenced distilling in 2008, and they now make a wide range of whisky, gin, vodka, and aquavit. The whisky comes in a distinctive flask-shaped bottle, like something lifted from a school chemistry lab, with the closures dipped in wax. In 2023, Spirit of Hven announced that they had agreed to cut off the drips of wax rolling down the neck of the bottles to avoid the prospect of any confusion between their bottles and a more famous whiskey dipped in wax. Their bottles are usually dipped in gold wax, but in the past, they have dipped some in green wax, some in blue wax, and for one product, they used red wax.

Spirit of Hven has a hotel, restaurant, and whisky bar on site for visitors, and over the years, they have added a laboratory, column stills to make grain whisky, and a wooden Coffey still to the distillery.

Henric Molin trained as a chemist, which explains the brand's bottle shape, and he runs a consultancy business using the lab to help other distillers improve the quality of their products. As an island distillery, the team are obliged to bring in raw materials by boat, so they now source organic grains and their gin botanicals on the island for some of their production. As master distiller, Molin has a track record of innovation and using his skills to make fine adjustments to his whisky-making process to explore how this affects the final flavor. He is always looking for the next big idea in whisky.

Hven is associated with Tycho Brahe, the 16th-century Renaissance astronomer, who was granted an estate on the island. Spirit of Hven produced their Seven Stars series of whiskies in honor of this connection, and they have subsequently embarked on a new series entitled Seven Angels. Their whiskies are exported to more than 40 countries, and in addition, they produce a core range of single malts, their Hvenus Rye whisky made from 78 percent rye, and their Mercurious Corn whisky made from 88 percent Swedish corn. Unlike some 21st-century distillers, Molin's vision is not to grow and grow to try to compete with the world's leading drinks brands; rather he wants to stay curious and focus on making the most interesting and unique spirits he can in the most sustainable way possible, sharing them with people who appreciate them when they call to the little island in the strait of Öresund.

Spirit of Hven's warehouse contains casks maturing single malt, rye, and corn whiskies.

Spirit of Hven Tycho's Star

TASTING NOTES

Spirit of Hven Tycho's Star
Single malt, matured in chinquapin oak, sessile oak, and European oak casks, 41.8% ABV
Molin combines heavily peated malt with pale ale malt and chocolate malt and matures it in air-dried casks of heavily charred *Quercus muehlenbergii*, heavily toasted *Q. petraea*, and a medium toasted *Q. robur*. The nose has a sweet composition of chocolate, cotton candy, and toffee apple, with flavors of dried banana, ginger, and citrus peel leading to a delicious finish of chocolate and cocoa.

Spirit of Hven Hvenus Rye
Rye, matured in American white oak casks, 45.6% ABV
Matured for around six years, the nose has caramel, vanilla cream, rye spices, and Andes mints, with a palate of peppery rye spices, mint, toffee, and cinnamon, and a distinctly dry finish.

Spirit of Hven Mercurious Corn
Corn whisky, matured in new American oak casks, 45.6% ABV
Aromas of ice cream wafer, salted caramel, and oak spice. The mouthfeel is glossy and smooth, with citrus peel, caramel, vanilla, and a little spice on the finish.

ICELAND

People have inhabited Iceland for a little over a thousand years, but when the Vikings settled, the island was forested. Land was cleared to grow barley and raise cattle, but the cooling effect of the Little Ice Age from the 13th century onward led to crop failures, and barley wasn't grown in Iceland again until the middle of the 20th century. Iceland also had Prohibition in the early 20th century, which was not overturned until 1989, with Icelanders still celebrating Beer Day on March 1 each year. Though some had learned to make their own alcohol during Prohibition, it still makes the country a surprising, but welcome, place to find a distillery.

EIMVERK

OWNER Thorkelsson family

FOUNDED 2009

WEBSITE www.flokiwhisky.is

Eimverk use dried, compacted sheep dung to smoke the barley for their whisky.

Founded by Halli Thorkelsson in 2009, Eimverk distillery produces Flóki whisky, brennivín, and gin, and the enterprise embodies that Icelandic spirit of self-sufficiency. Kría and Filippa are hardy two-row barley species grown and malted 56 miles away on the family farm in the shadow of the Mount Hekla volcano. Icelandic barley produces less sugar for the yeast during fermentation so has a lower yield and more grassy and peppery flavors in the spirit.

The traditional Icelandic culinary practice of using sheep dung to smoke foods certainly earned Eimverk some notoriety when they began to smoke barley with the dried, compacted dung and straw that builds up in the farm sheds where the sheep spend the winter. Unlike the making of peated malt in Scotland, the dung smoke is used in a dryer before the barley is malted. The grains can be damp from rain and dew by the time the farmer brings in the harvest each September. The distillery does two runs a year for their Flóki Sheep Dung Smoked Reserve and the smoky effect varies from batch to batch. The rest of their barley is dried without dung by more regular methods.

Unconventionally for a European distillery, they mash equal ratios of malted to unmalted barley and use recycled milk tanks for wash stills. In-grain fermentation and distillation is the Eimverk method,

so the worts are not drained from the mash. They use geothermal water, passing it through a heat exchanger to lower their carbon footprint. Charred virgin oak casks are the main cask type, but beyond sherry casks, they also use craft beer casks, birchwood barrels, and mead casks on their single barrel limited editions.

TASTING NOTES

Flóki Single Malt Icelandic Birch Finish
Single malt, finished in birchwood casks, 47% ABV
Peppery on the nose, with a balance of fruit and fudge measured against notes of burnt fruitcake and toasted coconut. The palate reveals caramel, honey, and stone fruit flavors, with a whirlwind of clove and pepperiness, and a finish of singed oak and cinnamon.

Flóki Single Malt Sheep Dung Smoked Reserve
Single malt, matured in refill casks, 47% ABV
The nose is intriguing and reminiscent of the countryside with earthy notes, mushroom, grass cuttings, tree sap, fresh barley, and herbal undertones. It's deliciously thick and chewy to drink, with flavors of toffee, banana, toasted almond, cinnamon, and hints of smoke.

Flóki Single Malt Icelandic Birch Finish

NORWAY

Norway's distilleries are located in some remote and challenging places, but with grit and determination, they have ensured this country has earned its place on the world whisky map.

AURORA SPIRIT DISTILLERY

OWNER Tor Christensen & Colin Houston

FOUNDED 2016

WEBSITE www.bivrost.com

Over 1,000 miles north of Oslo, Aurora offers an Arctic whisky experience at the world's most northerly distillery. Aurora uses glacial water from the Lyngen Alps to make vodka, aquavit, gin, vodka, and single malts using a hybrid pot and column still system. Their

Bivrost whisky has been released in limited quantities for their Nine Worlds of Norse Mythology series.

TASTING NOTE

Bivrost Alfheim
Single malt, aged in bourbon and virgin oak casks, 46% ABV
The eighth in the series has a nose of light vanilla, oak spices, coconut snowballs, white chocolate, and cinnamon sugar. Caramel sauce, vanilla, cinnamon, and toasted hazelnut, then clove, peppery spice and nutmeg, walnut cake, and toasted coconut, with caramel and five spice on the finish.

Bivrost Alfheim

FEDDIE OCEAN DISTILLERY

OWNER Anne Koppang

FOUNDED 2019

WEBSITE www.feddiedistillery.no

Northwest of Bergen, Fedje is the most westerly inhabited island in Norway. The settlement is known as the village in the ocean. Supported by hundreds of female investors, restaurant entrepreneur Anne Koppang makes organically certified whisky. The spirit is laid down in bourbon and sherry casks, and their inaugural single malt is due in late 2024.

MYKEN

OWNER Roar Larsen

FOUNDED 2014

WEBSITE www.mykendestilleri.no

This remote Norwegian island distillery is part of a small fishing community on the largest island in an archipelago of 40 islands at the northern end of Norway's Helgeland coast. Seawater is desalinated using reverse osmosis for the island residents' use and also used as Myken's production water. Peated and

unpeated whiskies are distilled slowly in direct-fired alembic-style stills and matured creatively in a diverse range of casks to explore their differences.

TASTING NOTE

Myken Arctic Single Malt Whisky Ocean Spirit 2023 Single Cask
Single malt, matured in a bourbon cask, 65% ABV
Sea spray, vanilla fudge, hard candy, grapefruit peel, and the minerality of dulse on the nose. A true taste of the ocean but dilute first; lemon, caramel, melon, banana, and vanilla, with pepper, chili flakes, and aniseed, and saltiness at the end.

Myken Arctic Single Malt Whisky Ocean Spirit 2023 Single Cask

DENMARK

Denmark may have other distilleries such as Thy, Fary Lochan, and Copenhagen making interesting whiskies, but only Stauning distillery, with its burgeoning range of rye and single malt whiskies, has truly shown the world it has box office potential.

STAUNING

OWNER 60% owned by the founders and 40% Distill Ventures

FOUNDED 2005

WEBSITE www.stauningwhisky.com

The inception of Stauning has all the makings of a good movie script, with a plot revolving around a crew of specialists who assemble for a specific purpose. It's a popular trope used in lots of films from *Ocean's Eleven* and *The Avengers* to *The Blues Brothers*. For Stauning, there would be a montage of each of the nine intrepid founders as they went about their jobs in their old lives, working in construction, medicine, aviation, engineering, hospitality, teaching, and meat-processing, before answering the call to down tools and make Danish whisky as if the future of planet Earth depended on it.

Stauning makes its home in the west of Denmark, a more agricultural and less populated area of the country, far from the urban bustle of Copenhagen. The climate is reminiscent of Islay, resulting in a slow maturation in cask not dissimilar to a warehouse in Scotland. In the early days, the founders were able to trade their skills and resources for pieces of equipment such as stainless steel tanks from old school friends who had gone into farming as they gathered together the basic equipment to attempt their first distillation. While it might have been more out of necessity than design, it helped keep the Stauning team grounded in the local community and helped them appreciate the rich abundance of resources on their doorstep, such as bountiful clear water, great quality local barley and rye, and the goodwill of their neighbors.

As self-acknowledged hobbyist distillers, they started in humble circumstances in an old butchery with a couple of small pot stills, spreading barley across the cold room floor to make malt, and pressing

an old meat grinder into service as a mill. They even sourced peat from a Danish folk museum that demonstrated traditional peat-cutting techniques to visitors and taught them about the industrialization of peat harvesting. The first Stauning spirit came off the direct-fired stills in 2006, with their first bottles going on sale in 2011.

Huge investment leads to a new era

By 2014, Distill Ventures, the Diageo-funded accelerator platform, had taken notice and made an approach, announcing a $12.6 million investment in the Stauning vision the following year to help them grow. The modern purpose-built Stauning distillery opened in 2018, designed to fit sympathetically into the landscape by drawing on the angular build of the local farmhouses and the fishing huts dotted around Stauning harbor. Cleverly, they upscaled without significantly changing their methods, staying true to their origins. Their automated floor malting system was designed in-house, with steeping and germination occurring at floor level, while massive motorized combine harvester–style blades patrol up and down the grain beds, flipping the sprouting barley grains over to keep the consistency of each batch in check. They bring in local heather to make their Stauning Smoke expression, burying it under chunky, loose peat to prevent it from burning in the kiln and allowing it to add its flavors.

Stauning is a heavy style whisky, thanks to the floor-malting process and their unique mashing methods, which creates thick worts full of solids. A long fermentation creates fruity esters, orchard fruit, and citrus flavors in their whiskies rather than the grainy, nutty characteristics that can arise from a shorter fermentation. As the 16 squat wash stills and 8 spirit stills are direct-fired by a biogas flame, they favor a slow distillation, being careful not to burn the thick wash while letting the direct fire work on the

Stauning Rye

solids, esters, and sugars to create a characterful, complex spirit.

The Stauning founders filled small casks when they were starting out, such as casks of 13.2 gallons (50 liters), a common practice at Nordic distilleries, though they discovered the initial results from the oak to be too intense. They swiftly moved to standard-

The new Stauning distillery has 24 small copper pot stills.

size casks when they could, though Danish fire regulations prevented them from filling larger 132-gallon (500-liter) sherry butts and puncheons. Eager to explore finishing, they experimented by sourcing three casks of every type of cask they could lay their hands on, from mizunara, rum, and Marsala barrels to mezcal and tequila casks. They tried different spirits in each one, discovering the speed at which rye spirit pulls flavor from the casks compared with the more sedate pace of flavor uptake from their single malt. Those trials that work are used in their active program of limited releases, such as their Stauning Rye Maple Syrup Cask, or their Stauning Dirty Bastard, where they start with their popular Stauning Bastard expression matured in new American oak and mezcal casks then finish it in Mexican hot chocolate imperial stout casks from contemporary Danish craft brewery To Øl.

Stauning Bastard

TASTING NOTES

Stauning Bastard
Rye, finished in Oro de Oaxaca mezcal casks, 46.3% ABV
Rye bread, herbal, and cinnamon spice aromas on the nose, laced with subtle smoke trails. Cinnamon sweetness, rye spices, and a more noticeable agave influence on the palate leave a lengthy flavor impact.

Stauning Kaos
Grain, matured in heavily charred new American oak and bourbon casks, 46% ABV
Scented with coffee beans, chocolate, green apple, and sweet peat smoke notes on the nose. The spices on the palate are a riot, with vanilla malt and chocolate flavors led astray by the last vestiges of smoke.

Stauning Rye
Rye, matured in new American oak casks, 48% ABV
Led by crisp rye notes, cardamom, peppercorn, cinnamon, and orchard fruits, this has a more pronounced rye whisky character on the nose. A soothingly creamy texture on the palate, with liberally spiced red fruit and cooking apple flavors.

ENGLAND

England's whisky industry is blooming, with the number of active distilleries and distillery projects now hovering around 50. Many are committed to traditional Scotch whisky practices in making their English single malts, while others are creating English rye and experimental bourbon-style whiskies drawing on American whiskey influences. The English Whisky Guild, launched in 2022, is helping to promote a diverse and innovative English whisky category. With locally grown barley, organic grains, and heritage rye varieties, England has got plenty of spirit to offer the world.

AD GEFRIN

OWNER Ad Gefrin Distillery Ltd

FOUNDED 2023

WEBSITE www.adgefrin.co.uk

Inspired by Yeavering's seventh-century royal palace, Ad Gefrin opened in nearby Wooler in March 2023 in Northumberland, near the border with Scotland. Founded by the Ferguson family, the distillery name means "by the hill of goats" and draws inspiration from this period of Anglo-Saxon history. It has been designed as a destination distillery incorporating a bar, bistro, and immersive AV museum celebrating the history of Anglo-Saxon Northumbria from 1,400 years ago.

A reasonably large distillery by modern English whisky standards, Ad Gefrin is equipped with four Douglas fir washbacks and a pair of copper pot stills manufactured by Forsyths Ltd of Rothes. The water is pure Cheviot water brought up from a borehole beneath the distillery. Ad Gefrin is distilling with locally grown Diablo barley malted in Berwick-upon-Tweed. Until their own single malt whisky is mature, at the earliest in 2026, they plan to release a series of sourced world blends under the name Tácnbora. Ad Gefrin will be one to watch in coming years.

ADNAMS COPPER HOUSE DISTILLERY

OWNER Adnams plc

FOUNDED 2010

WEBSITE www.adnams.co.uk

Beautifully positioned right in the center of the unspoiled Victorian seaside resort of Southwold, this innovative family company, with 150 years of history in wine, beers, and spirits, opened a distillery within the brewery site in 2010.

Head distiller John McCarthy oversees distillation using a beer-stripping column and copper pot still, using a wash made in the brewery from local grains. The initial range included a nonage statement single malt; a triple malt made from wheat, barley, and oats; and a rye malt made from 75 percent rye and 25 percent malted barley. Latterly, this has been joined by a Distiller's Choice range of 7-year-olds and their first 12-year-old single malt.

TASTING NOTE

Adnams Distiller's Choice 12-Year-Old
Single malt, matured in bourbon casks, 51.2% ABV
Best taken with a dash of water, the nose has notes of honey, barley, and fine peppercorn spices leading to a malty, toasty mouthful of baked citrus, pepper, cinder toffee, apple pie, and cinnamon. This has a longer maturation than the core range, and it really pays off with a greater depth of flavor.

Adnams Distiller's Choice
12-Year-Old

BIMBER

OWNER Bimber Distillery Ltd

FOUNDED 2015

WEBSITE www.bimberdistillery.co.uk

Using a hydrometer to determine the alcohol strength of new-make spirit at Bimber.

Bimber is first and foremost a single malt whisky producer, as founder and master distiller Dariusz Plazewski believes that the wider world will grasp the concept of English single malt more readily than other whisky styles. Bimber exclusively uses floor-malted barley from a single farm in Hampshire. Seven open-topped washbacks give them enough capacity to manage seven-day fermentation times, but the overall distillery capacity is only 13,200 gallons (50,000 liters) per annum, based on their initial two 264-gallon (1,000-liter) direct-fired pot stills. Expansion is planned, with a larger still and more washbacks, but requires the ideal site, and meanwhile, the company has opened a second distillery, Dunphail, in Scotland.

Demand outstrips supply

Bimber The First, their inaugural bottling, was bottled in 2019, and the distillery rapidly built up a loyal following eager for the next ballot to get a chance to buy a bottle. Each release is single cask or small batch, and demand currently outstrips supply, so to drink Bimber requires planning, loyalty, luck, and opportunity. That has made it very collectible, too, especially the attractively designed Spirit of the Underground series capturing the color and logos of the London Underground network. While in essence, Bimber follows a traditional single malt whisky pathway; they released a peated English single malt whisky in 2022, using their single farm origin malted barley peated with Aberdeenshire peat. In 2023, Bimber collaborated with Compass Box Whisky Co. to create a pair of blended malt whiskies called Duality, containing Bimber single malt combined with select Compass Box stocks of single malt Scotch.

In January 2024, Dariusz Plazewski was arrested and faced a number of serious charges when it was revealed he had been living in the UK under a pseudonym for 20 years. Lucasz Ratajewski, his real name, relinquished control of the running of the distilleries to his wife, Ewelina Chruszczyk, and Dunphail Director of Whisky Creation Matt McKay.

Bimber Apogee XII

TASTING NOTES

Bimber Small Batch Bourbon Oak
Single malt, matured in first-fill bourbon casks, 51.6% ABV
Vanilla, toffee, lemon peel, and a hint of Granny Smith apple on the nose indicate the American oak influence. The palate has citrus notes, spice, banana, and toffee apple, with spices and malted milk on the finish.

Bimber Apogee XII
Blended malt, finished in Bimber casks, 46.3% ABV
This 12-year-old, which combines Speyside and Highland single malts, has a nose of red apple, ginger nut, chocolate, malt and roasted pecans. Spicy on the palate with notes of deep citrus and orchard fruits, root ginger, and a finish of vanilla sweetness and apple peelings.

CIRCUMSTANCE

OWNER Psychopomp Ltd

FOUNDED 2018

WEBSITE www.circumstancedistillery.com

Liam Hirt and Danny Walker founded Circumstance in an industrial unit in Bristol in 2018. The distillery is highly experimental, using organic grains, brewer's yeasts, and a wide variety of casks and maturation techniques. The debut whisky appeared in 2022, and their first core range whisky in 2023. The Single Grain

Estate Whisky uses four organic grains and three brewing yeasts and is matured in bourbon, new European oak, and oloroso–seasoned casks.

TASTING NOTE

Circumstance Single Grain Estate Whisky
Single grain, matured in bourbon, new European oak, and oloroso–seasoned casks, 45% ABV
The nose brims with malty notes and rye spices, with aromas of ground coriander, cinnamon, nutmeg, digestive biscuit, burlap, hay, and a hint of warm porridge. A creamy texture, with malt, toasted cereals, rye, and lots of vanilla.

Circumstance Single Grain Estate Whisky

COOPER KING

Cooper King First Edition "Fruit + Spice"

OWNER Cooper King Distillery Ltd

FOUNDED 2016

WEBSITE www.cooperkingdistillery.co.uk

Chris Jaume and Abbie Neilson became hooked on the idea of a distillery while touring the craft distilleries of Tasmania. Learning from distillers, including Bill Lark, they bought a 238-gallon (900-liter) Tasmanian copper pot still with the intention of building a distillery just north of York. They use Maris Otter barley floor malted at Warminster Maltings, practice hand mashing and run long fermentations

lasting five to seven days. They double distill in their single pot still and are known to mature in small 26-gallon (100-liter) casks, like their Tasmanian mentors, to deliver a faster maturation time. The first whisky release in October 2023 sold out in 10 minutes.

TASTING NOTE

Cooper King First Edition "Fruit + Spice"
Single malt, matured in small-sized casks, including bourbon, refill sherry, red wine, and cognac casks, 48.1% ABV
Egremont russet apples, Seville orange peel, peach slices, blossom honey, and white pepper on the nose. This has instant appeal, with enough body and flavor to carry it all off. The malt shines through beautifully.

COPPER RIVET

OWNER Russell Distillers Ltd

FOUNDED 2016

WEBSITE www.copperrivetdistillery.com

In the historic Chatham Royal Dockyards, the Russell family transformed Pumphouse No 5 into the Copper Rivet distillery in 2016. Head distiller Abhi Banik sources wheat, barley, and rye from nearby Kentish farmers. Their set-up allows for several distillation options. The whiskies are bottled under the

Masthouse brand, named after the craft of making ship's masts in the dockyard. Their debut Masthouse single malt release arrived in 2020.

TASTING NOTE

Masthouse Single Estate Grain Whisky
Single grain, pot and column distilled, 42% ABV
The aromas include toasted almond, cracked black pepper, coriander seed, blanched hazelnut, meringue, and rye spices. Light-bodied on the tongue, with lots of vanilla sweetness, cereal notes, honey, and rye spices, growing in creaminess.

Masthouse Single Estate Grain Whisky

COTSWOLDS DISTILLERY

OWNER The Cotswolds Distilling Company Ltd

FOUNDED 2014

WEBSITE www.cotswoldsdistillery.com

Cotswolds distillery boosted its distilling capacity in 2022, adding two larger stills.

One of England's larger distilleries, Cotswolds distillery was the vision of New Yorker Daniel Szor, who built a distillery in one of the most idyllic parts of the country, guided by Dr. Jim Swan, who died in 2017. Their successful Cotswolds Dry Gin helped spread the word and built anticipation until the first whisky arrived in 2017. Szor sees Cotswolds as a world whisky distillery as well as an English one, part of a global revolution of new young distilleries such as Stauning in Denmark, Westland in the US, and Chichibu in Japan.

The site expands

The team uses barley grown in the Cotswolds, which is malted at nearby Warminster Maltings. Fermentation takes 90 hours, and they use two strains of dried yeast, Anchor and Fermentis, selected for the fruity flavors they produce.

The distillery underwent expansion in 2022, acquiring a 2-ton mash tun, a 2,600-gallon (10,000-liter) wash still, and 1,980-gallon (7,500-liter) spirit still, increasing production capacity sixfold up to 198,000 gallons (750,000 liters) per annum. As England's most available and bestselling single malt whisky, Cotswolds is going to need that extra distilling power.

The current range is comprehensive, starting with their Classics collection of Cotswolds Reserve and Cotswolds Signature; then their Cask Expressions collection that features a bourbon cask, peated cask, and sherry cask expression; with Szor's favorite, an STR cask expression named Founder's Choice. More recently, annual limited releases have appeared under their Hearts Series collection.

Cotswolds Reserve

TASTING NOTES

Cotswolds Reserve
Single malt, matured in first-fill bourbon and STR casks, 50% ABV
One of the Cotswold's finest whiskies, the cask recipe gives this a nose of apple, cherry, dried red berries, chocolate, vanilla, and dried vine fruits. Thick and chewy in the mouth, this has juicy flavors of red berries, Victoria plum, and vanilla fudge, with a spicy finish.

Cotswolds Sherry Cask
Single malt, matured in sherry-seasoned Spanish and American oak hogsheads and butts, 57.4% ABV
Szor seasons casks with oloroso and Pedro Ximénez sherry for this whisky, the nose revealing ginger loaf, chocolate cake, black tea, baking spices, and prunes. Thick textured with notes of sticky toffee pudding, clove, and dark fruits, this one is sherry heaven.

DARTMOOR DISTILLERY

OWNER Dartmoor Whisky Distillery Ltd

FOUNDED 2014

WEBSITE www.dartmoorwhiskydistillery.co.uk

Greg Miller and Simon Crow founded this distillery in Devon in 2014 following a stint at the Bruichladdich Whisky Academy. The pair salvaged a decommissioned 370-gallon (1,400-liter) alembic still from Cognac, lovingly restored it, and built a distillery in Bovey Tracey Town Hall. It's one of the most charmingly idiosyncratic stillrooms in England. A nearby cask ale brewer produces their wash from local barley malted at Warminster Maltings, not unlike several other English distilleries who get their wash delivered from a brewery.

The services of whisky legend Frank McHardy have been enlisted as master distiller. Producing spirit is a time-consuming process, as it takes three runs of the still to produce sufficient volume of low wines for each spirit run. The hard-won spirit is then matured in bourbon, oloroso sherry, and Bordeaux red wine casks, meaning every drop is quite precious.

TASTING NOTE

Dartmoor Whisky Single Malt
Single malt, matured in bourbon casks, 46% ABV
This has vanilla, marshmallow, meringue, and a hint of lime on the nose. It's a light, sipping whisky, with light vanilla notes, rum, and raisin flavors, toffee, and a lot of pepper. There are little glimpses of citrus peel, lime, white grapes, and vanilla fudge as it dilutes to a smooth finish.

Dartmoor Whisky Single Malt

EAST LONDON LIQUOR COMPANY

OWNER East London Liquor Company Ltd

FOUNDED 2014

WEBSITE www.eastlondonliquorcompany.com

From east London, there's a buzz about this urban distillery, bar, and restaurant, which hosts tours and tastings for gin and whisky fans alike. The single malt is fermented for 96 hours, fermented with a distiller's yeast, Belgian Ale yeast, and a Saison yeast, then double-distilled in copper pot stills and aged in bourbon casks, rejuvenated casks, and new American oak casks. Next

came a London Rye whisky made from malted rye and malted barley fermented for up to 120 hours using distiller's and Saison yeasts and matured in casks made from several oaks and London brandy casks.

With collaborations and more special editions on the horizon, there was a sense that ELLC was only getting started; however, the company briefly entered administration in December 2023 in debt to HMRC (HM Revenue & Customs). This enabled the board members to buy the company and eliminate sizable debts through transferring ownership to a new company, which enabled ELLC to save the employees' jobs and keep making whisky.

TASTING NOTES

East London Liquor Co. Single Malt Whisky
Single malt, matured in new American oak, sherry, and bourbon casks, 47% ABV
Lime marmalade, black pepper, banana, and a pinch of ground ginger on the nose. The palate has a superb evolution of citrus and stone fruit flavors, with baked apple, honey, marzipan, nippy pepper, caramel, candied citrus, and pineapple chunks, leading into a long fruity finish.

East London Liquor Co. London Rye Whisky
Rye, matured in rejuvenated casks, new American oak, chestnut, and brandy cask, 47% ABV
Beautiful active rye notes hit the nose, with toasted fruit scone, lots of nutmeg, cinnamon, cedar sticks, toasted hazelnut, and breakfast cereals. Lots of flavor, but the structure feels a bit loose, with apple, apricot, tangerine, malt, and pumping rye spices.

ELLC Single Malt Whisky 2022

THE ENGLISH DISTILLERY

OWNER The English Whisky Company Ltd

FOUNDED 2006

WEBSITE www.englishwhisky.co.uk

James Nelstrop founded St. George's distillery (now rebranded as The English distillery) in Norfolk, East Anglia, in 2006, the first new distillery in England for more than 100 years, realizing a long-held dream to make fine English whisky. They were up and running quickly; it took just 11 months to go from obtaining planning permission for a rural distillery in the depths of Norfolk to distilling spirit.

The English distillery in Norfolk was a pioneer of whisky production in England.

Moving on from traditional single malt

Recognized as the modern era's oldest English distillery, it is now approaching its 20th anniversary. James's son, Andrew, is now the managing director. Former Laphroaig legend Iain Henderson was in charge of their first spirit, monitoring the cuts as the vapors ran through the pair of 475-gallon (1,800-liter) copper pot stills manufactured by Forsyths Ltd of Rothes. Toward the end of his 10-month tenure, Henderson trained David Fitt, a former brewer at Greene King, to be his successor, and Fitt managed the stock profile as it matured into whisky from 2009 onward, negotiating the early years when there was a baffling array of different releases known as Chapters. Fitt also introduced some fascinating and delicious English grain whisky variants and liqueurs bottled under The Norfolk brand.

Until then, the distillery had largely followed the customs and methods of a traditional single malt Scotch whisky distillery, but The Norfolk has enabled them to flex their muscles and tackle bourbon-style mashbills and single grain variants ahead of other English distilleries. Following Fitt's departure in 2022, Nelstrop appointed Chris Waters as their third head distiller to help them write the next chapter of the distillery's story.

Given the farming heritage of the Nelstrop family and the setting of the distillery in the rich arable East Anglian landscape, much of the barley is locally sourced and malted nearby at the Crisp Maltings in Fakenham. The distillery draws water from Breckland Aquifer, England's largest underground fresh water source. Sustainability plays an important part in the operation, and the distillery is designed to reflect responsible water stewardship, energy efficiency, and waste recycling.

As part of a new signature range, The English Original and The English Smokey were released with new branding, with the arrival of The English Sherry Cask Matured adding to the lineup in 2023. The whole range is complemented by older limited expressions, including The English 11-Year-Old; single cask bottlings; special editions marking royal births, marriages, and coronations; and regular releases born out of the Chapters era such as the Triple Distilled, Rum Cask, Virgin Oak, and Sherry Butt Heavily Smoked editions.

The English Original

TASTING NOTES

The English Original
Single malt, matured in bourbon casks, 43% ABV
Their signature whisky has notes of malting floors, cornflakes, vanilla, and orange peel. Well balanced on the palate, with vanilla custard slice, marzipan, pear, melon, lemon zest, and black pepper on the finish.

The English Smokey
Single malt, matured in bourbon casks, 43% ABV
Made from malted barley peated to 45ppm, the smoke is expressed on the nose like a garden bonfire rather than being overly peaty. Creamy vanilla, ginger, pear, banana, and taffy candy on the palate, while the thick smoke of burning leaves infiltrates the flavors.

The English Sherry Cask Matured
Single malt, matured in Pedro Ximénez sherry casks, 46% ABV
Forest honey, fall leaves, fig, and seasoned sherry wood on the nose. A sherry-soaked experience but a well-structured whisky with a good flavor trajectory. Sultana, prune juice, fruitcake, baked apple, fig, and vanilla with a finish of Brazil nut, licorice, and hint of tobacco.

HENSTONE

OWNER Henstone Distillery Ltd

FOUNDED 2017

WEBSITE www.henstonedistillery.com

Chris and Alex Toller, two of the original co-founders, run this Shropshire distillery founded in 2017. Unlike some English distilleries, they produce their own wash and the original distillery is equipped with a 265-gallon (1,000-liter) Kothe pot and column hybrid still, nicknamed "Hilda."

Having outgrown the original site, entrepreneur Mike Harris acquired 50 percent of the business to help the distillery move to a larger location and meet its plans for growth. They make Old Corn Dog Liquor, a bourbon-style whisky, using a mashbill of

68 percent corn, 16 percent wheat, and 16 percent malted barley, which is matured in new American oak casks for 12 months. Whiskies are being bottled as single cask releases at 3–5 years old and include expressions matured in bourbon casks, peated Islay quarter casks, full maturation in oloroso and PX casks and firkins, and oloroso and Pedro Ximénez quarter cask finishes.

TASTING NOTE

Henstone Distillery Single Malt Whisky
Single malt, matured in bourbon casks, 43.8% ABV
Red apples, wine gums, cloudy lemonade, and cream soda, the aromas are light and almost effervescent. Sweet lemon, lime, candied citrus, and white pepper on the palate, it grows spicier. The finish is nutty with lemon biscuits.

Henstone Distillery Single Malt Whisky

HICKS & HEALEY

OWNER St. Austell Brewery & Healey's Cyder Farm

FOUNDED 2000

WEBSITE www.healeyscyder.co.uk

Healey's distills cider into apple brandy on its family-run farm in Cornwall. At the turn of the millennium, the company went into partnership with local brewer St. Austell to produce a small amount of whiskey. Today, the whiskeys are still made from Cornish barley brewed by St. Austell Brewery, then double distilled and matured by Healey's.

Their leading whiskey is a NAS single malt whiskey, made from Maris Otter barley, but they have offered a rare expression bottled at 15 years old.

TASTING NOTE

Hicks & Healey Single Malt Cornish Whiskey
Single malt, matured in bourbon casks, 40% ABV
A pleasant nose of creamy barley, floral notes, vanilla powdered sugar, cream soda, honey, a hint of pear, and light aromatic spices. Clean and sweet flavors with tablet, honey, pear, peppercorn, and brown sugar, with caramel and hints of tropical fruit, orange peel, and raspberry emerging.

New-make spirit is colorless when casks are first filled, but sampling Cornish whiskey straight from the cask shows how the spirit picks up color from the wood over time.

Hicks & Healey Single Malt Cornish Whiskey

THE LAKES

OWNER The Lakes Distillery Company plc

FOUNDED 2014

WEBSITE www.lakesdistillery.com

Co-founded by Paul Currie, who had co-founded Isle of Arran distillery (now renamed as Lochranza) in the 1990s, distilling began at The Lakes in 2014. The quatrefoil—representing faith, hope, luck, and love—was discovered in the stonework during the renovations to turn the mid-19th-century dairy farm into a distillery, and adopted as the distillery logo. Dhavall Gandhi was whisky-maker from 2016–2022, and during his tenure, the signature style became more clearly defined, with a preference for light, fruity, and elegant whiskies matured in sherry casks. In 2022, Sarah Burgess, former lead whisky-maker at The Macallan, became the new whisky-maker.

The Lakes use only unpeated malted barley, running fermentations over 96 hours using a combination of three yeast strains, distilling slowly, and choosing narrow cut points. A greater emphasis is placed on the quality of the cask types used and the meticulous art of the blending to layer the flavors behind each single malt expression. Riding on the success of its early releases, the distillery tripled its production capacity, adding eight further washbacks, developed extra warehousing space, and pushed into new export markets in the US, Asia, and Europe, with ambitions to be a luxury, sherry-led single malt whisky of world renown. The Whiskymaker's Reserve series ran for seven editions between 2019 and 2023 designed as a journey to follow as they refined their signature sherry cask–style while The Whiskymaker's Editions are limited-edition releases that are presented as new artistic interpretations, accompanied by some superb label designs. These whiskies are some of the more expensive English whiskies, often priced above well-known age-stated sherried single malt Scotch whiskies, but the quality and flavors show that The Lakes can take on the best in the world.

TASTING NOTE

The Lakes Whiskymaker's Reserve No. 6
Single malt, matured in oloroso, Pedro Ximénez, and red wine casks, 52% ABV
Saturated with fruity flavors, the nose is reminiscent of dried vine fruit, Christmas cake, fig, and chopped peel. The cask strength whisky delivers flavors of citrus, dried fruits, dates, fudge, and gentle spices on the finish.

The Lakes Whiskymaker's Reserve No. 6

LUDLOW

OWNER Ludlow Distillery Ltd

FOUNDED 2018

WEBSITE www.ludlowdistillery.co.uk

The town of Ludlow in Shropshire is known for its vibrant food scene, and this small distiller is building a solid reputation for both its gin and whisky. Now relocated to a farm shop two miles north of the town, distiller Shaun Ward combines English malt and peated Scottish malt, long fermentation times, and triple distillation in a wood-fired, 53-gallon (200-liter) German-made, four-plate column still. They are the only English distillery using peated malt in all of their mashbills. Column still whisky using 100 percent malted barley is also made at Copper Rivet in England, Loch Lomond in Scotland, and Miyagikyo in Japan. A number of young single malts have been bottled under the Distiller's Cut line, including oloroso sherry and Islay cask finishes. While their inventory builds up, releases are hard to find, with only 400 bottles being released every six months.

TASTING NOTE

Ludlow Single Malt Distiller's Cut Triple Cask No. 6
Single malt, matured in refill whisky casks, finished in Pedro Ximénez and ruby port casks, 42% ABV
English malt and Scottish peated malt are used here. Inviting with fruity port notes, spices, grist, malt, and earthy notes on the nose. A subtle influence from the finishing casks, this is light and sugary sweet on first sip, with caramel, raspberry, malt, vanilla, milk chocolate, and black pepper, leaving malt, dusty cocoa, and bramble fruit on the finish.

Ludlow Single Malt

THE OXFORD ARTISAN DISTILLERY

OWNER The Oxford Artisan Distillery Ltd

FOUNDED 2011

WEBSITE www.theoxfordartisandistillery.com

This distillery, its name shortened to TOAD, plows a different furrow to most of its English counterparts. In partnership with John Letts of Heritage Harvest Ltd, its ethos is based on the distillation of modern varieties of ancient grains.

A unique heritage of ancient grains

In 1994, Letts discovered perfectly preserved wheat and rye varieties dating back to the late medieval period while working on thatched buildings. These ancient grains grew much taller than modern varieties

Crafty Little Rye

and would have been perfectly adapted to the local growing conditions, centuries before the industrialization of farming and the commercial control over new seed varieties. Letts planted and harvested the grains over many years to bulk up supplies, developing more sustainable farming methods that helped enrich the soil and promote biodiversity. Within a 50-mile radius of the distillery, five farms now grow these ancient varieties of barley, wheat, and rye for the distillery, and they are the only distillery with access to them.

At the distillery, TOAD's stills are something to behold. Custom built from scratch by the industrial coppersmiths of South Devon Railway Engineering, they rock a steampunk aesthetic, taking inspiration from old diving helmets, Victorian engineering and Jules Verne's *20,000 Leagues Under the Sea*. They have two copper pot stills, the 634-gallon (2,400-liter) "Nautilus" and 132-gallon (500-liter) "Nemo," together with two 16½ft (5m) tall, 40-plate distillation columns.

Their first whisky was released in 2021, and labels such as Easy Ryder and Purple Grain show they love a good pun on their bottlings. In 2022, Distill Ventures, Diageo's spirit brand accelerator program, took notice and acquired a minority stake in the business, providing investment as it has done for Kanosuke, Stauning, Westland, and Starward distilleries.

In 2024, the distillery launched Fielden's Rye Whisky, emphasizing the agricultural practices on Fielden's Farm that support greater biodiversity, where heritage grains grow in soils naturally fertilized by clover, which they report results in grains with a fuller flavor than those grown under more industrial farming practices.

The Oxford Artisan Distillery is bringing heritage grains back to English whisky.

TASTING NOTES

Fielden Rye Whisky
Rye, matured in American oak and wine casks, 48% ABV
Warm berry notes of black currant and cranberry on the nose, with crisp rye, earthen musty floors, and scents of old barns. Fruity notes of red currant, cherry, and red licorice with toasty notes, caramel, toasted fruit loaf, ginger, and a hint of herbal notes and chocolate.

Crafty Little Rye
Rye, finished in Sauternes casks, 44% ABV
The Sauternes cask makes this whisky a real sweet treat. Made from 70% rye, 20% wheat, and 10% malted barley, the nose has a tickle of rye spice, but with creamy vanilla, crystallized honey, and poached pears in syrup. The taste buds are bathed in warm golden syrup, ginger loaf, herbal notes, baked fruits, and comforting sugary sweetness.

SPIRIT OF YORKSHIRE

OWNER Spirit of Yorkshire Ltd

FOUNDED 2016

WEBSITE www.spiritofyorkshire.com

Spirit of Yorkshire began distilling in 2016 as a field-to-bottle producer with a keen focus on environmental responsibility. Based on the Yorkshire coast, their whisky is named after the Filey Bay shoreline. Founders Tom Mellor and David Thompson engaged legendary global whisky

consultant, the late Dr. Jim Swan, who died in 2017, to formulate the design of the distillery to create the character of the whisky they envisioned.

A manual operation

Production is split between the working farm in the Yorkshire Wolds and the distillery, starting with the malted barley put through the mash tun and 2,640-gallon (10,000-liter) fermenters, equipment shared with their sister company Wold Top Brewery. Water is drawn from a chalk-filtered aquifer, the same private water supply used by the brewery.

Distilling takes place four days a week using their 1,320-gallon (5,000-liter) wash still and 925-gallon (3,500-liter) spirit still built by Forsyths Ltd of Rothes, which generate 106 gallons (400 liters) of pure alcohol per distillation. It's a manual operation with hand-turned valves controlling the pressure and temperature of the stills, with the cuts made by directly assessing the spirit, for the two styles of spirit they make, thanks to the optional four-plate rectifying column connected to the spirit still. Divert the vapor flow through the column, and a more purified spirit at 86 percent ABV can be collected over the typical 73 percent ABV from the spirit still alone.

Both styles are laid down in first-fill bourbon casks, with a smaller proportion filled into oloroso sherry casks and PX hogsheads. On the experimental side, they have filled casks of English oak, peated casks, and the brewery's IPA barrels. The relationship between brewery and distillery extends to filling Filey Bay casks with porter to make Rip Curl beer, then finishing whisky in the porter casks. Sufficient barley is grown on the farm to step up production to six days a week.

Filey Bay Flagship

TASTING NOTES

Filey Bay Flagship
Single malt, matured in bourbon casks, 46% ABV
Butter toffee, vanilla, ripe barley, banana peel, toasted oak, and dry oak spices on the nose, with fresh fruit and herbal notes as it opens up. The palate shows off the first-fill bourbon cask characteristics with vanilla, honey, apple, and orange flavors before taking it up a gear with toffee, hints of chocolate, clove, and ginger.

Filey Bay STR Finish
Single malt, finished in STR casks, 48% ABV
The STR cask imparts an explosion of pan-roasted spices and peppercorns accompanied by aromas of blueberry, strawberry jam, and rowan jelly. Flavors of licorice, gingersnaps, pepper, and clove give heat on the palate, adding to the red apple and rowan notes.

WEETWOOD BREWERY AND DISTILLERY

OWNER Weetwood Ales Ltd

FOUNDED 2018

WEBSITE www.weetwoodales.co.uk

Independently family-owned and run, Weetwood Ales Ltd had been running for 26 years when they decided to add a distillery to their brewery, taproom, and retail operations in 2018.

Equipped with a 106-gallon (400-liter) copper pot still, they produce gin, vodka, and brandy, and released The Cheshire, their first single malt whisky in 2022. This was finished in a European oak cask after undergoing its initial maturation in bourbon quarter casks. It's still early days for their initial batches, but their limited editions showcase their experiments in finishing such as The Cheshire Seaside Edition finished in Islay casks and The Cheshire Fireside Edition finished in oloroso sherry and PX casks.

TASTING NOTE

The Cheshire Single Malt Second Release
Single malt, matured in STR American oak quarter casks and finished in European oak casks, 46% ABV
Vanilla, honey, toasted cereals, earthy spice on the nose, as this really opens up well, with dried apple, mandarin, and hints of tropical fruit. Sweet and juicy, with honey, vanilla, peach, nectarine, dried mango, and mandarin, with cocoa, cinnamon, malt, citrus, and stone fruits on the finish.

The Cheshire Single Malt Second Release

WHITE PEAK

OWNER White Peak Distillery Ltd

FOUNDED 2016

WEBSITE www.whitepeakdistillery.co.uk

The White Peak distillery resides inside the former maintenance and storage sheds of the Johnson & Nephew Wire Works within the Derwent Valley Mills UNESCO World Heritage Site in the Peak District. The manufacture of wire and cable products took place on this site for 120 years.

Max and Claire Vaughan founded this Derbyshire craft distillery and designed it to ensure they could derive flavor at every stage of the process. They make a lightly peated style, combing 20 percent peated malt with 80 percent unpeated malt. Thornbridge Brewery delivers a live brewer's yeast every week, the same yeast used by the brewery to make their Jaipur IPA. White Peak distillery's luxuriously long fermentation time of 140 hours creates a lot of secondary flavors in the wash. It's a production decision that's much less likely to happen in a larger distillery where the patience for the development of these flavors may come secondary to volume, time, and efficiency considerations. The malt whisky side of White Peak's operations is equipped with a 792-gallon (3,000-liter) wash still and a 555-gallon (2,100-liter) spirit still fabricated by

White Peak distillery is equipped with a pair of copper pot stills for whisky production and a small spirit still used to make gin and rum.

McMillan Coppersmiths in Scotland. Distillation is run slowly with high cut points to capture the exquisite fruity flavors created during fermentation.

Adding to their range of Shining Cliff gin and rum bottlings made in "Betty," their 158-gallon (600-liter) spirit still, the team released their debut Wire Works whisky in February 2022. This was a cask strength single malt whisky matured in bourbon and shave-toast-rechar (STR) casks.

This craft distillery is doing everything on site, right down to bottling, labeling, and packing the spirits. To date, the lineup includes Over Smoke, a lightly peated single malt matured in STR-ROS casks, which are STR red wine casks recharred over smoke, a technique that captures the smoke within the barrel at the end of charring rather than letting it drift away. Take Alter Ego, an experiment to adjust the usual production parameters for their house style by taking deeper cuts during distillation, which is matured in a higher proportion of first-fill bourbon casks than their other lines. Thornbridge Brewery's Necessary Evil imperial stout casks, which previously held PX sherry, are used to add depth to the Wire Works Necessary Evil Finish.

Wire Works Caduro, named after a global cable brand once produced at the Johnson & Nephew Wire Works, uses a specific combination of American and French oak casks, both first-fill bourbon and STR casks, to create further complexity.

Caduro was also the first release to be offered as a distillery refill, launching their concept of a bottle for life. Each release is small batch and limited, sometimes just single casks, but the word is spreading as more people taste their Peak District craft spirits and discover the detail-orientated approach to making whisky practiced at the White Peak distillery.

Wire Works Over Smoke

TASTING NOTES

Wire Works Carduro
Single malt, matured in first-fill bourbon and STR casks, 46.8% ABV
Lightly peated, the nose is clean and fruity with jellied fruits, citrus, honeyed apple, and red grape integrated with a mild, sweet peat smoke. A pleasingly thick mouthfeel, with cherry, chocolate, toffee, roasted hazelnut, fudge, aniseed, and black pepper, with lingering notes of smoke and charred oak.

Wire Works Necessary Evil
Single malt, finished in stout casks, 51.3% ABV
With its stout finish, the nose has Ferrero Rocher, fresh roasted coffee, musty warehouse floors, and roasted spices. Date, prune, milky coffee, and lots of berry fruit to taste, with bramble, black currant, brown sugar, and chocolate, with malt and coffee leading a smooth finish.

Wire Works Over Smoke
Single malt, matured in STR-ROS casks, 52.7% ABV
A focused smoke, not peaty, but charred wood, with dried red fruits, Toffee Crisp, aniseed, and gingersnap. It's velvety smooth, with chocolate orange, malted milk balls, cask-strength spices, and little pockets of black currant fondant, and a lengthy finish. A dash of water brings out the fruitiness.

YARM

OWNER Yarm Distillery Ltd

FOUNDED 2018

WEBSITE www.yarmdistillery.com

Founded by the Marsden family, this small operation based at Eaglescliffe, County Durham, makes vodka, rum, gin, and liqueurs and then moved into making spirit for whisky in 2020. Just three years later in July 2023, Richard Marsden, Yarm's head distiller, released his first single malt whisky in a batch of 342 bottles at 43.1 percent ABV. The distillery brought in wash created by Cameron's Brewery made from 100 percent Golden Promise barley grown and malted near Berwick-upon-Tweed. This is a spring barley variety once favored by The Macallan, which had its heyday during the 1960s to '80s. Yarm distilled the new-make spirit in their pair of 132-gallon (500-liter) alembic stills, nicknamed "Boris" and "Doris," and matured in a Jack Daniel's Tennessee whiskey cask until it was legally allowed to be called whisky. The distillery's own whisky is also used as a component of their cherry whisky liqueur.

WALES

Penderyn is the flag bearer for Welsh whisky. It is a company that was ahead of its time in defining the Welsh whisky category, and it now has a successful Welsh export and internationally recognized brand. As the Welsh whisky category built its credibility, single malt Welsh whisky was finally granted protected geographical indication status in 2023, after a long and skillfully argued campaign led by Penderyn with the backing of fellow Welsh distillers.

PENDERYN

OWNER The Welsh Whisky Company

FOUNDED 2000

WEBSITE www.penderyn.wales

Whisky culture had been extinguished in Wales, so the opening of the Penderyn distillery in 2000 brought a great deal of interest and excitement. Penderyn has expanded significantly since then and now has a network of three distilleries in Penderyn

(the first), Llandudno, and Swansea. Global whisky consultant Dr. Jim Swan (1941–2017) helped the team set up the distillery and create their whisky, a feat he replicated for numerous distilleries around the world for the rest of his life. He was their first master distiller. The Penderyn Lloyd Street site in Llandudno is tasked with making peated whisky, while the Swansea Copperworks distillery matches the original distillery and boosts Penderyn's overall capacity to 238,000 gallons (900,000 liters) per annum.

Penderyn has always offered the whisky drinker a great deal of choice. Aista Phillips, Penderyn's current master blender, is responsible for creating new limited editions such as their Icons of Wales series. Penderyn Dragon is an eye-catching series and includes Penderyn Legend, their original Madeira cask finish; Penderyn Celt, the peated quarter cask finish; and Penderyn Myth. Their Gold range is bottled at the higher ABV of 46 percent and includes their Sherrywood, Portwood, Madeira, Peated, and Rich Oak expressions.

Penderyn Sherrywood

The new tasting bar *at Penderyn's Llandudno distillery.*

TASTING NOTES

Penderyn Portwood
Single malt, matured in ruby port casks, 46% ABV
Port casks are a superb match for the Penderyn spirit, and this carries aromas of dates, cocoa, and spicy dried fruits, with a beautifully concentrated, textured palate of dark honey, gingersnaps, and chocolate-covered cranberries and a smooth fruity finish.

Penderyn Sherrywood
Single malt, matured in bourbon and oloroso sherry casks, 40% ABV
Penderyn's spicy character comes to the fore as the baking spice aromas penetrate the rich sherry aromas characterized by dried vine fruits, black tea, and fruitcake. The palate is dense and malty, with melted milk chocolate, espresso, toffee, and further spices.

ABER FALLS

OWNER Halewood Artisanal Spirits plc

FOUNDED 2018

WEBSITE www.aberfallsdistillery.com

This compact distillery in Abergwyngregyn opened in 2018, becoming the first new whisky distillery in north Wales for 100 years. Named after the spectacular waterfall that supplies the water, they process Welsh malted barley using their stainless steel mash tun and six stainless steel fermenters. Following the first release in 2021, there is now a NAS single malt and regular exclusives, including rye whiskey.

TASTING NOTE

Aber Falls
Single malt, matured in bourbon, sherry, and new oak casks, 40% ABV
Light fruity aromatics, with a nose of apple, pear, nectarine, tangerine, and hints of spice. Light and juicy on the palate, but without much body at first. Orange jelly, dried apricot, chocolate malt, and peppercorns, leading into caramel, dried fruits, and spiced baking chocolate.

COLES

OWNER The Coles family

FOUNDED 2020

WEBSITE www.coles.wales

The Coles run the historic White Hart Inn pub, restaurant, and brewery in Llanddarog in Carmarthenshire, and added a craft distillery in 2020. The distillery fits snugly into a large shed. Their new-make spirit is filled into bourbon casks to mature. A NAS single malt whisky has been released.

TASTING NOTE

Coles Single Malt Whisky
Single malt, matured in bourbon casks, 42% ABV
Aged for over 5 years, the nose is slightly herbal with vanilla sponge and a hint of oak astringency. On the palate, there is sweet vanilla, candied orange, gooseberry, pineapple cubes, and hints of cilantro. It's pretty light initially, but tasty and develops a bit more body through to the finish of fleshy citrus and black pepper.

DÀ MHÌLE

OWNER The Savage-Onstwedder family

FOUNDED 2012

WEBSITE www.damhile.co.uk

Glynhynod Farm is home to this organic distillery near Llandysul, Ceredigion, where everything from the water for the spirits to the wood that burns to heat the still comes from their land. In 2012, they started making their own organic spirits, producing rum, vodka, gin, absinthe, and more, selling the spirits in local outlets and online. They have a single pot still, named Ceridwen, which is attached to a rectification column. The stills are steam heated, though a wood burner is used to create the steam.

TASTING NOTE

Dà Mhìle Organic Single Malt 2023 Limited Edition
Single malt, matured in two first-fill sherry casks, 46% ABV
The nose opens with a well-rounded barley note, with honey, butterscotch sauce, flaxseed, warm sweet pastries, and a pinch of white pepper. Full flavored and delicious, with sweet sherry notes and a dense texture, it shows red apple, clove, and peppercorn, adding chocolate Hobnobs, granola, date, and chocolate malt, with spices persisting throughout the creaminess on the finish. A highly recommended pour.

IN THE WELSH WIND

OWNER In the Welsh Wind Ltd

FOUNDED 2018

WEBSITE www.inthewelshwind.co.uk

Ellen Wakelam and Alex Jungmayr run this craft distillery in the former Gogerddan Arms pub, a few miles north of Cardigan in west Wales. They sell a wide range of Welsh gin, rum, and vodkas distilled with their copper pot stills named Meredith and Afanc. The spirit for their whisky is made in small batches, with the capability to undertake small scale malting on site.

The owners have invested in a high-tech iStill for their whisky production, which can help reduce energy costs and cleaning times and give greater control over distillation. Whisky will be released from the middle of the 2020s, using a wide variety of cask types and sizes.

FRANCE

Whisky-making has become more widespread in France, with hot spots in the Breton region, Bordeaux, and Alsace. Evidence that the French whisky industry is thriving and healthy can be found in the granting of Breton whisky with its own geographical indication status, the growth of fine luxury whiskies such as Alfred Giraud, and the increasing number of distillery and brand acquisitions by large companies. There is an increasing focus on growing and harvesting organic grains, with distilleries such as Domaine des Hautes Glaces embracing the circular economy to set an example of how to justify the environmental consequences of every action it takes.

DISTILLERIE WARENGHEM

OWNER Warenghem Company

FOUNDED 1900

WEBSITE www.distillerie-warenghem.bzh

In common with many other European distilleries, Brittany's Distillerie Warenghem was set up to make fruit liqueurs and to distill the local apple crop. When Léon Warenghem founded the distillery in 1900, they made a liqueur called the Elixir d'Armorique using 35 different plants, and it is still in demand today. However, like Distillerie des Menhirs, it adapted the Breton region's tradition of making cider brandy, and in the 1980s it embarked on the production of whisky.

A successful enterprise

Based in Lannion, the family-owned distillery enjoys great success under the direction of David Roussier. The team are dedicated to expressing the terroir in their whiskies, using only organic French malted barley since 2020, though their concept of terroir also embraces the spring water drawn from beneath the distillery, the maritime influences of their location, and the character of the Breton people.

The distillery is a popular destination for visitors to the area. Distillation is traditional, with a capacity to make 39,600 gallons (150,000 liters) per annum. They have six washbacks that are filled with clear wort drawn off the semi-lauter tun, which are then left to ferment over 72–96 hours. The copper pot stills would not look out of place in a rural single malt Scotch whisky

distillery. Double distillation takes place in squat stills with steeply downward-sloping lyne arms, and the vapors run through shell and tube condensers to be cooled into new-make spirit. A grain whisky is made, mainly from wheat, and used in their different blends.

Their Armorik single malt brand launched in 1998, and the modern range includes their Classic expression, matured in bourbon casks; Sherry Cask, matured in oloroso casks; and Double Maturation, which is initially matured in new Breton oak casks and then in oloroso sherry casks. Their stunning Yeun Elez Jobic is made from imported malt from Scotland. Age statements at 10 and 15 years have been released, and there is an active program of both limited edition and single cask bottlings.

Yeun Elez Jobic

TASTING NOTES

Armorik Double Maturation
Single malt, matured in Breton oak casks and finished in sherry casks, 46% ABV
A fruity bouquet greets the nose, with apple, citrus, vanilla, and digestive biscuits. The palate combines fruitiness with creamy caramel, maltiness, fine spices, and sherry fruit notes.

Armorik 10-Year-Old
Single malt, matured in bourbon casks and finished in oloroso sherry casks, 46% ABV
This draws on bourbon and sherry cask characteristics with toasted oats, vanilla, and cardamom. On the palate, there are notes of vanilla, dried red berries, and growing spicy notes and vanilla lasting into the finish.

Yeun Elez Jobic
Single malt, matured in bourbon casks, 46% ABV
Sizzled bacon fat by a peat fire, with lemon zest, pepper, and clove on the nose, which embody this peated whisky with a beach barbecue vibe. The texture is smooth as silk, with lemon, honey, and vanilla, fresh apple, and stone fruits, and a finish of peppery spice.

DOMAINE DES HAUTES GLACES

OWNER Rémy Cointreau

FOUNDED 2009

WEBSITE www.hautesglaces.com

Hautes Glaces is a high-altitude Alpine distillery in the Trièves region in the southern Isère department specializing in the production of grain-to-bottle organic whiskies. Founded by Frédéric Revol in 2009, the farm, distillery, malting house, and cellars were acquired by Rémy Cointreau in 2017, becoming a sister distillery to Bruichladdich on Islay and Westland in Seattle. The connection is obvious, with a common spirit that bonds all three distilleries together—a strong belief in terroir and a sense of responsibility to reduce the impact their activities have on the environment.

Beyond the spirits they make, there's a sense of spirituality here among the mountains: a place to reconnect with the environment, where you can put your hands in the earth. At 2,952ft (900m) above sea level, it's the right setting for a summit on the natural resources, energy costs, and land use that go into making whisky and consider the environmental impact of every action on the ecosystem and society.

Using as few resources as possible

Hautes Glaces is setting an example of how to make whisky using as few resources as possible. Organic barley seeds are selected for their suitability to thrive in the mountain climate and for their resilience to withstand the impact of climate change, as soils get warmer and drier. Flavor is prioritized over yield. Working with the Centre de Recherche Biologique, they are testing the suitability of lost seed varieties from the 19th and 20th centuries. The seeds that pass the test are then scaled up for use by some of the 19 farms that supply Domaine des Hautes Glaces with their raw materials. This farming collective rotates their crops, spreads spent grains back on the land, and practices regenerative agriculture methods through planting cover crops and periodically allowing the fields to return to grassland, helping prevent disease, promote biodiversity, bolster drought resistance, and enrich the long-term fertility of the soil. Together, the extra organic matter also helps the land store more carbon.

Using mountain yeast cultures

For a distillery looking closely at micro-provenance cuvées with their Epistémè range, through varying grain, yeast, cask, and maturation conditions, they have developed their own bank of mountain yeast cultures isolated from the fields, ending the need for commercial yeast deliveries. These natural yeasts can operate at lower temperatures and deliver longer fermentations of up to 140 hours, opening up the possibility of different flavor profiles. Releasing twin expressions that invite comparative tastings gives whisky drinkers the ability to make up their own minds about how significant each factor makes to the final flavor.

Conscious that more distilleries are disclosing their water efficiency in number of gallons per gallon of whisky made, water stewardship is a major focus here. Heat exchangers enable water to reach the required temperature with less energy, and surplus heat is supplied to keep the buildings warm. The distillery chooses not to use cleaning products on their equipment; their used water is clean enough to be used to irrigate the fields. Electricity comes from renewable sources, and the distillation is powered by burning wood from local sawmills. The distinctive flat-sided 50cl bottles have reduced their reliance on new glass and cut the carbon footprint of the bottle by nearly 40 percent.

The view of the L'Obiou mountain range from the distillery is replicated in miniature in the glass base, but the bottle transmits a stronger vision about purity, minimalism, and transparency. Tiny labels reduce ink and printing materials, the corks are made from spent grains, and they have abandoned foil capsules and branded boxes, simply shipping in recycled cardboard. When you buy a bottle of Domaine des Hautes Glaces, you are buying all of this.

TASTING NOTE

Domaine des Hautes Glaces Indigène
Single malt, matured in new sessile oak, new pedunculate oak, refill wine, Cognac, and Armagnac casks, 44% ABV
The nose is clean and pure and reminiscent of floral meadows, with hints of lime zest, yuzu, almonds, and clover. Refreshing to taste, with a dried grapefruit bitterness, lime juice, peach, chopped almond, and pepper, it develops more vanilla creaminess and citrus notes, with a finish of salted caramel and fading fruits.

Domaine des Hautes Glaces Indigène

CELTIC WHISKY DISTILLERIE

OWNER Maison Villevert

FOUNDED 1997

WEBSITE www.celtic-whisky-distillerie.fr

Established in an old farmhouse by Jean Donnay in the late 1990s, Maison Villevert acquired the Glann ar Mor distillery in 2020 and gave it a new name. The original name was the Breton for "seaside," which is apt given its picturesque location on the north coastline of Brittany, not that far from Jersey and Guernsey. At one point, Jean Donnay had reached an advance stage of planning for a second distillery at Gartbreck Farm, west of Bowmore on Islay, but plans fell through in 2017; Chivas Brothers now plan to build their first Islay distillery on the site. Jean-Sébastien Robicquet founded Maison Villevert, Celtic Whisky Distillerie's owner, and it has a solid reputation for innovation. The wooden fermenters are made of Oregon pine. The maritime influence on the maturing spirit in the warehouse is cherished as an essential element in shaping the whisky's character. The current range includes Glann ar Mor, peated expression Kornog, and their Celtic blend Gwalarn, with occasional cask-strength limited editions such as Kornog Sant Ivy and Kornog Sant Erwanun.

TASTING NOTE

Glann ar Mor
Single malt, matured in bourbon casks, 46% ABV
A sweet and light delight, summer in a glass, with soft canned pear, fluffy apple, sweet grapes, and berry fruits. Simple and straightforward and is pretty much blemish-free and bursts with fresh, fruity promise.

Kornog Sant Ivy

DISTILLERIE BERCLOUX

OWNER Les Bienheureux

FOUNDED 2014

WEBSITE www.bellevoye.fr

Distillerie Bercloux is a small artisanal distillery in the Cognac region of western France. Like a number of French distilleries, it has a Stupfler still made in Bordeaux, as well as the alembic still characteristic of the region. In 2019, Les Bienheureux, meaning The Blessed, acquired the distillery; they are a drinks innovations company formed by Alexandre Sirech and Jean Moueix in 2015.

The Bercloux stock was required as a component for their triple malt Bellevoye French whisky range—the name means "the beautiful path or the road less traveled." Triple malt is a slightly confusing term as it can mean a combination of three malted grains, such as barley, wheat, and rye, but in the case of Bellevoye, the term is used for their blend of three single malt whiskies from different distilleries. This would be a blended malt if this was Scotch whisky. The inspiration comes from winemaking in nearby Bordeaux, where wine is made from different grape varieties blended together to create a more sophisticated drink than the individual components. As well as whisky from Bercloux, the other malts include a fruity-style French whisky from Alsace made in Holstein stills and a light column still whisky made in northern France. The triple malt range is aged for 5–10 years and finished for up to a year to create the seven different colorful expressions, including Orange (unpeated, rum cask finish), Red (lightly peated, grand cru wine cask finish), Black (peated), Plum (old plum cask finish), and Green (lightly peated, Calvados finish).

TASTING NOTES

Bellevoye Blue
Blended malt, finished in new French oak casks, 40% ABV
A nose of beeswax and toffee, with a light fruitiness and a fine layer of spice. A complex palate, with flavors of mandarins, clove, and ginger with traces of milk chocolate.

Bellevoye White
Blended malt, finished in Sauternes casks, 40% ABV
Delicate flavors of vanilla custard, honey, brioche, and cumin, with a slight nuttiness. Ripe stone fruit flavors to taste, with cinnamon, marmalade peel, and an undeniably nutty finish with lingering spices.

Bellevoye Blue

DISTILLERIE DES MENHIRS

OWNER Le Lay family

FOUNDED 1998

WEBSITE www.distillerie.bzh

Brittany is noted for its apples and the drinks made from them, and it was these that former math teacher Guy Le Lay focused on before turning his hand to whisky. He invested in a new facility, building Distillerie des Menhirs in 1998—the name refers to local standing stones thought to be more than 5,000 years old. To produce a spirit with a unique flavor, Le Lay decided to make whisky with buckwheat, known as *blé noir* in French and *eddu* in Breton, the area's Celtic language. Buckwheat is a low-yielding cover crop and delivers only half of the alcohol yield of malted barley. Food researcher Pierre Duroset

developed techniques for malting and fermenting buckwheat, while Le Lay engaged the services of cognac master blender Robert Leauté to develop and teach him the art of distillation with direct-fired stills and to share his skills in maturation and blending. The distillery is now run by Guy's son Kévin Le Lay as cellar master. The Eddu range includes blends with whiskies made from barley, and pure buckwheat expressions named Silver, Gold, and Brocéliande, a whisky finished in new Breton oak casks.

TASTING NOTE

Eddu Silver
Buckwheat, matured in cognac casks, 40% ABV
Full-bodied and rich in flavor, after five years of aging. Floral and fruity notes, and flavors of cloves, cinnamon, and nutmeg, with a caramel note toward the end.

Eddu Silver

DISTILLERIE ROZELIEURES

OWNER The Grallet-Dupic family

FOUNDED 2000

WEBSITE www.whiskyrozelieures.com

Rozelieures is a family-owned farm-to-bottle distiller in Lorraine, eastern France. With five generations of farming behind them, including a history of distilling brandy and eau-de-vie from their own fruit, Christophe Dupic and his wife, Sabine, launched the whisky with the support of his father-in-law, the eau-de-vie maker Hubert Grallet.

The 740-acre farm harvests 120–245 acres of Laureate and Prospect barley specifically for whisky making, and the farm has converted to organic farming methods. Since opening the Malterie des Hautes-Vosges, they can now malt their own barley in-house. The malt is milled and mashed then fermented at the distillery in temperature-controlled washbacks. Distillation takes place slowly in a pair of Charentais stills, with a 845-gallon (3,200-liter) and 423-gallon (1,600-liter) capacity, and they produce a refined new-make spirit. Beyond filling sherry and bourbon casks to mature in their five cellars,

Rozelieures takes advantage of the availability of high-quality wine casks. Casks coopered from local *Quercus robur* and *Q petrea* are also in the pipeline.

Their vision for hyper-local whiskies has led to their single estate expressions, called Le Parcellaire Édition Spéciale, from different plots of land around the farm. The distillery has made strides toward greater sustainability and self-sufficiency and is taking French whisky to the next level.

TASTING NOTES

G. Rozelieures Tourbé Collection
Single malt, matured in bourbon and new French oak casks, 46% ABV
Peated whisky with a complex range of savory aromas with wood smoke, fragrant spices, and Worcestershire sauce. The palate revolves around vanilla, sweet malt, citrus peel, peat smoke, and black pepper and shows elegance and balance.

G. Rozelieures Subtil Collection
Single malt, matured in bourbon, cognac, and new French oak casks, 40% ABV
Unpeated, with attractive floral scents and honey, cereal notes, and cookie aromas. The Rozelieures full-bodied style is evident here with flavors of vanilla, honeyed oak, wood spices, and baked apple.

G. Rozelieures Tourbé Collection

BELGIUM

Belgium is well known for its beer and, to some degree, for its genever, a grain-based spirit. But the difference between genever and malt whisky is a fine one, and beer is the basis for whisky after all. Belgium whiskies are becoming better known as their producers tap into better distribution networks in new markets, often via importers run by world whisky aficionados eager to spread the word. By far and away, the Belgian whisky that enjoys the widest distribution is The Belgian Owl.

THE BELGIAN OWL

OWNER Etienne Bouillon, Luc Fobert, and Pierre Robert

FOUNDED 2004

WEBSITE www.belgianwhisky.com

Master distiller Etienne Bouillon installed one pair of stills from the closed Caperdonich distillery in Speyside, Scotland, while the other pair went to Falkirk distillery in the Lowlands.

Liège is a pretty, historic city in Wallonia, positioned at a key meeting point in the heart of Europe, which has made it a crossroads for an array of cultures. The region has been fought over repeatedly during the centuries, and the city has witnessed countless battles and hosted any number of peace ententes and victory celebrations, which it has celebrated with hedonistic joy. As a result, Liège is a city that knows how to party, and food and drink are woven into the fabric of the local community. That a whisky-maker should have laid out his stall here should come as no surprise.

Founder and master distiller Etienne Bouillon has come a long way from the original Belgian Owl micro-distillery. The building was more of a glorified lock-up decorated with bottle samples, packaging, posters, and newspaper articles about The Belgian Owl. The still itself was a historical curiosity, an oversize copper kettle on a wooden cart with wheels that would have been taken to vineyards to distill grape wine for brandy. In 2013, The Belgian Owl moved to Fexhe-le-Haut Clocher to the west of the city to open The Owl Distillery on a farm, next to fields of spring barley. Their crowning glory was the acquisition of one of the pairs of Caperdonich stills from the now demolished distillery in Rothes. These substantial stills from the Speyside region have found a very good home and now play their part in turning the Fair Trade barley grown in partnership with farmers in the Hesbaye region into a Belgian spirit

that Bouillon finds embodies the terroir of the area. The water table under the distillery serves all their water needs, so the move to this location has been truly ideal. Bouillon matures the whisky exclusively in first-fill bourbon casks from Heaven Hill in the US, and this young distillate-led dram exhibits a light, vanilla dessert style of whisky, which is rich in sweet apple and pear notes.

TASTING NOTES

The Belgian Owl Identité 3-Year-Old
Single malt, matured in bourbon casks, 46% ABV
Reflective of its bourbon cask and light, fruity distillate, this whisky belies its age with a nose of fresh floral notes, honey, vanilla, green apple, and freshly laundered linen. The palate draws together lemon bonbons, vanilla sponge, and citrus peel, with a hint of chocolate and espresso.

The Belgian Owl Evolution 4-Year-Old
Single malt, matured in bourbon casks, 46% ABV
The nose is complex with floral, lemon peel, and vanilla ice-cream notes mingling with scents of pine and snuff tobacco. The flavors play out a little unevenly, with sherbet lemons, creamy vanilla, and chewy nougat yielding to flavors of black pepper, grilled peach, and Walnut Whip.

The Belgian Owl Identité
3-Year-Old

FILLIERS

OWNER The Filliers family

FOUNDED 1880

WEBSITE www.filliersdistillery.com

Filliers in Deinze, southwest of Ghent, makes for a fascinating day out, and the production areas have an incredible range of distillation equipment. They now have three distilleries on site, each tasked with a different spirit: genever, gin, and whisky. In 2007, the late master distiller and co-owner Jan Filliers launched Goldlys, the first Belgian single malt whisky.

His son Benoit Filliers was promoted as the new master distiller and production director in 2023, and the whiskies rebranded as Filliers.

TASTING NOTE

Filliers 10-Year-Old Sherry Oak
Single malt, matured in sherry casks, 43% ABV
Nutty sherry notes on the nose with cherry, mixed peel, currants, and allspice. A smooth after-dinner dram with flavors of dried fruit, chocolate, bramble, vanilla essence, cinnamon stick, stewed apple, black currants, allspice, and herbal notes. Finish of dried vine fruits, orange zest, bitter chocolate, and walnut.

Filliers 10-Year-Old
Sherry Oak

PIRLOT BREWERY & DISTILLERY

OWNER Guy Pirlot

FOUNDED 1998; whisky since 2011

WEBSITE www.brouwerijpirlot.be

Guy Pirlot opened a micro-brewery in Zandhoven, east of Antwerp, and extended his beer-making activities to start distilling his own whisky. He specializes in peated Belgian whisky, bottled under his Kempisch Vuur label, using distilling malt from Castle Malting made using imported Scottish peat.

The natural beauty of the nearby countryside, known as The Kempen, has a history of harvesting peat, while Vuur comes from the Dutch word for "fire."

TASTING NOTE

Kempisch Vuur 3-Year-Old
Single malt, matured in Laphroaig quarter casks, 46% ABV
Cracking stuff. Gentle peat smoke, with hazelnut meringue and vanilla essence. Plenty of flavor with chocolate brownie, clove, peel oils, dried fruit, and lemon drops, and an intense finish of 70% dark chocolate and licorice.

WAVE DISTIL

OWNER Wave Distil Srl

FOUNDED 2010

WEBSITE www.wavedistil.be

Thierry Van Renterghem started working with spirits in 2010, subsequently launching his own vodka, gin, rum, and whisky ranges. The brand name August 17th serves as a reminder of his career-ending soccer injury sustained on that date in 1992. The distillery is located in Sorinnes southeast of Brussels. Benoît Bertholet came on board in 2018 to manage the business,

leaving Van Rentherghem to manage distillation and maturation. Casks are divided between the maturation cellar and finishing cellars, with finishing taking place in port, cognac, sweet wine, and peated casks from Laphroaig.

TASTING NOTE

August 17th Julius 7-Year-Old
Single malt, matured in cognac and port casks, 51.5% ABV
Sugared apple, baked citrus, gingersnaps, and aromatic smoke on the nose. On first sip, there are baked apple notes, with malt, ginger, peppery spice, followed by a mild, smoky finish.

NETHERLANDS

With a long history of beer-making, one might expect the Netherlands to have a history of whisky making, too. But the grain spirit made here is genever, which is often matured in oak barrels, and is an unbelievably popular drink in The Netherlands. The country has an enthusiastic whisky-drinking community, too, and hosts several whisky shows, and the seriously good whiskies made by Zuidam are worthy of these Dutch diehards.

ZUIDAM

OWNER Zuidam Distillers

FOUNDED 1975 (whisky since 1996)

WEBSITE www.zuidam.nl

When talking of emerging world distilleries, one of the recurring themes is the propensity to bottle whisky when it is too young in a bid to generate cash flow and cultivate an audience willing to follow your journey. At Zuidam, this isn't an issue. The family-owned and family-run distillery has been producing spirits for around half a century and has multiple product lines, so they have a solid range of age statement whiskies in their stocks, including releases over 20 years old. When it came to making whisky, their mantra is simple: good things come to those who wait.

Order out of chaos
East of Antwerp, the Zuidam distillery in Baarle Nassau isn't much to look at from the outside; it appears like any other industrial warehouse unit. But enter the building and you find yourself in an Aladdin's cave of pot and column stills, and large glass-extracting vessels containing everything from cinnamon and cocoa to roses and vanilla pods for the distillery's naturally flavored liqueurs. There are boxes of fruit, teams of workers cutting up oranges and lemons, piling up boxes of black currants, and squeezing casks in between distilling equipment.

Zuidam is very much a family firm. Fred van Zuidam set it up in 1975, with Hélène, his wife, designing the packaging and creating the look of the products. They have a rum brand called Flying Dutchman and a line of gins called Dutch Courage,

so while they are serious about quality, they are not averse to a little fun with their branding. These days, it's the second generation in charge; Patrick van Zuidam runs the distillery and genial brother Gilbert heads up sales. Patrick is obsessed with distilling and studies the process carefully to discern the origin of flavors in order to maximize the taste profile. The distillery allows him to experiment on a broad range of drinks, such as their oloroso cask–aged four-grain genever, made from malted barley, corn, rye, and winter wheat.

Single malt and rye
Their single malt whisky is made in traditional fashion. The grain is rolled in a rotary mill, and extremely clear worts are drained from the mash tun, much as they do in many Japanese distilleries. Clear wort gives a lighter flavor profile, with more fruity esters, and less high alcohols and grainy flavors than some Scotches. Zuidam has temperature-controlled fermenters, enabling the distiller to set the water jackets to exact temperatures and then pitch the yeast and control fermentation over the next five to six days as necessary.

Zuidam uses Belgian brewer's yeast, which gives a low yield but a lot of fruity esters, and M strain distiller's yeast, which is more conventional and high yielding. Overall, they have seven different strains of yeast in play across their wide range of products.

The Zuidam 100 percent rye mash uses 50 percent unmalted rye and 50 percent malted rye. Rye is notoriously difficult to malt and doesn't easily convert sugar to alcohol without a fight. Most rye whisky around the world is made with a proportion of malted barley in the mashbill to help the conversion process. It's not the easiest grain to work with—rye has a

Millstone 100 Rye

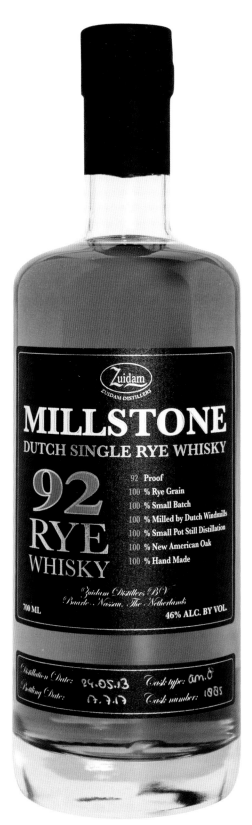

Millstone 92 Rye

Zuidam distillery is an Aladdin's cave of pot and column stills.

tendency to foam during fermentation, and it can turn into the consistency of wallpaper paste if you're not careful. Rye fermentations at Zuidam take eight or nine days, considerably longer than fermentation for their single malt. Unlike the majority of rye whiskey-makers in the US, Zuidam makes rye using batch distillation in copper pot stills, not with the typical column and doubler system more commonly seen in Kentucky and Tennessee distilleries.

From farm to glass

Zuidam styles itself as a farm-to-glass distillery these days, thanks to being able to harvest its own crops of barley and rye on a local farm. Whiskies are bottled under the Millstone brand name and include peated and unpeated single malts, mostly with age statements, and a pair of excellent rye whiskies. With single malt whiskies matured in oloroso sherry, Pedro Ximénez sherry, American oak, and French oak casks, they have ventured into using casks of tawny port, Moscatel, Amarone, and white port for their limited edition releases. With Zuidam, there's something for everyone.

TASTING NOTES

Millstone 100 Rye
Rye, matured in new American oak casks, 50% ABV
A powerful, impactful rye with an intensity of flavor and aromas, this has a nose of ripe plum and crisp rye, with a creamy sip that reveals chocolate and damson plum, surrounded by a swarm of cinnamon, spice, and rye flavors.

Millstone 92 Rye
Rye, matured in new American oak casks, 46% ABV
In contrast, this unspools from the glass with fragrant floral notes and aromas of fall fruits, treacle, dark chocolate, and a growing presence of rye spices. It's a well-paced rye with orange, chocolate, and vanilla on the palate, with a buildup of spices that ratchets up until it explodes into the finish.

AUSTRIA

Austria appears to have an active whisky-making industry from end to end, though many of the producers are local fruit brandy makers who have added whisky as a sideline. Those distilleries that major on whisky are making lovely spirits in interesting ways, leading to exports to more countries, but none of the brands are household names outside of Austria, and the country's whiskies definitely deserve more attention.

WALDVIERTLER WHISKY

OWNER The Haider family

FOUNDED 1995

WEBSITE www.waldviertlerwhisky.at

Johann Haider and his wife, Monika, established their distillery in Roggenreith, a little village in the Austrian region of Waldviertel, back in 1995. Today, it's one of the most picturesque distilleries in Austria, with both a museum and "Fire and Water Garden," and it even has its own helicopter pad for visitors. The Haiders are rye and rye malt specialists, but they also produce a range of single malts, gin, liqueurs, vodkas, and brandies. The apple doesn't fall far from the still either, as distiller Jasmin Haider-Stadler, daughter of the founders, took over as managing director in 2016.

Double distillation is practiced in a pair of Carl GmbH pot and column hybrid stills, which hold around 132 gallons (500 liters) each. Casks are made of sessile oak, grown locally in Manhartsberg, a species of oak known for its coarse grain. The cask interiors are charred before use, and the distillers fill them three times over their lifetime. The first-fill barrels are used for only three years, as the oak will give a lot of character to the whisky quite quickly, while a second-fill cask can last much longer and usually reaches its peak after six years of maturation. The coopers rejuvenate the barrels before using for them a third time, and then they will provide further service for another 18 years. Local wineries also supply them with wine barrels for their special editions.

Rye specialists

The Original Rye Whisky is made from 60 percent rye and 40 percent barley and has been their signature product since 1998, with its companion Rye Malt made from 100 percent malted rye. The distillery also works with dark roasted grains; their Dark Rye Malt is made from 100 percent dark roasted malted rye. Similarly, they make a single malt whisky from 100 percent malted barley, but also another made from 100 percent dark roasted single malt. They practice post malt smoking with local peat, too, which can be tasted in their Dark Single Malt Peated and Dark Rye Malt Peated whiskies. Age statement whiskies up to 18 years old have been released, and Waldviertler Whisky JH have also entered the crypto world of NFT (non-fungible tokens) whiskies.

Assessing the maturation of the Waldviertler spirit straight from the cask.

TASTING NOTES

Waldviertler Whisky Original Rye Whisky JH
Rye, matured in sessile oak casks, 41% ABV
Plenty of rye spice on the nose, with nutmeg, cinnamon, red apple, and chocolate notes, followed by a complex palate of vanilla, cocoa, rye spice, jammy dark fruits, and slightly herbal notes on the finish.

Waldviertler Whisky Single Malt JH
Single malt, matured in sessile oak casks, 41% ABV
The palate recognizes a light, crisp, malty, caramel flavor that dominates the whisky through to the finish, with a supporting role played by the honey, vanilla, peach, and nutmeg notes, which round it off nicely.

Waldviertler Original Rye

REISETBAUER & SON

OWNER The Reisetbauer family

FOUNDED 1998

WEBSITE www.reisetbauer.at

Hans Reisetbauer has always been fanatically driven by the quest for quality in his pursuit to create new and exciting products. Yet when he began distilling fruit brandies in 1994, he did not foresee that he would become Austria's first-ever whisky producer in 1998. The distillery is located in Axberg, south of the Danube and west of the city of Linz.

Reisetbauer's dedication to quality starts with the family's own organic barley, grown by son Hansi Reisetbauer Junior. Father and son now devise the flavors of their whiskies, and there is a lot to consider. The distillery was rebuilt in 2019 and is now a temple to modernity with temperature-controlled equipment that can be adjusted by smartphone. Sustainability remains at the center of all their production, with the distillery using solar energy and maximizing energy efficiency through the heat recovery systems in the production areas. Pure spring water comes from the Mühlviertel alpine pastures from the north of Upper Austria for their production water. The distillery has an impressive lineup of Carl GmbH copper hybrid pot and column stills on which they make the spirit for their whiskies, which are bottled at 7, 12, 15, and 21 years old, as well as a wide range of eau-de-vie, gin, vodka, rum, and brandy. The new-make spirit is matured in Chardonnay and Trockenbeerenauslese wine casks, giving the whisky a truly individual flavor.

TASTING NOTE

Reisetbauer & Son 7-Year-Old
Single malt, matured in Chardonnay and Trockenbeerenauslese wine casks, 43% ABV
Juicy ripe fruits hit the senses, with aromas of beeswax, menthol, and oak spice emerging from the glass. The whisky is light in texture but dances on the tongue with delightful notes of citrus, apple, and dried vine fruits, and hints of light spice and coffee on the finish.

RUOTKER'S HOUSE OF WHISKEY

OWNER David Gölles

FOUNDED 2016

WEBSITE www.davidgoelles.at

David Gölles opened Ruotker's House of Whiskey, Gin, and Rum in Riegersburg in a renovated inn. He trained and worked overseas in food processing before returning home in 2016 with the aim of writing the next chapter in the history of Stygian spirits. His parents, Alois and Herta Gölles, run a business producing fine vinegars and schnapps. The family factory has been able to make whiskey since 2003, and David Gölles produces his new spirits there.

He uses a wide variety of grains and cask types. Motivated to think laterally by the lack of locally grown barley, he looked to American whiskey culture for inspiration. Corn, wheat, spelt, rye, millet, oats, and buckwheat have been distilled, in addition to barley, and there are dozens of barrel types in play, from sherry, port, wine, tequila, mezcal, and shochu to new oak casks. He is a boutique producer currently honing his craft and defining his signature house style. He has the background, vision, and ambition to build an internationally respected Austrian whiskey brand.

TASTING NOTES

Ruotker's Whiskey Alois I Old Plum Brandy Cask Finish
Rye, finished in old plum brandy casks, 44.9% ABV
Bursting with rye character on the nose, there are notes of Ryvita, mint, and crisp spices. It is layered with plum and treacle on the palate, with expressive rye notes that lean into powerful clove notes.

Ruotker's Whiskey Ruediger II Lord's Reserve
Grain, matured in new American oak, refill oak, French oak, sherry casks, and sherry butts, 43.3% ABV
Here, David Gölles is aiming for a bourbon style, where he blends component whiskeys from five grains and five casks types, including corn, rye, barley, wheat, and spelt. The aromas project notes of cookie dough, brown sugar, pumpernickel, and stewed apple, and the waxy mouthfeel carries flavors of vanilla, rye spice, cinnamon, nuts, and characterful oak notes.

Ruotker's Whiskey
Ruediger II Lord's Reserve

GERMANY

The production of malt whisky in Germany began at Robert Fleischmann's Blaue Maus distillery in 1983, and the number of producers has increased rapidly during the 21st century. The number exporting in significant quantity to major whisky markets is still small in comparison to the number of producers, but the choice is growing and the styles of whisky are diversifying.

SLYRS

OWNER Slyrs Destellerie GMBH & Co KG

FOUNDED 1999

WEBSITE www.slyrs.com

It was in 1998 that the idea of making the first malt whisky in southern Bavaria dawned on Florian Stetter, who until that point had been engaged in brewing beer and distilling fruit brandies. With a skilled brewer's understanding of the relationship between hop and malt mashes, Stetter was well placed to fulfill his dream. After a visit to Scotland to learn the tricks of the Scotch malt whisky trade, he started producing his first whisky in 1999, using the stills formerly employed for fruit brandy and obtaining casks from local suppliers. Maturation took place in the clean fresh air in the town of Schliersee, known for its fine climate and panoramic views of the Alps.

A rapid rise to fame

The first distillate was released as a three-year-old whisky in 2002 and demand grew immediately; the new vintage expressions were released in early May each year and had usually sold out by the end of the month. The distillery rapidly became famous so expansion became necessary. A new distillery was constructed down the road and opened in 2007. Modern pot still distillation equipment was put in place for the double distillation and capacity was increased dramatically—a huge initial investment and a long-term, high-risk one, given the number of new whisky distillers on the German market.

Two-row summer barley grown in the Munich area is malted, though they have dabbled with Bavarian rye, and they draw mountain spring water from the Bannwald spring in the Schliersee Alps for their production. Mashing and fermentation are done in stainless steel vats opposite the two new copper pot stills. Master distiller Hans Kemenater uses slow fermentation and slow double distillation to retain the flavor profile from the Bavarian wood-smoked barley malt, while maturation takes place in the warehouse next door. New-make spirit is filled into toasted and charred casks made of American white oak; initial maturation typically takes three to six years.

While the complete range is available in Germany, the Slyrs Premium range of single malts contains the Slyrs Classic, Slyrs Fifty One, and Slyrs 12-Year-Old and are the most likely bottles to find outside of Germany. They produce a range of sherry-cask finishes, and other single malts finished in port, Sauternes, rum, Marsala, and Madeira casks.

Harder to find is their Bavarian Peat expression, and limited editions such as the Oktoberfest Edition and their annual Mountain Edition, which involves taking barrels to their Slyrs Altitude Camp up the mountain by ski lift, where they can breathe in the pure air for the next five years.

Slyrs Classic

TASTING NOTES

Slyrs Classic
Single malt, matured in American oak casks, 43% ABV
Freshly peeled citrus notes on the nose, with the sharp acidity of lime and gooseberry and a flicker of herbal undertones. Amid the orange, lime, and grapefruit that erupt in the mouth, there is balance from the sweet vanilla, runny caramel, and toasted wood sugars, with some dark berry fruits on the finish.

Slyrs Fifty One
Single malt, matured in American oak, port, sherry, and Sauternes casks, 51% ABV
Greater complexity with vanilla, blood orange, and pepper on the nose, and a thick texture with flavors of pear, cloves, chocolate praline, and black fruits.

EIFEL WHISKY

OWNER Stephan Mohr

FOUNDED 2008

WEBSITE www.eifelwhisky.de

Stephan Mohr's single malt and rye whiskies are admired for their innovative mashbills, maturation, and finishing regimes. Inspired by the German grain-distilling tradition, Stephan works with Feinbrennerei Sasse, where master distiller Hendrik Viefhus distills

the new make to Mohr's specifications, first distilling on the grain in a column still, followed by a second distillation in a copper pot still.

TASTING NOTE

Eifel Whisky 10-Year-Old Peated Single Malt
Single malt, finished in moscatel casks, 46% ABV
Clouds of fragrant smoke on the nose with tropical fruits, cinnamon bun, baked apple, and ginger. The malt was peated to 35ppm, and the whisky tastes of baked fruits, toffee, vanilla, and walnuts, with a swirl of active spices to finish.

Eifel Whisky 10-Year-Old
Peated Single Malt

STORK CLUB

OWNER Spreewald Distillers GMBH Co. & KG

FOUNDED 2016

WEBSITE www.stork-club-whiskey.com

Run by three friends with drinks industry backgrounds as bartenders, brand ambassadors, and spirit entrepreneurs, Stork Club Rye Whiskey acquired the Spreewald distillery in Schlepzig in 2016, around 37 miles (60km0 south of Berlin, and started to make German rye whiskeys.

They source rye from the Brandenburg region for their rye and malted rye recipes. The grain is ground to rye flour in a hammer mill, which is then mashed

and fermented over five days. Double distillation takes place in a small hybrid pot and column system, taking two batches to fill a 53-gallon (200-liter) barrel. The core range includes a straight rye, cask strength rye, a rye malt, and a smoky rye, plus a range of limited editions and rye collaborations.

TASTING NOTE

Stork Club Straight Rye Whiskey
Rye, matured in American and German oak casks, 45% ABV
Milk chocolate, sultana, espresso, pipe tobacco, nutmeg, and licorice on the nose. Core flavors of toasty rye spices, caramel, nutmeg, dried apricot, and chocolate, and a finish of rye bread, chocolate, and flashes of fruit.

Stork Club Straight
Rye Whiskey

ZIEGLER

OWNER GEBR. Josef & Matthäus Ziegler GMBH

FOUNDED 1865

WEBSITE www.brennerei-ziegler.de

They promise a whiskey like nothing else and given that Freud Whisky is matured in bourbon and German chestnut casks before finishing in old plum brandy kegs previously filled with Ziegler's Alte Zwetschge fruit brandy, it's safe to say they probably have the field to themself. The distillery is in

Freudenberg in the North Rhine-Westphalia, and until it was sold in 2020, the previous owners made the Aureum range of whiskies.

TASTING NOTE

Freud Whisky Distiller's Cut
Single malt, finished in old plum brandy casks, 41.5% ABV
The nose offers notes of varnished wood, whole plum, wood smoke, stewed rhubarb, and vanilla pod. Highly distinctive, there are bitter chocolate, plum mousse, marmalade, dusty cocoa, clove, tobacco, and leather on the palate, with a lighter finish of honey, vanilla, and peach slice.

Freud Whisky
Distiller's Cut

SWITZERLAND

Until regulations changed to allow the distilling of grain in 1999, Swiss distilleries were exclusively focused on the production of fruit brandies. Brewing beer, of course, is also a major part of the Swiss drinks industry, and the influence of beer culture on the flavor of Swiss whisky cannot be denied.

LANGATUN

OWNER Christian Lauper and Dr. Dolf Stockhausen

FOUNDED 2005

WEBSITE www.langatun.ch

The long history of Langatun began in 1857, when Jakob Baumberger returned home to Switzerland from his studies in Munich as a newly graduated master of brewing and founded a distillery at his father's farm. Three years later. he took over a brewery in the nearby village of Langenthal and developed both the distillery and the brewery into successful enterprises, subsequently purchasing the rights to a clear spring in the hills above the village and installing pipes to guide the water directly to his distillery.

Thanks to the farsightedness of his great-grandfather, master distiller Hans Baumberger III was able to rely on that fine spring water when he started making whiskies in 2005, launching the first Langatun bottling three years later. In 2014, the distillery moved to the Kornhaus in Aarwangen, a historic listed building, leaving behind St. Urbanstrasse in Langenthal. Christian Lauper and Dr. Dolf Stockhausen took over the distillery ownership from Hans Baumberger III in 2018, though they continue to honor the heritage of the Baumberger family and the whiskies they created.

They import the best quality barley from other parts of Europe and double distill in their gleaming pair of copper pot stills. One is a compact lantern-shaped still and the other, a small pot still-column hybrid still, the like of which can be commonly found in other European distilleries. Maturation adds complexity and finesse to the whisky, and casks are matured in the barrel warehouse at Langenthal,

traditionally racked and two barrels high. The distillery is open to visitors, and in addition to standard tours and tastings, they run distilling seminars and blend-your-own-Langatun experiences.

Their classic bottling is Langatun Old Deer, which is matured in sherry and Chardonnay casks, while Langatun Old Woodpecker is their organic single malt whisky. For smoky whisky lovers, their Langatun Old Crow is made with peated malt; while Langatun Old Wolf, also peated, aims to balance the smokiness with fruit with maturation in sherry and red wine casks. Germinating barley dried with beech wood smoke forms the basis for Langatun Old Bear, which is another red wine–matured expression.

From time to time, there are single cask and finishes, as well as a number of special bottlings, such as their Langatun Cigar Malt and Langatun Jacob's Dram, which is dedicated to their 19th-century founder Jakob Baumberger.

Langatun Old Deer

TASTING NOTES

Langatun Old Deer
Single malt, matured in sherry and Chardonnay casks, 58.5% ABV
An appealing nose of nectarine, cantaloupe melon, and floral notes, underpinned by cranberry, leather, and spice. Baked orange, ginger, and pepper on the palate, with black licorice and a hint of clove on the finish.

Langatun Old Woodpecker
Single malt, matured in Chardonnay casks, 46% ABV
An attractive nose of citrus peel and bright floral notes, with butterscotch, damson plum, and red wine notes on the palate, quite tannic, with malt and creamy cocoa, and red berry fruits to round things off.

Langatun Jacob's Dram
Single malt, finished in Pinot Noir casks, 49.12% ABV
Black cherry, black currant, and strawberry jam on the nose, with well-fired fruitcake notes, indicate the influence of the Pinot Noir cask finish. Those dark fruit notes form the core of the tasting experience, with oak tannins, black pepper, clove, and charred oak in support, with baking chocolate on the finish.

SÄNTIS MALT

OWNER The Locher family

FOUNDED 1999

WEBSITE www.saentismalt.com

Beer is the main product of Locher Brewery, the last remaining brewery of its kind at the foot of the Alpstein Mountains in northeast Switzerland, where it is well known for its Quöllfrisch Dunkel and other labels. When the Locher family established the brewery in Appenzell in 1886, they could not have foreseen that five generations later, their beer casks would be used not only for making beer but for single malt whisky too.

The man behind the idea of making whisky was Karl Locher. When turning 40, he conceived the idea of drinking his own malt by the time he reached 60 years old. Distillation had already been carried out in the brewery prior to World War Two, so it was just a matter of revitalizing the stills and returning to making spirits. The first distillation took place in 1999, after the legalization of grain distilling in Switzerland on July 1 that year.

Alpine whiskies

Säntis Malt is named after the highest mountain in the region, and they mature barrels of whisky at different altitudes. They also promote a testing Whisky Trek, which encourages those who love whisky and hiking to journey to different Alpine mountain inns serving unique Säntis whiskies. Maturing at altitude slows down maturation and alters the final alcoholic strength of the whisky in the casks. Some 5,600ft (1,700m) separate the altitude of their Brauquöll visitor center in Appenzell with the mountaintop retreat of Berggasthaus Alter Säntis.

What marks this distillery out from other European distillers is the use of beer barrels for maturation, in some case beer barrels as old as 130 years old. While most of their spirit is matured in regular beer barrels of 53 gallons (200 liters) or more, the Sigel matures in small oak barrels of 13–20 gallons (50–75 liters). The use of old beer casks for maturation is not the only method used to add flavor, as the maturing whisky is often filled into more active secondary casks, such as the Himmelberg, which is filled into red wine barrels. Dreifaltigkeit is their peated whisky matured in old beer casks, with peat taken from the Appenzell high moor to impart the smoke to the malt. There is an active program of limited editions and annual editions such as their long-running Snow White series, and their annual Triple Cask limited release, which is whisky from beer, port, and sherry casks.

Säntis Malt Edition Himmelberg

TASTING NOTES

Säntis Malt Edition Sigel
Single malt, matured in small oak casks, 40% ABV
The nose is compelling, with caramel, banana, vanilla, chocolate ganache, and nuts to savor. The whisky spreads across the palate with more chocolate and malty flavors, buoyed by hints of dark fruit, vanilla essence, and persistent spices at the end.

Säntis Malt Edition Himmelberg
Single malt, finished in red wine casks, 43% ABV
The combination of orchard fruit spiced with nutmeg, allspice, and cinnamon mark out the nose, with a palate of crisp apple, malt, and cherry and a finish of brittle toffee, chocolate-dipped brambles, and chewed leather.

Säntis Malt Edition Dreifaltigkeit
Single malt, matured in old beer casks, 52% ABV
The peat has conferred more wood smoke and singed stave notes than any of the medicinal notes associated with Islay peated whiskies, which should come as no surprise. It's spicy in the mouth at this strength, with invigorating notes of ginger, chocolate pralines, and lingering smoke.

ITALY

Whisky connoisseurs normally associate Italy with famous independent bottlers rather than Italian whisky. There was always something exciting, poetic even, in reading the words "Prodotto E Imbottigliato in Scozia" on a bottle, often clearly identifiable by the pink printed tax strips plastered over the bottle's closure. The import company and bottlers' names alone were enough to fire the imagination to aspire to La Dolce Vita; Samaroli of Rome, Sestante of Parma, Giovinetti & Figli of Milan, Soffiantino of Genoa, and Rinaldi of Bologna. Some distillery visitors will know the polished work of Italian coppersmiths, with stills made by Frilli, popping up in the Harris, Raasay, Inchdairnie, Starward, and Teeling distilleries among others. But for Italian whisky, there's only one name to know.

PUNI

OWNER The Ebensperger family

FOUNDED 2010

WEBSITE www.puni.com

The Ebensperger family founded Puni distillery in South Tyrol in 2010, taking the name from the river that flows through the Venosta valley. What they have now is one of the most spectacular-looking distilleries in Europe, with a cube-shaped building of offset latticed brickwork inspired by the area's traditional style of barn windows. Spirit first flowed from their sizable copper pot stills in 2012. In order to give them greater control, they designed a novel approach of using very hot water for distillation, rather than steam. Puni expressions are presented in pot still–inspired bottles and noticeably styled as malt whiskies, rather than single malt whiskies. Their malt whisky recipe involves malted barley, rye, and wheat, though they use unpeated and peated malted barley. The goal is to switch over to making more spirit from 100 percent malted barley as time goes on.

The core range and limited editions

The core range uses bourbon, sherry, and wine casks. Puni Gold is light and easygoing, matured in first-fill bourbon casks, with Puni Sole combining the bourbon with Pedro Ximénez sherry casks to bring in warm citrus and spicy notes. Puni Viña is matured for five years in carefully selected Marsala Vergine casks

from Sicily. An earlier edition called Puni Alba used the Marsala cask stock at three years old and finished it in peated casks. Limited edition lines so far are called Arte and Aura. Puni Arte was designed to give the company the freedom to bottle hand-selected expressions, drawn from experimental batches or specific rare casks, and included the first-ever Puni single malt whiskies made from 100 percent malted barley. Puni Aura is a range of cask-strength editions, often consisting of casks of their oldest stock to date. With a flair for beautiful design, Puni is trying to define what Italian whisky can be and hoping to convince a Scotch whisky–loving nation that it can find the quality it seeks closer to home.

Puni Gold

TASTING NOTES

Puni Gold
Single malt, matured in first-fill bourbon casks, 43% ABV
All the classic hallmarks of bourbon cask maturation are here, with honey, creamy vanilla, and ripe stone fruits. The flavors strike a balance between vanilla, orange honey, and custard creams with lemon and lime, and a hint of gooseberry that adds some tartness to the finish.

Puni Sole
Single malt, matured in bourbon and Pedro Ximénez sherry casks, 46% ABV
The PX sherry makes all the difference here, with dried fig and ginger adding to the heather honey, granola bar, and vanilla aromas. Though light in body, the flavors bring together notes of caramel, fruitcake, black fruits, and pepper.

Puni Vina
Single malt, matured in Marsala Vergine casks, 43% ABV
The Marsala gifts this whisky a greater richness, with dark fruits, leather, and some rye characteristics shining through on the nose, with flavors of black grape, blueberry, and cherry syrup on the palate, and some robust spices persisting through to the finish.

SPAIN

Spain plays a crucial role in the world of whisky, though it's not yet through its small but growing whisky industry. The importance of Spanish and American oak sherry puncheons, butts, and hogsheads to the Scotch and Irish whiskey industries cannot be understated. Distillers around the world rely on the country's world-class cooperages and the bodegas in Jerez for the best-quality sherry oak casks money can buy.

DESTILERÍAS ACHA

OWNER The Acha family

FOUNDED 1831 (whisky since early 2000)

WEBSITE www.destileriasacha.com

Euskal Herria or the Basque country has some of the most celebrated gastronomy in Europe in Donostia or San Sebastian, and the architectural marvel of Frank Gehry's Guggenheim Museum in Bilbao. South of Bilbao in Amurrio, Destilerías Acha is known for their Pacharán Atxa and range of vermouths. The company history stretches back to 1831 and has been under the ownership of the Acha family since the 1880s. Basque culture and spirits have enjoyed a renaissance in the 21st century, and Destilerías Acha

has diversified to include whisky. Distillation is in antique Hervé & Moulin Charentais alembic stills. The Haran range includes malt whiskies at 8, 12, 15, 18, and 21 years old, and the 12-Year-Old includes expressions matured in Iberian oak, as well as port, sherry, and cider cask finishes.

TASTING NOTE

Haran Whiskey Traditional 12-Year-Old
Single malt, matured in Iberian oak casks, 40% ABV
A nose of oak shavings, zested orange, pretty florals, and dried grasses. Perfect for a summer's day, the silky texture carries vanilla, honey, fondant, butterscotch, foam banana candies, and wood spices, showing toasty oak as the spices fade to a finish of custard creams.

Haran Whiskey Traditional 12-Year-Old

DYC

OWNER Suntory Global Spirits

FOUNDED 1958

WEBSITE www.dyc.es

Destilerías y Crianza, or DYC, is the leader of the Spanish whisky pack. It is based in the historic town of Segovia, a pretty town dominated by its stunning Roman aqueduct about an hour north of Madrid. In winter, it is bitterly cold here.

DYC founder, Don Nicomedes García, had been involved in the spirits business since 1919, when he took over the running of his father's small distillery at the tender age of 18. Yet it wasn't until 1958 that he

established the DYC plant, following several trips to Scotland to learn the secrets of Scotch whisky-making, and began distilling the following year, leading to the inaugural bottling in 1963. Owned by Suntory Global Spirits, DYC celebrated its 60th anniversary in 2019 and launched its first 20-year-old whisky in 2022.

TASTING NOTE

DYC 8-Year-Old
Aged blend, mix of various grains, 40% ABV
You can't help but admire how well it's put together, it hits the right sweet spots and is fruity in a good way, but it never really rocks out. Accept it as a light, fluffy, fun whisky that won't let you down.

DYC 8-Year-Old

MIDDLE EAST

Alcohol is prohibited and restricted in some Middle Eastern countries, but there are still many countries where alcohol sales are permitted. There is a thriving travel retail market for whisky in airports such as Dubai and Abu Dhabi, catering to long-haul passengers on a layover and international travelers departing the United Arab Emirates after business or leisure trips. The region now hosts its own consumer whisky show, too.

Israel's M&H Distillery is the best-known whisky producer in the Middle East, but there are other distilleries in Israel such as N.G.K distillery, which is M&H's second distillery, and David Zibell's Golani Heights and Yerushalmi distilleries.

Meanwhile, brands such as Ana Beirut, Athyr, and Levant Heights are emerging from Lebanon, though some of their techniques are pushing the boundaries of what is considered to be whisky. To make great whisky in the Middle East, as with Africa overleaf, means overcoming the challenges of the climate. This has an effect on the availability of raw materials such as water, barley, and oak, and the heat can play havoc on fermentation and distillation, while stifling hot conditions lead to high rates of evaporative losses from casks filled with whisky.

ISRAEL/M&H DISTILLERY

OWNER Gal and Lital Kalkshtein

FOUNDED 2012

WEBSITE www.mh-distillery.com

Founded by Gal & Lital Kalkshtein in 2012, M&H distillery, shortened from Milk & Honey distillery, was another distillery dream shepherded into existence, thanks to the expertise of global consultant Dr. Jim Swan (1941–2017), who helped the team navigate the perils and pitfalls of distilling and maturing whisky in Tel Aviv's hot climate with its 300 days of sunshine a year.

Water is a critical resource in this region, with the city relying on seawater and groundwater desalination plants; the distillery works with filtered and purified clean groundwater, which is also sustainable. Little barley suitable for distilling is grown in Israel, so head distiller Tomer Goren imports malt. He predominantly distills unpeated malt in their pair of copper pot stills, other than for peated malt campaigns, which run for two weeks twice a year.

M&H distillery is succeeding in making single malt whisky against the odds.

Rapid maturation in different locations

With an angel's share of 8–12 percent, maturation is understandably rapid, and comparable age statements to Scotch are essentially meaningless, though no whiskies are bottled younger than three years old. They utilize five maturation climates for their casks, from the city at sea level to the Dead Sea and the Negev Desert, to the Jerusalem Mountains and Upper Galilee—none of them are climate controlled. Cask selection is broad and experimental when combined with the maturation location options and has involved Swan's favored STR casks, kosher sherry casks, peated casks from Islay, beer casks, and Israeli wine casks. In addition to their signature M&H Classic, they bottle the Elements series, different twists on Classic, their experimental Apex series and single casks, and their Art & Craft line. Now a leading player in world whisky and another aspect of Dr. Jim Swan's legacy, M&H is showing the world how whisky-making can thrive against the odds in the most unlikely of places.

TASTING NOTES

M&H Classic
Single malt, matured in bourbon, new oak, and STR wine casks, 46% ABV
Delicate tones of golden syrup, marshmallow, jasmine, and nutmeg follow the nose, with a tempting balance of flavors between the vanilla, honey, and shortbread notes, and the developing juicy orange notes.

M&H Elements Sherry Cask, 46%
Single malt, matured in kosher-certified PX and oloroso sherry casks, 46% ABV
Black cherry, strawberry, plum, and black pepper on the nose. This shows an array of red berry fruits on the palate with chocolate, oak, and bourbon biscuits to finish.

M&H Elements Sherry Cask, 46%

LEBANON/
RIACHI WINERY & DISTILLERY

OWNER The Riachi family

FOUNDED 2013

WEBSITE www.riachi.me

The family-owned Riachi winery, based in Khenchara, 19 miles (30km) northeast of Beirut, started in 1839 and is known for fine wines, arak, and liqueurs. Then in 2013, master distiller Roy Riachi began to make whisky from floor-malted Lebanese six-row barley grown further inland in the Bekaa Valley. Compared with most whisky distilleries, Riachi unconventionally matures his whiskies in traditional clay amphorae with a capacity of around 32–28 gallons (120–180 liters), with cured branches of Lebanese oak slipped inside.

Beirut witnessed its first Lebanese whisky launch in 2019—Riachi produces the Athyr single malt and Levant Heights, their more experimental craft whisky range. This includes Espresso Roast Dark Malt, made from a malt normally used to make porter; Malt & Wheat, from malted barley and Lebanese durum wheat, which is triple distilled and aged in white oak; Dual Horizons, from a mashbill of malted barley from Scotland and Lebanon; and their Levant Highland King's Tower, a Lebanese corn whisky.

TASTING NOTES

Athyr Empire
Single malt, aged in clay amphora with Lebanese oak inserts, 55% ABV
Plenty of personality here, with dark, sweet aromas of vanilla, fig, brown sugar, root beer, and black pepper on the nose. It's bristling with heat, with chocolate, vanilla pod, and earthy, burnt spice notes, then it blooms with cola, oak, and Sachertorte flavors sliding into the finish.

Levant Heights Dark Malt
Single malt, matured in new white oak casks, 43% ABV
A compelling mix of aromas of coffee roasters, vanilla essence, bitter chocolate, and scorched pecan, and a mouth-puckering palate of molasses, coffee notes, brown sugar, and hazelnut—it's a bit of an acquired taste.

Levant Heights Dark Malt

SOUTH AFRICA

Africa is a growth market for Scotch, especially among consumers in South Africa, Kenya, Angola, and Nigeria. Like Lebanon, South Africa is also a wine-producing country, and this century, it has carved out a reputation for producing highly respected whiskies, too. We focus here on Drayman's and James Sedgwick, but they are not the only places making whisky. Pieter van Helden is working on defining an African-style whisky at Helden distillery, experimenting with using sorghum malt, African rice, and millet among others, while Qualito Craft distillery near the Kruger National Park bottle a Limpopo 10-Year-Old single barrel and add wood chips from the cask to their Heimer whisky bottles as a special aging technique.

DRAYMAN'S

Drayman's Highveld 5-Year-Old French Oak Reserve

OWNER Moritz Kallmeyer

FOUNDED 2000

WEBSITE www.draymans.com

Drayman's is a microbrewery and craft distillery based in Silverton, Pretoria, at 5,250ft (1,600m) above sea level. After being an amateur brewer for many years, the owner, Moritz Kallmeyer, opened the craft brewery in 2000 and released his own single malt whisky a decade later. Kallmeyer developed a solera system for making whisky, which he began by adding South African and Scotch whiskies to an eight-cask French oak solera system, drawing off the first bottling in 2009. Today, he makes wheat beers, smoked beers, lagers, and even mead. Oh, and Mampoer—a fiery indigenous spirit distilled from various fruits, which is made only in South Africa. The whisky is produced in tiny volumes, matured in French oak, and is only ever exported occasionally by dedicated world whisky proponents such as Fred Barnet of Anthem Imports in the US (drinkanthem.com), so buy it if you see it, as there is very little to go around.

TASTING NOTE

Drayman's Highveld 5-Year-Old French Oak Reserve
Single malt, matured in French oak casks, 43% ABV
The appealing fragrance of citrus, vanilla sponge, cereal, and spice notes on the nose, with a sip revealing marmalade, malt, and honey, with a dusting of cocoa and spices to finish.

JAMES SEDGWICK

OWNER Heineken Beverages

FOUNDED 1991

WEBSITE www.jamessedgwickdistillery.co.za

The pathway to the James Sedgwick distillery, the home of South African whisky.

Its history may stretch back to the 19th century, but its whisky production program started in earnest only in 1991, so there's nothing backward thinking about the James Sedgwick distillery. In 2009, the distillery in Wellington, northeast of Cape Town, was upgraded and expanded, with new equipment added to increase capacity for the production of its Three Ships single malt and Bain's Cape Mountain Whisky. The improvements included two new pot stills made by Forsyth's Ltd of Scotland and designed in the style of those at Bowmore on Islay to add to their considerable grain-distilling capacity. They have seven warehouses, and whisky matures more quickly in South Africa than Scotland, with an angel's share of 3–5 percent per year.

The role of Andy Watts

The Three Ships range now includes a broad portfolio of age and nonage statement expressions up to 21 years old, and a Master's Collection of special finishes. South African whisky owes a debt of gratitude to master distiller Andy Watts, the former cricketer for Derbyshire who came over from the UK, settled in South Africa, and joined the wine and spirits trade. Watts gained experience in whisky-making in Scotland from Bowmore, Auchentoshan, and Glen Garioch distilleries in the early years of his spirits career, thanks to a technical exchange program with Morrison Bowmore Distillers. Under Watts, the whisky made at James Sedgwick gained greater recognition and picked up international accolades, at a time when whisky drinkers were becoming more curious about whiskies made outside Scotland.

The South African drinks giant, the Distell Group Ltd was formed in 2000 and incorporated the Stellenbosch Farmers' Winery that Watts had worked for since 1984. In 2013, the Distell Group Ltd acquired Burn Stewart Distillers, giving it a major foothold in Scotch whisky through ownership of Bunnahabhain, Deanston, and Tobermory distilleries and the Black Bottle blend. Watts became Distell's Head of Whisky Intrinsic Excellence, taking charge of

the whole portfolio of whisky brands, as well as overseeing the production of grain and malt whisky at James Sedgwick. Then in 2023, Heineken acquired Distell along with Namibia Breweries Ltd, to form a new group called Heineken Beverages. After more than 38 years, Watts retired in 2021 to pursue his own projects, having become the best-known whisky figure on the African continent, though he continues to support the brands that he helped develop at the James Sedgwick distillery. The distillery has also opened to visitors, becoming a significant new attraction for local and overseas whisky tourists.

Three Ships 12-Year-Old

TASTING NOTES

Bain's Cape Mountain Whisky
Single grain, matured in bourbon casks, 40% ABV
Distilled from wheat or corn, the clever bit is the double maturation in first-fill bourbon casks over its 4–5-year maturation. There's aromas of honey, vanilla, oak shavings, ripening banana, and elegant florals, with the palate bringing sweet vanilla, candied citrus peel, ripe melon, toffee, and light spices, and a moreish velvety mouthfeel of melted white chocolate.

Three Ships 12-Year-Old
Single malt, matured in American oak casks, 46.3% ABV
Released by Andy Watts under the Master Distiller's Private Collection, the aromas open up with dried fruits, vanilla sponge, cherry pâte de fruits ,and new leather. Cherry soda, fresh cranberry, red apple, and black pepper, yield to juicy raisins and chocolate, with peat smoke, oak char, and black licorice edging into the finish.

LATIN AMERICA

Latin American countries are long-established markets for imported Scotch whisky, particularly blends, but distilleries making whisky are becoming a more common sight across the region. It's a land already revered for its incredible spirits, from rum, tequila, and mezcal, to cachaça, aguardiente, and pisco. Entrepreneurs are embracing whisky culture and launching their own brands, some like Argentina's La Alazana designed for consumers in their own countries, while others, like Peru's Black Whiskey and Mexico's Abasolo and Sierra Norte, are capitalizing on the interest in world whisky by tapping into export markets in the United States and beyond.

From large producers such as the Union distillery in Brazil, which makes 528,000–800,000 gallons (2–3 million liters) of alcohol a year, to the artisanal production at Tepaluma distillery in Chile, to craft distillers such as the Andean Culture distillery in Bolivia run by Fernando Marin and Felipe Gonzales-Quint, the number of whisky-makers and distilleries is growing steadily. Whether they use 100 percent malted barley or work with native varieties of heirloom corn, distillers are opening new frontiers across the continent.

MEXICO/ABASOLO

OWNER Casa Lumbre

FOUNDED 2019

WEBSITE www.abasolowhisky.com

Destilería y Bodega Abasolo is situated about 62 miles (100km) northwest of Mexico City in Jilotepec, a high-altitude location for a distillery, as it sits at 7,800ft (2,375m). While corn is strongly associated with the bourbon industry, master distiller Iván Saldaña applied traditional Mexican techniques of processing ancestral corn to make a unique new whisky. While not the first to be made in Mexico, its success was earned through better distribution than other brands, enabling a wider number of whisky drinkers to sample its charms.

This new-build distillery was built to make Mexican corn whisky, using Cacahuazintle corn, a native species that specializes in growing at high altitudes. The chunky kernels of this heirloom white corn look a little like pulled teeth and need to undergo nixtamalization before they can be ground into a corn flour to make tortillas or distilled into whisky. This ancient Mexican technique involves cooking these hefty kernels to high temperature in limewater. The protective outer husks dissolve in the alkaline solution, leaving the germ inside to soften. These are rinsed, dried, roasted, and crushed in a tortilla mill ready for mashing, where a little malted corn is added. Fermentation takes 120 hours, and then it is double distilled in a pair of adorable copper pot stills shaped like spinning tops. Maturation lasts a minimum of three years inside new toasted and used oak casks stored in an open-sided warehouse.

The distillate is also used to make Nixta Licor de Elote, a corn liqueur where the Cacahuazintle corn is mixed with the distillate to produce a sweet clarified wort, which is sold in corn-on-the-cob-shaped bottles.

TASTING NOTE

Abasolo
Corn, aged in new charred American oak casks, 43% ABV
The nose has buttered corncobs, light vanilla, honey on toast, and cooked vegetable and herbal notes. Lightly textured but also highly delicious, it tastes of buttered corn, sweet vanilla, and a dash of pepper, building up creaminess and texture to serve up flavors of cornbread and vanilla ice cream, which persist into the creamy finish. This whisky is a pure celebration of corn.

Abasolo

MEXICO/SIERRA NORTE

OWNER Douglas French

FOUNDED 1996; whisky since 2015

WEBSITE www.sierranortewhiskey.com

Douglas French is a maestro *mezcaleros* in Oaxaca, a master distiller known for his distinctive Scorpion mezcal range. And yes, there's a real scorpion in every bottle. Operating in San Agustin de las Juntas in Oaxaca, French turned his hand to making Mexican corn whisky. As well as being the heart of mezcal production, Oaxaca is a region that prides itself on having some of the finest cuisine in the country. With around 50 or so corn species in the region, Sierra

Norte whisky is made with heirloom corn varieties that would normally be made into tortillas and tamales. French swapped cooked *piñas* for cooked corn to make whisky, using a mashbill of 85 percent Oaxaca heirloom corn to 15 percent malted barley, which he double distills and matures in French oak casks, bottling everything as single barrel releases.

TASTING NOTE

Sierra Norte Native Oaxacan Yellow Corn
Corn, aged in French oak casks, 45% ABV
A floral bouquet with pleasing sweet corn notes and crushed red chili on the nose. The palate brings forth marmalade peel, spiced honey, and hot red chili notes.

Sierra Norte Native Oaxacan Yellow Corn

ARGENTINA/LA ALAZANA

OWNER The Serenelli family

FOUNDED 2011

WEBSITE www.laalazanawhisky.com

The Serenelli family are making Argentina's first single malt whisky in Las Golondrinas in Chubut Province, Patagonia. Lila Serenelli is in charge of production and trained in brewing and distilling in Scotland. Unpeated and peated malt was imported from Scotland initially, until sufficient quantities of suitable local barley could

be sourced. The volumes are modest, with much of the stock of aged and nonaged statement bottlings sold directly from the distillery.

TASTING NOTE

La Alazana
Single malt, aged in bourbon casks, 60% ABV
This cask strength sample has a nose of sweet malt, lemon and lime groves, and baked desserts, and with water, the aromas are clean and pure. At full strength, there's nectarine, pepper, tangy citrus, clove, lemon, and sweet fudge on the palate, with a lovely thick mouthfeel and dense texture.

PERU/DON MICHAEL DISTILLERY

OWNER Michael Kuryla

FOUNDED 2017

WEBSITE www.donmichael.pe

Michael Kuryla makes Black Whiskey from 60 percent Andean Black Corn, 30 percent malted wheat, and 10 percent malted barley at his impressive distillery south of Lima. The corn is first cooked and then pumped into temperature-controlled fermenters,

where the yeast is left to work its magic over the next 96 hours. After double distillation, the spirit is matured for two to three years.

TASTING NOTE

Black Whiskey
Andean corn, matured in small new charred American oak casks, 45% ABV
The nose is vanilla led, with treacle, chocolate, oak, and whole peppercorns. Loose structured, tasting of chocolate cake, coffee, black fruit, caramelized sugar, hazelnut, and fragrant spices.

GLOSSARY

ABV (alcohol by volume) This is the proportion of alcohol in a drink, expressed as a percentage. Whiskey is most commonly bottled at 40% or 43% ABV to over 60%.

Age statement The number on a label, e.g., 12 years old, which represents the minimum number of years the youngest whiskey has matured in wooden casks.

Angel's share The amount of liquid that evaporates from the cask during maturation, which can range from 1–2% per year up to 12% depending on the warehouse conditions, which can result in the alcohol strength going up or down.

Batch distillation Distillation carried out in batches, as opposed to continuous distillation. Each batch may be marginally different, which gives the method an artisanal quality.

Barrel *see* Cask.

Blended at birth The blending of various new-make spirits before aging in wood, usually single malts and single grains, rather than blending mature whiskeys together. While the end result is still a blend, it's no longer legal to make blended-at-birth products in Scotland.

Blended malt A mix of single malt whiskeys from more than one distillery.

Blended whiskey In Scotland, this is a mix of malt whiskies and grain whiskies. A blended Irish whiskey must include a minimum of two or more styles of whiskey, such as single malt, single pot still, and single grain. A blended whiskey in the US must include a minimum of 20% straight whiskey, but the remainder can include neutral grain spirit and other whiskey types.

Bourbon Produced in the US from a mash of at least 51% corn; distilled to a maximum of 80% ABV; and aged in new, charred oak casks at a strength no greater than 62.5% ABV. To be called straight bourbon, it must be aged for at least two years. Its heartland is Kentucky, but legally, it can be made in any US state.

Cask The oak vessel in which whiskey is matured, which comes in many different styles and sizes. The type of wood used is a principal distinction, e.g., American, European, or Japanese mizunara oak each impart different flavors. Some countries permit nonoak species for maturation or finishing casks, such as chestnut, cherry, and amburana. The other is the cask's previous usage and the flavor impact from those fillings as they seep into the wood, e.g., bourbon, sherry, wine, fortified wines, or beer. Casks can be used to fully mature other spirits, such as bourbon, or just seasoned with other liquids, such as sherry seasoned casks. In the US, whiskey is most commonly matured in barrels (40–44 gal/180–200 liters). American barrels are reused elsewhere; in Scotland, they are

often broken down and reassembled as hogsheads (55 gal/250 liters). Butts and puncheons (110 gal/500 liters) are the largest casks for maturing whiskey.

Cask finishing The practice of using a secondary cask for a further period of maturation with the goal of adding additional flavor and complexity. Sometimes called secondary maturation or just finishing, there is no minimum or set duration for a finish. It can take as short as a couple of weeks to several decades to achieve the perfect finish.

Cask strength Whiskey that is bottled straight from the cask rather than first being diluted down to a specific bottling strength. It is typically around 57–63% ABV but can be much lower in older whiskeys.

Column still Also known as a Coffey, Patent, or continuous still, this is the type of still used for continuous distillation.

Condenser The vaporized spirit driven off the stills is turned back into a liquid in a condenser. Condensers require a large volume of cold water to do their job. The traditional type of condenser is a "worm tub"—a tapering coil of copper pipe set in a vat of cold water outside the stillhouse. Worm tubs have largely been superseded by shell-and-tube condensers, usually situated inside the stillhouse, though some new distilleries have installed worm tubs to pursue a specific character in their spirit.

Continuous distillation The creation of spirit as an ongoing process, as opposed to batch distillation. Continuous distillation uses a column still (also known as a Patent or Coffey still) rather than a pot still. It has two connected columns: the Rectifier and the Analyser. The cool wash travels down the Rectifier in a sealed coil, where it becomes heated. It then passes to the head of the Analyser, down which it trickles over a series of perforated copper plates. Steam enters the foot of the Analyser and bubbles through the wash, driving off alcoholic vapor, which rises up the Analyser then passes to the foot of the Rectifier. Here it again ascends, to be condensed by the cool wash (which is thus heated) as it rises in a zigzag manner through another series of perforated copper plates. As the vapor rises, it becomes purer and of higher strength, until it is drawn off at the "striking plate" at 94% ABV.

Cut points In the process of pot still distillation, the operator divides the run into three "cuts" to separate the usable spirit from rejected spirit, which must be redistilled. The first cut contains the foreshots; the middle cut is the section of usable spirit; the end cut contains the feints or aftershots.

Doubler *see* Pot still.

Draff The Scottish name for the remains of the

grain after mashing. It is a nutritious cattle fodder, used either wet or dried and pelletized.

Drum maltings Large cylinders in which grain is germinated during the industrial malting of barley. The drums are ventilated with temperature-controlled air and rotate so the grains do not stick together.

Dumping Emptying the contents of a cask into a vat, either prior to bottling or before putting into a different kind of cask.

Dunnage Traditional low warehouse with earthen floors in which whiskey is matured in oak casks.

Eau de vie Literally "water of life" and usually used in reference to grape-based spirits. Compare with *uisge beatha*.

Expression The term given to a particular whiskey in relation to the overall output of a distillery or spirits company. It may refer to the age, as in 12-year-old expression, or to a particular characteristic, such as a cask-strength expression.

Feints The final fraction of the spirit produced during a distillation run in batch distillation. Feints (also called tails or aftershots) are aromatically unpleasant and are sent to a feints and foreshots receiver to be mixed with low wines and redistilled with the next run.

Fermenter Another name for washback.

First fill The first time a cask has been used to hold new-make spirit to mature into whiskey, it is referred to as a first-fill cask. A first-fill sherry cask will have held only sherry prior to its use for maturing whiskey; a first-fill bourbon cask will have been used once only to hold bourbon prior to its use in maturing whiskey.

Foreshots The first fraction of the distillation run in pot still distillation. Foreshots (also known as heads) are not pure enough to be used and are returned to a feints and foreshots receiver to be redistilled in the next run.

Grist Ground, malted grain. Water is added to grist to form the mash.

Heads *see* Foreshots.

High wines (US) A mix of spirit that has had its first distillation and the foreshots and feints from the second distillation. With a strength of around 28% ABV, high wines undergo a second distillation to create new make.

Independent bottler/bottling A company that releases bottles of whiskey independently of the official distillery bottlings. They order new-make fillings and may mature them in their own bonded warehouse and buy casks from brokers and individuals and bottle the whiskey as and when they choose. Independent bottlings can offer a different perspective on the signature style from that distillery by bottling at different age statements, strengths, or by using different cask finishes.

Kilning In the process of malting, kilning involves gently heating the "green malt" to halt its germination and thereby retain its starch content for turning into sugars (in the mashing stage). Ultimately, these sugars will be turned into alcohol. Peat may be added to the kiln to produce a smoky flavored malt.

Lomond still This pot still was designed so that a distillery could vary the character of spirit being produced. The level of reflux could be altered by way of an additional condenser on the still so that a heavy or light style of spirit could be made, as required.

Low wines The spirit produced by the first distillation. It has a strength of about 21 percent ABV. Compare with high wines.

Lyne arm (or "lye pipe") The pipe running from the top of the still to the condenser. Its angle, height, and thickness all have a bearing on the characteristics of the spirit.

Malting The process of deliberately starting and stopping germination in grain to maximize its starch content. As the grain begins to germinate (through the influence of heat and moisture), it becomes "green malt" (grain that has just begun to sprout). The green malt undergoes kilning to produce malt.

Marrying The mixing of whiskeys prior to bottling. It most often applies to blended whiskey, where whiskeys of different types and from several distilleries are combined for a period in vats or casks to fully integrate before the whiskey is bottled.

Mash The mix of grist and water.

Mashbill The mix of grains used in the making of a particular whiskey. In the US, there are specific, legal requirements about the percentage of certain grains for making bourbon, Tennessee whiskey, and rye whiskey, for example.

Mash tun The vessel in which the grist is mixed with hot water to convert starch in the grain into sugars, ready for fermentation. The fermentable liquid that results is known as wort; the solid residue (husks and spent grain) is draff.

Maturation For new make to become whiskey, it must go through a period of maturation in oak casks. The length of time varies: in Scotland and Ireland, the minimum period is three years; to be called a straight rye or straight bourbon in the US, the minimum maturation is two years.

Middle cut see Cut points.

Mothballed A closed distillery but capable of being returned to operation.

NAS or no age statement Applies to a whiskey for which the number of years of maturation is not stated on the label, usually because some or all of the component whiskeys are quite young.

New make The clear, usable spirit that comes from the spirit still. It has a strength of about 70% ABV and is typically diluted to around 63.5% before being put into casks for maturation. In the US, new make is called "white dog" and must come off the stills at 80% ABV or less.

Pagoda The distinctive style of roof found on distillery malting kilns in Scotland and elsewhere, e.g., Japan. The classic design is called a Doig's Ventilator and draws hot air up through the kiln from the furnace to dry the malted barley and stop further germination. It has been argued that cupola is a more accurate name, though pagoda remains the term in popular usage.

Peating Adding peat to the kiln when malting barley imparts a smoky, phenolic character that is adsorbed onto the husks. Barley that has undergone this process is known as peated malt, and the smoky flavor is refined through every stage of whisky production. Classically associated with Scotch whisky, it is now widely practiced in many whisky-making countries around the world.

Phenols A group of aromatic chemical compounds. In whiskey making, the term is used in respect of the chemicals that impart smoky and medicinal flavors to malt and the whiskey made from it, which may be described as phenolic. Phenols are measured in parts per million (ppm). Highly phenolic whiskeys, such as Laphroaig and Ardbeg, will use malt peated to a level of between 35 and 50ppm.

Poteen see Uisce poitín.

Pot still The large onion- or lantern-shaped vessels, nearly always made of copper, used for batch distillation. Pot stills vary in size and shape, and these variations affect the style of spirit produced. In the US, a doubler is a pot still connected to the column still used for a second distillation.

ppm see Phenols.

Proof The old term for the alcoholic proportion of a spirit, now superseded by ABV. The American proof figure, which is different to imperial proof, is twice that of the ABV percentage, e.g., 100° US Proof = 45.8% ABV.

Rectifier see Continuous distillation.

Refills Casks previously used to mature whiskey, used a second or third time.

Reflux The process by which heavier alcoholic vapors fall back into the still rather than passing along the lyne arm to the condenser. By falling back, these vapors are redistilled, becoming purer and lighter. The size, height, and shape of the still, and how it is operated, contribute to the degree of reflux, and therefore to the lightness and character of the spirit. Long-necked stills have a greater degree of reflux and produce a more delicate style of spirit than squatter stills, which tend to make heavier, "oilier" whiskeys.

Rickhouse A maturation warehouse, the term is largely used in the US. They can be constructed from brick and stone and may have wooden or metaled sides, which in turn, affect the maturation conditions for the casks stored inside.

Run In batch distillation—as carried out using pot stills—the extent of distillation is referred to as a run. The spirit produced during the run is variable in quality and is divided by cut points.

Silent distillery A distillery in which whiskey production has stopped—possibly only temporarily.

Single cask A bottling that comes from just one individual cask (often bottled at cask strength) and prized for its individuality.

Single malt A malt whiskey that is the product of just one distillery.

Spirit safe A glass-fronted cabinet through which the distilled spirit passes and which is used to monitor the purity of the spirit. The stillman operates the spirit safe during a run to assess its quality and make cut points.

Spirit still In double distillation, the spirit still is used for the second distillation of the batch, in which the spirit from the wash still is distilled again to produce new make.

Still The vessel in which distillation takes place. There are two basic types of stills: a pot still for batch distillation and a column still for continuous distillation.

STR The shave-toast-rechar cask is a former red wine cask that has undergone a three-stage process before it is used to mature or finish whiskey. A form of cask rejuvenation that extends the useful life of existing casks, it was popularized by the late whiskey consultant Dr. Jim Swan who advised many of his distillery clients to adopt it around the world.

Triple distillation Most batch distillation involves two distillations: in a wash still and in a spirit still. Triple distillation—the traditional method in Ireland—involves a third distillation, said to produce a smoother and purer spirit.

Uisge beatha/uisce beatha The Scottish Gaelic and Irish Gaelic terms, respectively, from which the word whiskey derives. The term means "water of life," as with eau de vie and aqua vita.

Uisce poitín Historically, the Irish Gaelic term for nonlicensed whiskey, usually known as poteen.

Vatting The mixing of whiskey from several casks. This is usually done to achieve a consistency of flavor over time (see also Marrying).

Wash The resultant liquid when yeast is added to the wort, fermenting into a kind of ale. Wash has an alcoholic strength of about 7% ABV. It passes into a wash still for the first distillation.

Wash still In batch distillation, the wash still is used for the first distillation, in which the wash is distilled.

Washbacks The fermenting vessels in which yeast is added to the wort to make wash. Called "fermenters" in the US.

Wood finish see Cask finish.

Worm/worm tubs see Condensers.

Wort The sweet liquid produced as a result of mixing hot water with grist in a mash tun.

Yeast An organism that converts sugar into alcohol and carbon dioxide.

INDEX

The mash tun at Indri Distillery, India. See page 253

PICTURE CREDITS

The publisher would like to thank the many distilleries and organizations who have provided images for inclusion in the book. Thanks also to The Whisky Exchange and Master of Malt who supplied images of various bottles. Finally, thanks to the following for their kind permission to reproduce their photographs:

(Key: a-above; b-below/bottom; c-center; f-far; l-left; r-right; t-top)

Alamy Stock Photo: Associated Press / Koji Ueda 185tc, Derek Croucher 20-21, dpa picture alliance 263, Horst Friedrichs 137tr, Robert Grim 162, Rasvan ILIESCU 14, imageBROKER.com GmbH & Co. KG / Peter Giovannini 119t, imageBROKER.com GmbH & Co. KG / Robert Seitz 19br, Rod Kirkpatrick 290cb, Iain Masterton 131, Iain Masterton 138, mauritius images GmbH / Novarc Images / Frame Focus Capture Photography 4, PA Images / David Cheskin 143t, Scott Hortop Travel 91tr, Ivan Vdovin 117t

Dreamstime.com: Helena Bilkova 266-267, Brina Bunt 178-179, Dmitry Serpakov 11tl

Getty Images / iStock: Roberto Vecchio 332–333

Shutterstock.com: Chapatta 228-229, DerekTeo 6-7, Lukassek 156-157, Jan Miko 8-9

Whisky Saga: Thomas hrbom 148cl

Map data from OpenStreetMap, available under the Open Database License.

All other images © Dorling Kindersley Limited

Page 2: Alembic copper pot stills at Aberfeldy distillery.
Page 4: The Valley of the Three Sisters, Glencoe, Scotland.
Page 332–333: The Black Lake in the Gap of Dunloe, Killarney National Park, County Kerry, Ireland.

PUBLISHER'S ACKNOWLEDGMENTS
DK would like to thank Marta Bescos for the picture research, James MacDonald for the cartography, Kathy Steer for proofreading, Ruth Ellis for indexing this 2024 edition, and Aaron Barker for consulting on the US edition. DK would also like to thank Jonny McCormick, Gavin D. Smith, Fiona Holman and Sunita Gahir for all their work on this edition.

ABOUT THE AUTHORS

JONNY McCORMICK

Writer and photographer Jonny McCormick is Contributing Editor for *Whisky Advocate* magazine (M. Shanken Communications Inc.), the largest spirits title in the US with a reach of more than a million whiskey drinkers. McCormick began writing for *Whisky Advocate* in 2006 and is their lead reviewer for blended Scotch, blended malt, grain, and Irish whiskey and their longest-serving Japanese and world whisky reviewer. He has written numerous features on whiskey for *Wine Spectator* and other books and international drinks and lifestyle publications. He was made a Keeper of the Quaich in 2013. McCormick has led presentations on whiskey in North America, Europe, and Asia and is an authority on whiskey auctions and the secondary whiskey market. He resides in Scotland surrounded by Scotch whisky distilleries and is possibly the only person to have driven a red sports car into Wolfburn distillery and parked it under the stills.

GAVIN D. SMITH

Gavin D. Smith has been writing professionally since the mid-1980s and is recognized as one of the world's leading whiskey writers. He acts as Contributing Editor Scotland for *Whisky Magazine*. He produces feature material for a wide range of international publications and regularly undertakes writing commissions for leading drinks companies. He is the author and co-author of more than 30 books, relating to whiskey, beer, Scottish history, and literature, including *Worts Worms and Washbacks, An A–Z of Whisky, Whisky Wit & Wisdom, The Whisky Men, Discovering Scotland's Distilleries, Goodness Nose*—written with Master Blender Richard Paterson—two editions of *The Micro-distillers' Handbook*. Along with the late Dominic Roskrow, he updated, revised, and edited three editions of Michael Jackson's *Malt Whisky Companion*. Recent publications include *The A9 Handbook, and a history of The Dalmore*. He lives in the Scottish Borders and is a Master of the Quaich, the highest honor bestowed by the Scottish whisky industry.

AUTHORS' ACKNOWLEDGMENTS

Gavin would like to thank the following people for their generous assistance in researching the book:

SCOTLAND John Fordyce, The Borders Distillery; Francis Cuthbert, Daftmill Distillery; Ewan Gunn, Diageo plc; Philip and Simon Thompson, Dornoch Distillery; Ian Palmer, InchDairnie Distillery; Peter Kwasniewski, Isle of Harris Distillery; Alisdair Day, Isle of Raasay Distillery; John Campbell, Lochlea Distillery; Malcolm Rennie and Leonard Russell, Rosebank Distillery; Angela Brown and Cara Laing, Strathearn Distillery; and Bruce Perry, Torabhaig Distillery.

IRELAND Alex Thomas, Bushmills and Causeway Distillery; John Teeling, Great Northern Distillery; Brendan Carty, Killowen Distillery; David Boyd-Armstrong, Rademon Estate Distillery; Ruairi Burns, Titanic Distillery; and Ned Gahan, Waterford Distillery.

Jonny would like to thank the network of distillers, importers, marketeers, PR teams, and couriers for their contributions from all over the world. Special thanks to Fred Barnet, Anthem Imports; Stephen Davies, Penderyn Distillery; Kris Elliott, High Road Spirits; Sam Filmus, ImpEx Beverages Inc.; and Raj Sabharwal, Glass Revolution Imports. None of this would have been possible without the support and understanding of my family and my colleagues, editors, and publishers at *Whisky Advocate*.

Finally, thanks to Lucy Sienkowska, Izzy Holton, and Marta Bescos from the wonderful team at DK, with particular thanks to our brilliant editor Fiona Holman for her meticulous work and stamina in bringing this edition to life.

Penguin
Random
House

DK LONDON

Editorial Director Cara Armstrong
Project Editor Izzy Holton
Senior Designer Glenda Fisher
US Senior Editor Jennette ElNaggar
Senior Production Editor Pushpak Tyagi
Senior Production Controller Luca Bazzoli
Jacket Coordinator Emily Cannings
Art Director Maxine Pedliham
Publishing Director Katie Cowan

Editorial Fiona Holman
Design Sunita Gahir
Cartography James MacDonald

DK INDIA

Assistant Art Editor Rajoshi Chakraborty
Senior Art Editor Devika Awasthi
Managing Editor Saloni Singh
Managing Art Editor Neha Ahuja Chowdhry
DTP Designers Manish Upreti, Satish Gaur
DTP Coordinator Pushpak Tyagi
Pre-production Manager Balwant Singh
Creative Head Malavika Talukder

FIRST EDITION

Senior Editor Alastair Laing
Project Art Editor Kathryn Wilding
Managing Editor Dawn Henderson
Managing Art Editor Christine Kielty

DK INDIA

Senior Editor Dorothy Kikon
Senior Art Editor Balwant Singh
Art Editor Anjan Dey
Senior DTP Designer Pushpak Tyagi
DTP Designer Saurabh Chhalaria
CTS Manager Sunil Sharma

This American Edition, 2024
First American Edition, 2012
Published in the United States by DK Publishing,
a division of Penguin Random House LLC
1745 Broadway, 20th Floor, New York, NY 10019

Copyright © 2012, 2024 Dorling Kindersley Limited
24 25 26 27 28 10 9 8 7 6 5 4 3 2 1
001-342228-Oct/2024

All rights reserved.
Without limiting the rights under the copyright reserved above, no
part of this publication may be reproduced, stored in or introduced
into a retrieval system, or transmitted, in any form, or by any means
(electronic, mechanical, photocopying, recording, or otherwise),
without the prior written permission of the copyright owner.
Published in Great Britain by Dorling Kindersley Limited

A catalog record for this book
is available from the Library of Congress.
ISBN 978-0-5938-4428-1

DK books are available at special discounts when purchased in bulk
for sales promotions, premiums, fund-raising, or educational use.
For details, contact: DK Publishing Special Markets,
1745 Broadway, 20th Floor, New York, NY 10019
SpecialSales@dk.com
Printed and bound in Italy

www.dk.com

MIX
Paper | Supporting
responsible forestry
FSC™ C018179

This book was made with Forest
Stewardship Council™ certified
paper—one small step in DK's
commitment to a sustainable future.
**Learn more at www.dk.com/uk/
information/sustainability**